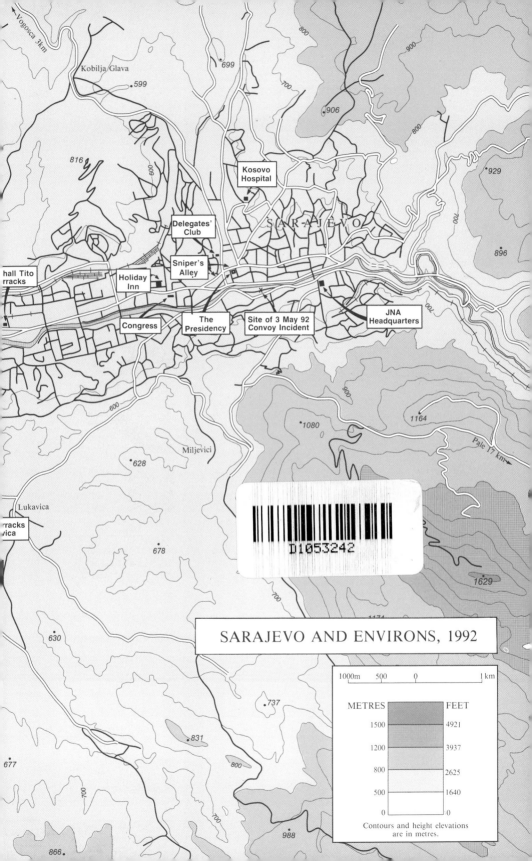

SARAJEVO AND ENVIRONS, 1992

PEACEKEEPER

PEACEKEEPER

The Road to Sarajevo

Lewis MacKenzie

Douglas & McIntyre
Vancouver/Toronto

Douglas & McIntyre
1615 Venables Street
Vancouver, British Columbia
V5L 2H1

Canadian Cataloguing in Publication Data

MacKenzie, Lewis, 1940-
  Peacekeeper

  ISBN 1-55054-098-X

  1. United Nations—Armed Forces—Yugoslavia.
2. Yugoslavia—History—Civil War, 1991-
3. MacKenzie, Lewis, 1940-   I. Title.
JX1981.P7M23 1993   355.3′57′09497 C93-091596-8

Editing by Roy MacSkimming
Jacket design by Rick Staehling
Front cover photo by Peter Bregg/*Maclean's*
Back cover photo by Sgt. Christian Coulombe/Department of National
  Defence
Text design by Tom Brown
Maps by William R. Constable
Typesetting by Vancouver Desktop Publishing Centre
Printed and bound in Canada by D. W. Friesen & Sons Ltd.
Printed on acid-free paper ∞

This book is dedicated to my wife, Dora, and daughter, Kimm, who for many years gracefully tolerated my long and frequent absences on peacekeeping tours of duty; and to each and every soldier who has served with me, particularly the magnificent international group in Sarajevo, dominated by the contingents from Canada and France.
Bless them all.

Contents

Acknowledgements

THANKS TO: General Satish Nambiar, for being such an outstanding boss; Cedric Thornberry for his sage advice; General Philippe Morillon for his friendship and example; Major Steve Gagnon for being the best assistant any general ever had; Warrant Officer Traclet and Corporal Leroux for keeping me sane; Colonel Vitali Petrounev for showing me how stupid I'd been to dislike Russians for the first fifty years of my life; Colonel Svend Harders for his magnificent support and cigarettes; Roy MacSkimming for his help and advice and for correcting my grammar; Linda McKnight for introducing me to the book business; Gerald Clark for introducing me to Linda; Doreen Potter for converting my pencilled scribbling into a legible manuscript; Martin Bell for unwittingly launching the idea for this book; and Scott McIntyre for believing I could write.

L.M.

List of Maps

Introduction

███████

IN JUNE 1992, when I was chief of staff with the United Nations Protection Force (UNPROFOR) in the former Yugoslavia, correspondent Martin Bell of the British Broadcasting Corporation was interviewing me in my office in Sarajevo. Martin's cameraman panned to a shot of my chronically cluttered desk. Sitting to the side of the desk was my brown, plastic-covered, one-year diary that I had bought for $4.29 back home, to record my hotel and meal expenses in a fashion that would satisfy the UN bureaucracy. Later that night, unbeknownst to me, Martin's commentary during his televised report referred to the "red, leather-bound diary on General MacKenzie's desk that will probably be a book someday".

Within weeks, I had received queries from a number of major publishing houses, all wanting to discuss the rights to my diary. One thing led to another, and this book was born.

Writing a book about my life in uniform was something I'd considered since I was a young officer. Military life is characterized by so many memorable and frequently humorous events that I thought a memoir would make interesting reading, and writing it would be good therapy in my waning years. But when the time came to sign a publishing contract, much sooner than I'd expected, I hoped that a ghost writer would assume the challenge of turning my rambling reminiscences into a coherent record of my career as a soldier and sometime peacekeeper.

No such luck. Unfortunately, my publisher and new friend, Scott McIntyre, decided that the book should be written in my own words. Scott set me to work, and a concerted effort between

Christmas 1992 and May 1993 produced what is contained between these covers.

The early chapters about my previous peacekeeping experiences were fun to write, because they reminded me of many old friends and incidents that had lain dormant in my memory for years. On several occasions, my wife, Dora, opened the door to my study and asked me what I was laughing about. With tears of nostalgia and joy, I would describe to her one of the more memorable moments of my life.

Lest the reader think that UN peacekeeping is all fun and games, however, please understand that I kept no records during my first eight peacekeeping tours, between 1963 and 1991 (actually seven, but Gaza was a double, two-year tour). If you try to remember what you did thirty years ago, the chances are pretty good that, like me, you will remember mainly the good times and the tragedies. The run-of-the-mill events and daily routines probably don't warrant description anyway. On the other hand, the pranks and disasters, the times when you were really scared, stand out as if they'd happened yesterday. They are the memories I've included here, and they are also the ones that inundated me with waves of nostalgia and feeling when I recorded them.

Until the Yugoslavian conflict erupted in 1991, United Nations peacekeeping, with a few notable exceptions, was pretty straightforward. Two or more countries, or warring factions within a country, decided they wanted to stop fighting and turned to the UN for help. A ceasefire was arranged, after which a multinational force of peacekeepers arrived with their white vehicles and blue berets and placed themselves in a demilitarized zone between the parties. The peacekeepers quickly established mechanisms to keep the peace: everything from telephone "hot lines" between the sides to regular conferences and meetings—in fact, anything at all that would keep the dialogue going between the combatants. The UN strategy was simple but pragmatic: if the fighting was to be kept under control, the best way was to keep talking. That's why I became so frustrated in Sarajevo when I couldn't convince the Bosnian President, Mr. Alija Izetbegovic, to talk directly with Dr. Radovan Karadzic, the leader of the Bosnian Serbs.

The whole idea of using lightly-armed forces to keep belligerents apart was developed by a Canadian, Lester Pearson, when he was Secretary of State for External Affairs. Great Britain and France had intervened in Egypt in 1956 to thwart President Nasser's move to nationalize the Suez Canal. The Soviet Union and the United States were on opposite sides of this conflict, and Canadians justifiably feared a superpower nuclear confrontation in the skies over our heads. Pearson, who subsequently became Prime Minister, suggested that a UN peacekeeping force consisting of lightly-armed infantry battalions could replace the British and French forces on the ground and defuse a potentially explosive situation. The strategy worked, and the concept of UN peacekeeping as we know it entered our vocabulary.

For thirty-six years, as the UN inserted its peacekeeping forces and/or observers in some thirty-three trouble spots around the world, the pattern of intervention remained reasonably consistent. Canada has participated in every UN peacekeeping mission and has supported a number of non-UN missions, such as the multinational observer force in the Sinai Desert, two missions in Indochina and Vietnam, and the European Community's military monitor mission in the former Yugoslavia.

As a rule, Canadians like serving on peacekeeping duty. A soldier's morale is directly proportional to what you can brag about. No one brags about the easy assignments, or about working at a desk in the Department of National Defence headquarters in downtown Ottawa. And nothing is worse than having to suffer in silence through your colleagues' war stories after their return from duty in one of the world's hot spots. I'm sure some military personnel do volunteer for peacekeeping duty for higher reasons, such as alleviating human suffering wherever it may be found; but for the majority of us, it's the excitement and camaraderie that beckon. I doubt soldiers will ever change in this regard, and hope they never will.

The early chapters of this book document one soldier's experiences of conventional modern peacekeeping. These were missions whose objectives were relatively definable and achievable. The United Nations Emergency Force in the Middle East was the first to utilize lightly-armed forces, and I joined that mission in 1963. Cyprus was the next hot spot to see large-scale UN involvement, and I managed to serve there three times—in 1965, 1971 and 1978. When the Middle East exploded yet again in 1973, the UN responded with another large peacekeeping contingent, which I joined during its first month in theatre. I also served with the

International Commission of Control and Supervision in Vietnam in 1973, and the UN Observer Group in Central America in 1990-91.

After Lebanon in the 1980s, the first major deployment of lightly-armed UN forces was to the former Yugoslavia in 1991. I almost missed that mission, but as we shall see, a fortunate (for me) sequence of events resulted in my placement as chief of staff in March 1992. Until Yugoslavia, the UN had normally been able to keep the peace because it had avoided becoming involved in civil wars. This policy was in keeping with the UN Charter, which precludes such involvement unless there is a definable threat to international peace and security.

All that ended when the Berlin Wall came down, dragging along with it the Iron Curtain. Almost immediately, numerous ethnic, religious, national and tribal factions started to redefine their borders and their political agendas. Very quickly, the so-called "New World Order" degenerated into the "New World Disorder", and just about everyone turned to the UN for leadership.

It is perhaps unfair and unwise to condemn the UN for failing to resolve the world's problems, because, when we do that, we are condemning ourselves. The UN is merely the sum of its parts: the best version we have of an international parliament. The Security Council, the primary decision-making committee within the UN, paradoxically now finds itself bombarded with demands for the type of action it was designed to undertake in the uncertain, postwar world of 1945 when the UN was created.

Following the Second World War, the "winners"—the United States, the Soviet Union, China, France and Great Britain—received permanent seats on the Security Council and told themselves to police the world. Almost immediately, the Cold War set in; the veto powers assigned to the Permanent Five, as they became known, handcuffed their decision-making. With the end of the Cold War in the 1990s, the Security Council could presumably fulfil its original mandate more easily—except that, in the intervening years, the world and the membership of the United Nations had undergone dramatic changes. Needless to say, since the majority of the members now come from the Third World, they are more than a little concerned about the powerhouses of the 1940s policing the world, and see a real danger of "UN colonialism".

The UN has not willingly or deliberately involved itself in civil conflicts where there is no peace to keep. In Yugoslavia, it literally backed into its new role, establishing a precedent that dominates its current activities in Somalia and Cambodia.

The Yugoslavian federation had begun to implode in early 1991, with declarations of national independence by the northern republics of Slovenia and Croatia. When fighting broke out in Croatia, the Serbian-dominated Yugoslavian National Army (JNA) went on the offensive and occupied territory with a view to protecting Serbs who lived in Croatian border areas.

In November 1991, former American Secretary of State Cyrus Vance, representing the United Nations Secretary-General, devised a peace plan that would see 14,000 UN soldiers assuming responsibility for protecting civilians in these border areas. The Vance Plan would allow the JNA to withdraw to what was left of Yugoslavia: Serbia, Montenegro and Bosnia-Herzegovina. Over objections from its military advisors, including myself, the UN insisted that headquarters for its peacekeeping operations in Croatia should be located in Sarajevo, the capital of Bosnia-Herzegovina—some 350 kilometres to the southeast. The rationale for this decision was that it would "cool things down a bit". It didn't.

Following the European Community's diplomatic recognition of Bosnia-Herzegovina as an independent state on April 6, 1992, war broke out all around us in Sarajevo, as the Bosnian Serbs sought to establish by force their own state-within-a-state. And so, like it or not, the UN found itself directly caught up in a new civil war.

The drafters of the UN Charter knew what they were doing back in 1945 when they precluded the UN from becoming involved in the internal affairs of sovereign nations. But unfortunately, nationhood and civil war came to Bosnia-Herzegovina after we had already established our headquarters in Sarajevo. UN peacekeeping will never be the same again. But I am getting ahead of myself: for that, ultimately, is what this book is about.

L.M.
Ottawa, May 1993

1

A Call from Home

THE 120-MILLIMETRE mortar bomb arched through the sky above Sarajevo and struck our headquarters about twenty feet from my office window. The bomb penetrated the building's metal facade and detonated against the support pillar. Shock waves passed through six feet of concrete and blew away all the paint in thousands of pieces from the interior walls of my office.

I had been standing fifteen feet from my desk in the doorway, talking to my Canadian executive assistant, Major Steve Gagnon, and one of our political officers, Adnan Abdelrazek. Steve and Adnan had been standing behind my desk, their backs to the window. They were both driven to the floor by the blast.

Within seconds, it was impossible to see anything—scorched paint chips filled the room like black confetti. For some reason I knelt on one knee, as if the gesture would provide some protection, and yelled, "Are you okay?"

Steve's voice replied, "Shit, I guess so, but that was close."

Adnan called, "Keep talking, General, so we know where the door is."

"Get your asses out of there! Those things normally travel in pairs! I'll keep counting out loud till you get here. One, two . . . ."

By the time I reached three, Steve had crawled to where I was kneeling. I had a very large office, so he must have made it in two bounds. Adnan was hot on his heels.

"We'd better get down to the bunker, they could be targeting us," I sputtered. By now my mouth was full of cordite dust and burnt paint chips. As Steve started down the hall, I yelled, "Wait a second!" I'd started smoking again after a twelve-year hiatus, and my cigarettes were on my desk in my office. Perhaps there was another mortar bomb on the way, but the prospect of hours in the bunker without my Rothmans was intimidating. "I'm going to crawl in and get my cigarettes, Steve. I'll be right back."

The floor was filthy, but the sunlight was beginning to penetrate the dust and I could identify the outline of my desk. I crawled over a couple of photographs of my racing cars, which had been leaning against the window before the blast. I remember thinking, "Bomb my building but don't screw around with my toys." I reached the desk and took up a position underneath it as my right hand searched the desk-top from below. The cigarettes had moved, but after ten seconds I found them—a bit filthy, but it's a filthy habit, so it didn't really matter.

I quickly crawled back into the hallway. Steve looked down at me and said, "General, with all due respect, now I know why smoking can be injurious to your health!" I tried to laugh but only got another mouthful of black confetti.

By this time, just about everyone in the building had written us off. As we descended the three storeys to the basement bunker, people emerged from their offices looking amazed and offered the revelation that our building had been hit. Not wanting to spend too much time discussing the obvious, the three of us, blanketed with a grey film of dust, merely responded in good soldierly terms: "You're f—ing right we were."

When you work on the third floor, you have to accept that by the time you reach the bunker, it's going to be full. This time was no exception. Under such crowded conditions, there was a natural tendency for our multinational UN force to gather in national groupings. Somehow it's easier to cope with stress if you can crack jokes in your own language. If you are from Russia or Nepal, you don't want to meet your Maker speaking English.

In a perverse sort of way, I enjoyed bunker time. Our 300 personnel were normally shut away in their offices, so you never really had a chance to see your colleagues together except during a meal in the cafeteria, where only about fifty per cent of us could eat at the same time, or in the bunker. It also gave you a chance see how people reacted under the stress of danger. For me it was always gratifying to notice how just about everyone from the twenty-nine nations represented in our headquarters made light of the miserable and dangerous conditions we were experiencing. I mean, there wasn't a lot of choice—they couldn't leave or go for a walk or anything like that—but they could have been sullen, bitter or bitchy, yet weren't. Perhaps the natural competition among nations convinced each of us not to let our side down. Perhaps it was a natural psychological defense mechanism. I don't know, and I guess it doesn't really matter; I'm just glad it happened that way.

Unfortunately, the bunker was not fitted for telephone communications, so our Dutch signallers had fabricated a crude but effective system that gave us a single-line connection to our switchboard upstairs. The area housing the switchboard had been well sandbagged for protection, so more often than not we left someone at the board during the shelling. (The same held true for our Swedish guards. At least ten of them remained above ground guarding the entrance to the building during any fighting or shelling. If this simple security precaution had not been taken, we would undoubtedly have emerged from our hole to find the building looted, or full of local citizens seeking asylum, or both.)

The Dutch field telephone rang, with an irritating sound that reminded me what a forty-foot rattlesnake would sound like if such a beast existed. Steve picked up the receiver. After about thirty seconds, a smile came over his face and he said into the mouthpiece, "Yes, he's around here somewhere; I'll try and find him and ask him." He released the prestle switch on the handset, which meant that the caller could not hear anything from our end until the switch was depressed again. "General, it's Michael Enright from *As It Happens* in Toronto. Will you give him a short interview—approximately ten minutes?"

As It Happens is one of the best-known programs on Canadian radio. It's heard on the Canadian Broadcasting Corporation network for ninety minutes every Monday to Friday, and broadcast on U.S. public radio and in Europe on Radio Canada International. The format is simple: the producers decide on several topics for each evening's show, and a team of callers gets on the phones and tracks down a cross-section of interviewees from experts to innocent bystanders regarding the chosen topic. On any particular evening, the host might interview the president of a country in his office to cross-examine him on human rights, and the next person interviewed could be a political prisoner detained in a room two floors below the president. The program will track down people in the most bizarre locations around the world; today was no exception.

I took the handset from Steve and depressed the prestle switch.

"Hello, Michael, congratulations on tracking us down. What can I do for you?"

"General MacKenzie, good evening. The line isn't that good, so let's get right into the interview in case we lose you altogether. Tell me, what's happening in Sarajevo right now?"

"Well, Michael, that's a bit hard to say. I know what's happening right now in this bunker, which I'm sharing with about 150 other people. I know shells are landing around and in a few cases on this building, otherwise we wouldn't be down here. Aside from that, perhaps you can tell *me* from your sources what *you* think is going on in Sarajevo."

"Not really, General, other than it sounds quite desperate. Tell me, in your previous eight tours of UN duty, did you ever come up against anything like this?"

Over the next few months, I was to hear that same question at least a hundred times, but this was the first. I was impressed that Michael Enright knew I had done eight tours of UN peacekeeping duty before Yugoslavia. Normally our cryptic military biographies are required reading only for our subordinates, or some poor soul forced to introduce us at the local Rotary Club. But as usual, *As It Happens* had done its research.

Eight previous tours. It hardly seemed possible. But then I guess I started younger than most. In fact, it has always seemed to me that when my UN peacekeeping career started, it was thanks to my passion for sports . . . .

2

Getting into Peacekeeping
the Hard Way

I WAS FIVE YEARS OLD at the end of the Second World War.
My father, Eugene MacKenzie, left the Canadian Army as an
engineer warrant officer first class in 1945 and returned to our small
farm in Princeport, Nova Scotia, near my birthplace of Truro. But
after the Korean War broke out, he joined up again, and in 1952
we moved all the way across the country to the army base in
Chilliwack, British Columbia.

During our first year in Chilliwack, I lied about my age to gain
entry to the local squadron of the Royal Canadian Air Cadets. At
six feet, I was tall for a twelve-year-old, so they accepted my word
when I insisted I was two years older. Three years later, at fifteen,
I earned my second uniform by persuading the local army militia
unit that I was seventeen.

In 1956 the military posted my father back to Nova Scotia: to
Sydney in Cape Breton. I completed grade eleven at Sydney
Academy, where I played on the basketball and volleyball teams.
Rather than attend grade twelve there, I followed the lead of my
basketball teammates and enrolled at Xavier Junior College in the
same city.

But I missed the friends I'd left behind in Chilliwack, and
particularly my girlfriend, so I joined Xavier's Canadian Officer
Training Corps as an engineer officer cadet, knowing that my first
summer of training would take place in Chilliwack. This undertaking had the appeal of gaining me a free trip back to my old high
school class graduation and, more importantly, a reunion with the

seventeen-year-old love of my life, who by virtue of the judges' good taste was then reigning as "Miss Apple Blossom Festival".

Strangely enough, I'd never really liked the army until then. Living near a large military camp for four years, I'd seen only the negative aspects: the drunken soldiers on the buses on Friday nights, and the unfair competition presented by the younger recruits to us local boys for the girls at our high school. After all, the soldiers had money and we didn't.

But once I got inside the camp gate as a naive officer cadet, I loved the army. I was enthralled by the challenge and responsibility of leadership. I transferred to the infantry in the following year; my engineer father accused me of "slumming".

By 1960, when I was twenty, I had completed my practical infantry officer qualifications at Camp Borden in Ontario and was scheduled to begin my third year of university, majoring in philosophy at St. Francis Xavier University in Antigonish, Nova Scotia. In early September, I heard that the Queen's Own Rifles of Canada (QOROfC) would soon rotate one of its two battalions to serve with North Atlantic Treaty Organization forces in West Germany. So I left university, was commissioned as a second lieutenant in the infantry, and reported to the Second Battalion, QOROfC, in Calgary, Alberta.

The following year, I was posted to the First Battalion of my regiment in Hemer, West Germany. By then I was comfortable in my role as a platoon commander, responsible for the leadership and welfare of some thirty-five soldiers. I didn't know very much; but a combination of ill-founded self-confidence, bluff and outstanding support and guidance from a series of unforgettable sergeants allowed me to create an impression of competence.

Good young officers who become good old generals are made by good sergeants, and I had some of the best as my tutors: Bob Plant, "Duke" Connelly, "Moose" MacDonald and Huey Graham got me started; Ken Snowden and Don Ethell kept the momentum going during my seven years as a lieutenant. I owe all of them, plus a number of other non-commissioned officers, more than I could ever repay.

IN ADDITION TO MY platoon-commanding responsibilities in West Germany, I was given the secondary duty of unit sports officer, the same assignment I had carried out in Calgary. Hence I had almost two years' experience as a sports officer under my belt when the army decided to send me on an officers' physical training course, conducted at the British Army School of Physical Training in Aldershot, just south of London—presumably to qualify me as a unit sports officer. This is normal military practice: you frequently get sent on a course after you have already done the job for which the course is designed to qualify you.

My plan was to drive from West Germany to Aldershot. I had recently purchased an Austin Healey Mark II. This was the fulfilment of a boyhood dream to own a sports car, and quite possibly the real reason I had joined the army. The Healey was worth every cent of the $2,375 it was supposed to cost me. Unfortunately, when I went to take delivery of the car, I was told the Canadian dollar had been devalued the day before, and since the payment was calculated in Deutschmarks, I owed another $250. The extra $250 represented over four months of my discretionary income, after my compulsory mess bill, compulsory tailor bill and monthly car-loan payments, so I was forced to operate on the cheap with regard to repairs and maintenance.

The Healey's fuel pump packed it in somewhere in northwestern Germany about an hour after I left our base. At that early stage of my subsequently long association with British sports cars, I knew next to nothing about mechanics. Survival dictated a steep learning curve. After much searching, I found the offending pump, located in what could be considered a logical place only by some perverse British engineer—mounted to the underbody of the car, where it could attract all the muck and debris from the road.

I knew the pump was supposed to click as it operated, and it appeared well and truly dead. No amount of hammering with a wrench (I had seen my more highly qualified colleagues use this technique) resulted in anything more than sparks. Delicately, I removed the cap from the end of the pump, horrified that whatever was underneath would fly apart and I'd be stranded in the middle of Germany. There, nice and clean, was a mechanism resembling a mousetrap, with a couple of points that looked like the one I had replaced in the Healey's distribution a few weeks earlier. I touched the moveable point and pushed it towards the fixed one. There was a spark, and the fuel pump clicked. A miracle!

Obviously I couldn't operate the fuel pump manually in its awkward location underneath the car. But, if I removed the tiny jump seat located behind the driver's seat and apparently designed for a four-year-old, I could drive with my left hand and, by twisting my upper body to the right, could get my right hand through the jump-seat opening underneath the car; then, with my index finger, I could just reach the points of the fuel pump. I decided to give it a try.

It took me a while to determine the rate at which the points had to be closed in order to maintain an adequate fuel flow. At relatively slow speeds through built-up areas, once every four or five seconds seemed to suffice; but once on the Autobahn, my index finger was a blur as it tried to keep up with the 85-90-miles-per-hour cruising speed. If the engine faltered, I just backed off for a couple of seconds until my finger caught up with the fuel demand of the engine.

Everything was okay until I hit Belgium, with its cobbled roads. In any other country, cobbled roads would necessitate a reduction in average speed. Not so in Belgium, birthplace of Jackie Ikyx, five-time winner of the Le Mans twenty-four-hour race. There, the roads were like a green flag to drivers who speeded up in order to enjoy the thrill of sliding their family sedans around corners at high speed, like one of their Formula One heroes.

I thoroughly enjoyed the competitive nature of the Belgian drivers and wanted to take advantage of the opportunity to joust with them for bragging rights. Unfortunately, the cobblestones set up a high-speed vibration throughout the Healey, which made it difficult for my right index finger, frantically searching underneath the car, to find the points on more than one in three attempts. As a result, I would be flying along a stretch of road in company with a couple of Belgian Walter Mittys, shifting with my left hand and maintaining directional control with my left knee on the steering wheel while my right hand operated the fuel pump, and always, it seemed, at the critical point rounding a corner, the engine would starve for fuel and my rivals would disappear at high speed or nearly ram me from the rear. What bothered me most was having them think that the guy in the Healey with the Canadian registration didn't know how to drive. They were also slightly bemused by my somewhat unconventional posture behind the wheel.

Fortunately, I survived Belgium and made it to the officers' mess in Aldershot on August 22, 1962. My injuries were nothing more serious than an index finger in need of a major rebuild, and a spine that would take a couple of days to straighten out, thanks to the contortions I had inflicted on it over some 500 miles.

Entering the mess, I was greeted by an indifferent silence. I considered this most unusual, given the British reputation for mess life, and the large number of single officers presumably living in the building. A larger-than-life picture of Field Marshall Montgomery of Alamein stared down at me as I walked towards some muffled sounds at the far end of a long hall. (As I would learn, Montgomery was the Honourary Colonel-in-Chief of the British Army School of Physical Training.) At the end of the hall was a tiny room containing a small television set. There was no picture on the screen, not even snow, just a plain green piece of useless glass in a wooden cabinet. A voice, however, was emerging from the set's speaker, and all ten people in the room were hanging on every word. No one acknowledged my arrival, preferring to stare intently at the blank screen, as if in the hope that a picture would appear.

As I concentrated, I recognized the voice of John F. Kennedy. Like the others, I listened with increasing excitement as the President explained in no uncertain terms that the United States was imposing an arms embargo on Cuba, and any Soviet missiles heading for Cuba would be intercepted by the U.S. Navy. At that moment, I was convinced I would soon be ordered to return to my unit to help defend against the Soviet hordes as they poured westward across the inter-German frontier.

"What the hell does he think he's doing—taking such action without consulting our Prime Minister!" A very large lady who took up most of the sofa had spoken. Everyone else was nodding in agreement. I couldn't believe my ears.

In my new home for barely five minutes, I blurted out, "Now, wait a second. Cuba is in the United States' backyard. If the world's two superpowers want to square off over Cuba, I don't see what it has to do with England."

I was evicted before I had a chance to introduce myself. The fat lady, I discovered on completion of my monologue, was the president of the mess committee, second in authority only to the commanding officer within the Mess itself. I also determined that she was a major, a scant few seconds after she determined that I was a mere lieutenant. I now found myself on the front steps of the mess facing my pathetic Healey, thinking how one of these days I'd have to stop saying exactly what I thought—particularly to military officers out of uniform.

I decided to try and find a duty officer so I could phone my unit in Germany to see if we were at war and if I should return immediately, index finger permitting. As I descended the steps towards the car, the mess door opened and a delegation of half a dozen young officers appeared with drinks in hand, including one for me.

"Don't pay any attention to the old girl," one of them said. "She's into the gin tonight and terribly upset about the demise of the Empire. Come on back in and buy her a drink and all will be forgotten."

I looked the group over. A few of them looked like "jocks", but the rest didn't fit the stereotype. "Are you all here on the officers' PT course?" I asked. They all nodded. I asked the frailest-looking of the group, "What's your sport?"

He responded, "Absolutely nothing. I look upon physical exercise as I do masturbation—self-abuse!"

"Then why are you here?" I asked.

"Oh, as punishment. My commanding officer was tired of giving me extra unit duties. He decided eight weeks of good tough physical training would sort me out."

Great, I thought. I've arrived at a young officers' penal colony masquerading as a school of physical training. "How many of you are here as a form of punishment?" I asked. To my considerable relief, only two hands went up.

"And about two or three more inside, but that's not bad out of fourteen," said a fit and tough-looking officer with a strong Scottish accent and a blond crewcut. "I'm a boxer," he said. This turned out to be an understatement a few weeks later, when the two of us squared off during the pugilistic phase of the curriculum.

The course at Aldershot turned out to be one of the most enjoyable experiences of my life. Apart from having to live on a diet of Mars bars due to the inadequate volume of food at every meal, it was paradise for anyone who loved sports. I had played many of the sports in the course for most of my life: basketball, volleyball, soccer. I adapted easily to rugby, having played in the backfield in college football. Boxing and judo were great fun, and I was able to beat everyone but the black-belt course sergeant-major, Mike Sheedy, who used to wipe the mat with me during judo class. I loved that sport so much that Mike and I would take coffee break and lunch hour to do judo groundwork when, occasionally and only occasionally, I would pin him. He probably let me win a few so I would be crazy enough to ask for more. He was a great instructor and a great person.

In addition to the course sports, I played for the Aldershot

Warriors, one of the top basketball teams in the British Army and the U.K. We were up to the standard of a medium-sized Canadian university team of the day: not great, but pretty good. Our biggest game was against the American students at Cambridge. We won 80 to 52, and I managed 36 points. It was the first time in my life that I'd been written up in my hometown newspaper. My mother wrote the article after I called her.

The course moved on to swimming, gymnastics, trapeze work over the swimming pool, and badminton. It was like being on holiday. There were exams on rules and organization, but it was relatively easy to get marks in the high nineties. It wasn't so easy for the less athletically inclined who had been sent to the school for punishment; they really took a beating early on. However, as in any military undertaking, group cohesion developed very quickly, and those of us who were there because we wanted to be made a pledge to get the other characters through. Every one of them made it; in a few cases, it turned their careers around. Their commanding officers had known what they were doing when they banished their troublemakers to the school.

As the course approached the end, Sergeant-Major Sheedy took me aside and told me to work as hard as I could for perfect scores on my exams. "If you get close to 100 per cent, you could leave here with the highest overall grade ever achieved in the history of the school." I took his advice to heart and ended up with a 98 per cent average. When that was combined with the practical side of the course and my extracurricular team activities, the course officer advised me that I had achieved the highest mark given to date.

MEANWHILE, IN THE GAZA STRIP, some 1,500 miles to the southeast, Colonel Don Rochester, commander of the Canadian Base Unit Middle East (CBUME), was frustrated. Colonel Rochester commanded over a thousand Canadians serving with the United Nations Emergency Force (UNEF), which had been established on the armistice demarcation line between Egypt and Israel in 1957. The UN border forces consisted of large infantry units from India, Brazil and Sweden; Denmark and Norway together formed a DANOR battalion; and two armoured reconnaissance squadrons came from Yugoslavia and Canada. Canada also provided the bulk of the administrative support to the entire force from a large base at Camp Rafah, situated in Egypt just outside the southern end of the Gaza Strip.

Since the inception of the Emergency Force, there had been an active inter-unit sports programme based on the most popular games played by the nations contributing units to UNEF. Basketball, volleyball, European handball and soccer were the major prestige sports, and winning a championship meant a great deal within the force. During its six years in UNEF, however, the large Canadian contingent had never won a championship—not even in one of the non-prestige sports like swimming or track. Colonel Rochester decided to do something about this: he would bring in a full-time sports officer to deal with the problem. If it meant sacrificing a position to make room for the sports officer, he would offer up his legal major.

Colonel Rochester's message requesting a full-time sports officer arrived at army headquarters in Ottawa and, after a few days of moving from one in-basket to another, found its way to a junior personnel officer for action. The officer's superior had scribbled across Colonel Rochester's message: "Make it happen."

Like most military officers during our days condemned to a desk, the personnel officer had developed a routine of putting difficult problems off to one side for consideration later in the day. Rochester's message qualified as difficult because the legal major's career manager would, without a doubt, protest to the highest authorities available about losing a plum legal position in a UN mission to a bloody jockstrapper.

At that point, Fate intervened to influence the direction of my career for the next thirty years. The next file in the personnel officer's basket was titled "Course Report—British Army School of Physical Training—ZF8294 Lt. L.W. MacKenzie QOROfc." As he reviewed the file with its somewhat flowery description of my athletic and leadership abilities, the spark of an idea began to glow. The officer reached for Colonel Rochester's request and removed it from the "Difficult—wait for later" pile. "Do I have a solution for Colonel Rochester," the officer mused.

By that time, thanks to a benevolent British Motor Corporation dealer in London who couldn't believe that I had driven from Germany operating the electric fuel pump on the Healey with my index finger, and had insisted on installing a new pump at no charge, I had returned uneventfully to my unit. I'd been back only a couple of weeks when I was told to report to the commanding officer. The C.O. was a gregarious and charming individual who had led a platoon ashore at Normandy; however, it was highly unusual for

Lieutenant MacKenzie to have an audience with Lieutenant-Colonel Hank Elliot in his office. I assumed I was in deep trouble.

"Lew, I've got a dumb message here from headquarters in Ottawa. It advises me you are posted to something called CBUME in the Gaza Strip. I don't like it: you're too young, you need a few more years with the battalion, and I need you on our basketball team. However, an order is an order. You had better get packed."

I spent the remaining few days in Germany trying to find someone who knew what CBUME stood for. I was unsuccessful. The favourite speculation was Canadian Base Units Medical Establishment. Great, I thought, I'm off to the desert to be sports officer for a MASH unit!

3

Tan-less in Gaza

▪

ON MARCH 10, 1963, I flew from Pisa, Italy, to El Arish, Egypt, in a Royal Canadian Air Force North Star. I had travelled to Pisa by train through major blizzards in Switzerland and northern Italy. About halfway to Pisa, I realized what was different about this trip: I was well and truly alone for the first time since I had joined the army.

The military is a bit like climbing a tree, with a big safety net underneath in case you fall: you are always surrounded by good people, a number of whom are much more experienced than you are. No matter what kind of problem you encounter, from attacking an "enemy" position on exercise to resolving a minor administrative problem, there is no shortage of advice from one or more in the group, which leads you towards an acceptable, tried-and-true solution. This trip, however, was fun; I was on my own.

Five hours after we took off, we were still roaring along over a vast expanse of the Mediterranean. The North Star was the tractor of our air force: loud, rough and slow, but reliable as hell. On the horizon, my gaze picked up what I thought was a sandy scum on the water. As we got closer, I began to realize it was landfall—using the term in its most generous connotation. The elevation of the desert was only a few inches above sea level. I could make out some sand dunes a few hundred metres back from the coastline; beyond that, the featureless sandbox extended to the horizon.

The North Star banked as we began a giant circle. The left wing dipped, and for the first time I was observing civilization in Egypt. Hundreds of square adobe shacks huddled together beside a black ribbon of highway parallelling the coast. A bit further inland, I could

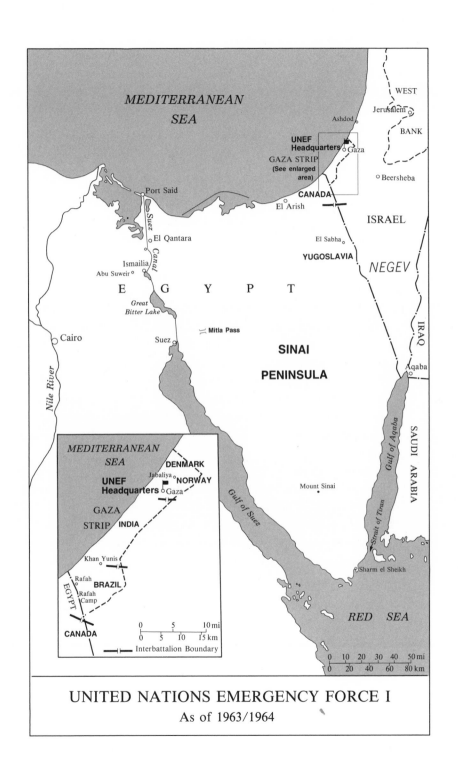

MEDITERRANEAN
SEA

WEST

Ashdod   Jerusalem
          BANK

UNEF
Headquarters   Gaza
GAZA STRIP
(See enlarged
area)   Beersheba

CANADA
Port Said   El Arish
                              ISRAEL

Suez   El Sabha
Canal   El Qantara
                         YUGOSLAVIA   NEGEV

Ismailia
Abu Suweir

E   G   Y   P   T

Great
Bitter Lake   IRAQ

Mitla Pass
Cairo   Aqaba

Suez   SINAI

Nile River   PENINSULA

MEDITERRANEAN
SEA   DENMARK
                    Gulf of Aqaba
UNEF   Jabaliya NORWAY   SAUDI
Headquarters   Gaza   ARABIA

GAZA
                                Mount Sinai
STRIP   INDIA
                                    Strait of Tiran
Gulf of Suez

Khan Yunis
Rafah   BRAZIL
Rafah
Camp   Sharm el Sheikh

EGYPT

CANADA   0   5   10 mi   RED   SEA
              0   5   10   15 km
              Interbattalion Boundary

              0 10 20 30 40 50 mi
              0   20   40   60   80 km

UNITED NATIONS EMERGENCY FORCE I
As of 1963/1964

see a more impressive collection of what appeared to be modern buildings, some of which were two or three storeys high. To the south of the built-up area was something that looked like a dragstrip: very straight, very black and not all that long. As our aircraft eased out of its bank and lined up on the dragstrip, I realized we had arrived at the El Arish runway.

Since that first trip to a desert environment, I've returned many times and know what to expect. But nothing prepared me for the first few moments. The door of the North Star was wrestled open by the load master, and immediately all we passengers broke out in a heavy sweat. It was as if someone had run a six-foot metal hose from a blast furnace and stuck it in the door of our aircraft. I took a couple of breaths, but nothing of value was reaching my lungs—there certainly didn't seem to be any oxygen mixed in with the dust and heat.

As I made it down the metal ladder, I couldn't see. Everything except the runway was the colour of sand, or just plain white. Just before my eyes welled up with tears from the glare, I thought I saw some white vehicles with UN markings, but I wasn't sure.

A voice from the other side of my closed eyelids said, "Hurry up, Mr. MacKenzie. We have to get to Camp Rafah right away." I stumbled into the arms of Sergeant Jack McBride, the sports NCO for the Canadian contingent. He handed me his sunglasses: "Bright, isn't it?"

Sergeant McBride was also a member of the Queen's Own Rifles of Canada, but because of his outstanding athletic abilities was employed with the army's physical education and recreation branch. "Mr. MacKenzie, we have to hurry," he repeated. "I've got the fastest jeep in the camp. There's a basketball uniform for you on the back seat. We play the Brazilians, the number-one team in UNEF, in less than an hour. We should be able to make it for the opening tip-off if we get a move on. Someone will bring your bags."

Operating on the theory that you never argue with a sergeant who has been in the theatre for six months compared to your forty-five seconds, I hustled to the jeep, losing a pint of sweat over the seventy-five metre jog. I don't remember a lot about the mad dash to Camp Rafah. It was a blur of camels, defensive positions, tanks, a lot of soldiers in sand-coloured uniforms, and more kids, burnt absolutely black from the sun, than I had ever seen before in one place. I also decided that the next time Sergeant Jack and I made a trip like this, I would drive.

We arrived at the outdoor concrete basketball court about two minutes before game time. I had changed in the jeep. The uniform fit; the shoes were a bit small, but they would do. There were about fifteen players warming up on the court, and they were all black. I knew that Brazil had a tremendous cross-section of skin colours, but I was surprised and pleased that the entire Canadian team was black also. My joy was short-lived as I got closer and realized I was observing the darkest tans ever seen on the face of the earth. Everything else in the area was white: the court, the backboards, the surrounding buildings, the vehicles and, of course, me.

My pasty-white body stood out like a spotlight. I thought I might gain an advantage by blinding our opponents by the glare from my skin. I ran over to the Canadian team and was advised I was starting at centre. I asked about the opposition and was told they usually beat us by about thirty points.

The first half was more like a dream than a game. I gradually found some oxygen in the heat masquerading as air, but it never seemed enough to permit normal breathing. It was fun playing outdoors, except that every time you went up for a shot, you had to search for a white backboard against the background of a white sky, a sandy-white desert or a white building. Occasionally you came down with the ball still in your hands, having failed to find your target.

As we neared the halfway mark, we were leading 38-32. I had managed about thirty points, strictly on adrenalin. The game was a lot rougher than I had expected; the Brazilians were not taking kindly to being beaten. Just before the end of the half, I tried a drive down the centre of the key. A large Brazilian defender stuck out his arm and knee and stopped me cold. Not appreciating his unorthodox technique, I grabbed him around the throat and threw him to the ground with my knee on his chest. A crowd of spectators and players quickly gathered, pushing and shoving in all directions. I felt something touch the back of my head; then just as suddenly it was gone. The crowd around me had shifted about ten metres to the rear and was moving towards a large building adjacent to the court. In the centre of the crowd, I could see the red collar-tabs of a Canadian full colonel bobbing up and down. Canada had only one colonel in the Middle East, and so I knew it had to be Colonel Rochester.

My Brazilian opponent and I decided to stop our mock battle; after all, there was no one around to keep us from fighting, so it didn't make a lot of sense to continue. I ran over to the crowd and grabbed the arm of a Canadian sergeant in uniform and asked him what the hell was going on.

"You mean, you didn't see it? A Brazilian military policeman didn't like you flooring one of their players, so he ran onto the court, drew his .45 and put it against the back of your head. Colonel Rochester shot out of his seat and decked him with a solid right. They're somewhere in the middle of that crowd."

Well, I thought, I've made my mark with the Canadian contingent. When I thought further about it, I wasn't sure hitting someone who had his finger on the trigger of a pistol aimed at the back of my head was a good idea; but what the hell, it had worked. Good for the Colonel.

After a few minutes, things were sorted out and everyone was shaking hands. After all, we were supposed to be a peacekeeping force. Half-time was declared, and I sat down with my new teammates to discuss our tactics for the second half. I started to feel woozy.

I woke up an hour later in the camp hospital.

I was covered with wet sheets, and a tall blonde woman in a white coat was attempting to pour fluid into my mouth. "Acute dehydration," she said with a strong Swedish accent. "You really should take some time to get acclimatized before you play around outdoors. Your body temperature is almost normal now, so you can spend the rest of the day in your quarters."

"Did we win?" I asked.

Another voice responded, "Almost. They beat us by a mere eight points. We'll get them next time."

The voice belonged to Captain Charlie Scott-Brown, who ran the Blue Beret, the UN equivalent of an American PX. In addition, Charlie was responsible for anything dealing with the troops' welfare—vacation arrangements, visits, tours, two beaches, sports facilities, movies, books, et al. He had been CANLOAN during World War Two—one of those Canadian officers who had been "loaned" to the British Army for the duration of the war. Charlie was now an officer of the famous Canadian regiment I was to join in 1970, the Princess Patricia's Canadian Light Infantry (PPCLI).

"Grab your things and I'll drive you to your quarters," he ordered, keeping up a visual exchange with the nurse. I discovered later that the six Swedish nurses were the only females in the entire camp of 1,200 men, and Charlie, like just about everyone else, enjoyed a face-to-face encounter, no matter how brief.

My "things" consisted of my uniform, since I'd left everything else at the airstrip. We went outside the hospital and I encountered my first Citroën *deux chevaux*. The name stood for two horsepower, *en français*, which was probably an exaggeration. The car was, however, a marvellous bit of French cost-effective engineering: front-wheel drive, a motorcycle engine, and a motorcyle gearbox operated by a rod with a large plastic ball that protruded from the centre of the firewall, requiring a sequence of pulls, pushes and twists to operate. It was a true convertible, since the roof was like a rubber mat that you rolled back and clipped in place if you wanted to experience the delights of 120 degrees F buffeting your face. The side windows were nasty little devices, with the glass split horizontally halfway up, designed to open by a doubtful arrangement of hinges and metal pins. The space provided was enough to let you stick your elbow out the window while bouncing along the highway on the vehicle's pneumatic suspension.

Unfortunately, as I was to learn, the rubber grommets holding the pins in place wore out very quickly. The window would stay open as long as the vehicle proceeded over a glass-like surface, but the slightest bump would jar the half-window loose, and it would swing down like some miniature, poorly aligned guillotine, slashing the elbow and forearm of the driver or passenger. You could recognize everyone in the camp who had a *deux chevaux* by the telltale scars around their left elbows. Damage to the right elbow meant you didn't rate a car and were a mere passenger.

Charlie drove me to an isolated spot beside barbed wire and a machine-gun post located at the extreme west side of the camp. There, tucked between a few cactii, was a decrepit, bleached bell-tent. Almost every panel had a tear, and the door flap was missing. The ropes were loose, and the tent was having difficulty coping with the prevailing winds blowing hard off the sea. There was a sand floor. An austere issue of furniture consisted of a faded canvas cot, a broken metal chair and a tiny table. My two boxes had been brought from the aircraft and were stacked on one side of the tent. A washbasin hung from the centre pole. This, presumably, would be my new home.

"Clean yourself up," Charlie ordered. "Get changed into civvies—open-necked, short-sleeved shirt is fine. I'll be back to pick you up in forty minutes. We'll go over to the mess so you can meet some of the gang." With that he disappeared in the direction of civilization, his *deux chevaux* bounding over the sand better than a modern-day dune buggy.

I found a jerry can of water and gave myself a sparrow bath from the washbasin. I opened my boxes from Germany and discovered they were not sandproof. I donned a wrinkled shirt and slacks and sat on my metal chair to do up my shoes. I had the strange feeling I was being watched; when I glanced at the entrance, I discovered why. Directly in front of where the door flap should have been was a bush resembling a tumbleweed from the North American west. Coiled around the centre of the bush, its triangular head protruding from the top, was a sandy-coloured, four-foot snake. Its beady eyes were watching my every move.

Just as I decided to sacrifice one of the legs of my metal chair as an anti-snake weapon, Charlie came bounding back over the dunes in the *deux chevaux*, and the snake disappeared in the opposite direction.

I jumped in beside Charlie and we drove almost a mile until we entered the built-up area of the camp. Considering the state of my quarters, I was amazed how well maintained and neatly laid out the camp was. The road system was paved and well signposted, and there were many relatively new buildings. We pulled up in front of a long walkway bordered by colourful flowers and some real grass—the first I had seen since Italy. We entered a beautiful patio with tables and chairs arranged as in an outdoor restaurant. Before we went into the mess building itself, I noticed an outdoor movie screen permanently installed on one side of the patio.

The mess was crowded with officers enjoying themselves. Everyone was very friendly to me, even though I was the most junior officer there. After my recent encounter with dehydration and my long trip in the North Star, it took only a couple of rum-and-Cokes for me to catch up with the party. I lasted until midnight, when I decided I would either make a fool of myself or go to sleep. I opted for the latter and asked Charlie if someone could drive me back to my tent. Everyone within earshot laughed and someone said, "Charlie, for God's sake, tell him!"

Charlie turned to me and said, "Lew, you can walk to your quarters from here; your room is only seventy-five yards away. Your boxes have been moved there from the tent. We pull this gag on most of our newcomers—at least the ones we like."

I considered grabbing my second throat of the day, but that would have been considered assaulting a superior, so I had a good laugh along with everyone else. After all, I was going to have my own room.

In fact, it barely qualified as a room; but after the tent, it looked like a palace. My tiny bed barely fit along one wall, which gives an indication of the room's dimensions. There was a small window cut through the adobe wall, and a bit of a closet. I pinned a couple of pictures of Ferrari racing cars onto the wall and crashed into a sleep resembling a coma.

THE NEXT MORNING, Colonel Rochester was sitting behind his desk, looking fresh and cool in spite of the 100-degree F temperature. I was sweltering as I listened to the Colonel outline my assignment:

"I gave up my legal officer to get a sports officer, Lew. Not just someone to organize the sports but play them too. You probably don't know this, but I was a sports officer in Petawawa when your dad was a sergeant-major there for a few years during World War Two. I remember him very well, he was a fine combat engineer. I'm an engineer also, so we're going to get along just fine.

"Lew, the officers and soldiers here are drinking too much. They have too much spare time. We work until early afternoon every day, and then it seems everyone disappears to the various messes and gets drunk. I want you to change that. Get them interested in some sports and let's win some championships. If you know of any good soldier athletes in Canada, let me know who they are and I'll get some of them posted over here to give you some talent."

I had my marching orders. I felt my first priority was to instil some pride in our men by winning a few trophies in the UNEF athletic competitions. It would take a while to gather and train the athletes necessary to win one of the prestige sports, so I decided to attack the problem another way.

At the next meeting of the UNEF sports committee in Gaza, where all national contingents sent their representatives, I argued that none of the sports currently being played was a Canadian sport. This was blatantly unfair, and the committee should agree to introduce at least two Canadian sports into the schedule.

The committee was chaired by a UN civilian welfare officer, an American by the name of "Hobbie" Holtzendorf. "That sounds reasonable," said Holtzendorf, "which two were you thinking of?"

"Horseshoes and darts!" I replied.

Two weeks later, the Canadian contingent won its first two trophies. Most of the other contingents had never seen a horseshoe used for anything but its intended purpose, and those who played darts didn't play them eight to twelve hours a day, like some of our mess members.

Unfortunately, the Indian battalion took all the UN sports seriously. The Indians put together two teams that started to practise darts and horseshoes full-time. Three weeks after our magnificent victories, the second round of both sports was held, and the Indians soundly trounced our very best. I considered lobbying for curling or ice hockey, but aside from the logistical problems, I feared that the Indians would learn how to skate.

The drinking problem in the camp required a more global approach. The most popular Canadian sport by far was softball, now referred to as fastball. The few softball teams we had were extremely good. Teams were organized along corps lines: Engineers, Signallers, Supply, Transport, Armoured Reconnaissance, etc. Each corps had a number of top players posted in on a regular basis, as they attempted to win the Canadian championship. I tried to encourage more teams to participate but had only limited success.

Later in my tour, Sergeant McBride was replaced by Sergeant Nick Procenko, a professional physical educational specialist and an outstanding infielder. After a few games, watching base hits turn into home runs as the ball rolled forever over the baked clay field, Nick said, "Why don't we put up an outfield fence?"

The fence was an immediate hit with both players and spectators. It improved the quality of the games, but interest and participation remained about the same.

I went to see Colonel Rochester. "Sir, let me put a hole the size of a dinner plate in the home-run fence in straight-away centre. If any player hits the ball through the hole, he gets thirty days' extra leave and a free return flight to Canada. I can virtually guarantee you that no one will hit the hole and we will double the size of our league. In addition, if any spectator wants to twin himself with any player on the field, he can do so for twenty-five cents; if his player puts the ball through the hole, the spectator gets two weeks' free leave and a return flight to Canada. We'll give the money to the UN Refugee organization in the Gaza Strip."

The Colonel, never a man to back off from a decision, merely said, "Do it."

In those days, Canadians serving with UNEF seldom got home during their one-year postings in the desert. So our incentives worked: we didn't double the size of the league, but we came close.

Our crowds got bigger, and we built some bleachers. No one hit the ball within two feet of the hole, but with the league profits we helped build a rehydration facility for Palestinian refugees in the Gaza Strip.

Gradually, some of the young jocks back home whom I had earmarked for the Colonel started to arrive on posting. All in their early-to-mid-twenties, and most of them well over six feet in height, they were a superb group of athletes. Probably the best example of the sheer athletic talent that came to exist within the Canadian camp involved our newfound prowess at the sport of outdoor European handball, a game unknown to North Americans in the early '60s.

If you place a ball in the middle of a field, most Europeans will rush out and kick it. North Americans will pick it up and find different ways to throw it around. European handball is somewhere in between and is, therefore, a slightly unusual sport for Europeans. You play the game with your hands, passing the ball, proceeding down the field by dribbling the ball a minimum of once every three steps, and throwing the ball through a soccer-sized goal from outside a curved restraining line. The harder you can throw the ball, the better.

I gathered my collection of young soldier athletes on a soccer field and explained the rules. We practised two hours a day for a week and then played our first match—against the Yugoslavians, the reigning UNEF champions at the time. To the shock of the Yugoslavians, and to my considerable surprise, we won a closely fought match. The game came naturally to us, and we threw the ball harder than anyone else in the league. The Yugoslavians, incidentally, were tough soldiers and good athletes. If one of them had predicted that three decades later I would be serving in his country in the midst of a bloody civil war, I'd have thought he was joking.

ABOUT SEVEN MONTHS into my one-year tour, Colonel Rochester called me to his office. "Lew, I've decided to take a one-year extension and I'd like you to stay with me. What do you say?"

Lieutenants rarely, if ever, say no to colonels; and if they do, they do so only once. I was still paying for the Healey, which I had written off hours after selling it and cancelling the automobile insurance in Germany. If I stayed in Egypt another year, I could probably save $2,000 towards the purchase of another sports car. "Okay, sir—I'll stay," I said, with limited conviction.

It wasn't until the first plane left, carrying people who had arrived after me going home at the end of their one-year tour, that

I realized what a mistake I'd made. But it was a bit like parachuting—once you leave the door, you can change your mind all you want, but you are still going to hit the ground. I had agreed to an extension, so I turned my attention to getting through my second year in the desert.

I can never pass up playing with anything that reminds me of a racing car. I hadn't started motor racing at that stage of my life, since I was always broke, but knew that someday I would give it a try. For now, in the middle of nowhere, the go-kart would have to do.

The Canadian Air Force at El Arish had bought a dozen go-karts but were not able to maintain them. At our base, on the other hand, we had an excellent workshop bursting at the seams with talented mechanics, so I bought the entire fleet of karts from the air force. We ran a series of races on the parade square, and occasionally rigged up some special air cleaners and ran races on the dirt ball field.

I parked my *deux chevaux* and started driving a go-kart from my quarters to the office—a run of three-quarters of a mile, with a couple of nice, sweeping high-speed curves along the way. Regrettably, there was a stop sign at the corner by the Blue Beret welfare complex, just before I reached my office. The view in the area of the corner wasn't obstructed, so if you looked in three directions very quickly, you could determine if there were any approaching traffic. Most of the time there wasn't, so you could howl through the stop sign and the junction at high speed. On a good day, I could make it to the office in under a minute: 53.7 seconds was my best time.

One morning, still trying to beat my best time, I came out of the last sweeping turn towards the stop sign and picked up the movement of something in the air off to my left, moving my way. It was what we affectionately called a "shit beetle". The creatures received this descriptive name because they would push balls of camel dung along the desert floor back to their nests. They wouldn't have been a problem if they had stuck to the ground, but unfortunately, for some bizarre reason that only Darwin would understand, they had developed the ability to fly—and even though they were about the size of a tennis ball, they flew bloody fast. In fact, they had been known to go through the windscreen of a *deux chevaux*.

Through some error in navigation, this particular specimen now embedded itself in my forehead. At a closing speed approaching eighty miles an hour, there wasn't much left of the beetle, at least in one piece. Its remains were running into my eyes and ears, and too late I lost all vision; I saw the stop sign and a large black car and heard the squeal of brakes. I brought the go-kart to a halt fifty yards beyond the sign, just in time to hear the familiar voice of Colonel Rochester yell, "Lew, that's the last time you will ever drive one of those contraptions on the street!"

I wanted to shout "Yes, sir," but part of what was left of the beetle had worked its way into my mouth.

For a safer form of diversion, we received movies from Canada on a weekly flight. They were shown in the camp every night, and the reels were passed in sequence between the Canadian messes in Camp Rafah and several recce squadron observation posts, which extended twenty miles into the Sinai Desert to the point where the Canadians linked up with the Yugoslavians. We started the showings as soon as the sun went down, so the third mess in the sequence usually started viewing about two hours after the first one.

Most of the movies were seriously dated and always seemed to be about war or infidelity or both. I decided to try to get some new ones, and wrote to a few American distributors. One responded with a magnificent idea: he would send us *Lawrence of Arabia* concurrent with its world premiere in the major cities of the world.

Everyone was terribly excited. Part of the film had been shot on location less than a hundred miles to the south of us, so I decided to orchestrate something special for our gala premiere. Everyone was in his seat as the sun went down. I was intentionally late with the first reel, and chants of "Where the hell is MacKenzie?" could be heard as I formed up with my detail outside the mess. I had rented a scruffy camel and an equally scruffy camel driver. A fellow officer and I were decked out in full Bedouin dress as I rode atop the camel into the mess. We proceeded through the crowd of cheering moviegoers until I reached the area of the projector. I gave what I thought was a signal for the camel to turn around and face the screen. Regrettably, he interpreted my attempt to control him as a signal to kneel down.

A new president of the mess had been appointed a few days earlier: an artillery officer, Major Grace, who had a weakness for things horticultural. During the last two days, the Major had planted a beautiful flower garden in the middle of the patio, right beside the spot where we set up the projector. The camel decided that if he was going to kneel down, he might as well do it on something soft instead of the patio stones. He took two steps to the right and started his articulated, three-phase kneeling process, which culminated in his four massive feet and bulging belly crushing every one of Major Grace's lovingly planted flowers. The Major was livid; but fortunately, before he had a chance to send me off to my quarters, Colonel Rochester started to laugh. Laughing is contagious when initiated by the senior officer, so I had my reprieve.

Lawrence of Arabia was a full four reels. Everyone wanted to see it on the first night, so arrangements had been made to deliver it reel by reel to the boys at the outposts in the desert, even though some of them would not see the first reel until two A.M. About midnight, I received a call from one of the desert observation posts. "It's a great movie, but I'm sure we're missing something. The story really jumped around between the second and third reel," the caller explained.

"Didn't you get four reels?" I queried.

"Nope—just three, and they're marked one, two and four."

My heart sank. When I told my boss, Captain Bob Muir, another PPCLI officer who had replaced Charlie Scott-Brown, he said, "Don't worry—you took out insurance on them, didn't you?"

Who the hell insures movies, I thought. "Why? How much do you figure a reel is worth?" I asked, not wanting to know the answer.

"Oh, I've heard around $60,000," Bob replied. At my savings rate of $2,000 a year, I'd be spending the next thirty years in UNEF with a blue beret permanently stitched to my head.

A phone call to New York the next day saved my life: the folks at UN headquarters had insured the film, and I was off the hook. An investigation revealed that the reel had probably fallen off the back of the jeep delivering it to the next outpost in the desert. A search the following day revealed nothing. I occasionally still have visions of a Bedouin holding the sixteen-millimetre film up to the sun and watching frame by frame as Peter O'Toole blows up the railway from Aqaba to Cairo, but without benefit of the marvellous soundtrack.

In October 1964, I left unef after twenty months under a blue beret. My first experience with a un peacekeeping mission had taught me little about the un itself, but a lot about human nature, particularly about people who are away from home for extended periods of time. The experience brought out the best in most of them, and the busier they were, the happier they were. This lesson was to be reinforced many times during the next three decades. And I had my first un medal, appropriately inscribed, "In the Service of Peace".

4

Cyprus—First Tour

I HAD ACCUMULATED over two months' leave during my time in West Germany and Gaza. Unfortunately, a salary of less than $300 a month did not permit me to stay on leave for the full time, particularly since I had bought another British sports car, a Triumph TR4, as soon as I touched down in Canada. I ran out of money after three weeks and reported to my old unit, the First Battalion, Queen's Own Rifles of Canada, which had returned from West Germany to Victoria, British Columbia.

I spent the first few months commanding an infantry platoon, in preparation for the first in an annual series of amphibious exercises on the west coast of British Columbia. My company commander was Major Charlie Belzile, a tough, single, charismatic French Canadian who, a mere eighteen years later, would be Lieutenant-General Belzile commanding the Canadian Army.

By a process of osmosis, Charlie had a significant impact on my leadership style. I admired his ability to be informal with his subordinates, right down to the most junior soldier; at the same time, everyone knew who was in charge. What separated Charlie from most other commanders was that he rarely had to *show* he was the boss. I liked that, and so, it seemed, did his soldiers, since they worked their tails off for him—as did I—and enjoyed doing it.

In January 1965, my commanding officer, Lieutenant-Colonel Kip Kirby, gave me the best lieutenant's job in the battalion. We had just been warned for UN peacekeeping duty in Cyprus, starting in April, and I would command the unit's reconnaissance platoon. I was disappointed to be leaving Charlie's company, but I knew that

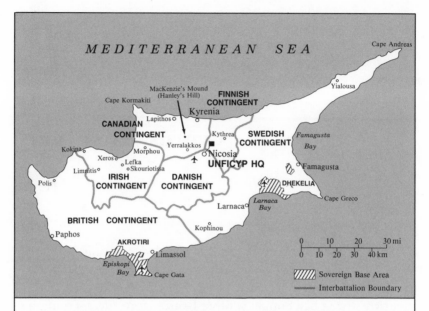

UNITED NATIONS FORCE IN CYPRUS
As of 1965

UNITED NATIONS FORCE IN CYPRUS
As of 1978

I wouldn't have received the appointment without his support, so I counted my blessings and started to study the history of Cyprus.

Everyone in the unit was excited about the prospect of serving with the UN. Despite the fact that Lester Pearson had originated the idea of UN peacekeeping units interposing themselves between belligerents, the Cyprus mission was the first deployment of a large Canadian infantry unit on such duty. Two Canadian battalions, from the Royal 22nd Regiment (the Van Doos) and the Canadian Guards, had preceded us. Both had been shot at on numerous occasions, so we took our training seriously.

I looked forward to this tour even more than most of my colleagues. Although my time in Gaza had been extremely enjoyable, our personnel there had been a large group of individuals who had come together for a year in pursuit of a common purpose, after which everyone had returned to another unit in Canada. Cyprus would be different: our unit was our family; we would train together, serve six months in Cyprus together, and return to Canada together. How we performed in front of our fellow regimental members in an operational theatre would stay with us for the rest of our careers, for good or ill.

MY FIRST IMPRESSION of Cyprus was that the place was absolutely magnificent. When the Greek and Turkish Cypriots weren't shooting at each other, a lot of people paid big bucks to visit the island as tourists, and here we were for six months with all expenses paid.

As we drove from Nicosia airport north to our headquarters in the mountains, we saw our first evidence of the ethnic tension that was tearing the island apart. Windows of houses were sandbagged; and along some streets, manned defensive positions squared off against each other as close as twenty metres apart. It all seemed so ridiculous: the place was so beautiful, and there seemed to be ample space for everybody.

I would have the same feeling thirteen years later, when I returned for my third tour. I'm also confident that the sons of a few of my fellow soldiers who served in Cyprus in 1964 and '65 had similar feelings when they too set foot on the island in Canadian peacekeeping units in the early 1990s.

The view from our base in the Kyrenia mountain range looking north over the Mediterranean towards Turkey was breathtaking. Just off my left shoulder was the dominating presence of St. Hilarion Castle. Everyone in our unit knew that Walt Disney had used it as the basis for the castle in his animated movie, *Snow White*. Below the castle on the coast was the jewel-like port city of Kyrenia. In spite of the tension associated with a shaky one-year ceasefire, Kyrenia harbour was crowded with exotic yachts from around the world. Since the mooring fees in Kyrenia were about one-quarter of those in places like Nice or Beirut, I could understand why.

As I mentioned, ours was the third Canadian unit to serve on the island since the UN had established a peacekeeping force along a "Green Line" drawn between warring Greek-Cypriot and Turkish-Cypriot factions in 1964. Cyprus had been a British protectorate, and the British still maintained a large presence on the island, supported by two large military bases in Dhekelia and Akrotiri. The Greek Cypriots were the majority of the population: most of them supported a policy of political union with Greece. An anti-British terrorist group, EOKA, representing the militant arm of the Greek-Cypriot union movement, was led by the charismatic George Grivas, who had assumed folk-hero status during the years when he had eluded British attempts to capture him. Since the ceasefire, Grivas had been given command of the Greek-Cypriot Army.

As if the situation weren't complicated enough, large contingents of Greek and Turkish soldiers were mixed in with the Greek-Cypriot and Turkish-Cypriot forces. Quotas governed the percentage of the Cypriot armies that could be filled by "mainland" Turks and Greeks. But no one paid much attention to the quotas, since it was impossible for an outsider to distinguish between a "Greek Greek" and a "Greek Cypriot", or a "Turkish Turk" and a "Turkish Cypriot". The mainlanders who fell within the legal quotas wore their national Greek or Turkish uniforms; those outside the quotas simply wore Cypriot uniforms.

All of this could have been frustrating as hell if it hadn't been for the simplicity of our job. The Green Line ran the entire length of the island. From the east, it traced its way along a mountain range until it was north of the island's capital, Nicosia, where it swooped down the mountains, across a desert-like plain, sliced through the city itself, and then headed off northwest in the direction of the mountains. Isolated pockets of Turkish and Greek Cypriots dotted the island like leopard spots. Kyrenia itself was predominantly Greek Cypriot, yet was located on the north coast and dominated by a number of Turkish-Cypriot positions. Our job was to keep the opposing forces apart within our unit's sector, which ran along the Kyrenia mountain range for some fifty miles.

"Recce platoon", as my command was termed, and as any self-respecting infantry officer will admit, is the best junior command in an 800-man battalion. In the 1960s, recce platoon was commanded by a lieutenant, supported by a large number of top-notch, hand-picked senior non-commissioned officers. I had an excellent staff sergeant by the name of Ken Snowden as my second-in-command; his experience would come to my rescue on a number of occasions. The platoon was subdivided into a number of jeep patrols consisting of a senior non-commissioned officer and a driver. Patrols usually travelled in pairs, but could work by themselves in the more secure areas. We were, in short, the eyes and ears of the commanding officer. We patrolled throughout the battalion's entire area, primarily during daylight hours.

Accommodation for my platoon was provided in an old bee farm owned by an eccentric retired British colonel named Charlie Simmonds. The Colonel lived in a beautiful mansion a few hundred metres down the road with his extremely attractive wife and two young and equally attractive (and eligible) daughters.

My driver was Rifleman Wiseman. He was the epitome of the Canadian soldier: tough, loyal and reliable. Wiseman and I drove over 5,000 miles together, negotiated many a mountain track, and generally got to know each other very well along the way. In fact, we established one of the closest professional relationships of my career, and I would gladly trust him with my life to this day.

When the un had drawn up the ceasefire agreement for the island, it had permitted both sides to declare certain areas out of bounds to un forces. Those areas were marked "restricted" on our maps, and it didn't take a genius to realize that both sides were hiding much of their most sophisticated military weaponry and equipment in there. Our job was not only to report developments from day to day, but to anticipate what might happen in the future; therefore the military dispositions in the restricted areas were of great interest to my commanding officer, Lieutenant-Colonel "Killer" Kip Kirby.

"Lew, you know that un headquarters in Nicosia doesn't want us going near the restricted areas," the CO explained. "You also know that we can't do our job properly unless we have some idea what both sides are up to. I want you and your platoon to make regular attempts to chip away at the boundaries around those areas. Make some personal contacts with the Greek and Turkish sentry posts. If you get a few feet deeper into the areas every day, you'll be driving right through them by the time we leave here in six months."

Lieutenant-Colonel Kirby was not one to accept willingly UN restrictions on what he considered the correct course of action. Kip was totally dedicated to his battalion and his profession. His priority was simple and clear: the unit should always be ready to fight, and the edge must not be lost while peacekeeping. He knew that minor penetrations of the restricted zones would provide us with some professional challenge, in addition to keeping a lid on secret manoeuvrings by both sides.

One particularly sensitive area was in the Turkish-Cypriot sector, about four miles northwest of Nicosia and close to a village called Yerralakkos. It was in the middle of a large sandy dustbowl miles from civilization, and surrounded by defensive fortifications. The temperature hovered above 100 degrees F every day; the area was the best replica of a desert I'd seen since Gaza.

Wiseman and I had tried to penetrate the area from the south a number of times during the previous week. Each time, we had encountered the same Turkish soldier at the entrance to the fortifications, who pointed his vintage submachine gun in our direction and waved us away. Each time, we had complied.

I hoped our next attempt would be different. The UN had, at last, issued us some Turkish and Greek phrasebooks. The Greek-English version was excellent, since it has been designed for use by the military. It contained translations of all the ranks and military equipment, and some useful phrases for a soldier, such as "Put your hands up" and "Stop or I'll shoot." Unfortunately, the UN had not been similarly successful in obtaining a military version of the Turkish-English phrasebook. All we had was a standard tourist version available at any newsstand in downtown Nicosia.

Armed with my newly acquired linguistic reference, Wiseman and I approached the Turkish restricted position from the south at about five miles per hour. Even at that speed, a thick chalky dust swirled around our jeep, interfering with our vision to the point where we could barely see each other. The area was devoid of human habitation, and the only signs of life were a few wild dogs. In the jeep we carried axe handles that the soldiers affectionately called "puppy pounders"; if and when one of the dogs tried to take a chunk out of your leg, you tried to take a chunk out of its skull.

When we reached a point about fifty metres from the forward line of trenches, our old friend, the Turkish sentry, emerged from behind the berm and pointed his weapon at us from the hip. Using the submachine gun as a pointer, he waved it about, presumably telling us to turn around. In response I motioned for him to come closer to us, making sure he could see both my hands. Wiseman had his FN rifle and I had my pistol, but they were both out of sight.

After a minute or two of ridiculous gesturing back and forth, the Turkish soldier ran towards us and stood about two feet from me, pointing his weapon at my chest. I said in English, "Where is your officer? I want to speak to him." I received nothing but a blank stare. "We want to drive back to Kyrenia. This is the shortest route. Let us through." Nothing further from the sentry, except that he was obviously getting more agitated and his weapon was beginning to shake.

I decided it was time to utilize my Turkish phrasebook—surely there would be a phrase in it somewhere that I could use. I held up my hand to signal a pause and started to thumb through the book. I searched for a full two or three minutes and found nothing of value. Out of the corner of my eye, I could see the sentry was livid; meanwhile, some of his fellow soldiers could be seen peering over the berm with their weapons at the ready. I decided to try another tack.

I flipped back to the beginning of the phrasebook and read out a sentence as slowly and accurately as possible. The sentry looked shocked, his pupils dilated, and his left hand went to his head. I was on a roll, so I read another phrase from the same page. Now his mouth was partially open, and he looked more scared than puzzled. Without warning he suddenly took a step backwards and waved us forward, in the direction of the restricted area. Wiseman slipped the jeep into gear, and we drove through the entire restricted zone without incident, noting a number of anti-tank positions along the way.

Halfway through the zone, after our heart rates had settled down a bit, Wiseman turned to me and said, "What the hell did you say to him, sir?"

I thumbed back to the page I had used. "Well, the first thing I said was, 'What's showing at the movie tonight?' And when he looked shocked, I followed up with, 'What flavour ice cream do you have?' I presume he thought he was dealing with a couple of madmen, so he wanted to get rid of us." Wiseman gave me one of those looks that could be interpreted as either disgust or respect. I decided to accept it as the latter and put the Turkish phrasebook away—for good.

EARLY IN OUR SIX-MONTH tour, I was struck by a rather obvious inspiration. I was sitting with my legs dangling over a sheer

2,000-foot drop behind the officers' mess and peering out at Kyrenia and the Mediterranean. The day was so clear and the sun so bright that you could see the coral reefs under the sea up to two miles offshore. I'd always wanted to try scuba diving, so I walked back to the mess and asked our Greek-Cypriot bartender if he knew anyone in Kyrenia who was involved with diving.

The response was immediate: "Andreas Cariolou. Turn left at the traffic circle and keep watching on your left. You will see a lot of sponges in a window—that's his shop."

When I walked through the door of the shop, I was greeted by a living, breathing Zorba the Greek. No single person has ever affected my life so much.

Andreas had been a successful sponge diver off the coast of Turkey until the tension surrounding the intercommunal troubles on Cyprus made him an unwelcome guest. He was a big, barrel-chested, swarthy individual with a mane of long, jet-black hair. His enthusiasm for life was unbridled, and it infected everyone with whom he came into contact.

Andreas agreed to take me and a couple of my fellow officers out for an initial diving lesson. If we liked it, Andreas would give us enough instruction so we could help him train anyone in the battalion who was interested. The next day, my two fellow officers and I left the harbour on board Andreas's boat, the *Glafmario*, named after his two sons, and set out to sea. About twenty minutes out, Andreas took a quick look at St. Hilarion Castle in the far distance and another mountain along the ridge line, and declared that we had arrived. I was impressed. As far as I was concerned, we were in the middle of nowhere.

"Lewis, you come with me first," Andreas ordered. I donned a crude lead-weighted belt, a single tank held by a military strap, a mask and flippers, and rolled into the sea some five seconds after Andreas. By the time I got my bearings and figured out how to clear my mask, I could see Andreas about fifty feet below me, going straight for the bottom, the tips of his flippers a virtual blur. It all seemed pretty simple, so I started down to join him, coming to a shuddering halt at about ten feet, when the pain in my ears became overbearing. Andreas had told me to swallow when I felt pain, so I tried it: sure enough, after a couple of loud cracks inside my ears, I felt fine and continued down.

It took me about ten stages to clear my ears, but eventually I reached Andreas at the eighty-foot level. He was peering under a ledge and seconds later emerged with an eighty-pound grouper skewered on the end of his fishing spear. I followed him in awe for the next twenty minutes as he speared at least five more fish and a moray eel. Suddenly he stopped, removed his mouthpiece, put his mouth to my ear and said in a surprisingly understandable voice, given that we were eighty feet under water, "We are going up now. Don't hold your breath; breathe out."

I found out months later from an expert that I shouldn't have been so ambitious on my first dive. When I discussed this with Andreas, his response was, "Look, I knew you were fit and could do it. I also knew you wouldn't panic, so I was confident I could get you to the surface if you had a problem." He was right. I was still alive; I had a new sport to love; and because of Andreas, we were introducing about ten soldiers a week to life under the Mediterranean.

More importantly, everyone who came into contact with Andreas had a greatly enhanced appreciation and appetite for life. I don't think Andreas ever used the word "tomorrow": it was alien to his vocabulary. Andreas squeezed every ounce of living out of today, and tomorrow would just have to wait. We all loved him for his carefree personality and attitude; we even tried to emulate him, but his philosophy of life didn't always fit our relatively structured military routine—which was too bad, since it certainly would have made for an interesting unit.

ALTHOUGH THE GREEK Cypriots represented the majority of the island's population, they were terribly concerned about the proximity of Turkey, a mere forty miles to the north, whereas Greece was 300 miles away. The Turks held the upper hand strategically; they could intervene with their air force to protect their minority population on the island long before Greece could react. On a clear day, you could see the Turkish coast from the Kyrenia mountain range, and the Greek Cypriots and their Greek national counterparts maintained lookouts at various points along the northern coast under their control. They also had a number of radar sites to give them early warning of any Turkish activities during hours of darkness or bad weather.

One large Greek radar detachment was located on the northwest tip of the island, on an isolated rocky point called Kormakiti, along our platoon's patrol route. Some of my patrol commanders and I were suspicious that it was a dummy radar site constructed entirely of wood. But none of us had managed to get any closer than 400 yards before the soldiers guarding the area started waving their weapons at us.

I decided to have a closer look. Rifleman Wiseman and I left early in the morning from the bee farm. We drove along the ridge line of the Kyrenia mountain range to its western limit, where we worked our way down the escarpment and started the dusty drive along the cliffs overlooking the sea towards Kormakiti. It was an absolutely beautiful drive apart from the dust. I was tempted to stop for a swim in one of the many inlets but decided to wait until our return trip.

As we came within a mile of the radar site, I indicated to Wiseman to slow down to reduce the amount of dust. The road went into a slight dip and emerged approximately 200 yards from the radar site. If we could get into the dip without being seen, we might have a couple of minutes on the hill directly overlooking the complex before being spotted. It worked. We stuck the nose of the jeep over the top of the hill and had a great view of the site.

On any UN peacekeeping mission, you are rarely allowed to take photos anywhere along the line of confrontation. Nor can you take photos of military installations. This restriction makes sense, since you are not there to spy on any of the parties to the conflict. On the contrary, you are there to help both sides by ensuring that neither secretly gains an advantage that might encourage them to take military action, thereby breaking the ceasefire. But no one had said anything against drawing pictures. I had done a little commercial art while attending college, and could sketch a pretty good likeness of simple structures in a few minutes.

As I started to draw, sitting in the jeep beside Wisman, the radar site still looked pretty phony. About a minute into the exercise, two bullets passed directly over our heads and one passed between us. It was the first time I had ever been shot at.

I didn't particularly like the experience. I said to Wiseman, "Let's get out of here." Wiseman reversed the jeep for twenty yards, spun it around, and we took off towards the main track.

Twenty seconds and 200 yards later, it hit me that this was not the right way to handle the situation. If the UN ran off every time it was shot at, pretty soon everyone would be taking potshots at us. In addition, I wanted to have a few words with the idiot who had nearly killed us.

"Stop and turn around, Wiseman. No—come to think of it, just stop. Keep the jeep pointed this way. We will walk back to the radar site, it will be less threatening. Bring your rifle." Without any change in expression, Wiseman brought the jeep to a stop, grabbed his rifle, which was held upright by a clip on the dash, cocked it and jumped out onto the road facing the Greek position.

The ability of the Canadian soldier to tolerate some really dumb decisions by young junior officers never fails to amaze me. In Wiseman's case, walking back down a road towards a group of soldiers who were shooting at us probably didn't make a lot of sense; but I could tell he was ready to go, and I had the sense he was enjoying the challenge.

Before we left the jeep, I got on the radio and called Major Charlie Belzile's company headquarters. We were in Charlie's area of responsibility, and if we needed help it would come from his organization. "We are being fired at from the Kormakiti radar site. I'm going to talk to them along with my driver. I should call you in about ten minutes—out."

Wiseman and I started the long walk towards the site. I could detect a dozen people in uniform manning a line of trenches just in front of the large radar disk, which was rotating once every ten seconds. It took us about five minutes to reach the position. On the way, our friends fired a couple of rounds well over our heads.

As we stopped in front of the centre trench, I noticed that everyone was wearing the blue uniforms of the Greek-Cypriot Air Force. With all due respect to my air force colleagues, this really bothered me. I had a certain amount of faith that if the army was shooting to miss us, they would miss; I didn't have the same confidence in the air force.

"Does anyone speak English?" I yelled. No response. I reached into my pocket, extracted my Greek military phrasebook, and found the phrase, "I want to see your leader." It worked. A sergeant moved towards us from the left and took up a position directly in front of me.

"Why the hell are you shooting at us?" I asked him. "We are on this island to try and help you."

"Because you are spies for the Turks," came the response in perfect English.

"Balls, we aren't spies for anyone. And except for the radar site, this entire area, including where we were shot at, is not restricted to the UN. I'm going to report your actions to my headquarters," I said.

"You will be shot," was the reply.

Well, I had got us into this mess, and we certainly didn't seem to have the upper hand. There were about ten men within twenty metres of us, pointing their weapons in our direction. "Wiseman, we are leaving." With that, I brought my right hand up from my hip and nailed the sergeant on the temple. He dropped to his knees, and I said, in a somewhat shaky voice, "Don't ever shoot at UN personnel again. If you do, they will put you in the army. Let's go, Wiseman!"

Rifleman Wiseman and I turned and walked back towards our jeep. We reached it without incident. Wiseman started it up and we began to roll. A hundred yards later, two shots cracked over our heads. Wiseman looked at me as if to say, "Are we going back?"

I responded, "We've pushed our luck enough today. We'll let them have the last shot, and maybe they'll be sorted out by their own people once they see our report. By the way, Wiseman—well done and thanks."

A few months later, Lieutenant-Colonel Kirby was advised that the Greek-Cypriot sergeant had indeed been courtmartialled and found guilty of firing at the UN. He was sentenced to a stiff prison term, during which he would receive a series of lashings. I was invited by the Greek Cypriots to observe the first set in the series. I accepted; however, I was overruled by Colonel Kirby, who thought it would be in bad taste.

ONLY THE GREEK CYPRIOTS had tanks on the island. The tanks were pretty old, and there were just fifty-four of them, but they were of great concern to the Turkish enclave centered on Bogaz Junction, located on the south side of the Kyrenia range where the Nicosia-to-Kyrenia road entered the mountains. In the latter half of our six-month tour, rumours started that the Greeks were going to move their tanks east towards Yerralakkos and then attack north in an attempt to capture Bogaz Junction. Our UN headquarters in Nicosia obviously had some hard intelligence on the matter; the chief of staff, Canadian Brigadier Bruce MacDonald, arrived at our headquarters one night, and I was roused from my bed at one A.M. and stumbled down the hill to the commanding officer's villa to be briefed.

Apart from saying "thank you" to a few generals when we had received sports trophies for various unit championships, this was the first time I had actually had a conversation with a brigadier. It seemed the rumours were right. The Greeks had plans to move their tanks out of the compound beside the UN Austrian field hospital and, following a short drive to the east to make it appear that they were doing a simple administrative move to Nicosia, they would attack north to secure Bogaz Junction. Brigadier MacDonald wanted us to establish a new observation post midway between Bogaz Junction and the place where the tanks would probably turn north. In order to complete their attack, the tanks would then have to overrun our UN observation post, which, while certainly possible, was unlikely to be attempted (we hoped). The location chosen for the post was on a hill in the middle of a Greek-Cypriot battalion's defensive position. The Greeks would never accept a UN post in that location, so we would have to infiltrate the area with our vehicles and personnel under cover of darkness. The new observation post would have to be in place within twenty-four hours.

At six A.M. I briefed the platoon on our assignment. All of the day's normal patrols were rerouted so that we could gather as much information as possible, from a distance, on the new position we were to occupy. Regrettably, just about everything we discovered was bad. The hill had to be approached from the south. If we came at it any other way and were discovered, the Greeks would logically assume we were Turks and would open up with everything they had. But if we came from the south, they might assume that we were one of their own patrols, lost at night in search of our unit. The hill itself was not occupied, which was favourable for our approach, but it was ringed by prepared defensive positions, some of which were manned at least during the day. We could get within two miles of the hill using the main road without arousing suspicion, but after that our butts would be hanging out a mile.

We decided to make our move after midnight when, we hoped, just about everyone would be asleep. Both sides were confident that the ceasefire would hold, so they were not particularly alert at night. Although our vehicles were white, we blackened our faces in case we had to sneak around in the dark on foot. We took some extra ammunition, which we had to borrow from our colleagues. The UN restricted each soldier to one twenty-round magazine, so there was not a lot of spare ammunition available in the unit. We packed a short flagpole and a large UN flag to make the new observation post recognizable from a distance.

Just before we left for the hill, we gathered around, and for one of the few times in my life, I worked my way through the sequence of command if any of us were shot. "If I'm killed, Sergeant Snowden is in charge; if he gets it, Sergeant Ethell takes over; if Sergeant Ethell goes down, Sergeant Muller is in charge. If Sergeant Muller buys it, it's probably time to come home." You should never lose your sense of humour in the military; at the same time, I was impressed by how closely everyone was paying attention.

We left our headquarters at midnight and drove over the Kyrenia pass, down through Bogaz Junction and out onto the flats towards Nicosia. Just before the city, we turned hard right and started to move northwest towards Yerralakkos. There were a few lights on in the village as we drove through, and a couple of the bars were still active, with a dozen soldiers milling about. Just after the village, we pulled over to the side of the highway and turned off all our lights. After pausing for five minutes to get our night vision, we idled off up the highway looking for a small pile of stones that one of our patrols had placed earlier in the day. From that point, we would proceed on a compass bearing directly to the hill.

It took us about ten minutes to reach the pile of stones. I got out to get a close look at them in the dark. There was a small piece of paper crushed under the top stone. I pulled it out and read its short but meaningful message: "Good luck. Safe trip."

From that point we left the road and proceeded on a bearing of 28 degrees for two miles. We put the differential of each jeep in low range and the transmissions in first gear, which meant that there was no need to touch the accelerator, since the idling speed of the engine would move the vehicle forward with virtually no sound at about two miles per hour. Progress was frustratingly slow, but for forty minutes everything went fine. It was a bright night, and with our binoculars gathering in some extra light, we could see pretty well: too well. Directly in front of us was a series of slit trenches; fortunately, they were facing away from us, but stood between us and our objective nonetheless. I motioned to Sergeant Ethell, and we crept forward on foot, until we were standing among the trenches. Every one of the occupants was sound asleep.

Ethell and I motioned the jeeps forward and walked in front of them, while guiding them between the trenches. A few sleeping bodies turned over, but no one even sat up, let alone picked up a weapon. If they had done so, our first line of defense would have been a large flashlight taped to a pole at the back of the jeep, which carried a large UN flag. The flag was wrapped around the pole with an elastic band to keep the noise down, but in the event of trouble it could be pulled loose and the light switched on, and we would all pray that the soldiers in the area recognized and respected the UN badge. Somehow I doubted it: it would be too blatantly obvious that we were up to no good, sneaking through the middle of their position at night.

Two minutes later, we all started breathing again, after we cleared the position. Sergeant Ethell and I jumped back in our jeeps and proceeded at less than walking pace towards our hill.

In half an hour, we came to the base of a fairly large, flat-topped feature. There were trenches all around its base, but none of them was occupied. We eased our way along the track, which ran up the west side of the feature, and were rewarded with a magnificent nighttime view of the lights of Yerralakkos and Bogaz Junction. We were well and truly in between the two: we were sitting smack on our designated location.

After installing our flagpole and running up the UN flag, we placed a jeep with a flag flying on three of the four corners of the feature. Anyone approaching the hill from any direction would see it was under UN control. We took turns on sentry duty while the others curled up on the ground for a few hours' rest.

First light brought a number of irritated visitors from the Greek-Cypriot battalion. Presumably they had found our tracks and deduced that we had moved through their position the previous night. Fortunately, they appeared to be more than a little impressed by our audacity, so we played the gracious hosts.

Ours was only a temporary occupation. Around noon, the commanding officer sent the nearest company commander, Major Jack Hanley, along with one of his platoons to relieve us. My lads had kindly named the hill and the observation post "MacKenzie's Mound". I was touched. An hour after we left, Major Hanley changed it to "Hanley's Hill". It kept that name for over eleven years.

MY TOUR IN CYPRUS would turn out to be the first of three on the island, and it was a real eye-opener. It was the first time I'd been shot at; and it was the first time I'd seen Canadian non-commissioned officers and soldiers under danger-induced stress. I was extremely impressed by the calm, resourceful and courageous way they reacted. It convinced me that our soldiers deserved the most loyal and dedicated leadership. Leadership was without a doubt a two-way street; I vowed never to forget that, and to try and live up to the expectations of the Wisemans and Ethells of the world.

5

Cyrus—Second Tour

—

SIX MONTHS AFTER our unit's return to Victoria in October 1965, I was sent to the School of Infantry in Camp Borden, Ontario, to instruct officer cadets during their second phase of training. One Friday evening I had gone to bed early after a particularly physical day with the cadets. A friend and fellow officer, Bob Newman, was visiting the camp and, following happy hour at the mess, dropped by to ask if he could borrow my car for a trip to Toronto, about an hour's drive away.

I have never been terribly keen about lending my car to anyone, so I told Bob I would go with him. He wanted to visit a well-known rollerskating rink in downtown Toronto. I hadn't been on rollerskates since my "skate cop" days at an outdoor rink during the early '50s, and it sounded like fun.

Since the rink was packed with people displaying a wide range of skating skills from incompetent to professional, every circuit of the floor was entertaining. Early on, I noticed a tall, slim, dark-haired young woman wearing the miniest of miniskirts and bearing a marked resemblance to a young Jackie Kennedy. Her good looks were attracting more attention than she seemed to want, so I decided to come to her "rescue". I told her this was my first time on skates, and she graciously held me up for the rest of the evening. Her name was Dora McKinnon.

As we came to know each other better, Dora was like thousands of women before her, in the sense that she didn't heed the warning that her life would be both hectic and lonely if she was crazy enough to marry a soldier. Later in 1966, I was posted on a two-year exchange tour with the British Army. I reported to the Third

Battalion of the Queen's Regiment in Lemgo, West Germany, and lasted only three days in my new surroundings before deciding that Dora and I should get married sooner rather than later. Six days later, I was back in Lemgo with Dora, having made a quick visit to Canada, which included an even quicker wedding ceremony in a church not far from the rollerskating rink.

A few months later, Dora started to take my warnings about long separations seriously. Our unit departed for desert-warfare training in Libya fewer than twenty-four hours after Dora announced she was pregnant.

Our daughter, Kimm, was born in a British military hospital in West Germany in October 1967. Her arrival had a big impact on our lives, but not enough to keep us grounded. At that stage, I was twenty-seven and Dora a mere twenty. Concurrent with our marriage, I had taken delivery of a brand-new E-Type Jaguar sports car. It cost $5,700 duty-free, and I had to borrow $2,500 to pay for it. It was the only possession we owned, so we spent a lot of time on the road. With room for only two seats, I was always concerned that Kimm would grow up deformed from being crammed into the tiny space just behind our seat backs. Fortunately, the experience had a positive effect on her development, since she has become a race-car driver in adulthood.

I entered the Canadian Army's one-year Command and Staff College course in Kingston, Ontario, in 1969 and graduated in the summer of 1970. By some miracle of miscalculation, I obtained an A grading and was advised by the commandant that I would be promoted to major as a result. Two days later, I was advised that because I had left university voluntarily (rather than failing!) in 1960, I would not be eligible for promotion until 1971. I was devastated and considered submitting my release. A few close friends, including Charlie Bezile, talked me out of it.

Meanwhile, we in the combat arms had been shellshocked by the actions of Prime Minister Trudeau's government. Under the Minister of National Defence, Paul Hellyer, the navy, army and air force had been forced to integrate into a single service, to be known as the Canadian Armed Forces. One result of this unification was the elimination of a number of regiments from the regular, full-time army. My own regiment, the Queen's Own Rifles of Canada, was swept away at a stroke of Mr. Hellyer's pen.

It's not easy to explain the role of a regiment to someone who has never served in one. I always say that, in the end, soldiers do not put their lives on the line for God, Queen, country or their general; they do so for their fellow soldiers a few metres on either side of them. The regimental system creates the human bonds and commitments that make such selfless acts not only possible, but to be expected.

By serving with the QORofC for ten years, I had been blessed with exposure to Second World War vets who had more than paid their dues, and who pointed us all in the right direction; it was also a regiment renowned for establishing the closest of bonds between its officers and soldiers. Fortunately, those of us in the QORofC were assigned to the Princess Patricia's Canadian Light Infantry (PPCLI), a regiment that welcomed us with open arms, immediately made us feel at home, and gave us a tremendous amount of support. Unlike some other amalgamations that were forced upon the army, the merger of the QORofC and the PPCLI created a synergy that continues to have a positive impact on the army over twenty-three years later. In my own case, following Staff College I was posted to the First Battalion, PPCLI, in Calgary, Alberta.

THERE ARE TWO TYPES of work for officers in the military. One is termed "line" duty, and officers fortunate enough to be so designated are somewhere between the commander and the soldiers in the chain of command; they command the people working under them. Most line officers want to stay line officers for their entire careers. There is another category of officer employment, designated "staff". Staff officers support line officers, but rarely have the privilege of commanding anything. In war, staff officers can lose a battle by screwing up the commander's orders, but they will never win one.

When I went back to Cyprus in the summer of 1971, it was as a staff officer: my battalion's operations officer, to be exact. I was delighted to be back in Cyprus again, but a little disappointed not to be commanding soldiers. My job was to convert the commanding officer's general directions into coherent, detailed orders to the unit. It wasn't much of a challenge: Lieutenant-Colonel Bill Hutchinson, who was the commanding officer for the first three months, and Colonel Bill Hewson, who followed him, are by nature more articulate and precise than I am, and they usually included all the necessary details in their various orders. All I had to do was make sure the orders were carried out in accordance with their wishes.

Dora had accepted my first UN assignment since our marriage

with her usual good grace. Kimm was only four and quite a handful, but Dora didn't fight the problem and organized herself for a long period on her own. She had no idea, nor did I, that this Cyprus tour was to be the first of six similar separations over the next twenty years.

The Canadian battalion had moved from its idyllic location in the Kyrenia mountain pass, where I had served in 1965, to the heat and confusion of the island's capital, Nicosia. There had been very few problems along the Green Line over the past few years except in the area of Nicosia itself. The line of separation wound its way through the centre of the old walled city like the path of a drunken soldier. In some places, the Greek and Turkish Cypriots were separated by a mere ten feet—unlike the countryside, where it was not unusual to find their lines up to a mile apart.

Soldiers get bored with nothing to do. As a Greek or Turkish Cypriot, you got particularly bored when all you had to look forward to for the next few months was staring at your adversary a scant ten feet away, peering out at you from behind a sandbagged defensive position. Every time there was a problem on the Green Line, UN Headquarters tried to read some deep political meaning into the event. There would be much speculation that one side or the other was posturing for purposes of future political negotiations. In fact, the disturbance was usually nothing more than bored soldiers having a bit of fun.

The favourite verbal gambit was to accuse the enemy conscript opposite your position of arriving on this earth as a result of frequent out-of-wedlock activities by his mother or, better still, as the result of a liaison between his mother and a farm animal. This frequently drew a response that North Americans would refer to as "mooning"; however, between Greeks and Turks, including their Cypriot brethren, exposing yourself in someone's direction was about as insulting as you could get. Frequently the "exposee" would attempt to strike the exposed part or parts of the "exposer" with a well-aimed rock. If he missed, the game would probably end amidst a flurry of insults regarding the enemy's sexual inadequacy, resulting from attempts at procreation with a herd of goats. All good clean fun.

Both sides had powerful slingshots that could, in the right hands, be deadly accurate. The soldiers knew they would be in deep trouble with their own officers if they fired their guns at the other side, and every round of ammunition had to be accounted for at the end of each day. But nobody worried about stones. Occasionally, the exposed body part would suffer the damage of golf-ball-sized stones travelling at 100 miles per hour. The result was not a pretty sight and frequently resulted in an all-out stone war in the immediate area. It was the standard job of our Canadian soldiers and young officers to wade into this Biblical re-enactment and cool it down before some idiot laid down his slingshot, picked up his rifle, and started a major incident that could jeopardize the ceasefire along the island's entire length.

The Canadian battalion had been moved to Nicosia because that was the major potential trouble spot on the island. Canadian soldiers were good at sorting out problems before they became crises. Troubleshooting that would be done by officers in other armies was done equally well by corporals in the Canadian battalion. We had a tremendous pool of negotiators who helped keep a lid on the situation during our six-month tour.

This second Cyprus tour gave me an opportunity to renew my friendship with Andreas Cariolou and scuba diving. Andreas was only six years older, but his hair, still long and thick, was beginning to grey. In spite of his carefree exterior, I knew from hours of private talks with him that the island's troubles bothered him deeply. He agonized over the ethnic and religious fanaticism that had the potential to destroy one of the most beautiful mini-civilizations on the face of the earth.

Andreas had taken delivery of a new and much larger boat, the *Glafmario II*, which he had purchased from a company in Norway. It could easily handle twenty divers at a time. The roof of its tall wheelhouse provided a great platform for free-diving into some of the clearest and most beautiful water in the world.

Andreas had graduated from a hand spear to the more modern spear gun. Most of these guns were operated by bungee rubbers, and cocked underwater by hand like a bow. Once the trigger was pulled, the spear shot out fifteen feet, skewering anything in its way until the tether stopped its flight. Andreas also had an older type of spear gun, which he didn't particularly like; one afternoon after a dive together, he gave it to me. It was about three feet long, with a round barrel lined with a powerful spring. You inserted the tail of the two-foot spear into the barrel, and then pushed the tip of the spear against something solid, compressing the spring; when the spear was fully loaded, the locking mechanism clicked, and you were ready for action.

The adjutant of our unit (another staff officer) was a close friend of mine, Captain Cris Smith. We had attended the same officer training course and both loved diving. Cris was with me when Andreas handed over the spear gun. We jumped into Cris's jeep and headed off for Nicosia. As we were leaving the built-up area, Cris asked, "Are you sure that thing would have enough punch to penetrate a large fish like a tuna?"

"I don't know, but let's see," I said. I compressed the spear into the barrel of the gun, finally hearing an audible click as it locked into place. I rested the barrel on top of the windshield at a 45-degree angle, in order to give us maximum range. "I'll fire it when we have a straight stretch of highway, so we can find the spear on the road," I said. "It probably won't go more than fifty metres."

A few moments later, we turned a corner and started along a 300-yard straightaway before the road jogged to the left. "Okay," I said, "here goes."

Regrettably, neither Cris nor I had taken into account the fact that the gun was designed to be fired underwater, where there is a good deal of resistance—to the spear and to the spring. The spear took off splendidly and quickly disappeared into the clear blue sky. We lost sight of it while it was still rising, at the far end of the straightaway.

Cris and I looked at each other. He said, "I guess you should have tied a rope to it."

"If I had, it would have pulled me out of the jeep," was the best retort I could manage. "Damn," I said, "now the gun is useless. That was the only spear."

We carried on to the end of the straightaway. We did quick turns to the left and right, starting a climb up the north face of the mountain range that stood between us and Nicosia. About fifty yards after the second corner, we spotted a crowd of people gathered around an old tractor. The driver, an elderly white-haired gentleman, was gesturing wildly with both hands towards the sky; the crowd, following his story, were staring straight upwards as we drove past. Imbedded at an angle of 45 degrees in the top of the exposed tractor engine was my spear—still vibrating. Discretion got the best of my desire to reclaim my projectile, and we carried on to Nicosia at increased speed.

I spotted the tractor twice more over the next few months, my spear still solidly in place. Undoubtedly, it could have penetrated a tuna.

Our tour ended without any major incidents. The unit played a lot of sports, got terribly fit, and developed a good operational reputation, thanks to the day-to-day professionalism of our soldiers and junior leaders. It was becoming crystal-clear to me that boredom is a soldier's worst enemy. No one ever left our unit for civvie street because military life was too hard; but over the years, lots of soldiers left because it was not as exciting as they'd expected. Soldiers like to be busy, and in Cyprus it was becoming increasingly difficult to provide them with an adequate challenge.

6

Slumming in Saigon

DURING SUMMER 1972, my promotion to major came through.
I left my staff job as operations officer and took command of "B"
Company in the First Battalion, PPCLI.

There is a strong argument to be made that company command
is the best job in the army. It is the last appointment where you are
really close to the soldiers. In a properly sized infantry company,
there are over a hundred soldiers, and you eat, sleep, work and play
together as a team. If you are a weak leader, good subordinates may
get you through, but the soldiers will always know they were poorly
led; the word will get around, and you will never command a
battalion as a lieutenant-colonel—nor should you.

My year in company command was the culmination of a dream.
When I'd joined the army in 1960, all my officer role-models had
been captains or majors. That was what I'd wanted to become, and
I'd always thought I'd retire happily as a major.

For just under a year, it was like being on holiday. It seemed
every day was spent on good, hard training, or sports, or a
combination of both. The company was fit, tough and always ready
for a challenge. My company sergeant-major, Jack Murray, and I
got along well, and the soldiers responded willingly to our direction.
I wanted to stay with the company as long as possible; but then, out
of nowhere, came the possibility of peacekeeping duty in Southeast
Asia. I couldn't resist.

WHEN U.S. SECRETARY OF STATE Henry Kissinger and the North
Vietnamese delegation signed the Paris Peace Accord in 1972, the
protocol established an international observer force to oversee the

VIETNAM
INTERNATIONAL COMMISSION
OF CONTROL AND SUPERVISION, 1973

ceasefire, the withdrawal of U.S. forces, and the return of prisoners of war. The observer force would consist of contingents from Canada and Indonesia representing the West, with Poland and Hungary looking after the interests of the Eastern bloc. I got my commanding officer's permission to call my career manager in Ottawa to volunteer.

During the next few days, over 200 Canadian officers were nominated to serve with the International Commission of Control and Supervision (ICCS) in Vietnam. Major-General Duncan A. MacAlpine was appointed to command the Canadian contingent. I was extremely disappointed when the Canadian officers were called to Montreal for processing and I wasn't included. They left for Saigon just before Christmas.

Over the next few months, I called my career manager at least once a week to remind him I was available. I knew that some of the observers had contracted malaria and thought I might be lucky enough to be selected as a replacement. I couldn't stand the thought of 200 of my colleagues coming back from Vietnam and telling me how exciting it had been: "Boy, you should have been there!"

Meanwhile, the mission was experiencing difficulties dealing with all sides in the conflict. These problems came to a head when one of the mission's helicopters was shot down by a North Vietnamese missile. A Canadian captain, Charles Laviolette, was killed in the incident, and a public debate started in Canada regarding the wisdom of our participation. The newspaper in Calgary, where I was based, ran an article suggesting Canada should leave the peace mission because it was too dangerous. Upset by this attitude, I wrote a letter to the editor stressing that if the mission were fruitless, then yes, we should leave. On the other hand, if the mission were deemed worthwhile, we certainly shouldn't leave simply because it was dangerous. After all, we were soldiers, and the Canadian public paid us to take risks in support of our foreign policy.

I was posted to Vietnam the day after the letter was published. It's amazing how many people thought my posting was the result of my letter. In fact, the letter had nothing to do with it; my career manager had been asked to replace an officer who had been evacuated from Vietnam, and he knew how much I wanted to go. Perception has a momentum of its own, however, and to this day, a number of my friends think I was sent to Vietnam as "punishment" for speaking out.

I went to a regional headquarters of the observer force in the central highlands of Vietnam, and shortly thereafter to a team site in Cheo Reo, close to the Cambodian border. Most team sites were organized with double "C.H.I.P." representation—two officers each from Canada, Hungary, Indonesia and Poland. Cheo Reo was no exception. Our job was to investigate complaints from either side about breaches of the ceasefire. It was all a little ludicrous, since a war was still going on concurrent with the American withdrawal. Some of our luckier colleagues were up in Hue facilitating the exchange of prisoners, but for a lot of us, the routine was just that—routine.

Fortunately, our team site had a tennis court within the barbed wire. I had never played the game, but one of the Hungarian majors was quite keen to play, so I let him humiliate me every day for two weeks. Gradually I started to match his limited ability, and on one particular day, I beat him six games to four.

That evening, my Hungarian tennis opponent came to see me and with tears in his eyes said he would not be allowed to play me in future. When I asked why, he explained that his Polish colonel had told him that if he couldn't win each and every day, he was not to play anymore. This was my first experience of the win-or-else attitude of our friends behind the Iron Curtain, and I was shocked by it. I explained that I would be happy to lose more games than I won, but the Polish colonel had spoken, and that was it. I retired from tennis.

EACH TIME A COMPLAINT was delivered by either the North or South Vietnamese, a C.H.I.P. team was despatched to carry out an investigation. In over 90 per cent of the cases, the complaints alleged breaches of the ceasefire, some of them involving thousands of troops. Following each investigation, a report was prepared. The protocol for the observer force dictated that a report could be submitted to the International Commission in Saigon only if there was unanimity among the four C.H.I.P. delegations comprising the investigation team.

In over 800 investigations, there was never unanimity that the North Vietnamese were at fault. The Poles and Hungarians always found that the South Vietnamese were to blame, no matter what the circumstances or facts, and therefore not one report was submitted condemning the North Vietnamese for their actions. On the other hand, the Canadian and Indonesian team members found the South Vietnamese to be at fault about 20 per cent of the time, and therefore approximately 150 reports were passed to Saigon condemning the South for breaking the ceasefire. The reporting system became such a farce that the Canadian Secretary of State for External Affairs, Mitchell Sharp, visited the mission on a fact-finding trip, and secret plans were developed for the Canadian withdrawal.

One of the best examples of the mission's futility involved the destruction of a South Vietnamese bridge and an adjacent village by large-calibre artillery and rocket fire. When the c.h.i.p. team arrived on the scene, the bridge was destroyed and still smoking as it gradually settled into the river. The edge of the village closest to the bridge was on fire, and bodies littered the landscape. The ground contained a large number of shell craters, with the telltale indications that permit one to calculate the direction of fire. The Canadian and Indonesian officers completed their calculations and explained to their Polish and Hungarian colleagues that the fire had originated from a North Vietnamese position about ten kilometres to the west. The Polish colonel smiled and said, "Absolutely not. It appears that the bridge was blown down by the wind." The report was never submitted.

On July 27, 1973, the word was passed to all 250 Canadians with the iccs throughout Vietnam that the Canadian government had decided we would leave the mission and return to Canada on the last day of the month. Every time a helicopter arrived at a team site, just about every Canadian except the poor soul designated to stay behind on duty watch snuck on board with the hope that he could make his way to Saigon for a forty-eight-hour break before leaving the country.

Early on July 28, an Air America Huey helicopter settled onto our landing pad at Cheo Reo. Major Bill Decant, my Canadian ppcli colleague, and I jumped on board with all of our kit, along with two Poles, a Hungarian and an Indonesian. It was a blistering-hot day, so we flew with the side doors pinned back on the chopper. Wherever you flew in Vietnam, the view was breathtaking. It always amazed me how difficult it was to see the war damage from the air. Except for areas that had been defoliated, the jungle grew so quickly that a few weeks after a battle, the war scars were already starting to heal and blend into the surrounding foliage.

An hour into the flight, our Polish colleague's body language indicated that he was experiencing some sort of discomfort. We all thought it was probably stomach cramps, which afflicted everyone at least once a week, but a short discussion revealed that he had to relieve himself in the worst way.

We were over dense jungle, so it was impossible to land. After much consideration, which eliminated the possibility of urinating out the open door of the helicopter, since outside air was being pushed into the helicopter by the main blade at a rate of about 60 miles per hour, we decided on a more practical solution. Every helicopter carries a number of air-sickness bags; if they could hold vomit, they could hold urine. We passed one to the Polish colonel, and, with a surprising degree of modesty, he turned away from us as best he could (a number of us were taking pictures) and filled the bag. The top of the bag had a ridge reinforced with a thin piece of wire, which allowed the bag to be sealed by folding back the top and securing it with a tab on each side. The sealing procedure was successfully completed by the colonel.

Now that we had a bag of urine in the helicopter, we had to do something with it for the two hours remaining in our flight. As we set our collective mind to work to solve the dilemma, the colonel cocked his arm and, ignoring our urgent pleas to reconsider, threw the bag out the door of the helicopter.

Six pairs of eyes watched the bag advance four feet into the air turbulence that was keeping us aloft and moving us forward. Then, in a scene resembling slow motion, we watched the tabs of the bag release their grip and the top of the bag unfold, open and turn in our direction before, at something approaching the speed of light, it was driven back into the helicopter, exploding as it re-entered the door. I would never have believed what a half-litre of vaporized urine could do to the inside of a helicopter, its six passengers and three crew, if I hadn't seen, felt and tasted it myself.

When we arrived in Saigon, we unloaded our own kit. None of the ground crew would come closer to us than fifty feet before inexplicably turning away.

THE DEPLOYMENT OF observers in the ICCS was quite different from any other peacekeeping mission in which I served. After an initial few days in Saigon following their arrival, officers were sent to one of the many team sites throughout Vietnam, and there they stayed. As a result, officers who had arrived six months earlier had not seen the majority of their colleagues for their entire period in Vietnam. We were quite lucky in the region where I served, because the commander, Colonel Keith McGregor, decided to rotate officers throughout his region; every month or so, teams would move from one site to another. Keith felt quite rightly that this was a good idea, since some team sites were bloody miserable, with a high incidence of malaria, whereas others, such as Na Trang on the coast of the South China Sea, were comfortable and relatively pleasant.

With over 200 Canadian officers gathered together in Saigon, most of whom were seeing their colleagues for the first time in six months, the potential for a good time was considerable. We all lived up to expectations. Parties, planned and spontaneous, erupted throughout our spartan accommodations. War stories got better with the telling, and everyone scoured downtown Saigon for the standard "peace-offering" gifts to give our families when we got home. Porcelain elephants and jewellery were the most popular items; the local merchants were delighted.

Two days before we were scheduled to depart, Major-General MacAlpine called us together and told us what a great job we had done. He quite accurately explained that our departure was directly related to the inability of our Hungarian and Polish colleagues on the mission to maintain their impartiality. Because so few investigation reports were reaching Saigon, and because only those condemning the South Vietnamese had a chance of surviving the filtering process, the Canadian government had decided we should depart. Our duties would be assumed by an Iranian contingent, which was scheduled to arrive a couple of weeks after we left.

As he reached the end of his presentation, General MacAlpine said, "And I want every vestige of Canada removed from Saigon, particularly all those maple-leaf decals that seem to be stuck on everything."

I had two close regimental friends in the mission, Major Bill Minnis and Captain Wayne Dehnke. Bill later served as my deputy commander when I commanded a battalion of the regiment, and subsequently commanded his own battalion; Wayne was to serve as one of my company commanders some five years later. We knew what the General had meant to say: remove all the decals from our *base* in Saigon, Tan So Nut. But he *had* said to remove them from all of Saigon.

Bill, Wayne and I didn't think any more about the General's remarks until the second bottle of rum was opened approximately four hours later. "You know, all those Saigon warriors have been living the good life while we've been out at the team sites over the past six months. They've left Canadian decals all over town, especially in the steam baths and massage parlours. In accordance with the General's wishes, I think we should commit ourselves to removing each and every one of them by morning." Bill had spoken, and Bill was the senior of our group: we prepared ourselves for action by polishing off the second bottle of Bacardi.

Just after ten P.M. we rented a "hoptac", an ingenious Southeast Asian invention which is, quite simply, a motorcycle with two rear bicycle wheels supporting a trunk-like box with seats for up to six passengers. Holding on for dear life, we set forth on our mission.

My memory of the remainder of the evening is a bit hazy; however, I do recall smooth-talking our way into at least twenty steam baths or massage parlours where, inevitably, we spotted two or three Canadian flag decals stuck to one or more of the ubiquitous full-sized mirrors. By the second or third establishment, we had worked out a basic but impressive ceremony for removing the decals, involving a bit of foot drill, some saluting, and a few bars of the song that my mother always felt should have been our national anthem, "The Maple Leaf Forever". Most of the establishments' staff were duly impressed, having been briefed by us on our mission; however, some of their clientele were more than a bit bemused by our presence in their naked midst.

By the time the sun came up, we had removed approximately 150 decals, which were now rolled into a sticky mass the size of a soccer ball. After a few hours of well-earned rest, we delivered our evidence to General MacAlpine with a brief report: "Your orders have been carried out, sir."

The Canadian contingent departed Saigon forty-eight hours later. As a short-timer, I had contributed very little to the mission. Others, who had endured six months under some very difficult and dangerous circumstances, had every reason to be proud of their accomplishments and to feel a certain sense of relief at having survived.

The ICCS was an example of a good idea within a ceasefire protocol that was itself, unfortunately, impractical in its application from the beginning. Being a non-UN peacekeeping mission, the ICCS made the most basic mistake of employing officers from countries who had a natural and overt affiliation with one of the sides in the conflict. This handicap was further aggravated by the requirement that reports had to be unanimously endorsed by the four nationalities making up each investigation team. Although this inherent inefficiency made life extremely frustrating to those of us on the ground, the mission did serve its purpose in the much larger global context. Without the ICCS or something like it, Kissinger's Paris Peace Accord on Vietnam would never have been signed; the American military forces would not have left in an orderly manner, and prisoners of war would not have been exchanged.

This was a peacekeeping lesson that was slowly etching its way into the area of my brain where unequivocal truths are kept. There would always be serious, practical problems at the sharp end of a mission. In reality, you were rarely, if ever, an important part of the solution to an armed conflict; but you were a critical factor in getting the entire peace process rolling. It was a lesson that gave me a certain amount of solace later in my career, as I dealt with the expanding scope and ensuing frustrations of peacekeeping.

7

Back in the Middle East

FROM VIETNAM, I RETURNED to the PPCLI in Calgary just in time to take some leave, after which I accompanied my battalion to Wainwright, Alberta, on our annual summer training. By now a good friend, Lieutenant-Colonel John Sharpe, had taken command of the unit, and he tasked me with conducting the final exercise.

On return to our base in Calgary, John said he intended to give me command of the battalion's administration company. I asked to return to my rifle company; but John, quite rightly, insisted that I'd had my "fun" and it was time to learn the nuts and bolts of unit administration by commanding the biggest company in the battalion—the one that kept everyone fuelled, fed, maintained and otherwise administered.

I barely had time to organize my office.

In early October 1973, on Yom Kippur, the Egyptian Army carried out a picture-perfect crossing of the Suez Canal and attacked Israeli defensive positions on the East Bank. Simultaneously, the Syrians attacked the Israeli forces on the Golan Heights. Approximately a week later, the Israeli forces counterattacked across the Canal and cut off the Third Egyptian Army. The UN established United Nations Emergency Force II (UNEF II), with a mandate to position itself between the two protagonists in the Sinai and to facilitate the exchange of the dead and prisoners of war. Canada, along with Poland, agreed to provide logistical support to the force.

The Canadian communications and logistics units established themselves at the Shams horse-racing track, adjacent to Cairo International Airport. Living conditions were spartan under canvas, and the 1,000 Canadian troops experienced severe frustration as they

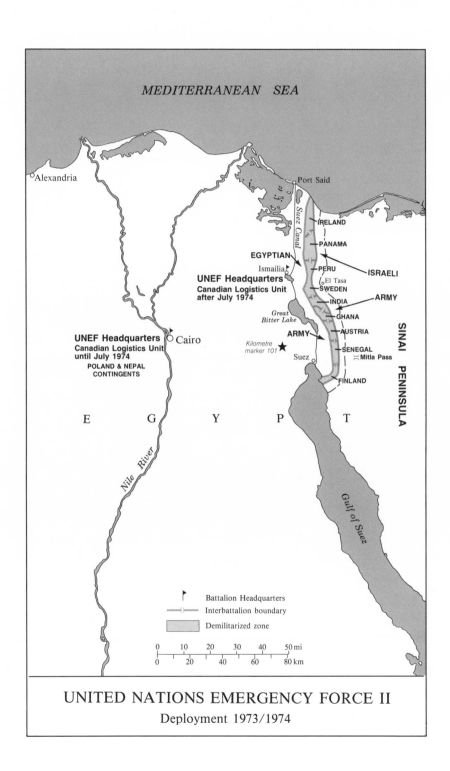

MEDITERRANEAN SEA

Alexandria

Port Said

Suez Canal

IRELAND

PANAMA

EGYPTIAN

Ismailia

UNEF Headquarters
Canadian Logistics Unit
after July 1974

PERU

El Tasa

SWEDEN

INDIA

GHANA

Great
Bitter Lake

UNEF Headquarters
Canadian Logistics Unit
until July 1974
POLAND & NEPAL
CONTENGENTS

Cairo

ISRAELI

ARMY

ARMY

AUSTRIA

Kilometre
marker 101

SENEGAL

Mitla Pass

Suez

FINLAND

SINAI PENINSULA

E   G   Y   P   T

Nile River

Gulf of Suez

Battalion Headquarters
Interbattalion boundary
Demilitarized zone

| 0 | 10 | 20 | 30 | 40 | 50 mi |
| 0 | 20 | 40 | 60 | 80 km |

UNITED NATIONS EMERGENCY FORCE II
Deployment 1973/1974

attempted to execute their duties. As the logistics unit, the Canadians were responsible for providing the UN infantry battalions manning the line of separation in the Sinai with their day-to-day requirements. As usual, the UN was incapable of providing the various supplies, ranging from food to construction materials, in a timely manner. In spite of the fact that the deficiency was not the fault of the Canadian logistics battalion, they understandably bore the brunt of criticism from the forward troops, who were forced to operate with less than adequate basic supplies.

Morale among the Canadians hit rock-bottom, culminating in an unfortunate incident in late November. A jeep carrying three Canadians had been involved in a serious traffic accident in downtown Cairo. The city was still under black-out in anticipation of Israeli airstrikes. Traffic was more chaotic than usual, and it was hours before a Canadian miltary doctor, Major Jean-Paul Vézina, arrived at the Egyptian hospital caring for the Canadian casualties. There had been one fatality; Major Vézina was shocked and disgusted by the apparently superficial and crude autopsy that had been carried out prior to his arrival. He managed to remove the two seriously injured Canadian soldiers to an ambulance and started back to Camp Shams, located on the outskirts of the city. Regrettably, the ambulance was stopped at a number of roadblocks along the way, frequently for hours at a time.

By the time Major Vézina reached his medical facility at the camp and had given the medical treatment required, he had been working for over twenty-four hours and was extremely upset. He went to his tent a few feet from his operating room and had a drink. A number of fellow officers dropped by to see how the injured soldiers were doing. By that time, the combination of fatigue, frustration and alcohol was taking its toll, and Major Vézina started to expound in a relatively loud voice about the miserable living conditions at Camp Shams.

A Canadian journalist sleeping in a neighbouring tent was awakened by the noise. He dressed quickly and sauntered over to Vézina's tent where, during the next few hours, he participated in the type of camaraderie born of common suffering in a foreign land. The next day, many Canadian newspapers carried the headline: "Canadian Soldiers Living like Pigs, Says Canadian Major".

The next day, at about nine in the evening, the phone rang in our home at 38 Arras Drive in Calgary. As I reached to pick it up, my wife said, "You're going to Egypt." I chuckled at her pseudo-psychic powers and put the receiver to my ear. It was the brigade commander, Brigadier-General George Brown: "Lew, they have a morale problem with the Canadians in UNEF II. Ottawa has asked me to provide a major with some UN peacekeeping background to get over there right away and check it out. Will you go?"

I put my hand over the mouthpiece. Looking Dora in the eyes with new respect, I said, "Well, Madame Crystal Ball, you got it dead right. Should I go?"

Military wives are a special breed of humanity. At first they don't believe you when you explain what it will be like married to a soldier, sailor or airman; they think you're exaggerating to make yourself look more important in their eyes. Within a few short years, however, they realize they are destined to share life with someone who would be impossible to live with if an operational assignment, particularly a challenging one overseas in a war zone, were passed up due to domestic concerns. Dora was definitely getting used to the unpredictability of it all. To those who simply couldn't abide that kind of life, she always had the inner strength to say, "I'd rather have him happy overseas in a UN mission than miserable at home brooding about it." Now she nodded—bless her.

"Certainly, General, when do I leave?" I said into the phone.

"Come and see me at eight," was the reply.

The following morning, I spent thirty minutes in General Brown's office and was disturbed by his briefing. It seemed that our Department of National Defence headquarters in Ottawa was seriously concerned about the morale of our troops in Cairo and wanted someone to sort the problem out before more draconian measures were necessary. When I asked what type of action was being considered, General Brown avoided answering directly; however, I had the distinct impression that heads would roll if things didn't improve for our troops in Cairo.

With a few notable exceptions, the majority of UN peacekeeping missions have been carried out in warm climates. Perhaps that's why Canadian and Scandinavian armies are such staunch supporters! It's hard to elicit much sympathy from your colleagues or family when you abandon Calgary at minus-30 degrees F in early December and fly off to Cairo, which, although suffering through an abnormally cold winter, was still managing an average daily temperature of 60.

As I stepped off the Canadian aircraft in Cairo, I was greeted by Brigadier-General Nicholson, the commander of the Canadian contingent. We shook hands and he asked, "What job have you been sent to do?" I was shocked. General Brown had told me I would fill the position of executive assistant to the contingent commander; here I was meeting the contingent commander, and obviously no one had told him.

"I'm your executive assistant," I blurted out.

"Great," the General replied, "just what I need, another major. Take a few days to settle in and then come and see me."

I was taken to Camp Shams by one of the commander's staff. The camp occupied the infield of what must have been a magnificent horse-racing track. The area under the grandstands was being used for storage, and the few administrative buildings had been converted to offices for senior Canadian and Polish officers. The middle of the infield looked like a Bedouin encampment; hundreds of tents had been set up, apparently without the kind of order and control that would have been imposed by a good sergeant-major. The tents served various purposes: kitchens, hospitals, three messes, offices, storage; but, the vast majority were dedicated to accommodation.

I was dropped off in front of a two-man tent. Inside was a dusty cot, a metal chair and a wash basin. "Ah," I thought, "I've been here before. I'll just wait: in twenty minutes or so, someone will come by, tell me it's all a big joke, and take me to my room." Two hours later, I decided that no amount of wishful thinking was going to make history repeat itself, so I started to unpack, halting when I realized my clothing was much better off staying in my barrack box than hanging from the single tent pole. I unrolled my sleeping bag and went to sleep.

The next morning, after breakfast in the officers' mess kitchen, I wandered about the camp for a few hours. It was unseasonably cold for Cairo. I was shocked to find our soldiers quartered in large marquee tents, in groups of twenty to thirty. They had no electricity and very little heat. I struck up conversations with the soldiers and determined that a large number of them did not know whom they worked for, and didn't have any meaningful employment scheduled for that day. On the other hand, the officers and non-commissioned officers were living in two-man tents complete with a single light bulb and an oil heater. I started to form the opinion that Major Vézina had been right; the troops *were* living like pigs, their conditions apparently the result of bad organization.

I discovered that these observations applied only to our logistics and headquarters personnel. Our contingent also included a signals unit, responsible for communications, a homogeneous grouping under their regular commanding officer, Lieutenant-Colonel George Simpson. They were tucked away in a corner of the camp and were well organized; their soldiers were properly cared for and their morale was good.

The logistics battalion, on the other hand, had been created by bringing together individuals from existing units across Canada. Their recently appointed commanding officer had been taken by UN headquarters in Cairo to act as UNEF II logistics officer. Since no one had filled the leadership void, the unit was operating without clear direction, and the soldiers were suffering the consequences.

Later that day, General Nicholson held a meeting in which I participated. After an hour of discussion on various matters, the floor was thrown open to questions and comments. I waited my turn, and when the moment came, reported my observations from my morning walkabout. I stressed the need for the soldiers to have electricity and heaters available if we were to motivate them to work in support of their unit. I didn't see why we couldn't organize the camp along conventional military lines, with company commanders, company sergeant-majors and basic platoon organization to give structure to what seemed to be chaos.

One lieutenant-colonel was particularly offended by my outspoken criticism. "He's been on the ground for less than a day and already he's an expert. What the hell does he know about our problem?"

I responded, "Not a lot, sir. But I did almost two years in UNEF I, where we had a similar task. This is not nuclear physics; we can improve morale dramatically with a few basic changes. I'm told everyone is forced to wear uniforms downtown. The Egyptians are extremely friendly. With the General's permission, I'll set up a rest centre downtown where people can go on a forty-eight-hour pass and have a hot shower and a good meal. That, combined with getting out of uniform for a day or two, and creating a conventional military organization in this camp, will be a positive step in the right direction."

General Nicholson gave me his full support. The next day, I drove to downtown Cairo and visited 26 Kaser El Nile Street, where we had had a few rooms booked back in 1963 for convoy personnel, so they could spend the night in Cairo before returning to Gaza. The hotel was under new management; however, the manager was an ex-Egyptian Air Force colonel, who was delighted with the prospect of UN soldiers making regular use of his establishment. We despatched our medical-hygiene team to check out the kitchen, and after two days of scraping and scrubbing, they declared it open for business.

SOON AFTER MY ARRIVAL, we were joined by two more officers of my regiment, Captain Chris Wellwood and Lieutenant Tony Stasiwic. Tony was fluent in Polish and became the General's aide-de-camp. The three of us informally organized ourselves into Canadian Patricia Delegation Cairo (CANPATDET-CAIRO), and as the only infantry officers in the camp, started to socialize together.

At that stage of our deployment, the UN had yet to establish a proper outlet for duty-free items such as liquor and cigarettes. We had some Canadian beer shipped aboard each of our regular flights from Canada, but were in need of so much operational equipment that there was not a lot of space for such luxuries, and the beer had to be rationed. Our neighbours in the Polish contingent were better organized in the liquor department. Their logistics battalion was not scheduled to arrive for another few months. In the meantime, one of their airborne battalions was sharing the camp with us. The Poles spent most of each day lining up tents and whitewashing rocks. Their side of the camp looked immaculate, whereas ours still resembled the same Bedouin encampment. Mind you, we were executing our logistics duties, such as they were, given the dearth of supplies; the Poles were not.

We got along well with the Poles, and with Tony's fluency in Polish, CANPATDET-CAIRO benefitted from favoured-nation status. We became fans of Polish vodka, which is closer to a liqueur than to the North American version of vodka. The bottle is easily recognizable by the large piece of green glass that the makers insert into each bottle before they cap it and ship it off to the unwary. The Polish officers met our requirements for about two months, until they too suffered the consequences of a flawed resupply system, and their stock ran dry.

We reluctantly suffered through our withdrawal pains until a Polish colonel advised us that one of their resupply ships was scheduled to arrive at the Egyptian port of Alexandria on the coming weekend. If we wanted a few bottles right away, we could drive up to the port; otherwise, it might be a week before their supplies would reach Cairo. The colonel was virtually certain that there would be some vodka as part of the shipment. All we had to do was speak to the ship's captain, who would gladly slip us a few bottles—particularly in exchange for U.S. dollars.

Two days later, Chris, Tony and I set off on our adventure a mere hour after sunrise. The route north from Cairo to the coast, along the west side of the Nile, is a magnificent trip; the road winds its way through the most fertile area of Egypt, culminating in a final dash through the lush Nile delta. Alexandria itself is a beautiful and cosmopolitan city. As we drove along the quay, we passed a dozen ships flying a dozen different flags of registration. We were about to ask for help in finding our freighter when we spotted the Polish flag flying from the stern of an impressively large ship. We parked our jeep and proceeded up the gangplank. Tony explained to a sailor that we were Canadians from the UN peacekeeping force and would like to speak with the captain.

The captain's quarters were magnificent—spacious, tastefully appointed and warm. Thinking of my tent, I wondered for a moment if I should reconsider my career choice. The captain, much to our surprise, was no more than thirty. Tony introduced us, and before we could get a word out, a bottle of that clear liquid with its telltale sliver of green glass was produced. We decided it would be impolite to make our request for a handout before getting to know the captain better, so we took up his offer to sit down and relax.

Over the next ten hours, we relaxed quite a bit. After the second bottle, we all grabbed a taxi and proceeded downtown into the mayhem of Alexandria, with its numerous bars and dives along the waterfront. One can only assume that this part of the city was designed by a sailor—who knew exactly what he was doing. Just before midnight, we ended up at a hotel swimming pool. For some obscure reason that only three inebriated soldiers and the captain of a Polish frigate would understand, we entered the pool in our underwear by jumping from the ten-metre diving tower. Regrettably, the captain did not anticipate the force with which he would strike the water and decided to jump with his legs apart. The resulting injury, temporary and superficial, but extremely painful, brought the evening to a fitting close. We hailed another cab and, dripping wet, made our way back to the ship.

By now it was past midnight. Chris, Tony and I decided, via a series of winks and nods, that it was time to raise the issue of the vodka.

Tony explained, "Captain, the Polish officers serving with us in Cairo said there would be some Polish vodka on their resupply ship.

A Polish colonel told us that if we drove up here and offered to buy five or six bottles with U.S. dollars, we would probably be looked after. Can you help us?"

The captain stared quizzically at Tony; gradually, his tiny smile became a full-fledged laugh. When he had regained control of himself, he said, "I can't help you. But perhaps the captain in the next berth can—his is the Polish resupply ship, not mine!"

We slept in the captain's quarters until the sun came up. Accompanied by three raging headaches, we drove back to Cairo empty-handed, but with a new friend behind the Iron Curtain.

Shortly after our excursion to Alexandria, General Nicholson was replaced by Brigadier-General Don Holmes. General Don was an infantry officer and a decorated veteran of the Second World War and Korea. I forgave him the fact that he was a member of the Royal Canadian Regiment—my regiment's rival for glory among the English-speaking infantry regiments of Canada's regular army.

General Don was revered as an outstanding leader by all members of the military who weren't jealous of his popularity with the soldiers. He lived for his soldiers, and they, in turn, loved him. He had endeared himself to just about everyone in uniform, except the Chief of the General Staff and the Honourable Douglas Harkness, the Minister of National Defence on the night when President Kennedy imposed the blockade on Cuba (and when I was being evicted from the officers' mess in Aldershot, England).

At the time of Kennedy's ultimatum, General Don had been a Lieutenant-Colonel commanding the First Battalion of his regiment. His battalion was Canada's standby force for peacekeeping assignments, prepared to move on short notice on any new UN peacekeeping operation that the Canadian government decided to support. The unit was on exercise in Petawawa, Ontario, at the time, and there was a bit of a party at their field officers' mess during a break in the training. When General Don heard President Kennedy's words, he became more than a little agitated. "How dare that SOB Kruschev put his bloody missiles in our North American backyard," he exclaimed to his adjutant, or words to that effect: "Get him on the phone, I want to talk to him."

Over the next two hours, using a military field telephone plugged into the camp switchboard, General Don spoke with a senior ranking official in the Kremlin, an assistant to Cuban President Fidel Castro, and, to cap off the evening, the Colonel-in-Chief of his regiment, an honourary position held by his Royal

Highness, Prince Philip. The General told all three more or less the same thing: "If those Soviet missiles don't move out of Cuba, and soon, I'll go in there with my battalion and sort out the problem myself!"

My first commanding officer, a tremendous leader and motivator of soldiers, Dan Osborne, once told me, "Lew, screw up or do well, but make sure they know who you are." Everyone now knew who Don Holmes was. Unfortunately, Minister Harkness failed to see the humour of General Don's prank, and he was relieved of his command. A few years later, Don found himself serving as the Canadian military attaché in Warsaw, Poland.

Well, our group of Canadians in Cairo needed a strong leader. In a brilliant and unfortunately rare example of typecasting, Don Holmes was brought out of Warsaw, promoted to brigadier-general, and joined us at our racetrack in Cairo. With his knowledge of Poland, both the people and the language, he was the ideal person to smooth over any difficulties with the Polish battalion that shared our camp. On the first afternoon at his headquarters, he sequestered himself in his office with the two Polish colonels and a forty-ounce bottle of Canadian Club whisky, and that was the end of any turf battles with the Polish battalion.

A GOOD THREE MONTHS into the mission, the UN had still failed to provide us with anything approaching an adequate level of supplies. Its self-imposed requirement to source supplies through international civilian contracts was proving once again to be too slow and hamstrung by UN bureaucracy and inefficiency. People in the UN system meant well; however, there were too few of them, and they couldn't meet the expanding and legitimate needs of the soldiers on the ground in a timely manner.

From my new vantage point on the seniority ladder as a major with some, albeit limited, authority, I began to realize that the UN's inadequacies were seriously eroding the reputation of our Canadian logistics battalion. Every demand for supplies from the forward infantry battalions in the Sinai should have been filled by the Canadian battalion. In turn, the battalion should have been kept in stock by the UN civilian-contract system. Since it was not, legitimate demands from the forward battalions for building and construction materials, cooking equipment, heaters, generators, lights, etc. were always being met by the irritating response, "Sorry, we don't have any stock."

This would not have been a major problem for the Canadian battalion's credibility, except for the fact that Canada refused to tolerate its own soldiers' suffering as a result of UN inefficiency. The type and quality of supplies desired by all members of UNEF II, particularly wood for construction, started to arrive on Canadian aircraft, paid for by the Canadian taxpayer, but intended solely for the use of Canadian soldiers. These highly desirable supplies were secured at our camp.

Each time a supply sergeant from, say, the Senegalese or Nepalese battalion would arrive at our camp with his unit's request for supplies, he would be told, quite accurately, that the UN cupboard was bare. But on his way in and out, he would see stacks of lumber stored throughout the Canadian compound; naturally, his perception was that the Canadian logistics battalion was hoarding the UN supplies for itself. The senior commanders throughout the force probably understood that the supplies were our own national stocks—God knows, we told them often enough—but I don't think the average soldier from Ghana, Indonesia, Peru, Senegal or Nepal ever believed we were anything but a bunch of spoiled, white, overpaid rip-off artists.

Midway through my tour, the UN, Egypt and Israel agreed to a plan that would see the Israeli forces withdraw from Suez City on the West Bank of the Suez Canal, turning the city over to the UN for a matter of hours, after which the Egyptian Army would reoccupy it. I decided this would be a historic moment that should not be missed. On the appointed day, I drove from Cairo to Suez City early in the morning, arriving an hour before the noon deadline for the Israeli withdrawal.

There was only the occasional burst of machine-gun fire in and around the city, so I decided to sightsee. I turned down a sidestreet towards a particularly putrid canal literally stuffed with rotting animal carcasses. I reached the canal with some difficulty, since the road, as narrow as it was, was partially blocked by three mangled Soviet T55 tanks, belonging to the Egyptians. I was amazed that anyone would try and manoeuvre tanks down such narrow streets; the crews must have been trying to sneak around an enemy position or get away. Whichever it was, it hadn't worked. I didn't like the smell as I drove past.

I parallelled the Canal for a mile and came upon a graveyard with the characteristic headstones of a British Commonwealth cemetery. I stopped and climbed over the low adobe wall, checking for trip wires or mines, and walked up to the first grave marker. Following a quick glimpse, I took a deep breath, turned and hurried back to my jeep. The inscription on the stone read, "Major L.W. MacKenzie, At Peace at Last". Omen or no omen, there was no sense pushing my luck.

By now it was getting closer to the hour for the Israeli withdrawal, so I started to move east towards the main Suez Canal. About a hundred yards before the Canal, I came upon an Israeli half-truck with its crew frantically loading everything they could into the limited confines of the vehicle. They had probably started loading their kit too late and, with their radio crackling orders for them to get moving, they were debating the merits of making one last trip into the bunker. Their sergeant won the argument, so they mounted up and took off in a cloud of dust and smoke towards the Canal.

Considering the obvious interest of the Israeli soldiers in returning one more time to their bunker, I decided to investigate. I eased myself down the narrow steps, checking for booby traps and mines along every inch of the entrance. It was not beyond the realm of possibility that the Israelis would booby-trap some of their own positions, just to teach the Egyptians a nasty lesson about the merits of caution. Soldiers don't always agree with political decisions, particularly when territory that has been paid for with blood is returned to the other side. I was aware that some Israeli soldiers and officers were not happy with their government's decision to turn Suez City over to the Egyptians.

As I reached the bottom of the steps, I edged around a 90-degree corner and entered a square, solidly sandbagged room the size of half a tennis court. This had likely been a bunker for an entire platoon. As my eyes grew accustomed to the dim light, I made out an object at the far end of the bunker that could only be one thing—a bed.

For over two months, I had been sleeping two inches above the dirt of the racetrack infield on my military-issue cot. I'd searched for a bed of some sort, any sort, but without success. Thanks to the firm decision taken five minutes earlier by the Israeli sergeant, I now had an opportunity to improve my quality of life—provided the Egyptians didn't arrive early.

Over the next ten minutes, I disassembled the bed and lovingly secured it, piece by piece, in the back of my jeep. The coil springs looked a little ridiculous and out of place, but considering that some fifteen local citizens were killed over the next thirty minutes as the

Egyptians celebrated the reoccupation of the city by firing into the general direction of the sky, my version of the Beverly Hillbillies did not draw much attention as I headed out of Suez back towards Cairo.

UST PRIOR TO MY ROTATION to Canada in April 1974, plans were made for the Canadian and Polish logistics battalions to move to the town of Ismalia, on the West Bank of the Suez Canal. We were to occupy an old British camp, which had been severely damaged in the 1972 war. I was part of the reconnaissance party that visited the camp, and our Canadian team determined that the most habitable part was on the west side. We would try and stake out that portion of the camp, leaving the east side to the Poles.

On decision day, I proceeded to Ismalia with General Holmes. We stopped in the middle of the camp and laid a map of the area on the hood of the General's jeep. I briefed General Don on our plot: the west for us and the east for the Poles.

The Polish colonels arrived, and General Holmes briefed them on our proposal. "Colonel, my staff has looked at the camp and we feel you would be best served by occupying the west side of the camp. We'll take the east." My God, I thought, the General has it backwards! I took up a position behind the Polish colonels and gestured frantically at General Don that it was the other way around. He ignored me.

The Polish colonels whispered to each other, moving their fingers about the map. Finally one said, "General, we think it should be the other way around. You take the west and we will take the east." General Holmes smiled and said, "Well, I'm not happy about that, but in the interests of international co-operation, I agree." Don winked at us. I was impressed; General Don knew his Poles.

I returned to Canada just before the move to Ismalia. UNEF II had been a real learning experience. I was absolutely convinced that, given any choice in the matter, only formed units should be sent on peacekeeping duty. Throwing together a heterogeneous force of individuals from across the country at the eleventh hour created an almost impossible problem for the unit's leadership. As Canadians, we always bragged about the cohesion of our units and the strength of our regimental system. In UNEF II, we had defied the principle of unit cohesion, and the soldiers had suffered the unpleasant results. Thanks to the personal leadership of General Holmes, things had ultimately worked out, but it was an important lesson for the future.

I was also persuaded that we'd have to suffer the inadequacies of the UN supply system along with the less well-off contingents, if we were to avoid developing a reputation as the spoiled brats of UN peacekeeping. God bless Canada for looking after our needs with national money outside the UN supply system; it certainly made our spartan existence more comfortable; however, at the same time, it had the potential to erode our reputation within the mission, particularly if we were responsible for logistics supply.

Finally, I had witnessed what outstanding leadership could do for a group of soldiers living under relatively miserable conditions. General Holmes was an inspiration: he got close to his soldiers without being overly familiar, and he genuinely put their needs first. Officers and noncommissioned officers were put on this earth to look after their soldiers, to make sure they are not only cared for, but put in danger only if the end result warrants the risk. Watching Don Holmes, I appreciated that commanding soldiers as a general in difficult circumstances was a rare privilege, granted to very few. Those officers fortunate enough to have the opportunity were truly blessed.

8

Cyprus—Third Tour

IN APRIL 1974, I returned to Calgary from Cairo, ready to settle down for a couple of years as the brigade major at our unit's superior headquarters. I had been advised that would be my next assignment, so it was a bit of a shock when I discovered that the rank for the position had just been elevated to lieutenant-colonel, and I was therefore out of a job.

Our commanding officer, John Sharpe, came to my rescue. He called Major-General Jim Quinn, who was on his way to Germany as commander of the Canadian forces in Europe. John had been Jim's brigade major in Petawawa, Ontario, a few years earlier, and he was good enough to talk General Quinn into taking me on as his executive assistant.

At last, Dora would be insulated from the likelihood of short-notice postings for a while. We spent two very enjoyable years in Lahr, West Germany. When Jim Quinn was promoted and returned to Canada a year after our arrival, I stayed on for a year with Duncan A. MacAlpine, my former commander in Vietnam.

Life was so stable in Lahr that it was almost boring at times, so I went to England and bought my first racing car, a vintage Lotus Elite. Dora agreed with the purchase on the grounds that it would be a one-year fling with motor sport, after which I would sell the car. (We've been working on extensions of the original contract ever since; I'm now on my seventeenth year of racing and sixth racing car since the Lotus.)

In summer 1976, I was advised that I would probably take over command of Three Mechanized Commando, an infantry battalion located at Canadian Forces Base Baden, a short drive up the

Autobahn north of Lahr. But no sooner had I started thinking about my promotion and new responsibilities than it was announced that Three Mechanized Commando was being eliminated in Prime Minister Trudeau's continuing cutbacks on defense spending and our NATO presence in Europe.

By this time, General Quinn was in charge of all personnel matters in the Canadian Armed Forces. He called me with the good news that I would be taking some French-language training in Lahr until February 1977, at which time I would proceed to Rome with my family to attend the six-month course at the NATO Defence College.

Although I didn't realize it at the time, taking the course in Rome was a tremendous stroke of good fortune. The Defence College is attended by both military and civilian students from every NATO nation. The various military members of the alliance send officers ranging in rank from major to major-general. I was a brand-new lieutenant-colonel, so I fit the mould. More importantly, the civilian students came from a wide range of backgrounds, including substantial representation from the diplomatic corps. This was my first opportunity to go head-to-head with diplomats during discussions of world affairs. Not only was this a very entertaining experience, in one of the most beautiful cities in the world, but it proved to be an invaluable preparation for my frequent dealings with heads of state and senior UN diplomats over a decade later in Central America and the former Yugoslavia.

Dora continued to demonstrate her flexibility during our six months in Rome, taking on the role of teacher, and tutoring Kimm in the intricacies of Ontario's grade-five curriculum. One thing was evident—both of them had a harder assignment than mine.

In July 1977, we flew from Rome to Canada and, with the Lotus in tow, drove to Calgary, where I would take command of the First Battalion, PPCLI. Command of a battalion of your regiment is a privilege desired by all infantry officers, and regrettably experienced by very few. Scores of deserving officers never get the chance, due to bad luck, poor timing, or losing out in a very subjectively judged competition.

A regiment's senior executive chooses its battalion commanders from the pool of lieutenant-colonels produced by the Canadian Forces' central promotion system. Although the regiment does not exercise control over who gets promoted, it does have a strong influence over assignments and therefore indirectly influences promotion. If you put a good officer into a high-profile job, and he does well, it will do him a lot more good than doing well in a relatively obscure appointment. There are many rolls of the dice before you have the good fortune to be entrusted with the command of a battalion, and I had enjoyed more than my share.

ORIGINALLY, IPPCLI WAS NOT scheduled to serve on peacekeeping duty in Cyprus until the late fall of 1978.

Tragically, in early 1977, my dear friend Andreas Cariolou died while attempting to rescue a Canadian soldier off the south coast of Cyprus. The accident occurred at a depth of over 100 feet, during a dive organized by the soldier's unit. Andreas and his oldest son, Glafcos, had nothing to do with the dive, apart from providing the boat and some of the equipment; however, they were in the area doing some spear fishing when the soldier got into difficulty, and characteristically, Andreas came to the soldier's assistance. Glafcos did a free ascent for a fresh tank of air for the soldier, and when he returned, both his father and the soldier were dead.

Over the next few months, rumours circulated on the island that Andreas's equipment had been inferior and that the dead soldier's family might sue the Cariolou estate. There was little basis for the rumours; however, they took on a momentum of their own, and relations between the Canadian unit and the Greek-Cypriot community deteriorated.

By now, Major Charlie Belzile, my friend who in 1965 had been standing by to rescue Rifleman Wiseman and me from our confrontation with the Greeks at the Kormakiti radar site, was Major-General Charlie Belzile, in command of all our troops in Germany. Charlie too had been a close friend of Andreas's and was disturbed by the rumours circulating around the island about the two deaths. Charlie used his influence so that my unit's rotation into Cyprus was moved forward to the spring of 1978, instead of the fall; Charlie felt that my presence, as a close friend of the Cariolou family, might help to put the rumours to rest.

Under my previous commanding officers in Cyprus, Kip Kirby in 1965 and Bill Hutchinson in 1971, I had seen pre-Cyprus training programmes that included everything from the history of the Crusades to the geological structure of the island. It was all good stuff, but much of it was unnecessary. Soldiers wanted to know where the Greek Cypriots, Greek nationals, Turkish Cypriots and Turkish Army personnel were; how to tell them apart; the locations and operational instructions for UN observation posts; and which direction was north. Just about everything else was superfluous. This time around, our only pre-Cyprus training exercise lasted a mere three days.

Since this was my third tour of Cyprus, I erroneously felt that I knew just about everything that had to be done to organize the unit before we left Calgary. Over the last few years, the maximum number of soldiers permitted to serve with the unit in Cyprus had gradually been reduced. The imposed ceiling for my forthcoming tour was to be approximately 560 personnel, of which some thirty positions would be filled by specialists posted in from across the country. I had over 720 people in the battalion and would therefore have to leave almost 200 of them behind in Calgary.

A large number of our noncommissioned officers had done multiple tours in Cyprus, and a few had been there six or seven times. I had an excellent regimental sergeant-major, Bill Colbourne, whom I called into my office. "RSM, with all the soldiers we're going to leave behind, why don't we give some of the sergeants and warrant officers who've been there many times an opportunity to volunteer? They've paid their peacekeeping dues. They should only have to go back if they really want to."

"Right on, sir. I'll get the word out this afternoon," replied the RSM.

The following morning, when I arrived at my office, I found a line of sergeants and warrant officers extending from inside the front entrance of our headquarters building out onto the sidewalk.

The RSM was waiting for me in my office. "Sir, we have a problem," he explained. "Every one of those warrant officers and sergeants lined up in front of your office has the same story. They all want to go to Cyprus. But if their wives find out they volunteered, they will never hear the end of it. In some cases, I wouldn't be surprised if it breaks up the marriage. They all respectfully request that you order them to go to Cyprus!"

And so my dumb idea regarding volunteers was cancelled; we ordered most of the soldiers in the RSM's line-up to Cyprus, and I filed away another lesson in human nature.

SINCE MY LAST TOUR IN 1971, the political and military situation on the island had undergone a profound change. In 1974, the Greek-Cypriot National Guard had orchestrated a short-lived coup and, in a monumental political blunder, had attempted to install Nikos Sampson as a figurehead president. Nikos had been an EOKA terrorist and was outspoken, to put it mildly, in his criticism of the Turkish-Cypriot minority.

There were three national guarantors of Cypriot security and independence: the United Kingdom, Greece and Turkey. If one of the two ethnic populations on the island were threatened, the other reserved the right to intervene. With Sampson as president-designate, Turkey declared the minority Turkish-Cypriot population threatened and intervened with a massive military operation that ultimately succeeded in occupying the northern half of the island. Many called it an invasion; however, from another perspective, the Turks had reason to be concerned about the security of their Cypriot brethren with Sampson as president and, in accordance with the protocol that existed at the time, had the right to intervene. For the world, this was a moot point; for most Cypriots, the Turkish intervention changed their lives, perhaps forever.

Consequently, the Green Line now ran across the middle of the island, splitting the country into two roughly equal halves. Many Greek Cypriots were driven from their homes in the north into the south, and the Turkish Cypriots in the south fled to the sanctuary of the north. It was an early form of "ethnic cleansing", to use the term that would become chillingly familiar eighteen years later in the former Yugoslavia. In a number of relatively humane examples, friends from the two ethnic communities actually exchanged homes so they could live on the "right" side of the Line. In Nicosia itself, however, the Green Line had changed very little, since few territorial gains had been made in the city by either side during the fighting.

After our arrival, we set to work trying to make our soldiers' lives more than an endless schedule of routine observation-post duty. Leave centres were established on the south coast in the lively Greek-Cypriot tourist towns of Limassol and Larnaca. Although the Greek Cypriots had turned their commercial attentions to the south coast only since 1974, it was already a booming success. On the other hand, the Turks had occupied the former tourist mecca of Kyrenia in the north, and for all intents and purposes it was a ghost town. Senior Turkish Army officers admitted quite freely, in private, that their people were not very good at running tourist facilities—even when they took over one of the most popular tourist areas in the world. They envied the Greeks their business acumen.

· · ·

WE STARTED THE STANDARD inter-company sports leagues and prepared Canadian teams for the various UN competitions among the British, Swedes, Danes, Austrians, Finns and ourselves. We won nearly every championship, thanks to a talented collection of young officers I was fortunate enough to have in the unit.

We also had a good supply of movies, which were rotated through the various messes every night. Nothing much had changed in this respect since Gaza, except that we received new movies soon after their North American release. When the word was passed that we were to receive *Saturday Night Fever* with John Travolta, the local diplomatic set and the expatriate Brit community went wild. We received numerous phone calls and notes from people asking if they and their families could attend our first showing on the patio outside the officers' mess. The movie had yet to appear in the local Cypriot theatres; however, its reputation as good entertainment was well-known, so I decided it would be excellent public relations to open up one mess to expatriates who wanted to bring their spouses and children.

On the night of our premiere, we arranged for a cold buffet and lots of popcorn for the kids. Soft drinks were free, and we put on extra bar staff. About thirty families arrived with kids ranging from babes-in-arms to teenagers. Everyone was in a festive mood; as the sun disappeared behind the built-up area of Nicosia, the kids were especially excited.

I was having a discussion inside at the bar with the president of our mess, Major Charlie Jurek, and through the doorway we could see the glow from the projector set up on the patio. As the crowd settled down, we could hear the familiar strains of the Bee Gees' music on the opening soundtrack. Charlie and I continued talking at the bar, when a few minutes later there was a virtual stampede of mothers and kids from the viewing area. They hurried through the mess and out the front door to the parking lot. Not one of them said even "Good night" or "Thank you". In fact, their facial expressions and body language led me to believe they were pretty upset.

I stuck my head out the side door and had a quick look at the screen. In the ten seconds or so that I watched, Travolta was having a discussion with his buddies, and I picked out at least six "f—ks" and a couple of "c—ksuckers". Our viewing audience was down to males over voting age, and I began to think I was jinxed whenever it came to mixing movies with peacekeeping.

• • •

A FEW MONTHS INTO my tour, the UN chief of staff, a British brigadier, was replaced by a Canadian, Brigadier-General Jim Cotter, an artillery officer. A few days after his arrival, I was patrolling the Green Line with RSM Colbourne when I received a message over my radio to report to General Cotter.

Entering his office, I hadn't had a chance to sit down when General Cotter said, "Lew, you have a serious problem in your unit. Your officers and soldiers are wearing their plastic name-tags flush with the top of their pockets. The dress regulations clearly indicate there should be a quarter-inch gap."

I thought he was kidding and said, "Well, General, if that's my only problem, I guess we're in pretty good shape."

Unfortunately, that was the wrong thing to say; and it marked the beginning of my first and only personality conflict with a superior in my entire military career. Our relationship hit rock-bottom a month later, when General Cotter counselled me on my leadership style: "Lew, your problem is that you are leading by example. You are leading your companies. Leave that to your company commanders. You should be thinking of your career five to ten years hence."

"On the contrary, General," I replied, "I'm a commanding officer, and my responsibilities are contained in my title. My priority is my unit and my soldiers. The future, if I have one, will look after itself as long as I look after my soldiers."

One of my major weaknesses is my inability to accept criticism. This encounter was no exception. General Cotter and I continued our adversarial relationship for the next four months. He documented his concerns regarding my shortcomings and sent them to my brigade commander back in Calgary, Brigadier-General Pat Mitchell, who was responsible for preparing my annual efficiency report. When General Mitchell debriefed me following my return to Canada, he said, "Lew, everything that Cotter criticized you for in his report is what I like about you. Here's what I think of his comments." With that, he ripped up General Cotter's letter. Needless to say, I'm a fan of General Mitchell, who epitomized the tough and compassionate leader that Canadian soldiers deserve.

ABOUT MID-TOUR, a large package, about the size of a portable television set, was delivered to the officers' mess on a Friday afternoon. Even though we worked seven days a week, we held "happy hour" every Friday from four P.M. until the last officer went to bed. We eyed the unopened package for over an hour, noting its return address was our officers' mess in Calgary. The handwriting looked suspiciously like my wife's.

After a couple of brandy sours, we decided to open the package. You can imagine our surprise when we discovered thirteen sets of women's panties and nine brassieres. A short note from Dora explained that the unit officers' wives had been having a little party in Calgary and had decided that we might appreciate receiving a token of their support.

We laid the items out on the floor, and I suggested we try to match the underwear to our wives. Obviously, four of them were liberated and not wearing a brassiere, but I thought we could do a matching job through a process of elimination. After half an hour of unsuccessful attempts in front of a spectators' gallery of single officers, who heaped sarcasm and other abuse on us, we returned to the bar, leaving the garments on the floor.

The next morning, when we returned to the mess, we discovered that all the underwear was missing. A superficial investigation failed to reveal the culprit. I can only imagine and hope that he enjoyed himself during the remaining three months on the island.

AS A RESULT OF MY deteriorating relationship with General Cotter, the UN military police unit was not particularly tolerant when it came to the questionable actions of my soldiers. Close to the end of our tour, my two best master corporals attended a strip show at one of the local dives on Regina Street in downtown Nicosia. Part-way through the performance, according to the military police, the two of them "mooned" the stripper. They were arrested and incarcerated in our makeshift jail across from my headquarters.

The next day, I conducted a military trial of the two soldiers. After hearing the charge and the evidence, I asked each of them, "What do you have to say for yourselves?"

The first corporal explained, "Sir, it was about halfway through the performance when I realized I had to use the washroom. When I returned, I must have inadvertently left my fly open."

His colleague continued with this miserable history of the event. "Sir, at some point during the evening, I noticed that I was improperly dressed, as my shirt was not tucked in. I stood up, undid my belt and while I was adjusting my shirt, I was arrested."

I turned to the RSM and said, "I need a couple of minutes to consider all of this. March these two out and we will recall them when I've made a decision. Come back in yourself; I want to talk to you."

When the RSM returned, I explained what I was about to do. The two corporals were marched back and stood at attention in front of my desk.

"Gentlemen, what you did was an insult to the regiment. The RSM will find some extra duties to keep you busy. Unfortunately, what you exposed was too small a thing on which to base a finding, and I therefore have no choice but to drop the charges. Dismissed."

With that, the RSM bellowed, "Flashers, right turn, quick march!"

We watched the two from our vantage point overlooking the parking lot. They were halfway across it before they realized they had gotten away with their prank. They let out a yell and took off at a trot to their place of duty. Both of them are sergeant-majors today, and two of the best in the regiment.

I left Cyprus for the third and last time in September 1978. I was unhappy with the confrontational relationship I had developed with General Cotter, but terribly proud of the job the unit had done—without one fatality, which was unusual in that high-risk area at that time. My high opinion of Canadian soldiers had been reinforced; I was sure they were as good as any in the world.

9

Observing in Central America

■

AFTER TWO VERY SATISFYING years in command, I wondered, like most ex-commanding officers, what black hole would suck me away from the troops. Unlike the American military, the Canadian Armed Forces have very few command positions at the rank of full colonel; therefore a thirty-nine-year-old lieutenant-colonel who had already completed his battalion command could realistically look forward only to a long series of relatively bland staff appointments.

In August 1979, I was fortunate enough to be posted to the Canadian Forces Command and Staff College in Toronto, where I remained a member of the faculty for three years—the longest period that Dora, Kimm and I have spent in one place in our lives together. The work was challenging and enjoyable. Young majors selected from competition with their peers attend the Staff College to prepare themselves for more senior rank. They study everything from strategy to domestic and international affairs, and improve their communication skills. As a tutor, I probably learned more than I taught.

In September 1981, Kimm and I ventured to Gimli, Manitoba, where I won the Canadian Sports Car Championship for GT3 cars. Earlier in the year, my trusty Midget had won the Ontario Road Racing Championship in the same class. As I accepted the trophy, I couldn't help but think of my experiences with my old Austin Healey and its finger-operated fuel pump.

My promotion to colonel came in May 1982; the MacKenzie family reported to Carlisle, Pennsylvania, where I completed a one-year fellowship at the United States Army War College. There

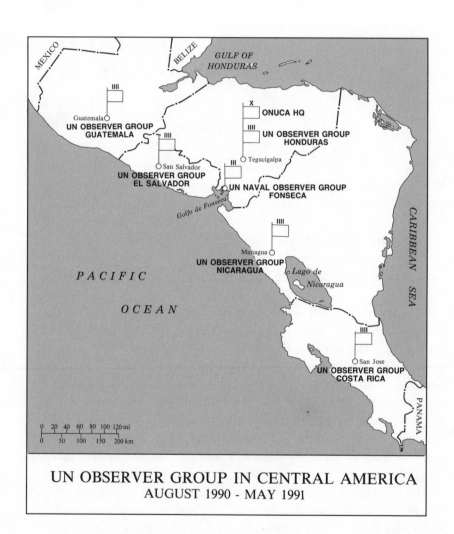

MEXICO

BELIZE

GULF OF
HONDURAS

IIII

Guatemala○
**UN OBSERVER GROUP
GUATEMALA**

X
ONUCA HQ

IIII
**UN OBSERVER GROUP
HONDURAS**

IIII
○ San Salvador
**UN OBSERVER GROUP
EL SALVADOR**

III
○ Tegucigalpa

III
**UN NAVAL OBSERVER GROUP
FONSECA**

Golfo de Fonseca

IIII
Managua○
**UN OBSERVER GROUP
NICARAGUA**

*Lago de
Nicaragua*

PACIFIC

OCEAN

CARIBBEAN   SEA

IIII
○San Jose
**UN OBSERVER GROUP
COSTA RICA**

PANAMA

0 20 40 60 80 100 120 mi
0   50   100   150   200 km

UN OBSERVER GROUP IN CENTRAL AMERICA
AUGUST 1990 - MAY 1991

were 250 American lieutenant-colonels attending the course and sixteen international fellows, most of us holding the rank of colonel. The course was equivalent to a post-graduate degree in political science, and was of considerable value in preparing me for the political intrigue of Central America and the Balkans.

Following Carlisle, I was posted to army headquarters in St. Hubert, Quebec, where I was placed in charge of army training. Dora and Kimm moved to Ottawa, so Kimm could carry on with an educational curriculum closer to the one she had followed in Toronto and the U.S.

In summer 1985, I completed my two years at St. Hubert and was assigned to "capital punishment" in Ottawa. Mind you, my good fortune continued, since I was given what I still consider to be one of the best colonel's jobs at our National Defence headquarters—Director of Personnel Careers Officers (DPCO). As DPCO, I was responsible for managing the careers of 16,000 majors, captains and lieutenants. I had an excellent staff, who made my job easier, and I enjoyed the instant feedback you got from your "customers" in the personnel world.

Over the years, the Canadian Armed Forces had come under increasing pressure to integrate women into all areas of the military, including the combat trades. The Minister of National Defence, Perrin Beatty, decided to proceed with operational trials to see if the idea was practical. He asked the Chief of the Defence Staff, Paul Manson, to nominate a general to be placed in charge of the project.

Generals were not beating down the Chief's door to volunteer for the job, and so I received the "good news/bad news" call: "The good news is you are promoted; the bad news is we have an interesting job for you."

My promotion was almost concurrent with that of Sheila Helstrom, Canada's first female general. Some ill-informed reporter on the staff of an Ottawa newspaper assumed that a female general would be placed in charge of my project, and wrote an article headlined, "Brigadier-General L.W. MacKenzie, Canada's First Female General, to Head up Women in Combat Trials." My friends have called me "Louise" ever since.

I spent a year with the trials and received a lot of practice dealing with the media. The trials were just about to commence when the federal government's Human Rights Tribunal took the problem out of the military's hands by declaring that we were not allowed to discriminate by sex when recruiting into any trade in the Canadian

Armed Forces. In the short term, the decision was a step backwards for women, since very few would be likely to pass the current operational physical standard for the infantry (to date, only one female private soldier has been accepted); whereas, under our proposed trials, we would have had almost 200 women trained and employed as a critical mass within the infantry for a period of two years. In the long term, however, the decision made a lot of sense, for there are very few women who want to serve in the infantry in the first place—so why make such a big deal about it?

In the spring of 1988, I was back on French-language training when a general at National Defence headquarters had a heart attack. In a small army, the ripple effect is significant when someone has to be replaced out of sequence. When the dust had settled, I was on my way to New Brunswick to command Base Gagetown, which is the largest military installation in Canada, and also houses the army's Combat Training Centre.

The posting was a marvellous two years. Kimm had left home and school, but decided to join us in New Brunswick. She returned to school and started training for her pilot's licence. She also get her first taste of motor racing; this involved a horrendous accident in my Formula Ford, but thankfully she walked away in one piece.

During those two years in Gagetown, I was back with the troops. The Combat Training Centre was responsible for training noncommissioned officers, warrant officers and junior officers in combat skills, building them up to combat-team level. In civilian terms, that means teams of infantry, armour and artillery personnel, supplemented by combat-engineer and signals support numbering around 200 personnel, with all the necessary equipment including tanks and armoured personnel carriers. It was very satisfying work; three years later, I would send my successor a message from Sarajevo saying, "Don't change a thing, the training you are giving our junior leaders is saving lives every day—keep up the good work."

My command tour was due to finish in the summer of 1990, so early in the year I started to lobby for a one-year extension—until I heard about the United Nations Observer Group in Central America (ONUCA). After all, it had been some twelve years since my last UN assignment . . . .

ONUCA WAS CREATED in November 1989, when the UN Security Council acceded to the request of five Central American governments to establish an observer force in their region. Costa Rica, El

Salvador, Guatemala, Honduras and Nicaragua had pledged to cease all aid to irregulars and insurrectionist forces. In addition, the five countries agreed that they would not allow their territory to be used to launch attacks against a neighbour. Reading between the lines, it was easy to deduce that the primary objective of the UN's resolution was to stop the war in Nicaragua, where the American-backed Contras operated from their bases in neighbouring Honduras.

Within four months of ONUCA's deployment to the area, Violeta Chamorro won a surprise victory in the Nicaraguan elections, ousting the Sandinista leader, Daniel Ortega, from the presidency. ONUCA's mandate was expanded to include the demobilization of the Contras, monitoring of the ceasefire in Nicaragua, and the separation of the opposing forces.

Between April 16 and June 29, 1990, ONUCA assisted in the demobilization of 22,000 members of the Nicaraguan resistance and destroyed an equal number of their weapons. This operation was conducted in a flawless manner, except for the chronic, serious lack of logistics and communication support provided by the UN. In spite of this critical shortcoming and its negative impact on the health and morale of the UN troops, and thanks to the dedication and professionalism of the military components, the operation was one of the most successful in the history of UN peacekeeping.

Early in the spring of 1990, I advised my career manager at National Defence headquarters that I would be pleased to accept an assignment to ONUCA in the coming summer. At the time, a colleague and friend, Brigadier-General Ian Douglas, was serving as the deputy commander and chief of staff for the mission. I had been told by one of my friends in low places in the personnel world that Ian would return home to Canada in a few months, so I volunteered to take his place.

As usual, I was told "no". I had more UN tours under my belt than most Canadian officers, and someone else should get a chance. However, again as usual, I was called in April and told to get to Ottawa for a two-week crash course in Spanish, after which I would replace Ian Douglas in Central America.

Armed with my new, largely inadequate, competence in Spanish, I reported to UN headquarters in New York in June for briefing. After a quick chat with a good friend, Colonel Doug Fraser, the military advisor to Canada's UN ambassador, I reported to the military advisor to the UN Secretary-General, Major-General Timothy Dibuama from Ghana. General Dibuama had graduated from the Canadian Army Staff College as a major in 1971 and had been with the UN ever since. He explained that I would encounter something called the "Spanish connection" when I arrived in ONUCA; Spain was participating in UN peacekeeping for the first time, and the Spanish commander of ONUCA, Major-General Augustus Gomez, an engineer by profession, had little command experience and was uncomfortable dealing with the eleven national contingents comprising ONUCA; as a result, he tended to pass along the majority of his orders and instructions by way of his Spanish officers, who were located throughout the mission area.

I arrived in Tegucigalpa, Honduras, on August 7 and completed the handover with General Douglas. Ian had done an outstanding job as the key ONUCA negotiator during the Sandinista and Contra talks leading to the demobilization of the Nicaraguan resistance. He had also been primarily responsible for the detailed planning and supervision of the actual demobilization process and the destruction of a large number of Contra weapons.

The successful conclusion of the Contra demobilization in June, and its resulting high profile in the international media, were, paradoxically, counterproductive to the continued effectiveness of ONUCA itself. ONUCA's involvement in the Nicaraguan reconciliation process had not been foreseen in its original mandate. Although the UN Security Council expanded the mandate to accommodate the window of opportunity provided by President Chamorro's surprise victory, it did so for a limited period only. Shortly after I arrived in the mission area, we were back to the original mandate, which required us to ensure that the five Central American countries were not supporting, in any way, revolutionary movements among their neighbours. This was a low-profile mission, which generated little media attention. Hence it was not surprising that the majority of people on the street openly wondered why we were still in Central America, now that the Contras were no longer a destabilizing force in the region. We were a victim of our own success.

As in most mission areas, however, there were also influential people who wanted us to stay, frequently for the wrong reasons. ONUCA was an observer mission, with the majority of its observer duties carried out by unarmed officers. In such missions, the UN does not provide accommodation or meals for the officers, preferring to pay them a daily subsistence allowance. The allowance is quite generous; and so, if two or three officers went together and shared accommodation, they could rent, at reasonable cost by North

American standards, a very nice house complete with caretaking staff and a maid, while still saving a good deal of their allowance. Most did so. Consequently, rental rates skyrocketed throughout the region, as local landlords in all five countries discovered the relatively high prices that UN personnel were prepared to pay. In some cases, local families moved out of their own houses to make room for UN personnel, in order to take advantage of a windfall in U.S. dollars.

The leadership of the five countries also wanted us to stay, but not enough to live up to their collective promise to the Security Council to provide us with free office accommodation. As a result, we were paying some stiff rental fees for both personnel *and* office accommodation for our team sites throughout the countryside.

Many of our operational needs, such as civilian staff, construction materials, fuel, maintenance and airport services, were obtained by local contract. Needless to say, the local entrepreneurs who were satisfying those needs didn't want us to leave either, even if our contribution to the Central American peace process was now somewhat limited.

The Contra demobilization had justified a modest increase in the overall strength of ONUCA. Many extra officers had been added to the mission for a period of about six months. Now that the demobilization was complete, I submitted a proposal to reduce the overall strength of the mision by some eighty observers. General Gomez approved the idea and submitted the plan to the UN in New York.

General Gomez and I had established a good working relationship. I'd found that the "Spanish connection" did exist; however, it resulted from General Gomez's shyness and awkwardness when dealing with members of other nations. He tended to explode with rage when anyone challenged his authority, but this was just camouflage for someone who was uncomfortable in command.

The UN approved our proposed reduction in the size of the mission within weeks. I was a bit embarrassed when the approval was accompanied by a direction that the rank of the force commander would be reduced from major-general to brigadier-general, and that General Gomez would return to Spain. Ultimately, he would be replaced by a Spanish brigadier-general; in the meantime, I would be appointed "acting" commander of the mission.

An "acting" commander takes over temporarily in the absence

of a person more qualified for the job. Since Spain was new to the peacekeeping process, whereas I was into my fifth year of peacekeeping and held the appropriate rank for the position, it was a fairly safe assumption that I was, at a minimum, as well qualified as any Spanish brigadier-general. I asked General Gomez to advise New York that I would not accept the qualifier "acting" in my title. If the UN couldn't live with that request, I would ask to be returned to Canada.

A series of nauseatingly childish exchanges by message and telephone took place over the next few days, and ultimately the inevitable UN compromise was reached: my title was adjusted to "commander, ad interim". Since I wanted to stay with the mission, I bit my tongue; but starting on the day General Gomez left the mission, I ceased using the qualifier "ad interim". I assumed that this personality-driven altercation would keep me from serving on any other UN mission in the future.

AFTER I ASSUMED COMMAND on December 21, 1990, I came face-to-face with the realities of directing a UN peacekeeping mission. The job on the ground was relatively straightforward, and I had excellent military officers to carry out our mission. Spain had provided a first-rate contingent of officers, along with Brazil, Argentina, Colombia, Ecuador and Venezuela. These officers provided us with strong Spanish-language skills. A number of officers from the other countries represented in the mission—India, Ireland, Sweden and Canada—became quite fluent within a few months. French-speaking Canadian officers were particularly successful in mastering Spanish in double-quick time. However, the joy of command quickly waned as I discovered how little authority I really exercised.

We had to channel any ideas to improve our effectiveness through the political net to New York. Given the potentially negative implications of any change from the status quo, I understood why this had to happen, but it was frustrating nonetheless. Fortunately, this characteristic of UN decision-making did not affect our people deployed throughout the region. Like any commander, I considered that one of my primary responsibilities was to insulate my people in the field from the political problems of our job, doing the real work myself on any problems we might have in our own headquarters or with New York. Except for a large-scale ambush of a mini-battalion of the Salvadorean Army by left-wing guerrillas, which resulted in Salvadorean soldiers escaping across the border into Honduras and into one of our team sites, the situation throughout the region remained tense but quiet.

OUR FRUSTRATION caused by the slow and complex decision-making system in New York palled in significance when compared to the ire evoked within our military component by the UN's system of administrative support.

Normally, when you take over any command in the military, you are responsible for just about everything, including the budget. You might not get as much money as you want—in fact, you rarely do—but in most instances, you decide how it is going to be spent. Not so in the UN. There are two bosses in UN New York who have a powerful impact on your day-to-day life in the field: the Undersecretary for Peacekeeping Operations, who provides you with your operational direction; and the head of the Field Operations Division, who controls your budget through your mission's chief administrative officer. In the UN, unlike the military, operations does not reign supreme. If you need fifty vehicles to do the job, but the beancounters decide you can have only fifteen, you get fifteen.

To be fair to the UN beancounters, you occasionally run up against the same problem in the military. There is, however, a dramatic difference. In the military, the commander can play around with his budget and realign priorities as necessary; the commander, not his administrative and financial staff, determines the operational imperatives, and once he makes his decision, everyone mobilizes all resources to support him. Fortunately, I was blessed in ONUCA with an outstanding chief administrative officer, Noel François. We established a good working relationship; consequently, the mission prospered in relative terms, in spite of the bureaucratic hurdles imposed by the UN.

Noel was keen to support the operation, yet even he, with his intimate knowledge of the UN system, was stonewalled a number of times. I took some solace in the fact that he seemed as frustrated as I was. In most cases, I decided, the problem was systemic and had little to do with the personalities or dedication of the people comprising the UN civilian administration. But excessive bureaucracy was a UN shortcoming that would have dire consequences two years later in Yugoslavia.

• • •

ONCE I ASSUMED COMMAND of the mission, I was entitled to bring in my family from Canada. Dora and Kimm, then twenty-three, arrived in Tegucigalpa and moved into my somewhat palatial, Spanish-style residence perched on top of the highest mountain overlooking the city. It was a massive house with a magnificent view. It was also vulnerable to break-and-enter artists, so we hired armed guards from the Honduran Army, who controlled the gate entrance and patrolled the grounds twenty-four hours a day.

It took about twenty minutes to drive from home to my headquarters in Tegucigalpa. On the way home after work, I would drop my driver, Rico, off at his street at the bottom of the mountain and drive home by myself. In fact, I would race home. ONUCA represented my first break from active racing competition in eleven years, so I used the run up the side of the mountain every night for practice and therapy. I drove a UN-supplied Toyota Crown that was underpowered and heavy but had good handling characteristics. My times in the beginning were around eleven minutes, but by the end of my tour, I was breaking the seven-minute barrier on a regular basis.

A number of record-setting runs were aborted due to a large black cow that had a habit of resting in the middle of the unlined black road. She enjoyed settling down to cool off in the midst of a spring-fed stream that ran across the road and down the mountain-side. I would come around a high-speed right-hand turn at over eighty miles per hour, arms crossed to apply some opposite lock to the steering wheel, only to find her bulk in the middle of the road. Fortunately, she got used to me and never bolted in panic, providing me with enough space to get around her. Compared to the cow, fallen rocks, potholes the size of a small nuclear crater, and agonizingly slow, overloaded local buses were child's play.

About a week before our return to Canada, I was in my office finishing off the daily paperwork just prior to a helicopter visit to our Argentine naval squadron. (This outstanding naval unit patrolled the Gulf of Fonseca, maintaining a UN presence among the three countries bordering the Gulf—Nicaragua, Honduras and El Salvador—and at the same time intimidating gun-runners.) My phone rang, and it was Dora, breathing heavily and sounding very excited: "We've been robbed! There are two of them. Rosa [our maid] and José [our gardener] are chasing them. José has got Gus's pistol and tried to shoot one of them but the gun won't work. I'm here by myself with a switchblade!"

I yelled to Captain Gus Garant, my Canadian aide in the outer office, "Gus, Dora says your pistol won't work."

Gus entered the office. "It works fine but I unloaded it last night—it's empty." If nothing else, I supposed José could beat the robber over the head with it if he caught them. I told Dora to stay put and lock the door to the bedroom, and I'd be there right away. I put Rico in the passenger seat and drove as fast as the traffic allowed back up the mountain. Fortunately, the cow had taken the day off.

Arriving at the residence, I noticed there were no guards, and the gate was open. Dora saw us drive in and came rushing out of the house with a switchblade in her hand. "Rosa and José chased the banditos over the back fence. José was still trying to shoot them when they all disappeared down the hill. They've been gone for at least thirty minutes."

"Where the hell are the guards?" I asked.

"Don't you remember? You decided to cancel the contract a week ago so we could tidy up the bill!" Dora exclaimed. Dumb decision, I thought.

Rosa and José appeared at the front gate, from the opposite direction in which they had chased the robbers. Both were sweating heavily, and José was still carrying Gus's pistol. Excitedly they described the chase; I gradually understood that the banditos had made a clean getaway, although one was limping quite badly, having damaged his ankle when they jumped over the wall surrounding the house.

Dora accompanied Rosa and José as they retraced the robbers' path from the house. I called the office and asked them to hustle up the police. They had been called by my secretary Claudia as I left the office, but had yet to appear.

I heard a shriek from behind the house and rushed out onto our bedroom balcony. Rosa had jumped over the wall to the spot where the robber had twisted his ankle. There she found her wallet, with her month's pay undisturbed. But she wasn't entirely relieved, for we discovered that her pistol and small portable radio were still missing. I promised to replace them and thanked her and José for being so aggressive. I also had new respect for Dora, who must have looked absolutely intimidating with her switchblade at the ready. I reminded myself not to upset her in future.

ON MAY 17, 1991, I HANDED OVER COMMAND of ONUCA to a first-class Spanish officer, Brigadier-General Victor Pardo. He came to the mission from an impressive series of command appointments in his own army; he also had the human touch so essential to multinational command. He would command the mission until it closed down in January 1992.

I left ONUCA with some new concerns regarding the overall cost-effectiveness of UN peacekeeping operations. Host countries were not forced to live up to their responsibilities to provide accommodation for the UN. In addition, the process for modifying outdated Security Council mandates was agonizingly slow. There was a strong feeling that ONUCA had stayed in Central America beyond its requirement because the Peruvian Secretary-General of the United Nations, Xavier Perez de Cuellar, was reluctant to leave Central America over the objection of the region's presidents while the international community was paying so much attention to the Gulf War and its aftermath. All I knew was that there had to be a better way to look after the military component of a UN peacekeeping mission in the field.

On the positive side, this had been the first time that I had dealt with heads of state on peacekeeping matters. President Chamorro of Nicaragua was charming and tough, and presided over what must have been the youngest collection of cabinet ministers in the world; several of them were graduates of McGill University in Montreal, so they had a warm spot for Canadians. President Callejas of Honduras was friendly and graciously assisted a number of my officers in working their way through the bureaucratic maze associated with the adoption of local children. President Cristiani of El Salvador had by far the most difficult task during my time in command; his country's civil war was far from over, and serious clashes took place almost every day. Since our mandate covered only conflicts that crossed borders, civil strife was outside our legal responsibilities. My dealings with the presidents of Guatemala and Costa Rica were limited to protocol visits, and we discussed little of substance. But as someone who has always considered national leaders a special form of humanity, I found it a revelation to realize that relatively ordinary people occupy these extraordinary positions, with their extraordinary problems.

10

Rumours of Yugoslavia

FROM CENTRAL AMERICA I reported in July 1991 to the headquarters of the Canadian Army's Land Forces Central Area in Toronto, to take up the position of deputy commander. Since my boss, Major-General Nick Hall, was a reserve officer and would continue to live at his home in Whitby, my family and I moved into the commander's residence.

Two months after my arrival in Toronto, I started to watch the self-destruction of Yugoslavia on the late news. Slovenia and Croatia had declared their independence from the federation. Yugoslavia's Serb-led National Army (JNA) was taking territory in Croatia by force in order, in Belgrade's words, "to protect" the ethnic Serbs living in those areas. Considering the Croatian mistreatment of the Serbs during the Second World War, in collaboration with the Nazis, one couldn't blame the Serbs for being fearful and even a little paranoid; but they were obviously trying to even the score with a very heavy hand.

Because this conflict was in Europe's backyard, I assumed that the European Community would take the lead in any peacekeeping measures. They did so very slowly, however, and then invited Canada to participate. Colonel Don Ethell, my former sergeant from the 1965 Cyprus mission, was selected as the operations officer for the European Community's military monitor mission located in Zagreb, Croatia. I was envious when Don phoned me from the Toronto airport on his way to Yugoslavia. I called National Defence headquarters in Ottawa the next day.

A day later, I received a call from the Commander of the Army, Lieutenant-General Jim Gervais, thanking me for volunteering for

UN peacekeeping in Yugoslavia; but, he explained, once again, that other officers deserved a chance, so I wouldn't be going on this one. I didn't argue the decision but felt disappointed. Many officers still thought that UN postings were good fun. They hadn't been to the Middle East or Nicaragua, and it was hard to change their perceptions after twenty-eight relatively easy years of peacekeeping in Cyprus.

That evening I was to attend a dinner at the Canadian Institute for Strategic Studies, hosted by its director and an old friend of mine, Alex Morrison, and featuring a lecture by Alex's opposite number from the Beijing Institute. I gave Dora the news: "Well, dear, I guess Central America was it for my peacekeeping career. General Jim says they're going to choose someone else to be chief of staff of the Yugoslavia mission, so you can relax. I'm off to Alex's dinner and should be home around midnight."

Dora saw that I was disappointed. She said, "Don't worry, you'll get there in your own good time."

The content of the lecture that evening was interesting; however, it was eclipsed by an agonizingly slow and monotonous delivery. Mind you, the lecturer was speaking in one of his many languages other than his native Chinese, so he deserved my patience and close attention. Nevertheless, I found my mind drifting off into other areas, not the least compelling of which was the current situation in what was soon to be known as the former Yugoslavia.

Our distinguished lecturer was about forty-five minutes into his presentation, and I could see by his neat stack of unread pages that we had at least another hour to go, when my assistant's cellular telephone beeped. Captain Bonnie Goldbeck was sitting close to the door and quickly stepped outside. I assumed the caller was my driver, checking to see if she should position the car in front of the Institute for our scheduled departure time. At the current pace, we were going to be leaving a couple of hours later than expected.

The door opened again and Bonnie pointed to her cellular, indicating that I had an important call, or at least a call from someone more important than I was. My eyes made a silent apology to Alex for the disturbance, and I tiptoed out of the room. Bonnie handed me the phone, saying, "It's General Gervais."

"Yes, General, thanks for rescuing me from strategic planning in China. What's up?" I asked.

Jim sounded a bit subdued. "Lew, we have a problem. We screwed up when we submitted the name of our general to go to

Yugoslavia as the mission's chief of staff. We told New York he'd been a unit commanding officer in Cyprus in the early '80s. That more or less satisfied their criterion of recent UN peacekeeping experience. This afternoon we discovered we were wrong. He last served on peacekeeping duty in Cyprus in '67 as a lieutenant. The UN has told us that would not qualify.

"It seems the Indian general nominated as the force commander and the French general who will be his deputy have never served with the UN before. So they want a chief of staff experienced in the workings of the UN.

"Now, we have two choices. You know who our nomination was—Ray Crabbe. We can say to the UN, look, we're giving you one of our very best generals, he'll do a great job, take it or leave it, and lose the position to some other country. Or we can accede to their wishes and provide them with a UN-experienced officer. My initial reaction was to say it's Ray or nobody; however, we'll have the second-largest number of soldiers, about 1,400, in the mission area, so we really should have a Canadian general in the headquarters."

I knew what was coming . . . .

Jim concluded: "Would you be prepared to go?"

We in the military pride ourselves on the efficient way we manage the careers of our personnel. For almost two years, I had been responsible for the career management of over 15,000 second lieutenants, lieutenants, captains and majors. My staff of over forty worked long hours, travelled constantly and turned themselves inside out to make sure our officers could plan their moves at least a few months in advance. Ideally, they should know where they are moving six months before the actual transfer.

Don't try and explain this theory to my wife. She won't believe you. Over the previous ten years, the warning time for our moves had remained about the same, but the proposed destination and job had sometimes changed four or five times between January and May. Now it had come down to, "Would you be prepared to go?"

"When?" I asked. I couldn't think of anything better to say.

Jim explained: "The UN will have to approve your nomination. I'm pretty sure they'll be delighted, considering you were a UN commander in Central America last year. I would imagine they'll want you in New York on Monday—that's in four days. And you'll have to be briefed in Ottawa before that."

My mind was spinning, trying to put the various considerations into some order of priority. I'd already decided I would agree to go; after all, I had volunteered only a day earlier. Now, what could I ask Jim to do for me before I hung up?

"General, I'll go, but I think we should protest the UN's rejection of Ray Crabbe. Ray would do a great job, probably better than me. And the point should be made that *Canada* picks its officers for senior peacekeeping appointments, not the UN. I doubt very much if many other countries would tolerate such interference.

"Now, I need your co-operation, General. Based on your call earlier today, I told Dora I wasn't going to Yugoslavia. I've got some fancy explaining to do when I get home, so give me until midnight to do that. In the meantime, please make sure some keen member of your staff doesn't call her with the good news." That was about all I could think of.

"Thanks, Lew. I'll let Ottawa know, and good luck with Dora," Jim said as he signed off.

I waited a few minutes to collect my thoughts, then crept back into the dining room. I whispered in Alex's ear as I passed behind the head table, "It looks like I'm off to Yugoslavia." After the dinner was over, I didn't stay around for the usual drink and discussion of the lecturer's thesis.

As my official car approached our residence, I noticed that all the downstairs lights were on. It was past midnight—unusual for Dora to be up at such an hour. She normally went to bed and watched the television news at eleven, and was asleep if I arrived home much after eleven-thirty.

Not so tonight. The front door opened abruptly just as my hand was reaching for the knob. Dora got in the first word: "What the . . . is going on? You told me you weren't going to Yugoslavia. Now Nick Hall says you are!"

It turned out that General Gervais had felt badly about approaching me directly, rather than going through my immediate boss, Major-General Nick Hall. Following his telephone conversation with me, Jim had called General Hall to advise him of my pending assignment to the UN. Whether he remembered to tell Nick not to call my house until I got home in a few hours, I will never know. All I know for sure is that Nick called Dora right away and asked her what she thought about the assignment. He even turned his telephone speaker on, so that his wife could hear Dora's reaction.

Needless to say, Dora was a little miffed. After Nick's call, she had assumed it must have been out-of-date information still flowing through the system. I had told her some eight hours earlier that I wasn't going to Yugoslavia, and that was that.

"I'm afraid there's been a change in the last few hours," I explained hurriedly. "The UN has rejected Canada's first choice for the chief of staff job, and I've been asked to go—probably in three days."

It was time to start my selling pitch, which would come back to haunt me within the week. "I assume that being in the headquarters, I'll be on some sort of UN military subsistence allowance. I've heard figures of at least $150 a day. If that's the case, I can probably save a good deal of it while living on my Canadian overseas allowance. With any luck, I could save $40,000 during the year—and that's U.S. dollars."

I had played my trump card. No mention of the inconvenience of yet another year on her own; no reference to another move for Dora; no consideration of the impact on our daughter's continuing education; just a quick stab to the heart of the matter—the money.

I could see Dora waver when I mentioned $40,000 U.S. The rest of the early morning was dedicated to persuading each other that this assignment was actually a good idea. This was strictly self-administered therapy, since it was too late to change anything anyway. But, like everyone else in the military who receives an unpopular or controversial posting, we took only a few hours of rationalization and soon began looking forward to the change and the challenge. By sunrise, we had eliminated all the negatives and were praising the positive aspects of the assignment.

We were the beneficiaries of the coping mechanism that most military families possess. Over the years, I've decided that it's probably a natural part of the genetic makeup of soldiers and their spouses. Without it, we would all go a little crazy—at least once every two or three years, when we are warned of a pending move to a new and sometimes unpopular location.

At eight A.M., I went to my office and dropped the bombshell that tomorrow would be my last day at work. I called my replacement, Colonel Gary Thompson, who would be promoted to brigadier-general on my departure, and arranged to meet with him the following day.

While the staff went into high gear to facilitate my departure, I went home for the afternoon to sort out the garage. Once Kimm had completed her night-school course at York University in April, she and Dora would move into our house in Ottawa. A lot of our furniture and effects would go into storage in Toronto, anticipating my return in a year's time. Unfortunately, I was the only one who could organize all the racing-car bits and pieces spread about the garage. Some of them I would need as soon as I returned in a year, in order to prepare for the next few races; the rest could go into long-term storage. By the end of the afternoon, the garage's contents were organized into the two categories.

That evening, Dora and I went shopping, primarily for items to fill up my shaving kit. I had no idea what to expect in Yugoslavia. The televised reports I had seen on CNN suggested that some of the more basic items might not be available. I had no idea at that time where our headquarters in Yugoslavia would be located.

On the way out of the shopping mall, we passed a bookstore. I mentioned to Dora, "I should buy a simple one-year diary. The UN is a real stickler for precision when it comes to claiming expenses. The easiest way to keep track of what they owe me is to enter the amounts every day."

I bought a brown, plastic-covered, one-year diary for $4.29. Four months later, it was widely reported on television and in the print media as "the red, leather-bound diary on his desk". It was still the same brown, plastic model; if I had known it would capture the imagination of the media and become the genesis of a book, I would have bought the more expensive version.

11

New York, New York

▬

THE BALANCE OF THIS BOOK is devoted to my experiences as chief of staff of the multinational United Nations Protection Force (UNPROFOR) in the former Yugoslavia—and in particular, to my command of UN peacekeepers in Sarajevo in the summer of 1992, after what is now known as the Bosnian civil war had erupted in April.

My sources for retelling these events include UN communiques and news releases; the texts of ceasefire agreements among the combatants; and correspondents' reports in newspapers and magazines. But the chief source is my personal memory, aided and abetted by the somewhat cryptic entries in my diary, which I kept faithfully up to date between my departure from Canada in March and my return in August.

Consequently, I have chosen to follow the diary's path by telling the story chronologically. I hope the result, if not the method, will remind readers a little of a book that has served as something of a model for this one, William Shirer's classic, *Berlin Diary*. Not that I have pretensions to be the reporter that Shirer was; but there is at least the attempt here to be, like him, an eyewitness to history in perilous times, in addition to having been briefly a protagonist.

The reader may sometimes feel, exactly as I did at the time, swept along by sudden and unexpected incidents, bombarded by unfamiliar players and foreign-sounding names, rather than being guided through the maelstrom of events by the more structured overview of a historian. But the advantage of a daily narrative is that it places the reader at one end of a telescope observing history in the making.

My interpretation of events will undoubtedly upset some of the players involved in Sarajevo's continuing plight. While I can understand their frustration, I could not bring myself to sanitize the record of what I saw on the ground in order to avoid upsetting my critics. I have merely tried to document from the inside one person's view of UN peacekeeping efforts in the turmoil and tragedy of Sarajevo.

MARCH 2   On Monday, March 2, 1992, I made the first entry in my diary:

> 0540   A.M. Reveille
> 0630   Departure—emotions

Few professionals experience or even comprehend the implications of long family separations as well as military people. This was to be my sixth extended separation from Dora and Kimm, and once again I found it never got any easier. At least I had the excitement of a new challenge to motivate me. All Dora had was yet another move staring her in the face—this time to Ottawa. Not only that, but Kimm would eventually be moving herself, to be with her boyfriend Gus in Gagetown, New Brunswick (you remember Gus, he was my aide in Central America with the empty pistol), so Dora would be absolutely on her own for the first time since we were married.

As usual, she put on a brave front. We parted amid tears, a kiss and a wave—only to repeat the sequence ten minutes later, after I realized I'd forgotten my wallet and had to turn around halfway to the airport. Although it was below freezing, Dora had run down the street in her bare feet, waving my wallet, trying to catch my attention, but to no avail. I was thankful for the second goodbye.

My first stop was Ottawa, where I spent much of the day reading briefing materials at National Defence headquarters. The more I read about the situation in the former Yugoslavia, and the UN's plans to intervene on the side of peace, the more I became convinced that the planners, whoever they were, were being unrealistically optimistic.

The republics of Slovenia and Croatia had declared their independence in 1991. The Yugoslavian National Army (JNA) had been forced to withdraw from its bases in Slovenia and had moved south to Croatia. Major fighting broke out between the JNA and soldiers of the fledgling Croatian Army (a large number of whom had recently served in the JNA, but had affiliated themselves with their ethnic homeland when Croatia had declared its independence).

But the Croatians, although performing admirably with their brand-new army, were incapable of purging the JNA with its heavier weapons from Croatian soil. The JNA reinforced its units and occupied a good deal of southern Croatia, claiming that it had to protect fellow Serbs in the region from Croatian atrocities.

In November 1991, Mr. Cyrus Vance, the UN Secretary-General's special representative, appeared on the scene. Vance worked out a deal with Croatian President Franjo Tudjman and Yugoslavian President Slobodan Milosevic. The Vance Plan would see 14,000 UN soldiers located in three "UN Protected Areas" (UNPAS) in southern Croatia. The UN soldiers would be responsible for protecting the civilian population, primarily Serbs, within the UNPAS. When the UN took over this protection role, the JNA units would withdraw to Bosnia-Herzegovina or Serbia, or their personnel could demobilize and stay in the UNPAS as unarmed civilians.

The Vance Plan left many details unresolved, such as the ethnic composition of the local police forces in the UNPAS; these details were referred to as "technical issues" to be worked out on the ground by the United Nations Protection Force commander. They were to become the bane of our existence after we arrived in Yugoslavia.

Like all ceasefire agreements, the Vance Plan was developed on the assumption of a modicum of trust and goodwill existing on all sides. Regrettably, the Serbs and Croats had their own nationalistic agendas, which didn't augur well for the peaceful implementation of the plan. The Serbs ruling in Belgrade, the former federation's capital, didn't trust the Croats, and lacked confidence in the UN's ability to protect the Serbs living in the UNPAS. The Croats, for their part, didn't believe that the JNA would actually withdraw from Croatia, and understandably looked upon the UNPAS as Croatian territory occupied by the Serbs under UN supervision. Nonetheless, the plan's objective was to create an atmosphere conducive to political negotiations between the two parties, leading to a lasting ceasefire and eventually to peace.

The UN is one of the world's largest committees, and UN decision-making can be a painfully slow process. It was fully four months later, in February 1992, before the Security Council approved a resolution authorizing the creation of UNPROFOR. And here it was the first week in March, and UNPROFOR commanders and senior staff were only now preparing to gather in New York for our instructions.

In the meantime, fighting was continuing between the JNA and the Croatian Army. The boundaries of the UN Protected Areas drawn up by Mr. Vance, which in most instances were based on a combination of ceasefire lines and municipal boundaries, had been overtaken by the shifting battles. In some areas, the JNA had advanced up to twenty kilometres, bringing additional Serbian minorities outside the UNPA boundaries under their "protection".

The idea that the UN could now intervene in a timely manner, or that the JNA would turn its protection role over to a lightly-armed UN force, seemed terribly naive to me. However, those were diplomatic decisions; our job in the military was to get the Protection Force over there and make it operational as quickly as possible. Over four months had already been wasted since the signing of the Vance Plan. From what I had been watching on television over the past few weeks, I doubted that the ceasefire was holding in more than a few locations. Perhaps it would all make more sense when I got to New York.

MARCH 3   This would be my last day on Canadian soil for many months. I spent the morning taking care of administrative, legal and financial matters.

One of the few people you can pretty well select for yourself in the Canadian Army is your executive assistant or personal staff officer. As a brigadier, I would normally be entitled to a captain; however, the people who had put together the UN organization for Yugoslavia had assigned major's rank to the position. I was delighted.

Usually an infantry officer, like myself, would choose an armour or artillery officer to help balance his own professional knowledge. But my previous UN experience told me in no uncertain terms to reject this temptation and select a signals officer. The UN had always had communications problems wherever I had served; to ensure that I could at least talk to Ottawa on Canadian administrative and personnel matters, I went to Lieutenant-Colonel Lew Evans' office and reviewed the files of five signals officers. I had about two minutes for each file and quickly selected a Major Gendron.

I rushed up one floor to see the legal people and signed over my power of attorney to Dora.

Then it was time to see the people at Compensation and Benefits. They had the latest data from UN New York and told me that my UN subsistence allowance would be $180 U.S. per diem for the first thirty days and $150 U.S. thereafter. That would be in addition to the Canadian allowances of approximately $1,000 a month. I felt extremely gratified knowing I would be able to live up to my promise of financial benefit made to Dora.

In the afternoon I flew to New York and checked into the Roosevelt Hotel. It didn't take me long to realize I was back with the UN, where double standards abound. While the UN civilian and military staff live comfortably in New York and its environs, military personnel on our way to or from a mission in the field receive minimal support. The paint was peeling off the ceiling and walls of my room at the Roosevelt, and there was barely enough room for my luggage; on the plus side, the hotel was within walking distance of the UN.

I dined that evening with Colonel Doug Fraser, then military advisor to Canada's UN Ambassador, Madame Louise Frechette, who was also present. I learned that Brazil and Pakistan would not be providing battalions to UNPROFOR after all, as previously suggested, but that Jordan and Poland would probably take their place. It seemed a little late to be finalizing the participating nations, given that our advance group was due to depart for Belgrade and Zagreb within the week. I knew that, once a country agreed to provide a contingent of soldiers, it could take the UN up to two months to get them into the mission area. I had an uneasy feeling and didn't sleep well on return to my cubicle at the hotel.

MARCH 4   Early the next morning, I attended my first briefing. The UN would start sending in the lead battalions a few weeks after we arrived in Yugoslavia with our advance party. Everyone was expected to be on the ground within approximately six weeks.

It all looked good on paper, but every experience with the UN over the past twenty-nine years told me it wouldn't work. I made a mental note to try and influence the sequence of battalion arrivals, if not the specific dates, when it came time for me to comment.

I met the general who would be UNPROFOR commander and my boss for the next year, Lieutenant-General Satish Nambiar from India. General Nambiar was a very pleasant surprise. Indian generals have commanded numerous UN missions since the 1940s and have usually been quite elderly, having in some cases been called out of retirement for the job. Nambiar, on the other hand, was young, fit and, to judge by the numerous rows of campaign medals on his chest, an experienced field commander. I immediately liked him when he told me, "For God's sake, Lew, pay attention to all this. I have no idea how the UN works." I didn't have the heart to tell him we would all be learning the hard way, since each mission has its own unique problems. I felt certain that UNPROFOR was going to have more than its share.

The force's deputy commander would be French Major-General Philippe Morillon. Philippe and I struck it off right away. He reminded one of a young version of Jacques Cousteau. Outspoken and honest, he had good political antennae, essential for a senior officer in France, but not so critical to Nambiar and me in our armies. Philippe struck me as being impulsive, which meant he and I were probably cut from the same cloth. He was also tough, having served with the French Foreign Legion in Algeria as a young officer, so I anticipated (correctly, as it turned out) that he would be good under pressure.

(Philippe would earn an international reputation a year later, several months after my departure from Sarajevo. He would take command of the UN follow-on forces in Bosnia and capture the imagination of the international community when, by force of personality and bravery, he tried with significant success to alleviate the suffering of the civilian population in eastern Bosnia.)

I would be number three in UNPROFOR's military hierarchy, after Nambiar and Morillon. I also met my chief operations officer, who would be a godsend—Colonel Svend Harders from Denmark. Experienced, tough and articulate, Svend could write English as well as a native speaker. It would be the two of us who would put most of the plan in place for UNPROFOR's deployment.

Later that day, I received the devastating news that we would be receiving the subsistence allowance of $180 U.S. for only one month. It would then drop to $1.28 a day!

Well, this was going to be an interesting phone call to Dora. So much for my theory of fiscal benefit in return for the year's separation. I dialled her number.

I figured I'd better get to the point: "Dora, I'm afraid our financial folks were wrong about the UN allowance. Members of UNPROFOR will only receive the standard $1.28 once we're settled in the mission area, not the $180 I promised you."

There was a very long pause, and I felt guilty for having misled her, albeit unknowingly. "You get your butt back here if they can't live up to their promises," she said.

"Unfortunately, the fault rests with our Canadian staff, Dora. They assumed all of us in the headquarters would receive subsistence allowance. But it's impossible to back out now. Not only that, but I think they really need people like Harders and me. This mission has the potential to be a major organizational disaster—it's going to take a lot of hard work to bring it off. I know you'll understand."

I threw in the last remark in the futile hope that Dora would soften. She didn't.

My telephone message light was still flashing when I finished my call to Dora. The front desk advised me that Lieutenant-Colonel Evans had left a message for me to call him at home as quickly as possible.

"Lew, it's Lew, what's up?" I began, somewhat impatiently. After a pause, Lew Evans gave me the bad news: "Sir, I'm afraid I've got a problem with Major Gendron. It looks like he might not be able to go to Yugoslavia. I will probably have to send you somebody else."

I was starting to feel really discouraged—nothing was working out, and my temper got the better of me: "Damn it, Lew, I don't care what his problem is, you obviously thought he was okay or you wouldn't have shown me his file. Tell Gendron I'll see him in Belgrade!"

Lew responded, "I'll do my best, General. Have a good trip."

Lew and I were old friends, and I felt badly taking my frustration out on him, but it had been a particularly miserable day. I hoped that Major Gendron would be worth the effort.

I spent another restless night, with the sounds of New York magnified by my open window and tight surroundings.

MARCH 5 UNPROFOR's disjointed and frequently interrupted planning process continued. Our personal administrative arrangements were pure chaos. We had to go to several different offices to pick up our traveller's cheques, airline tickets, etc. General Nambiar was very understanding: if I had been he, I'd have blown my top by now. Svend Harders and I worked late into the evening putting the final touches to the plan, since we had to brief the UN Secretary-General's Undersecretary for Peacekeeping the next day.

We only had time to produce a very simple plan for the force's deployment. We had twelve battalions to play with; the UN staff had decided for political reasons where some of them would be located. The three UNPAs had been subdivided into four UN sectors, since the Krejina region of Croatia was too large for one commander. Two battalions were assigned to Sector East, four to Sector West, and three each to Sectors North and South.

The Canadian Combat Engineer Regiment would support mine-clearing operations in all four sectors; the Finnish construction unit would help develop our infrastructure throughout the mission area. We would try and get the Dutch signals unit, French logistics unit, and Canadian and Finnish engineers into the mission area early, followed by the bulk of the infantry forces.

Our medical capabilities would be very limited. The U.K. had promised a field ambulance unit, but it appeared to be on hold until after that country's pending national election.

We had two major concerns: the site designated by the UN for UNPROFOR headquarters—Sarajevo—and the site chosen for our logistics base—Banja Luka.

MARCH 6   Svend and I finished off our planning in the morning, prior to briefing Mr. Goulding in the afternoon.

Marrick Goulding is an Irishman who was at that time the UN's Undersecretary for Special Political Affairs, which included peacekeeping. As such, he was responsible to the Secretary-General for all UN peacekeeping operations around the world. I had come to know him quite well while commanding the UN observer mission in Central America a year earlier. Goulding was understaffed and overworked, as a result of a dramatic increase in the number of UN peacekeeping missions. A structural fault in the UN organization, which placed financial and administrative responsibilities for peacekeeping under the Field Operations Division and outside of his control, robbed him of the capability to resolve many serious problems.

Our briefing of Goulding went quite well until it came time to discuss our two main points of concern. As chief of staff, I was leading the discussion, having cleared my remarks with General Nambiar before I started.

I began with Sarajevo. "Mr. Goulding, we honestly feel that Sarajevo is a poor choice as the location for our headquarters. Our 14,000 troops will be 350 kilometres away from us in Croatia. We have no mandate in Bosnia, and you couldn't pick a worse location to get in and out of. The airport has one of the worst weather patterns in Europe; the local roads are marginal and probably blocked in the winter. Resupply will be difficult. More importantly, once we put the UN flag up in front of our headquarters, it will be a lightning rod for every problem in and around Sarajevo; yet we'll have neither mandate nor resources to deal with the inevitable requests for help. We recommend you reconsider. We'd like the authority to investigate some other possibilities on the ground."

I had been warned that Sarajevo was not negotiable; however, it was important that we give our professional military opinion. If the UN, in its wisdom, wanted us to go to Sarajevo, so be it. It seemed they did; Goulding told us in no uncertain terms to forget about putting our headquarters anywhere else.

Following the rejection of our recommendation on Sarajevo, our chief administrative officer (CAO) gave a brilliant presentation on why we should not be forced by the Vance Plan to put our logistics base in Banja Luka. Keith Walton had been named the force CAO; this was to be his first mission as CAO and, since ours was the second-largest mission in the history of UN peacekeeping, it was going to be a hell of a challenge. Keith had just returned from a reconnaissance trip to Yugoslavia and had a good understanding of the administrative and logistical problems we would all face in a matter of days.

Forcing us to put our major logistics base in Banja Luka— which, like Sarajevo, was located in Bosnia-Herzegovina, and absolutely crammed with JNA units—was a dumb idea. Keith was much more articulate than I; thanks to his persuasive arguments, we at least received authority from the UN staff to investigate other options once we were on the ground. In fact, for all the reasons Keith cited at the briefing, we never were able to put any of our logistics in Banja Luka; but it took two months for us to persuade UN New York to give up on the idea. We ended up doing it the way Keith had proposed at this very first meeting.

After the briefing, we went out for a drink with some of our staff to a place called Charlie O's. I remember being amazed that there was no toilet in the establishment. We celebrated having our overall plan approved, and I started smoking again after a break of twelve years. Sarajevo, here we come!

MARCH 7 Originally, we had been scheduled to leave JFK Airport at ten P.M. on a Yugoslavian Airlines flight to Belgrade. Starting early in the evening, a series of telephone calls delayed our departure for a variety of obscure reasons. Our arrival at the airport at midnight was followed by another series of delays. Just before two A.M., it became clear why we were on hold: arriving late was the president of the "Yugoslavian UN Co-operation Committee", Borislav Jovic, who would fly with us to Belgrade. I whispered to

General Nambiar, "This won't do our impartial reputation any good. The Croatians will probably accuse us of collaborating with the Serbs on our way to the mission area."

MARCH 8　We took off from JFK shortly after two A.M. As we levelled off over the Atlantic, we had our first chance to talk informally about our mission. Svend and I used the opportunity to get to know our sector commanders a little better.

We had three generals and a Russian colonel who would command our four UN sectors in Croatia. The Russians do not have the rank of brigadier-general in their army, and therefore Colonel Alex Khomchenkov would command Sector East. His English was a bit weak, but he was a tough and dedicated soldier, and his English communication skills would improve significantly over the first few months. Alex's Russian battalion commander, Lieutenant-Colonel Viktor Loginov, was an Afghanistan veteran whose English was quite good.

Sector West would be commanded by Brigadier-General Carlos Maria Zabala from Argentina. I took an immediate liking to Carlos. He was a sophisticated, gregarious officer with an excellent sense of humour. Mind you, he was having a hard time laughing at some of the UN's administrative policies, and had been with the organization for only four days. Carlos would be good for Sector West; I was happy that the Canadian battalion would be working under him.

Nigerian Brigadier-General Musa Bamaiyi would command Sector North. Musa had been a few days late getting to New York and was, therefore, a bit behind on his reading. Since he'd been told to proceed to New York while on a duty trip outside of his country, and therefore had never had a chance to say goodbye to his family or pack for the mission, it was little wonder that he felt disoriented.

Sector South would be run by Brigadier-General Arap Rob Kipngetich from Kenya. Rob was a well-trained and confident professional. He knew exactly how things should be run, and for that reason I felt a little sorry for him. I knew he would probably be the most frustrated of our group when he and his soldiers were forced to endure the chronic administrative and logistical deficiencies that haunt the first six months or so of any UN peacekeeping mission. Thank God he had a sense of humour.

By now the group was beginning to jell, at least on a personal level. We were united in our common disappointment with the inadequate preparation we had received in New York. Here we were, off to a country that was in the midst of violent self-destruction, and all we had was a two-page outline of a plan that I knew in my heart would not unfold as we would like. Its execution was predicated on the arrival of the twelve infantry battalions in Croatia in accordance with the schedule we had requested at the UN briefing. I had worked on enough peacekeeping missions to know that the UN had to charter ships and aircraft to get the battalions from their home countries to Croatia; consequently, the arrival schedule would change on a daily basis until the units were actually on the ground. If any of the twenty-nine armies represented in our group had been planning this operation, it would have taken at least fifty of their officers a good month to put the plan together. As chief of staff, I was a little uneasy having only an outline concept of operations, developed by our tiny team in just forty-eight hours, tucked away in my briefcase.

Midway over the Atlantic, I went forward to speak with General Nambiar. His seat location in first class was the first perk the UN had voluntarily arranged for a military officer in our group since our arrival in New York. All of us had been shocked two days earlier when the UN administrative staff had told us we should take taxis to the airport to catch the flight. Not only was such an idea a waste of money, since a dedicated bus would have been less expensive, but it was an insult to our commander, General Nambiar.

Civilians frequently misinterpret the pomp and ceremony that surround military life. The strict protocol is not perpetuated for the benefit of the individuals who, by virtue of their rank, are entitled to the various perks; it exists to identify clearly the chain of command, and to let everyone know who is in charge, and who has the final responsibility for making those tough decisions on which human lives depend. If leaders benefitting from the perks start to believe the perks are for them personally, rather than for their rank and the overall good of the organization, they are well on their way to becoming bad leaders.

Lieutenant-General Satish Nambiar was the commander of a 14,000-member multinational force. To suggest that he arrange his own taxi to the airport was an insult to all of us. I protested to the UN administrative staff, who were incapable of resolving this simple problem. In the end, General Nambiar was transported to the airport in a car provided by India's permanent delegation to the UN.

While talking to Nambiar, I noticed there were six or seven women seated in the same area. I could tell from overhearing bits of their conversations that they were UN employees. Since they were in first class, I assumed they were senior UN officials with whom I would be working, so I introduced myself. I was more than a little surprised when I discovered they were some of our secretaries. My fellow generals were not amused when I revealed my discovery on return to economy class. Each of them would soon command between 1,600 and 4,000 soldiers under difficult circumstances; they were understandably expecting to be treated as well as they would be in their own countries.

Dipping into my reservoir of UN trivia, I explained to my astonished colleagues serving on UN duty for the first time that the rules were different, and the benefits significantly more generous, for the civilian employees within a peacekeeping mission. It was a fact of life and, while frustrating, not worth getting too excited about—particularly as there was absolutely nothing that we, the military, could do about it.

This minor observation was one of many that have persuaded me that the UN civilian bureaucracy in support of peacekeeping has created a relatively comfortable niche for itself, frequently at the expense of the soldiers who do most of the dirty work. There are many dedicated and competent civilian employees involved with peacekeeping, but there are also some who look upon the military component as an inconvenience at best. This was to create a major morale problem in our force, as highly-paid civilian staff members demonstrated their inability to provide the most basic services to the military component. We all knew the real problem rested with UN New York, but New York was a long way away, so we vented our frustration by criticizing our administrative colleagues. It created unnecessary tension in our mission and detracted from our operational efficiency.

12

On the Ground

▬

TWO MINUTES AFTER OUR ARRIVAL in Belgrade, I knew what it must be like to travel with a rock star. General Nambiar was inundated with demands from approximately seventy members of the international and Belgrade media, who bombarded him with questions about our mission. He made a few appropriate comments to the effect that we were on a "mission of peace", and we inched our way towards our waiting convoy. Throughout the entire process, Mr. Jovic of the Yugoslavian UN Co-operation Committee was at Nambiar's side. I knew how badly this would play on Croatian television later in the day, but there was nothing we could do about it.

Our convoy to the Hotel Yugoslavia was my first experience of a Communist-style escort, and it was embarrassing, to say the least. The accompanying military police would run innocent people off the road if they didn't notice us in their rearview mirrors and get out of the way. Several times, the escorts leaned out of their windows and beat upon the window or fender of some poor unfortunate soul who hadn't pulled over—all of this at speeds around 120 kilometres per hour. I had the distinct feeling that this was not going to endear us to the local population. Unfortunately, we had large UN decals prominately displayed on the doors and windscreens of all our cars.

The UN had maintained a peacekeeping presence in the former Yugoslavia since January 16, 1991. Following approval of the Vance Plan, an organization called UNMLOY (United Nations Military Liaison Officers Yugoslavia) had been established in Belgrade and Zagreb. It was a small group of some fifty unarmed military officers, commanded by a tough Australian officer, Colonel John Wilson.

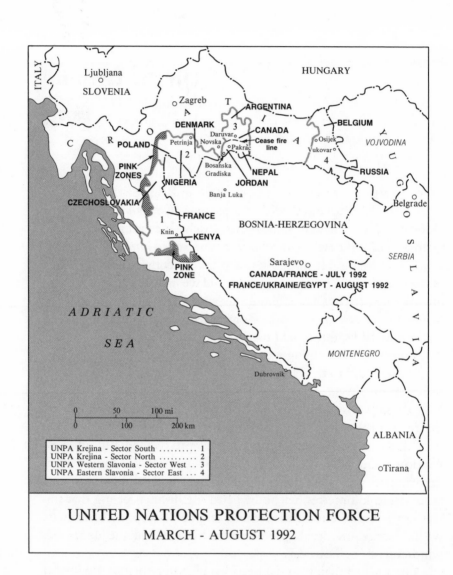

ITALY

Ljubljana
○
SLOVENIA

HUNGARY

○ Zagreb

ARGENTINA

BELGIUM

DENMARK

Daruvar
Petrinja Novska ○
○

CANADA
Cease fire
line

○ Osijek

Vukovar ○

VOJVODINA

POLAND

CANADA

PINK ZONES

Bosanska
Gradiska

NIGERIA

NEPAL
JORDAN

RUSSIA

CZECHOSLOVAKIA

Banja Luka

Belgrade

FRANCE

Knin ○

KENYA

BOSNIA-HERZEGOVINA

SERBIA

PINK ZONE

Sarajevo ○

CANADA/FRANCE - JULY 1992
FRANCE/UKRAINE/EGYPT - AUGUST 1992

ADRIATIC

SEA

MONTENEGRO

Dubrovnik ○

0	50	100 mi
0	100	200 km

UNPA Krejina - Sector South 1
UNPA Krejina - Sector North 2
UNPA Western Slavonia - Sector West .. 3
UNPA Eastern Slavonia - Sector East ... 4

ALBANIA

○ Tirana

UNITED NATIONS PROTECTION FORCE
MARCH - AUGUST 1992

John had come to New York for our planning session and was an invaluable source of information. His officers had maintained close liaison with the leadership of the warring parties in both Belgrade and Zagreb and had paved the way for our arrival. John and I exchanged horror stories about previous UN missions over a couple of beers and felt better, having fulfilled the genetic need of every soldier—to criticize your headquarters.

I had dinner with Philippe Morillon and General Nambiar's UN political advisor, Cedric Thornberry. Cedric was the senior civilian with UNPROFOR and, as such, number three behind Nambiar and Morillon in the overall mission, whereas I was number three in the military component. Cedric was a senior and very experienced UN official, having played a key role in the recent and unusually successful UN operation in Namibia. He was an Irishman and rightly proud of it.

You don't like Cedric Thornberry when you first meet him. He is brusque, acerbic, sarcastic and frequently cranky. Apart from that, he's a nice guy. Fortunately, you soon discover that his gruff exterior is a facade masking a kind and compassionate man, who finds it impossible to hide an infectious sense of humour. I would discover that he was a skillful diplomat, as much at home with the pen as the spoken word. Although he camouflaged it quite well, he was frequently as frustrated with the UN as were those of us in uniform. The UN could use more civilians like Cedric—a lot more.

MARCH 9   We began our first full day in Belgrade with industrial-strength briefings by the Serbian authorities at the Presidential Palace. With Mr. Jovic in the chair, we received a two-hour history lesson on why everyone but the Serbs were to blame for the current troubles.

I came face to face for the first time with the intransigence of the parties in the Yugoslavian conflict. The pattern of the meeting would be repeated scores of times over the next six months by all sides. The opening statements were always rational, conciliatory and unemotional. It didn't take long, however, for voices to be raised, emotions to boil over, and the issues to be painted in black and white. Second World War atrocities were recalled, and the side making its case became dogmatic and inflexible. Compromise became difficult if not impossible to achieve; neither side was prepared to consider modifying any aspect of the Vance Plan, which had already become dated by some four months.

In the afternoon, we were briefed by the JNA (Yugoslavian National Army), after which we met with Judith Kuhn, the regional head of the United Nations High Commissioner for Refugees. She knew more about what was happening than most UN officials. According to the local news, there was increased tension in Sarajevo. Roads were being blockaded throughout the city by the various ethnic communities there.

MARCH 10   We had held our first meetings with the Serbs in Belgrade; now it was time to visit the Croatian leadership in Zagreb.

It was impossible to drive from Belgrade to Zagreb on the main highway. The ceasefire line crossed the highway between the two capitals at several locations, and those areas were heavily defended and mined. We were surprised to discover we couldn't fly between the two capitals either. In accordance with international air-traffic rules that had existed before the war, Belgrade still controlled all airspace over the former Yugoslavia. This provided the Serbian authorities with powerful leverage over their opposite numbers in Zagreb; to date, they had given absolutely no one permission to land in Croatia. The only way to get to the Croatian capital was overland from a neighbouring country, and so we flew to Graz, in southern Austria, then drove south to Zagreb.

The "rock-star" media reception accorded to General Nambiar on our arrival in Belgrade was repeated as we pulled up in front of the Hotel Intercontinental in Zagreb. You could spot the glow from the camera lights a good kilometre from the hotel. On arrival, I stood back from the mob scene and covered the event with my own eight-millimetre video camera.

During a reception hosted by the Croatian government, I met Croatia's Minister of Communications, Ivica Mudrinic. An extremely tall, dark, good-looking man in his forties, he surprised me by saying he was from Mississauga, just outside Toronto. I had lived there from 1979 to 1982 when I had taught at our Staff College, so we exchanged some recollections of the bedroom community. It seems Ivica had visited Croatia on holiday two-and-a-half years ago, and had remained to become an important cog in the new nation's government. I was to find out later that he was a trusted advisor to President Tudjman and never far from the President's side.

Midway through our initial discussion, Ivica said, "I called the Croatian community in Toronto last night and told them we would be in good hands, since there's a Canadian general in UNPROFOR.

Everyone was delighted." I was shocked. Ivica obviously didn't understand that a peacekeeping force could only be effective if it was seen to be totally neutral. Praise from one side in the conflict was as damaging to the UN's impartiality as condemnation from the other. This principle was to be reinforced in spades a few months later in Sarajevo.

For the moment, all I could muster was, "Thanks, I'll be as fair as possible." I silently hoped that the Serbian community in Canada didn't discover the overt Croatian endorsement of my presence in UNPROFOR. I could see it was going to be difficult to persuade the warring parties that we were UN first—and Canadian, Russian, Nigerian, or whatever, a distant second.

MARCH 11 We spent most of the day meeting with the "Government of Croatia's Working Group for Support of UN Peacekeeping Operations in the Republic of Croatia". Mr. Ramljak, the Deputy Prime Minister, was president of the group and quickly revealed himself to be a tough but likeable individual. It was clear that the Croatians were frustrated with the laboriously slow arrival of UN forces. We found ourselves explaining the mechanics of how a peacekeeping force is put together, and rationalizing why our battalions wouldn't be able to arrive "next week".

At the same time, it was also explicitly clear that the Croatians were offended by the prospect of our occupying the United Nations Protected Areas on what they considered to be their territory. They might have lost those areas to the JNA during the recent war; but it was obvious that they intended to return them to Croatian authority at the earliest opportunity. I got the distinct feeling that they had signed the Vance Plan for reasons well beyond the basic one of stopping the war. Once the UN Protection Force was in place, the plan called for the JNA to withdraw to what was left of the former Yugoslavia. The Croatians barely camouflaged their intention to regain control over the UNPAs with the JNA out of the way, using force if necessary.

The Vance Plan, which we had been sent to implement, would clearly benefit the Croatians in the long term; the question was, how long would they wait before they took matters into their own hands? A lot would depend on the efficiency of the UNPROFOR operation, and the strength of the diplomatic support we would receive from the Security Council.

The Croatian Working Group invited us to the ballet that evening. I am not a ballet fan, so I worked late in my hotel room fleshing out our concept of operations, and dropped into a local pizza parlour for dinner.

MARCH 12 More meetings with the Croatian Working Group in Zagreb. The commander of the Croatian forces, General Tus, emphasized his desire that our battalions arrive as soon as possible. I didn't have the heart to tell him that they would probably arrive later than scheduled, rather than earlier.

After a fine lunch hosted by the Croatian Prime Minister, we met with the Minister of Interior Police. The Vance Plan called for the police forces within the UNPAs to return to their "original ethnic composition", but no one knew what "original" meant. It depended on which date one picked, and both sides wanted to pick a date that would benefit its own ethnic population: another "technical issue" that would cause us problems.

An impressive reception was held for us in the Rathaus (mayor's office), a magnificent thirteenth-century house that Dora would have loved.

Tomorrow we would cross the line of confrontation.

MARCH 13 Friday the Thirteenth appropriately turned into a wild day. During the drive from Zagreb to Banja Luka in northern Bosnia-Herzegovina, we crossed the line of confrontation on foot.

I got an idea how spies must have felt when they were exchanged at Checkpoint Charlie in Berlin during the Cold War. We crossed at Novska, where the JNA and the Croatian Army were separated by a No Man's Land of a mere 100 metres in the middle of the town, devastated by the recent fighting. We dismounted from our cars and formed up on the Croatian side of the line, along with two of John Wilson's military officer observers, unarmed except for two very large flags, one UN and one white. We could see our welcoming committee on the far side of the line, also displaying the obligatory two flags.

Weighted down with our suitcases and bulging briefcases, our two parties slowly approached each other at a walking pace. As we entered No Man's Land, we could see that the ditches were lined with surface-laid anti-tank mines. Several destroyed fighting vehicles, including one tank, provided ample encouragement for us to pick our way carefully down the very middle of the road.

The houses on either side of the street were totally destroyed. It struck me that the houses immediately to the rear of those on the street were in pretty good shape. It was as if a unit had driven down the main street firing indiscriminately at the houses lining the way. It didn't seem as if there had been a major battle for the town itself.

After two or three minutes at a slow shuffle, we reached the centre of No Man's Land and married up with our reception party. The observers exchanged flags. We proceeded to the JNA side, where we were greeted by the local commander and the Belgrade media. There was a convoy of vehicles waiting for us, so we mounted up and departed for the airfield at Banja Luka, where we would be provided with a JNA aircraft to fly to Sarajevo.

General Nambiar had agreed to a short meeting with the JNA lieutenant-general who commanded the corps deployed in north-central Bosnia. We drove southeast through village after village of destroyed homes, until we arrived at the JNA corps headquarters close to the Sava River. Nambiar had scheduled fifteen minutes for a short courtesy call; however, as soon as we entered their headquarters, I could see that there had been a misunderstanding, intentional or otherwise.

The full JNA staff was standing by to give us a comprehensive briefing, and a four-course luncheon awaited us in their dining facility. The more we insisted that we had to get to Sarajevo as soon as possible, the more the corps commander insisted we partake of his hospitality. Since he controlled the aircraft that would be flying us to Sarajevo, discretion ruled the day, and we settled in for a two-and-a-half-hour visit.

As the time drew close for us to depart, I noticed the corps commander pick up the phone and pass some pretty direct instructions to whomever was on the other end. I don't understand Serbo-Croatian, but I know when a direct order is being given in any language.

It was another thirty minutes before we started the last leg of our overland trek to the Banja Luka airport. The corps commander accompanied us on the drive, along with six outriders on motorcycles, complemented by a number of military police vehicles. We immediately accelerated to 150 kilometres per hour and stayed there. All traffic, including pedestrians, had been halted and pushed off to the side of the road. Klaxon horns blared and lights flashed as we hurtled down narrow country roads and through towns and villages. Curious onlookers strained to get a view of the cause of all the fuss and inconvenience. Unfortunately, they saw the large UN decals on the doors of our vehicles and the blue UN pennant flying proudly from General Nambiar's staff car. I began to understand that this was part of the Communist legacy—if you were important, you owned the roads, and everyone else had better get out of the way. The techniques in Belgrade and Zagreb were identical. Regrettably, the incident reflected poorly on the image of the UN. There was nothing we could do about it in these early days except object, which General Nambiar did, but with little consequence.

Thanks more to luck than good driving skills, we arrived unscathed at Banja Luka airport and took off for Sarajevo. The flight lasted less than an hour and took us over some absolutely magnificent countryside. As we started our final approach, I couldn't help thinking of the thousands of Olympic athletes who must have been pumped up with adrenalin as they touched down at the Sarajevo airport in 1984. From the air, the city was beautiful: its red tile roofs contrasted with the lush green of the mountains and forests which bracketed three sides of the city. I could see why the '84 Winter Olympics had set the standard for convenience and efficiency. No competitor had needed to drive more than twenty minutes to his or her event—the mountains were literally attached to the city. I was surprised by how little snow there was. Some of the mountains were over 1,300 metres high, yet there was only a dusting of snow on their peaks.

We were arriving in the capital of the Yugoslavian republic of Bosnia-Herzegovinia. Bosnians were rightfully proud of the fact that they defied the external perception of chronic ethnic tension in Yugoslavia; they lived together in ethnically mixed communities, of which Sarajevo was the jewel in the crown. Almost half the population was Muslim; approximately a third was Serbian; and, except for a substantial Jewish population in Sarajevo, the remainder was Croat.

The President of Bosnia was Alija Izetbegovic, a Muslim, and his vice-president and cabinet ministers were variously drawn from all three ethnic communities. President Izetbegovic had visited Bonn in November 1991 and requested that the European Community withhold recognition of Slovenia and Croatia. He had been convinced that once Croatia became an internationally recognized state, it and Serbia would fall upon Bosnia and share the spoils of war. His pleas had been ignored: formal EC recognition had been granted Slovenia and Croatia on January 15, 1992.

President Izetbegovic had now been placed in a "lose-lose" situation. No matter what he did, the potential for violence was high. He had decided to go to the people of Bosnia-Herzegovina and obtain their opinion on independence. A referendum had been held in February. The Muslims and Croats had chosen independence; however, the Serbs had boycotted the referendum. Their leaders wished to establish a Bosnian Serb state within Bosnia-Herzegovina, with some sort of link to Serbia, which, along with Montenegro, was about all that was left of the former Yugoslavia. Tensions were high in Bosnia: considering the serious external threats, compounded by internal ethnic disagreements regarding the constitutional future of the republic, it was easy to understand why.

And so, into this political morass tip-toed the headquarters of UNPROFOR, looking for a nice, tranquil, neutral location from which to control our operations in Croatia, up to 350 kilometres away. We had voiced our concerns unsuccessfully in New York, and were now more convinced than ever that it would be difficult if not impossible to maintain proper contact with either our 14,000 troops in Croatia, or the Serbian and Croatian authorities in Belgrade and Zagreb. Of course we hoped the UN was right, and our modest presence would keep the lid on the ethnic tensions in Sarajevo. None of us was actually persuaded of this, but what the hell: soldiers do what they are told. Perhaps the diplomats knew something we didn't.

13

Getting to Know Sarajevo

———

AFTER MOVING INTO the Holiday Inn Sarajevo, which would provide our interim headquarters, I met with the UNPROFOR signals officer and our four sector commanders.

Lieutenant-Colonel Haans Vermass was commanding officer of the Dutch signals battalion that would provide the military communications for UNPROFOR. Haans had laid out and equipped a temporary base of operations for us on one of the floors of the Holiday Inn. The hotel was located in downtown Sarajevo, directly across the street from the Bosnian Congress. The hotel's reception area was packed with hundreds of people resembling extras from a movie about the KGB. The bulges under their arms were a little obvious, and some of them were carrying automatic weapons in plain sight, although wearing civilian attire. There was a definite feeling of tension throughout the hotel.

I had a short chat with the four sector commanders, Colonel Khomchenkov and Generals Rob, Musa and Carlos. They had spent the past few days in their respective sectors in Croatia, while Nambiar, Morillon and I had been in Belgrade and Zagreb. Although they had yet to find adequate accommodation for their battalions, they had been well received by both sides and were optimistic about devising an acceptable deployment plan for their troops when they arrived.

In my room, I had a call from Cedric Thornberry, who advised me we had a meeting with Ambassador Cutileiro, Lord Carrington's assistant in the peace negotiations. Lord Carrington, the former British foreign minister, was the European Community's representative in Bosnia-Herzegovina. It was the EC's responsibility to broker a peace settlement by helping to find a constitutional solution for Bosnia-Herzegovina before violence broke out. The presidency of the EC rotates through its membership; at that time, it was the turn of the Portuguese, and Cutileiro was their point-man in Bosnia.

Nambiar, Morillon, Thornberry and I arrived in Cutileiro's suite. We were immediately advised, in Cutileiro's arch diplomatic language, that there would be no role for us in Bosnia-Herzegovina, since he had resolved the Bosnian problem by virtue of his plan for cantonization, which all three ethnic communities would soon endorse.

Nambiar and Thornberry proceeded to explain that we would be delighted to see that happen. After all, the UN had no mandate to get involved in the affairs of Bosnia-Herzegovina; our responsibilities were restricted to command of the 14,000-man UN force in Croatia. Sarajevo had merely been selected by the UN as a good, neutral location for our headquarters.

As the discussion neared its end, Captain Thomas Jarnahed, our Swedish security officer, entered the room and motioned me aside. In hushed tones, he explained that he had just been briefed by the head of government security that an attempt would be made to kill an UNPROFOR general that night. He also gave me the disturbing news that the group of heavies in the hotel lobby were the security men for the Bosnian-Serb leader, Dr. Radovan Karadzic, and his party, who were also staying at the hotel.

Captain Jarnahed had been given a photograph of the potential assassin, which gave the threat a little more substance and elevated my concern for Nambiar's safety in particular. I told Thomas to see the hotel manager and advise him that if the armed mob in the hotel were not disarmed or removed immediately, we would have to move elsewhere. Thomas and I agreed that he would assign Swedish soldiers to guard General Nambiar around the clock, and to maintain a roving security watch on the rest of our generals. Copies of the suspect's picture were to be distributed to our modest security force made up of Swedish soldiers. If the individual entered the hotel, he would be shadowed and apprehended if he tried anything representing a threat to UN personnel.

I went to bed on my first night in Sarajevo, remembering that it was still Friday the thirteenth.

MARCH 14 I flew back to Belgrade to prepare for the advance parties of the twelve infantry battalions, which were to start arriving the next day. Advance parties were due, in alphabetical order, from Argentina, Belgium, Canada, Czechoslovakia, Denmark, France, Jordan, Kenya, Nepal, Nigeria, Poland and Russia. Each army has slight variations on the theme, but generally a unit advance party comprises the lieutenant-colonel commanding officer, his four or five major company commanders, the operations officer, logistics, medicine and communications experts, and the senior noncommissioned advisor, normally referred to as the regimental sergeant-major.

In addition, smaller groups would arrive from Canada, Finland, the Netherlands, Norway and Sweden. Those nations would provide, respectively, the combat engineers, construction engineers, and communications, movement–control, and headquarters–guard personnel.

It was impossible to bring the twelve infantry battalions into Sarajevo, primarily because of the difficulty of moving them from there to their deployment areas in Croatia. They couldn't land in Zagreb, which was the preferred choice, since Zagreb airport was not functioning. We were stuck with Belgrade, which meant Nambiar and I would be spending a lot of time shuttling back and forth between Belgrade and Sarajevo. Driving was impractical, so we were constantly beholden to the JNA for providing us with aircraft. Our own UN "air force" would not arrive for at least five months.

Thank God I had left our chief operations officer, Svend Harders, in Belgrade while the rest of us were in Zagreb and Sarajevo; otherwise, the reception for the advance parties would have been a complete disaster.

The UN had refused to pay for hotel accommodation for the advance parties; however, Svend had persuaded the JNA to provide a barracks close to the airport. It was spartan, to say the least, and our personnel would sleep on the floor in unheated buildings. Food would be provided by the JNA, and while it certainly wouldn't be up to North American standards, it would be tolerable for a couple of days.

This entire exercise highlighted the double standard imposed by the UN. The headquarters personnel, civilian and military, were accommodated in a hotel in downtown Belgrade, whereas the military, who were en route to the UNPAs to do the dangerous work, had to put up with sleeping on the floor in an old army barracks. That's what happens when the financial people, rather than the operational commanders, dictate policy. General Nambiar didn't like the arrangements, but there was little if anything he could do about it. In the UN, it's frequently the beancounters who drive policy in the field.

MARCH 15 It was noon before I realized today was Sunday. I guess you can get used to a hectic routine. Nambiar and I went to the JNA barracks to meet the advance parties. In good military tradition, we held a modest parade. General Nambiar greeted our new colleagues and explained the challenge they were about to undertake. The parade was covered by CNN; a few hundred families around the world checked their television screens that night for a glimpse of their beloveds.

We also had another administrative crisis on our hands. The approximately 200 advance-party personnel were expecting to be paid military subsistence allowance at a rate of $180 U.S. a day for the first few weeks, until some sort of accommodation could be provided for them in the UNPAs. Our administrative staff didn't have any money, so I had to go through the embarrassing exercise of asking the senior representative of each battalion if they could survive over the next few weeks without any UN allowances. Fortunately, most of the parties had been paid an advance before they left their home countries, and they agreed to live on the cheap until the UN found some cash. The few groups who were strapped for money said they would try to have funds sent by their governments to tide them over. None of us was impressed with the UN's administration, but morale remained high because of the scale of the challenge.

MARCH 16–17 With the battalion advance parties settled in, I flew back to Sarajevo with Svend and Nambiar. We spent the rest of the day working flat out, looking for permanent accommodation for our headquarters.

The next day was my regimental birthday. The Princess Patricia's Canadian Light Infantry had been founded on this date in 1914.

General Nambiar and I proceeded to the headquarters of the JNA's second zone in Bosnia. Colonel-General Kukanjac (equivalent to a lieutenant-general) was the zone commander for the Yugoslavian government. His headquarters was located in the downtown area, across the river, just over a kilometre from Mr. Izetbegovic's

Presidency. Everyone at the JNA headquarters was a little tense; they could easily be blockaded and cut off if the situation in Sarajevo deteriorated. We were exposed once again to a black-and-white version of history; General Kukanjac was particularly outspoken in his condemnation of the Croatians. He had little to say about the Muslims.

Following the meeting, we visited the Delegates' Club, a Bosnian government facility operated for visiting VIPs, which was being offered to UNPROFOR for some of our senior officers. It too was very close to the Presidency and the Old City; it was a beautiful building, with a magnificent patio that doubled as an outdoor extension of a very fine private restaurant operating on the ground floor. We were told that, before the troubles in Yugoslavia, the club had been the favourite gathering place of academics and intellectuals when they wanted to discuss politics—which was almost always. One of the 1984 Olympic stadiums was only a kilometre up the road.

Philippe Morillon and I paid close attention during the tour and decided we would live at the Delegates' Club if the Bosnian government were serious about their offer. There was only one catch: some of Dr. Karadzic's bodyguards who had been evicted from the Holiday Inn because they wouldn't surrender their weapons were now living in one of the club's service buildings. We seemed to be following each other around. They would have to go (again) before we moved in.

MARCH 18   Keith Walton, our chief administrative officer, and I continued to deal with the Bosnian government regarding accommodation for our headquarters. As in all other UN missions, the host country was responsible for providing free accommodation less any operating costs. Host countries rarely lived up to this obligation; however, in Sarajevo, the situation was even more difficult than usual. At that stage, Bosnia-Herzegovina was still part of Yugoslavia. Yugoslavia had agreed to provide free accommodation, but Bosnia was flexing its independence muscles and didn't agree that it should provide us with anything for nothing. We were therefore negotiating with people who were not obliged to succumb to pressure from the UN and were not inclined to do what Belgrade ordered.

Into this dilemma strode Keith, who, by virtue of his persuasive personality and forceful negotiating techniques, managed to obtain five accommodation sites. With a little overcrowding, they would just house our 300 UNPROFOR staff.

Our main headquarters would be located in the PTT building, on the main road on the west side of town. "PTT" was an acronym for a government technical group that supported the telephone industry, among others. It had a five-storey tower, connected to a three-storey building and a number of sub-floors. The basement contained the obligatory bunker required by law in all government buildings; the bunker was as solid as a rock and could hold up to 150 people. If, for any reason, the building was shelled, I anticipated that it could hold a lot more. The building also had a large underground parking lot that could double as a crude bunker in the event of overflow. It wasn't an ideal building for our headquarters, but it was to prove quite bullet-proof in the days ahead. We were lucky to get it.

Most of our soldiers from the Swedish guard platoon, the Dutch signals component and the Norwegian movement-control unit, plus all the officers with rank of major and below, would be housed in a new and still-unoccupied old folks' home about 800 metres west of the PTT building. The home was painted in the most garish, ugly colour scheme ever devised. When I saw it for the first time, I was reminded of a motel Dora and I had frequented many years earlier in Angus, a small town north of Toronto. It had been called the Rainbow Motel, so I christened this architectural aberration the Rainbow Hotel, never anticipating it would become seen around the world on the television news when it was shelled two months later.

Keith tracked down a motel/hotel complex called Stojcevac, about two kilometres to the southwest of Sarajevo, tucked up against a formidable mountain. This would house our fifty-plus lieutenant-colonels, colonels and a few majors who didn't fit into the Rainbow. The complex had been used by officials during the Olympics and was built in the Austrian style, very practical. About a ten-minute walk away was a large, comfortable house said to have been used by Marshall Tito when he visited Sarajevo. It would be our commander's residence; and once he saw it, General Nambiar could hardly wait to move in. He hated living in the Holiday Inn.

Because Sarajevo remained relatively peaceful at that point, it never crossed our minds to consider the dispositions of the ethnic enclaves around the city, and how their locations might eventually relate to our dispersed accommodation. The fact that our colonels and our commander were sitting smack between the Muslims and

Serbs at Stojcevac was to become a significant factor as the situation in Sarajevo deteriorated.

After a few days of reduced tension in the Holiday Inn, new concerns about our safety were raised by the Bosnian government security forces. It seemed that any number of people were threatening to kill UN personnel. I had a feeling this was merely tit for tat: the Bosnian Serbs were telling us that the Muslims wanted to kill us, and once the Muslims heard about that, they told us there was a Serb plot to do us in. The next day, it was the reverse again. We had only fifty guards for five sites and almost 300 personnel, so all we could do was keep a vigil at night and keep an eye out for each other during the day.

MARCH 19 · 20 · 21   For the first time, I began to feel we had actually started the mission. A long-time Canadian colleague, Lieutenant-Colonel Jamie Arbuckle, gave us our first operations briefing. Jamie was the senior staff officer for operations and reported directly to Svend. He is one of the smartest and most articulate officers in the Canadian Army, but his acerbic style and outspoken nature had held him back from attaining his career potential. I was delighted to have him running our operations centre, since I knew his vast operational background would be a source of much strength and stability where and when we needed it.

Rumours were rampant that our move into the Rainbow Hotel would prevent a number of local pensioners from achieving their dream of being provided decent accommodation. I could see the headlines around the world: "UN soldiers displace Sarajevo elderly." The Bosnian government's UN Co-operation Committee assured us that the building was ours and that no one in Sarajevo would be disadvantaged; however, to this day, I'm not sure we did the right thing by moving in.

Meanwhile, with good intentions and some operational justification, Canada had approved a reorganization of our infantry battalion, the First Battalion of the Royal 22nd Regiment of Canada (known as the Van Doos), who were due to arrive in Croatia in less than a month from their base in southern Germany. There was just one problem: the UN had requested that the battalion consist of five small companies, including some armoured reconnaissance capability, whereas Canada had decided to organize the unit into two large companies.

Needless to say, General Nambiar and the sector commander who would command the Canadian battalion were not pleased; nor was I. The two-company organization may have made sense for the mission that the unit was anticipating in Croatia; however, one of the characteristics of UN service is that you rarely end up doing only the job you prepared for, as we were soon to discover in Sarajevo. I felt that the two-company organization reduced the unit's flexibility to take on other tasks.

There is also, however, a principle of leadership that says, "Don't screw the troops around more than you have to." I was advised by the Van Doos' brigade commander in Germany that the armoured regiment had previously been told they would not be going to Croatia, and that the infantry battalion had just completed its reorganization. I was not prepared to order them to reorganize yet again, so I slipped into my persuasive mode and convinced General Nambiar that the two-company organization would probably work out fine. He was gracious as usual and agreed to give it a try.

One evening, we took our first break in over two weeks and attended a reception in downtown Sarajevo hosted by the UN Co-operation Committee. Following the reception, we saw a play presented in the ancient Greek style, with the audience joining the performers on the stage floor. The play was performed in Serbo-Croatian, so we had a hard time following the story. What really confused the issue was that a white goat kept crossing the stage. We all agreed afterwards that the goat probably represented the passing of the various stages of life. I'm not sure if we were accurate, but all in all, it was a most enjoyable evening and a pleasant break from the daily pressure.

The next day, I was approached by a delegation representing the Norwegian, Dutch and Swedish units who were trying to occupy the Rainbow Hotel. They were concerned about the standard of accommodation for their soldiers and junior officers. I was a bit short with them, pointing out that we had yet to find *any* accommodation for our troops about to arrive in the UNPAS in Croatia. Like the good officers they were, they endured my less than sympathetic attitude and got on with sorting out the problem themselves.

"Whatever happened," I wrote in my diary, "to 'War is hell'?"

14

Prelude to War

—

MARCH 22 I made my first comprehensive visit to UNPROFOR's new headquarters in the PTT building. The Sarajevo media congratulated us on our choice, saying that we were not being "ostentatious". They were right about that! The building might have been only seven years old, but it was very tired and looked as if it had been occupied for much longer than its actual life span. Not only that—it was filthy.

On arrival in Sarajevo, I had noticed a definitely offensive taste to the air. When I got up in the morning, I was startled to see that my saliva was black. I asked others about it and they all had the same story. One of our interpreters explained that the homes in Sarajevo were generally heated by a soft bituminous coal, so that during the winter months, the contamination of the air was very high. The PTT had air vents in every office; for two feet around each vent, the ceiling was jet black from the recirculated coal dust. The windows were almost opaque with the stuff, and every interior surface had its thin film of black dust. The entire building would need a good scrub-down just to make it habitable.

With my Canadian executive assistant, Major Steve Gagnon, I moved into the Delegates' Club. We were met by thirteen staff at the door, in a scene reminiscent of the British television series, *Upstairs, Downstairs*. As we were introduced to each staff member, I had a sinking feeling that the UN was going to be stuck with a large bill that it would reject. But since I was not authorized to dabble in the UN's administrative arrangements, I decided to let Keith Walton sort it out.

On the club's second floor, there was one suite with a self-contained bathroom complete with a barber's chair. As my senior in rank, Philippe would occupy that room. Adjacent to his suite was a very large dining room. During our first visit to the club a few days earlier, I had requested that the staff convert the dining room into a bedroom for me. They had done a masterful job. A double bed had appeared, along with a chesterfield, a dining-room table to be used as a desk, and a variety of chairs. The entire room was dominated by a large painting of a nude hanging precariously over the bed. I was advised that a hand-held shower would be installed in the toilet across the hall. I was impressed, and called Dora with the good news about my new digs, explaining that the beginnings of the Old City were visible some 300 metres away through the French doors leading onto my balcony. I remember thinking the room would make the time in Sarajevo more pleasant than I had anticipated.

MARCH 23 · 24 · 25   We spent the next three days setting up our offices in the PTT building, cleaning the place from stem to stern, and preparing for and conducting our first major conference to co-ordinate the work of our four sector commanders in Croatia. As it turned out, this would also be the last conference during my time with UNPROFOR where we had all the commanders and senior headquarters staff in one room at the same time. We didn't know at the time just how unique the experience would be.

Each of the sector commanders reported on the results of his reconnaissance of his sector, done in concert with his battalion commanders. Colonel Alex Khomchenkov from Sector East started off. He would have the small Belgian battalion and the Russian battalion in his sector, and he made a plea for some additional troops. His sector was a difficult one, because of the large number of ceasefire violations on a daily basis around Osijek. Nambiar reserved judgement on Alex's request until he heard from the other commanders.

Carlos Zabala, who commanded Sector West, was next. He had his own country's battalion and three more from Canada, Jordan and Nepal. He indicated that he had adequate resources for the work at hand. We all nodded wisely, knowing full well that he probably had more than he needed; however, UN New York had told us to put four battalions in Sector West and, at least in the beginning, we would do exactly that.

General Musa Bamaiyi followed. Musa had command of Sector North, and his battalions would be provided by Denmark, Nigeria

and Poland. This was a sensitive sector, since there was a large
Muslim pocket around Bihac, and the potential for a growing
refugee problem was extremely high.

The final report was given by General Arap Rob Kipnegetich,
who commanded Sector South. Arap gave a very professional
briefing, reflecting his British-style staff training, and quickly
convinced me that he knew his business. He would have battalions
from France, Czechoslovakia and his own country, Kenya, to carry
out his mission.

All four sector commanders expressed variations on the same
theme: "I can do the job with the troops at my disposal; but there
is a critical shortage of accommodation. The weather will be
warming up soon, so by the time the bulk of the soldiers arrive, they
can live in tents. Some units will be self-contained for sixty days and
able to feed themselves. Others won't have that capacity, even
though it was ordered by the UN. Our sector headquarters has no
authorized support personnel, so we'll have to set up in a location
where we can hire local help to look after our basic needs—and
we're still broke!"

I reminded General Nambiar that winter was only seven to eight
months away. He regarded me with a certain curiosity, wondering
why I bothered to inject such an obvious statement of fact into the
discussion. I continued, "My experience with the UN combined
with our civilian staff shortage tells me we'd better start worrying
about heated accommodation for our troops this winter. If it can be
organized within eight months, I'll be surprised and impressed."
Nambiar was beginning to appreciate the military inadequacies of
his new employer; but, true to form, he would give the organization
a chance to react to our needs before passing his own judgment.

Nambiar agreed that, in due course, we would ask the Belgians
through the Security Council to augment their small battalion in
Sector East with another hundred personnel. I promised to examine
ways to get some support personnel for the four sector headquarters,
and Keith Walton gave the sector commanders authority to
negotiate contracts for their soldiers' accommodation. This was
necessary since Keith had not been given the civilian support who
were supposed to deal with accommodation matters. To Keith's
credit, his decision helped us out of a mess, but as we shall see, he
paid dearly for it later; big bureaucracies don't like people who bend
the rules and use their initiative.

As we listened to each of the sector commanders, we realized we had a serious problem with the boundaries of the United Nations Protected Areas in Croatia. When they had been drawn by Mr. Vance in November 1991, the boundaries had followed a combination of municipal borders and the ceasefire line between the Yugoslavian National Army (JNA) and the Croatian Army. The boundaries had made sense at that time; but, during the intervening five months, the war had continued, the "ceasefire line" had moved, and some municipal governments had actually changed their borders in anticipation of our arrival. In cases where the JNA had advanced and seized additional Croatian territory, there were indications that they would not withdraw (thus leaving their fellow Serbs under Croatian control) unless we expanded the boundaries of the UNPAS to match the new ceasefire line, thereby placing the Serbian enclaves under UN protection. But we knew the Croats would never agree to such an adjustment of the UNPA boundaries; they felt they had already given up enough control of their national territory to the UN.

The disputed areas between the original Vance Plan boundaries and the March 1992 ceasefire line became known as the "Pink Zones". They were to become a major irritant for the combatants and ourselves, and still threaten to be the spark that could set off a major resumption of fighting between Serbia and Croatia.

MARCH 26 We continued our conference, spending all day with the sector commanders in sequence, recording what the two sides in each sector had said about the UNPA boundaries.

The Vance Plan called for the boundaries to be finalized by General Nambiar, after consultation with local Serbian and Croatian commanders on the ground. Our sector commanders had indeed consulted with the local commanders of the two sides; however, neither the Serbs nor the Croats were going to be happy with an arbitrary decision by General Nambiar. We advised UN New York of our dilemma and, pending their reponse, told our sector commanders to work from a boundary option based on a consideration of all the points raised during the previous day's conference. Little did we know that this first cut at determining the boundaries would, for all intents and purposes, represent our last. We were about to be overwhelmed by far more pressing challenges.

During the afternoon, we had a call from our Swedish guards at the Delegates' Club. Two of them had been patrolling the grounds when the occupants of one of the service buildings—the bodyguards assigned to the Bosnian Serb leader, Dr. Karadzic—had cocked their assault rifles and pointed them in a distinctly threatening manner. The Swedes had backed off and returned to the main building. The Presidency had agreed that the bodyguards would leave two days earlier; however, from this incident, I assumed they were still there and immediately wrote a note of protest to the Presidency, indicating that we would be forced to move to another location if the heavies weren't removed.

MARCH 27 It was becoming clear that arranging for the basic necessities of existence took much longer in a former Communist society than in the West. The Presidency had guaranteed that the previous occupants of the PTT building would be entirely moved out three days earlier. But at least fifty of them were still occupying their offices, and the halls and entrances were littered with antique file folders, partially filled boxes, and the occasional picture of Marshall Tito. Our administrative staff was also having difficulty arranging the contract to supply and service the building. It seemed the entrepreneurial spirit was alive and well in Sarajevo; estimates from potential contractors were exorbitant, to say the least. As a result, a good number of the basics were still missing.

It had been a particularly hectic morning, with numerous conferences to attend and messages to write. I had just received two highly classified documents from UN headquarters in New York when I was struck by the urgent need to visit the toilet. Wanting to take advantage of every available minute, I took the two messages with me. They raised some key issues, and I became so engrossed in their contents that I failed to notice there was no toilet paper in the wall holder. I kept a roll in my desk, but unfortunately I'd neglected to bring it along in my hurry. I finished the messages and my other activity at the same time. Anxiously, I reached behind the toilet bowl—nothing! Not even some paper towel that other visitors frequently left behind. I toyed with the idea of trying to sneak back into my office, but there was so much traffic on the floor that the odds were pretty good I'd get caught with my pants down. It was then that I noticed, in a different light, the two classified messages I was holding. I decided to sacrifice one of them in the interests of my dignity. As quickly as possible, I committed the text to memory and proceeded to finish the task at hand.

MARCH 28 We were being well and truly spoiled by the staff at the Delegates' Club. A small dining room had been fitted out next to my bedroom on the second floor. Philippe Morillon, his assistant, Captain José Fernandez, Steve Gagnon and I would arrive for breakfast or dinner, and the entire restaurant staff would spring into action. Since there was no other entertainment, dinner became the high point of our day. As the only anglophone in the group, I felt a little embarrassed when my three colleagues had to express themselves in English in order for me to understand anything more complex than the basics, but they were extremely understanding of my linguistic deficiency.

I will always look back on those few evenings before the storm of civil war as a time when I enjoyed some of the best dinner conversations of my life. Our topics were a delightful mix of business and humour; at times it was difficult to distinguish between the two. We had more problems with the arrival of UNPROFOR than we could handle in a sane manner, so we were forced to employ a soldier's best defence—humour, augmented by a good Beaujolais.

MARCH 29   I decided to celebrate Sunday and our first break from work with an afternoon walk from the Delegates' Club through the downtown area. At that time, Sarajevo was still a beautiful city, with magnificent architecture and imposing period buildings. The city is divided from east to west by the Miljacka River; thirteen bridges connected the two banks. I walked past the bridge where Archduke Ferdinand of Austria was assassinated in 1914, sparking the First World War. Numerous Olympic facilities dating from 1984 were located in the downtown area; I imagined Katarina Witt winning her gold medal for figure skating as I walked past the site of her victory.

In spite of all the beauty, there was an obvious tension in the air; I didn't see one person smiling during my two-hour stroll. When I returned within sight of the Delegates' Club, one of the Swedish guards ran towards me and told me I had an urgent call from Cedric Thornberry.

Cedric had received the UN's draft submission to the Security Council on our $633.6-million budget. It recommended a 4.1 per cent reduction, and we were obliged to respond with our own recommendations by not later than tomorrow. As we were scheduled to go to Zagreb to meet with the Croatian authorities early the next day, we had to put our comments together tonight; we'd fine-tune them in our Zagreb hotel tomorrow, then FAX them to New York.

MARCH 30 We worked feverishly on our budget submission until our departure at 1230 hours by jet to Banja Luka. Our return trip to Zagreb was less eventful than our journey in the opposite direction two weeks earlier; at least we didn't get "kidnapped" for lunch by the local JNA commander. We did our Checkpoint Charlie routine at the Novska crossing and drove without incident to Zagreb. Cedric and I worked flat out on our budget submission and, with a certain degree of relief, FAXed it off to New York just before dawn.

MARCH 31 We spent over ten arduous hours discussing the deployment of our UNPROFOR battalions with the Croatian authorities. No matter what the subject, the discussions kept coming back to the contentious matter of the Pink Zones. The Croatians were adamant that there would be no compromise: the boundaries of the UNPAS must stay as outlined in the Vance Plan, and not one foot of additional Croatian territory would be given up to UN control, temporarily or otherwise.

We could understand their point of view. However, we were equally aware that the Yugoslavian leaders would not abandon their Serbian enclaves, which were now stuck between the new ceasefire line and the Vance UNPA boundaries. This was obviously going to be a major stumbling block to peace.

APRIL 1 April Fool's Day. No one noticed—very appropriate. Our discussions with the Croatians started to be eclipsed by reports from our people back in Sarajevo that tensions there were rising. The roadblocks that had been appearing at night, erected at strategic points by the various ethnic groupings, were now staying up during daylight hours. It was getting more and more difficult to move about the city.

APRIL 2 We left Zagreb, driving across the line of confrontation at Karlovac and proceeding to Bihac, where we met a JNA executive jet that flew us back to Sarajevo. There we discovered that the operational needs of our mission were running up against the budget realities of the UN. The Canadian battalion wanted to bring additional vehicles, weapons and ammunition necessary to do its job with UNPROFOR and, more importantly, to deal with any violence resulting from a deteriorating situation on the ground. The UN authorities refused to approve any increase over the modest scale of supplies already dictated, because, they said, they couldn't afford to pay for it. The government in Ottawa supported the battalion's "wish list", as did I, so we started working on a deal that would see Canada paying the additional costs.

Three-and-a-half months later, the UN would come begging to use the additional vehicles and weapons that the Canadian taxpayer had funded to get to Croatia. If the UN does not find a way to fund an adequate scale of vehicles and equipment in future missions, the pool of countries, such as Canada, which normally volunteer soldiers for UN missions will quickly dry up.

APRIL 3   We flew to Belgrade for a meeting with Serbian authorities. Our fears were confirmed by Mr. Jovic, the President of the Yugoslavian Committee for Co-operation with the UN. He and his colleagues were firm in their insistence that they would not abandon the Serbian enclaves in the Pink Zones. In fact, they had a number of other areas with significant Serbian populations that they now wanted included within the UNPA boundaries. The thought crossed my mind that Mr. Vance's presence would have been invaluable at this meeting, since he was the one who had convinced President Tudjman of Croatia and President Milosevic to sign the ceasefire agreement, and he alone understood all the nuances of the final contract. In the absence of Mr. Vance, Cedric Thornberry was doing a masterful job of speaking eloquently and saying nothing. We all knew we would have to await New York's guidance on the Pink Zones before we committed ourselves one way or the other.

APRIL 4   We arrived back in Sarajevo early in the afternoon. The city was deathly quiet and there was very little traffic on the streets. It reminded me of a ghost town.

Rumours were starting to circulate that the European Community would recognize Bosnia's independence on April 6. Although we were not diplomats, all of us in uniform were pretty sure that fighting would break out around us as soon as independence was announced. There was little chance that the Bosnian Serbs would accept the consequences of a referendum they had boycotted a month-and-a-half earlier.

APRIL 5   Amid the deteriorating political situation in Sarajevo, most of my morning was spent trying to sort out the contract for our headquarters. We assigned a couple of local employees to listen to the radio and watch television and keep us briefed. Their descriptions of what was happening seemed incoherent; we discovered later that was because the actual situation was totally confused and out of control, and even the local media had a hard time making sense of it.

At approximately 1500 hours, some 2,000 Bosnian peace demonstrators, many of them bussed in from outlying areas, marched down the main road past our headquarters in the direction of downtown. As they passed, they chanted, "Nambiar, Nambiar". I assumed and hoped this was an endorsement of our presence, not a condemnation.

An hour later, we received the bad news. The marchers had reached downtown and taken up a position in front of the Congress building, diagonally across the street from the Holiday Inn. Their specific objective was never entirely clear; however, it appeared they wanted to stress the need for peace and understanding, and hoped to soften the hardening attitudes of the ethnic communities against each other. If the people showed they were prepared to compromise, perhaps the politicians would follow.

They never got a chance. As the crowd formed up in front of the Congress, snipers on the roof of the Holiday Inn opened up. Sixteen demonstrators were hit, some fatally. Skirmishes broke out around the city, and roadblocks went up around those areas clearly defined as "belonging" to a specific ethnic group.

The JNA in Bosnia-Herzegovina now found itself in a bizarre position. It owed allegiance to the army of the former Yugoslavia—now being referred to as "Serbia" more often than not. At the moment, Bosnia was still a republic of the Yugoslavian federation; but if recognition of Bosnia's independence was conferred by the European Community the following day, as rumoured, the JNA forces commanded by General Kukanjac would be stuck in the middle of a foreign country. Not only that, they would undoubtedly be requested by the Bosnian Serbs to assist them in their quest to establish their own state within Bosnia, with close ties to Serbia. As far as Belgrade was concerned, Bosnia was still constitutionally part of the former Yugoslavia, and the JNA was responsible for maintaining law and order there. That was fine in theory, but in reality, General Kukanjac knew he was in a no-win situation. To make matters even more awkward, he was a long way from Bosnia's border with Serbia.

In UNPROFOR, our problem was equally pressing. We had no mandate from the UN Security Council to get involved in the affairs of Bosnia, yet the situation was deteriorating all around us. The European Community was supposed to be taking the lead in peacemaking; the EC's Lord Carrington had a special representative in Bosnia, Colm Doyle, an Irish army major, who was doing his best, like the rest of us, to find out what was actually happening. Until we knew that, there was little we could do, except to offer to provide our "good offices" if a neutral setting were required for intercommunal discussions.

Meanwhile, we ordered our personnel to concentrate at our four accommodation areas. We also mounted extra security to complement our fifty Swedish guards, who were stretched to the limit. All UN vehicle movement would be accompanied by armed escort, and everyone would report in and out of our operations centre when they made an essential trip anywhere. Our civilian staff left their rented accommodations and moved into our military locations, so we could look after their security.

Philippe Morillon, Steve Gagnon, José Fernandez and I returned to our digs at the Delegates' Club before dark. As we drove by the Congress, we could see the blood stains on the street where the wounded peace marchers had been dragged to civilian cars that took them to the hospital.

That evening, we watched on television as over a thousand citizens occupied the Congress. They called themselves "the People's Assembly" and elected a "Committee of Salvation", which immediately pledged itself to organizing another round of elections. What followed was some of the most compelling television I have ever witnessed. Anyone who could work his way to the stage in the Congress could speak, but only for as long as the people crammed into the massive hall would tolerate what he had to say. Average citizens, academics, professionals and politicians all took their turn over the next thirty-six hours—without a break. I couldn't understand what was being said, but it was obvious that the people were trying to hold the country together through their own grassroots democratic movement. It was hugely entertaining stuff, and I watched it until early morning.

Unfortunately, the background noise across the street from the Delegates' Club was not so encouraging. Mortar and heavy machine-gun fire kept up a steady beat from midnight onwards, frequently complemented by more distant flashes of massive explosions that lit up the city. Munitions were being utilized to destroy entire buildings in the downtown area. The blasts must have been extremely powerful, since they shook our building and rattled our windows throughout the night. It is always hard to be precise about the direction of noise at night, but I was pretty sure that the predominantly Muslim Old City was taking a pounding.

APRIL 6 Before leaving the Delegates' Club for the PTT building, I received a call from Svend Harders. There had been a lot of shelling and small-arms fire in the area of Stojcevac last night, where Svend and about fifty of our other officers were housed. Everyone was okay, but the Muslim staff there reported that the JNA had moved in under cover of darkness and occupied the Sarajevo airport; there had been sightings of tanks and anti-aircraft guns around the runway.

Svend said he and his officers were about to leave in their bus for a run to the PTT. He had been talking to General Nambiar next door, who was about to depart also.

Philippe, Steve, José and I left the Delegates' Club escorted by Captain Thomas Jarnahed and a 4x4 full of Swedish guards. Thomas had become key to our attempts to find out what was going on around the city. He had established valuable contacts with each of the ethnic communities and with the Bosnian government; this initiative, combined with his boundless energy, made him the best-informed member of our staff concerning the hour-to-hour situation in Sarajevo. From this, the second day of the fighting, I tended to deal directly with Thomas. It was good for me, since I got the information I wanted firsthand; unfortunately, it wasn't good in the long term for Thomas. His immediate supervisors resented his direct access to me, and, without my knowledge at the time, he was ostracized by some of his colleagues and superiors. I tried to sort out the misunderstanding a number of times, even writing to his superiors in Sweden; however, perception had overtaken reality and the damage had been done. It was too bad, because Thomas always did his very best and risked his life on a number of occasions to get us critical information, or to help countless citizens of Sarajevo of all ethnic affiliations.

Our drive to the PTT building normally took about ten minutes. Today, our first experience of being fired on by snipers, we did it in under seven. We ignored stop signs and red lights; there was no good reason to give anyone an easy shot.

By early afternoon, the word came through that the European

Community had recognized Bosnia's independence; however, just before that announcement, the Bosnian government collapsed. What a paradox. The Prime Minister resigned, and most of the Serbs serving in the government left the Presidency and started their move to Pale (pronounced Pa-lay), a town seventeen kilometres east of Sarajevo, where Dr. Radovan Karadzic would establish his Bosnian Serb headquarters.

From today forward, there would be two categories of Bosnian Serbs: those who were loyal to Dr. Karadzic's self-proclaimed Serbian Republic run from Pale, and those who stayed in Sarajevo and remained loyal to the Bosnian government. The majority of Bosnian Serbs lined up behind Karadzic, but those who stayed in Sarajevo were still a significant element, known as "tame" Serbs.

The People's Assembly and the Committee of Salvation continued their marathon session throughout the day. Various resolutions were passed, indicating that secession from Bosnia and division of Bosnian territory were not acceptable, and calling on the JNA to recognize Bosnia and convert itself into the Bosnian Army. This latter idea was not as bizarre as it might sound, since a large number of the JNA conscripts had been born in Bosnia.

The crowds in front of the Congress grew throughout the afternoon, the previous day's tragedy notwithstanding. Once again, some snipers made it to the roof of the Holiday Inn and started picking off innocent demonstrators below. This time, however, the crowd took matters into its own hands. Hundreds rushed across the main street, some of them shot in the process, and stormed the Holiday Inn with nothing but their bare hands.

The Holiday Inn had been a fine hotel, but the same designer who had selected the colours for the Rainbow Hotel must have had something to do with the Holiday Inn project also. It was painted a horrible mustard colour, and stood out like a sore thumb against the surrounding period buldings. We still had some of our civilian staff living in the hotel. They were gathered in one of the rooms on the south side, watching the events live on television, the coverage a mixture of the CNN network and the local Bosnian TV. They watched in horror as the unarmed crowd stormed across the street. Another camera from a vantage point in front of the Congress showed the crowd as it moved towards the mustard-coloured building. One of our staff said, "Doesn't that building look awfully familiar?" Everyone realized at the same time that they were in the building actually being attacked by the crowd. Forgetting the television, they rushed to the window and observed the carnage four floors beneath them. Glancing back at the TV set, they could discern themselves standing in the window. One of them told me later that it was the eeriest feeling she had ever experienced.

The crowd swarmed into the hotel. Many worked their way to the roof, where by virtue of their numbers they overwhelmed the snipers, trussed them up and dragged them down ten flights of stairs. The snipers were a mess by the time they reached the lobby.

The chaos in the area of the Holiday Inn meant we couldn't drive to the Delegates' Club that evening. We opted to spend the night at Stojcevac with Svend, Jamie Arbuckle and the rest of the colonels. We felt badly about not being able to get to the club, for the staff there associated our presence with greater security for themselves. I hoped we could get back there soon. Apart from everything else, I had left a load of underwear in the laundry.

15

Anarchy Takes Over

APRIL 7 Bosnia was now a country. But conditions were bordering on anarchy, and the thugs were coming out of the woodwork. A good deal of the shooting and looting was being carried out by criminal elements devoid of any political motive. In fact, there was virtually none of the public celebration that normally accompanies the birth of a nation. It was becoming harder by the hour to determine who the players were in and around Sarajevo.

General Nambiar was due to fly to Banja Luka and continue by road to visit General Musa, UNPROFOR commander in Sector North. But the Bosnian government, or at least the bureaucratic component of the Ministry of the Interior, couldn't or wouldn't guarantee the security of the airport; and the JNA, who occupied the airport, reported it was under sniper fire. I sent Thomas Jarnahed out to the area to confirm the JNA's claim, and he reported that the airport was indeed not safe. With the Bosnian government in a state of transition, it was impossible to find anyone to take responsibility for security.

Rumours were going around about a big Serbian offensive. When I asked our information staff about this—"Bosnian Serb offensive? JNA offensive? A combination of both?"—I got an understandably blank stare. The opposing sides had yet to be clearly drawn. One thing was for sure: the indiscriminate shelling of the city after dark was the work of the JNA. The rounds that landed every few minutes could have been fired by one or two guns; at that stage, only the JNA had weapons of the calibre being used.

Presumably Dr. Karadzic had talked General Kukanjac into shelling the city, in the hope that President Izetbegovic would capitulate to the Bosnian Serb demands for secession. It didn't make a lot of sense to someone conditioned to a more painstaking way of resolving constitutional disputes, of which we have our share in Canada; but then we have never experienced civil war.

Steve Gagnon and I spent our second night with our fellow officers in Stojcevac. The phone rang most of the night with reports of heavy fighting in Sarajevo. We agreed that we would get back into the Delegates' Club some time the next day. We both needed underwear.

APRIL 8   Steve and I drove into the PTT with Svend. All along the route there was plenty of evidence of the previous night's fighting. Armoured vehicles were dug in, and both the Muslim and Bosnian Serb soldiers manning their positions looked tired and tense. But no one interfered with our passage.

We decided to bite the bullet regarding General Nambiar's visit to General Musa in Sector North. I advised the Presidency and the JNA that we would accept the fact that they couldn't guarantee Nambiar's security, but that he wanted to fly to Banja Luka anyway. A flood of objections and warnings ensued. But Nambiar insisted, and the JNA finally agreed to provide him with an aircraft. When we delivered him to the airport, there was no aircraft in sight, so we cooled our heels for over an hour until one arrived. During the waiting period, I counted seven JNA tanks and a couple of anti-aircraft guns positioned around the terminal and runway. An occasional sniper opened up from the Muslim village of Butmir, located approximately 500 metres from the far side of the runway, but no damage was done. We crossed our fingers, and Nambiar took off without incident.

Following the commander's departure, I had a chat with the airport manager in his office. Looking out his window, I mentioned that a race circuit could easily be laid out on the runway and parking apron. He immediately became animated and exclaimed, "We had a race two years ago. Let's have another this year! If you promote the event, I'll arrange to get you a car so you can compete." We agreed that if the troubles ever died down, it would be a good idea. That night, I called Dora and asked her to ship me my helmet and racing suit.

Steve and I made it back to the Delegates' Club and our laundry. Philippe and José were away visiting the Croatian sectors, so we had a quiet dinner and an early night. It was comparatively peaceful until

0300 hours, when a constant din of heavy machine-gun fire started from the general direction of the Old City.

APRIL 9   The city was relatively quiet during the daylight hours this day, so I got lot of work done. I decided to take advantage of the absence from Sarajevo of Cedric Thornberry and Generals Nambiar and Morillon to send a strongly worded message to New York regarding our pathetic state of administration. As I noted in my diary, this was a potentially career-ending message, but the lack of administrative support for our mission was criminal. We still had inadequate money to pay our people in the UNPAs in Croatia; the little we did have had to be carried back to the sectors in bulk by our officers following their rare visits to our headquarters.

Our own headquarters in Sarajevo and the four sector headquarters were still operating without the simplest essentials. The system couldn't even keep up with our needs for paper and pencils. The commanding officers in the UNPAs were still without adequate accommodation for their battalion personnel, who were starting to arrive 800 at a time. Our outstanding French logistics battalion was ready to deliver supplies forward, but there was little if anything to deliver, since the contracts had not been let. We were woefully short of vehicles and radios, and it would probably be months before we saw any more.

In my message, I asked New York to place a priority on our needs and not to place the blame on our chief administrative officer, Keith Walton. I explained that Keith was working his butt off but had only 10 per cent of his authorized staff. To blame him for our dilemma would be like blaming me for failing to seize a battalion objective when I had only eighty soldiers, rather than the 800 called for. I didn't expect the message would improve things (and I was right), but at least I felt better sending it. Unfortunately, rather than doing Keith any good, the New York Field Operations Division bureaucracy circled their covered wagons and got their knives out for him. I still feel badly about that; my aim had been to give him the credit he deserved, but I ended up being counter-productive.

Later I received the good news from Dora, who had been suffering from swollen glands, that her blood-test results were normal.

I spoke to Chief Warrant Officer Fournier in Ottawa and got an update on the forthcoming Formula Ford racing season in Canada. He promised to keep close contact with Dora in case she needed anything.

APRIL 10   The fighting had spread from the downtown area and was now going on around our headquarters in the PTT building. The JNA were on a hill one kilometre south of us; the Presidency's forces held the high ground directly north of us. Unfortunately, their disagreement was taking place directly over our heads. Artillery fire was passing overhead, and a television transmission tower nearby was hit. I couldn't help but think of Canada's concerns if the former Soviet Union and the United States had decided to have it out; the ensuing exchange of missiles would have met somewhere over our country.

The JNA fire appeared designed to take out a Presidency mortar position about 200 metres north of our building. Because of their lack of firepower, the Presidency forces had very limited ability to silence the JNA on the hill, unless they decided to mount an infantry attack; but at that early stage of their military development, I doubted they could succeed at such a sophisticated task.

Sarajevo was now pretty well shut down. People were reluctant to venture out onto the streets. All roads leading into the various ethnic areas were blockaded, and access was controlled by nervous, and in most cases untrained, paramilitary guards. We were advised that food and gasoline were about to be rationed throughout the city.

We received reports that JNA personnel were being attacked throughout Bosnia as they moved about in buses and cars. Presidential forces were allegedly demanding that the JNA turn over their weapons in return for safe passage. The JNA barracks had reportedly been blockaded with the soldiers inside.

Late in the afternoon, the small-arms fire intensified, and a number of small-calibre rounds struck our building. One bullet hit the window of Svend's office, just above the desk of his assistant, Major Eric Schwensen. When we first saw the hole with the starburst cracks around it, we thought the bullet had gone all the way through. On closer inspection, we discovered that the windows were double-paned, and that the inside pane was virtually bullet-proof, at least to small-calibre fire. This was a boost to our morale. I began to think the exorbitant rent demanded of us was justified!

Dora called at midnight. My racing gear was on the way.

APRIL 11   Philippe Morillon returned by road from his visit to Sector North. I briefed him on the deteriorating situation in Sarajevo. The European Community and Lord Carrington's representative, Colm Doyle, were having a hard time getting the parties together to discuss a ceasefire.

True to form, Philippe took the bull by the horns. He immediately got on the phone to the Presidency, to Dr. Karadzic, and to the JNA, requesting they all meet that afternoon at our headquarters. When he told me about the arrangements, I expressed some concern that we would be seen as taking on the European Community's role of peacemaker. Since we had absolutely no mandate in Bosnia, we could be getting in over our heads. Unaccustomed as I was to assuming the voice of caution, I recommended that we advise New York and see what they had to say. The UN responded to my FAX in a matter of minutes, tearing a diplomatic strip off us for getting involved where others feared to tread. As usual, a compromise was developed; we were told to provide our "good offices" for a meeting to be chaired by the European Community. We rescheduled the meeting for the next day, since General Nambiar would be back by then.

Later that afternoon, I drove to the airport to confirm rumours of a mass exodus of the Jewish community from Sarajevo. The reports were correct. The tiny terminal was packed with over 500 people loaded down with their personal belongings. They were all trying to talk themselves onto a single Boeing 707 that was doing shuttle runs to Belgrade.

At the airport, I met Major-General Milan Aksentijevic, the chief of the JNA's co-ordination group with UNPROFOR. General Aksentijevic was a hero in the JNA, having been taken prisoner during the recent war with Croatia but never surrendering his dignity while captive, and constantly speaking out for understanding and compassion by all sides. In a bizarre turn of events, he had been exchanged in a complex deal involving a Canadian 707 full of arms. Thanks to his moderate views, the General had a good deal of credibility with all sides in the emerging conflict in Bosnia. This factor would get me out of an extremely tight situation within the month.

Milan Aksentijevic was a cultured man with a good sense of history. He explained, "General MacKenzie, this is not a good sign. The Jewish community is an excellent barometer on which to base predictions of the future. If they are leaving Sarajevo in large numbers, it does not augur well for the next few months. I fear it is the beginning of the end." I reserved comment, but had an uneasy feeling that he knew far more about the situation than I did. And of course he would turn out to be dead right.

APRIL 12 "Philippe's" meeting was scheduled for 1000 hours. Philippe, Cedric Thornberry and I gathered in General Nambiar's office to await Ambassador Cutileiro of the European Community, who would chair the gathering.

Our elevators had been out of order for over a week, so by the time Cutileiro burst into Nambiar's office on the second floor, he was out of breath and flushed. As he approached the table where we were all sitting, he launched into a tirade: "Look, General Nambiar, the next time you want to get involved in dealing with all sides and broker anything, let me know. That's our job. I don't appreciate having to rush here to run a meeting I had nothing to do with setting up!"

I was sitting at the end of the table, and so had an excellent view of the participants. General Nambiar, always the gentleman, was about to pacify Cutileiro with a few kind words of explanation when Philippe cut the Ambassador off in mid-gesture. I had seen the blood rising in Philippe's face ever since Cutileiro had opened his mouth; he could restrain himself no more. "Mr. Ambassador, don't you dare talk to my commander that way! You are a guest in our headquarters and I, for one, will not tolerate your bad manners. It was I who arranged the meeting. Your people were not making any progress and we were getting calls from all sides for help. I suggest you take advantage of this opportunity to speak to all sides and try to arrange a ceasefire."

A pregnant hush fell over the room as Philippe glared at Cutileiro. I wanted to applaud but didn't. Fortunately, Cutileiro found his voice and, in the language of diplomats, explained that it was all a gross misunderstanding and he was delighted to be meeting with us. I detected a tiny smile at the corners of Cedric's mouth.

A long discussion followed regarding the wisdom of putting all the parties in the same room, at the same time. Cutileiro felt it would be inappropriate to give Dr. Karadzic, as the leader of the breakaway Bosnian Serbs, a seat at the table. President Izetbegovic represented a legitimately recognized government, whereas Dr. Karadzic led a self-proclaimed republic with no international standing. General Kukanjac would be welcome, however, as the representative of Serbian interests, since he commanded the JNA and was therefore a key player in resolving the conflict.

Although I was no diplomat, I considered this rationale to be extremely shortsighted. It seemed to me that if you wanted to stop the fighting, you had to deal with all sides in the conflict. Perhaps the JNA could speak for Dr. Karadzic and his SDS party, but I was not convinced of it. After all, it appeared the JNA wanted to get out of Bosnia as soon as possible, whereas Karadzic wanted to establish his own republic in Bosnia with Serbian support. The two objectives did not seem compatible.

It was agreed by Cutileiro and Nambiar that the question of attendance at the meeting could be resolved by holding bilateral discussions with each of the parties. I was beginning to learn a little about diplomacy, and I wasn't sure I liked it.

Throughout the remainder of the day, small subsidiary meetings took place throughout our building. General Nambiar and the rest of us from UNPROFOR backed off. The European Community folks took over and brokered a ceasefire agreement, which was signed in my office and went into effect at midnight. It had been a long day; however, it marked our first participation in negotiating a ceasefire. Naively, we all thought it might be our last.

APRIL 13 Firing started at 0330 hours. Our dreams were punctuated by shelling and small-arms fire in and around the Old City.

Steve Gagnon and I left for Croatia by road immediately after breakfast, joined by Jim Baldie, the chief administrative officer from the United Nations' Interim Force in Lebanon. Jim has been sent to us for a few weeks by the UN in New York to help Keith Walton with our administrative woes. Jim was going to visit each of the sectors and had decided to start with Daruvar in Sector West, where the Canadians were located.

This was my first drive through the Bosnian countryside, and I was impressed by its wild beauty. Unfortunately, it also struck me as ideal country in which to conduct a civil war: rugged, hilly and almost totally forested, with very narrow roads cut through sheer rock faces.

When we arrived in Daruvar, I dropped in to see Lieutenant-Colonel Mike Gauthier, the commanding officer of our recently arrived Canadian Combat Engineer Regiment. Mike's unit would be responsible for the touchy job of lifting thousands of mines in the UNPAs, once the Croatian Army and the JNA agreed to the details. My father had been a combat engineer sergeant-major, so I watched the ease with which they settled into their spartan accommodation with a good deal of interest and admiration.

Following my visit with Mike, I met with Lieutenant-Colonel

Michel Jones and toured his unit's accommodation. Michel's unit was the First Battalion of the Royal 22nd Regiment, known as "the Van Doos", an anglicization of the number twenty-two in French. The unit had a strength of approximately 850, which included a large company from another Canadian infantry battalion belonging to the Royal Canadian Regiment. They had taken over an abandoned JNA camp now in Croatian hands. A large number of buildings had been destroyed, and there were mines everywhere; however, after only a few days, the Canadians had made a good start on cleaning up the place.

The Canadians had started arriving in large numbers a few days earlier and were just settling in. Since their permanent accommodation was not ready, they were living in tents. Late in the afternoon, I visited both company locations and spoke to about 200 soldiers in each. Standing on a table, I reminded them, "You are here as peacekeepers. All sides in the conflict want you here. There is a ceasefire in Croatia, so you should not be overly concerned about your safety—you're located in a very peaceful area."

Less than an hour later, both company locations were shelled by heavy mortars and artillery, and my credibility became seriously eroded! Fortunately, no one was hurt, and the companies spent the rest of the night doing what infantrymen do best—digging in.

APRIL 14   Steve and I had breakfast with Michel Jones and a few of his officers and headed back to Sarajevo. We were joined by Canadian Sergeant "Chico" Traclet. Steve and our Corporal Leroux were having a hard time keeping up with the typing demands I was generating. The UN had not yet provided me with a secretary; but as chief of staff, I was producing a fair amount of paperwork, so Michel kindly agreed to lend me Sergeant Traclet, who was one of his best clerks. At the time I didn't realize I was also getting one hell of a soldier.

I decided to drive for therapy and had a lot of fun speeding along the narrow roads, with our Swedish guard escort in hot pursuit. We arrived back in Sarajevo just in time to see and hear a mortar attack on the streetcar terminal, located a kilometre from us in the direction of downtown. If the Bosnian Serbs, or the JNA, or a combination of both, were trying to shut down the city, they were doing a good job; public transit was now pretty well out of commission. There were a few casualties, and the attack had a demoralizing psychological impact on the citizens of Sarajevo. The city seemed to be self-destructing.

Shortly after the attack on the streetcars, the apartment complex directly across the street from our headquarters came under machine-gun fire. We waited for a break in the action and made a high-speed run back to the Delegates' Club. The sounds of firing and demolitions continued throughout the night.

APRIL 15   The day started off with a crisis: two of our unarmed officer observers were missing on a routine patrol. It was difficult to send vehicles out to retrace their intended route, since snipers were active all over the city. We called the Presidency and the JNA for information. A few hours later, we were relieved to discover the observers were alive and well—less their kit and Toyota 4x4, which had been stolen, with them in it. They had subsequently been released and would be delivered back to our headquarters by the Presidency's forces, now officially referred to as the Bosnian Territorial Defence Forces (TDF). This was the first of many vehicles we would lose to hijackers. Since the observers had to be unarmed, in accordance with UN operating procedures, they made easy pickings. After this incident, they started travelling in paired vehicles.

During the day, I received an excited call from our Norwegian movement-control personnel in Belgrade. They had been informed by an airline charter company that up to 900 Nigerian soldiers would arrive at Belgrade airport the following day. I immediately got on to New York and asked for clarification. We had heard nothing about the Nigerian battalion for over two weeks. Their advance party had arrived a week late, and General Musa had been unable to find out when his country would send the rest of its battalion. New York was likewise in the dark and advised me that a ship had yet to be chartered to bring the Nigerians' heavy equipment to Croatia. I explained that a battalion without its equipment would be more bother than it was worth, and that I intended to send them back to Nigeria as soon as they landed in Belgrade. We would be pleased to have them join UNPROFOR, but only when they had their weapons and equipment.

Somehow the message got through. No Nigerians landed at Belgrade airport the following day.

We were advised by New York that the UN Secretary-General's Special Representative for Yugoslavia, Cyrus Vance, would visit within twenty-four hours. He would spend about seven hours with us, for the primary purpose of being brought up-to-date on our deployment in Croatia in support of his peace plan. Since we had no mandate in Bosnia or Sarajevo, Mr. Vance would be less interested in what was happening immediately around us.

A few weeks earlier, before the fighting had begun, Philippe had suggested to General Nambiar and me that we should have some armoured cars for mobility. I had forcefully pointed out that peacekeepers should not be seen to be hiding in armoured vehicles: we were impartial and therefore not directly threatened. Philippe, as a lieutenant-colonel ten years earlier, had been the French Army's project manager for a three-seater, turbo-charged armoured car built by Panhard and called by its French acronym, VBL; it had just come into production, and the French infantry battalion deployed in Croatia had a couple of VBLs that they would lend us. Nambiar and I turned down Philippe's offer.

Now, with my tail between my legs, I approached Philippe and said, "You remember those armoured cars we discussed?"

Philippe smiled: "It's okay, Lew, they're on the way."

When we reached the Delegates' Club that evening, we were greeted by a wonderful sight. Not only had the French battalion provided us with a gleaming new VBL; it had also seen fit to give up a magnificent ex-French Foreign Legion Montenegran sergeant-major by the name of Mihilov, an over-qualified cook, and two excellent drivers for the VBL. All in all, not a bad day.

APRIL 16   At mid-morning, we all rolled out to the airport and met Mr. Vance. It was just a little bizarre: he was in Sarajevo to be briefed on how the implementation of his peace plan up in Croatia was getting on. Presumably he appreciated the paradox as we explained, to the background noise of mortar fire a few hundred metres from our building, that things were going quite well, albeit slowly, in Croatia. No one brought up the question of why the UN insisted our headquarters be located in Sarajevo. We all knew it was too late to do anything about it anyway.

My paperwork had piled up to a point where it was threatening the structural integrity of my desk, so following my part of Mr. Vance's briefing, I begged off and attacked the pile of messages with a vengeance. There were numerous messages from the sector commanders, pointing out for the umpteenth time that their people were still owed money by the UN, and in some cases couldn't check out of their accommodation to move to their new operational locations, because they couldn't pay their hotel bills. If it hadn't been so pathetic, it would have been funny: here we were in headquarters, where things are normally routine and safe, worrying about the security of our administrative personnel, while our troops, who we thought we were sending into a war zone, couldn't check out of their hotels because they didn't have any money.

I experienced my tenth flashback to the briefing we had given in New York, when we had explained that locating UNPROFOR's headquarters in Sarajevo was not one of the UN's better ideas. Regrettably, there was not a lot we could do about the money concerns at this moment, since all the banks were closed and we couldn't reach the UNPAS from Sarajevo. I sent the sector commanders a FAX trying to put a humourous spin on their dilemma, hoping that their reservoirs of tolerance had not run dry. It was becoming all too obvious that we were not doing a good job of supporting our troops in the UNPAS from our current location.

APRIL 17 (GOOD FRIDAY) *Cross Canada Check-up* is a CBC radio program with a large audience, so I was happy to record an interview for the program. It gave me a chance to allay the fears of those Canadian mums, dads, daughters, sons, wives or girlfriends who had loved ones serving with us in Sarajevo. I stressed that we were not being intentionally targeted by the combatants, and that we were looking after each other, and everyone was okay. I hoped listeners would spread the word that we were better off than they might assume from all the exaggerated reports they were hearing.

APRIL 18 A foreshadowing of the painful times that lay ahead: the United Nations High Commissioner for Refugees requested permission to store 200 tons of food and medicine in our underground garage. We approved the request.

Thomas Jarnahed and I ventured out to the Bosnian Serb security headquarters, located in what appeared to be an old police station. The staff looked very tired and dejected. Their building was well-protected by a combination of 1950s-vintage tanks and a couple of Soviet-style armoured fighting vehicles. The chief of security pledged co-operation with UNPROFOR.

No matter what the political implications of such co-operation might be, I felt it necessary to make and maintain contact with the Bosnian Serbs, if we were to be in any position to influence what was happening in the city and to co-ordinate the relatively safe movement of our personnel as they undertook a growing list of humanitarian tasks. Both sides were after us to reconnect power lines and water mains, recover bodies from areas of conflict, and deliver flour to their bakeries and chlorine to their water supplies. Nine out of ten such missions were fired at and ultimately aborted, because the local people would permit such assistance only if it benefited their side. Anything else was considered collaboration with the enemy.

I discovered early in my military career that it's important to get all the staff together once a week on a social basis. In Canada, we do it during "happy hour", which normally occurs at 1600 hours every Friday. Liquor was in short supply in Sarajevo, but I had given instructions to our chief of military personnel and administrative officer, Polish Lieutenant-Colonel Prokopiuk, to organize our first happy hour on the 18th. We all gathered in our austere eating facility and downed a few drinks as we listened to the small-arms fire less than a hundred metres from our headquarters. We agreed that happy hour was a good idea and decided to make it a weekly event.

APRIL 19   After five weeks in theatre, I decided it was time to bring people back home up to date on what was happening in UNPROFOR. I spent some of this Sunday morning writing a letter, which Steve's computer addressed to approximately fifty of my friends and colleagues. I believe the letter is worth quoting here as documentation of this moment in history:

> From Brigadier-General L.W. MacKenzie C.D.
> Sarajevo
> 19 April 1992
>
> Dear _____,
>   Well, it's springtime in the Balkans, and history is repeating itself as the various ethnic groups (Muslims, Croats and Serbs) seek to exterminate each other; except this time it's by artillery rather than swords.
>   The deployment of our twelve infantry battalions and two engineer regiments is pretty well on schedule into the United Nations Protected Areas (UNPAs) in Croatia. So far the Canadians (both infantry and engineer battalions), and the French, Russian, Belgian (with a platoon from Luxembourg), Czechoslovakian and Danish battalions are on the ground, and

hopefully the Polish, Nepalese, Argentine, Jordanian, Kenyan and Nigerian battalions will arrive within three weeks.

The UNPAs are relatively quiet, with *only* 100-200 ceasefire violations per day. In my estimation, there is no ceasefire; however, the UN likes to say it is "holding". Both major players, the Croatian Army and the JNA (Yugoslavian Army), have picked up the habit of moving close to UN positions to protect themselves from counter-artillery fire. I have asked them to keep at least a kilometre away—time will tell. Once we have all the battalions in each one of the four sectors, we will assume responsibility for protecting the people in the sectors and will monitor the local authorities and police forces. Sounds simple but execution will be difficult in the extreme for a number of reasons.

Most of the villages in the various sectors are dominated by Serbs, who are currently executing a policy of "ethnic cleansing"—that is to say, evicting the non-Serb occupants at gunpoint and destroying their homes once they leave. If the occupants don't leave, the Serbs destroy the houses and the occupants. The Croats are carrying out similar actions in their area of Sector West, which the Canadians partially occupy.

The other major problem results from the move of the line of confrontation since the Vance ceasefire in December. In a number of sectors, the JNA has moved forward up to twenty kilometres from the boundary of the UNPA since the ceasefire and are protecting the Serb villages in what we affectionately call the "Pink Zones". Our responsibilities are legally confined to the UNPAs and it would take the Security Council to change them. Obviously the Croatian authorities would object, as that would be an encroachment on their territory. The JNA are equally adamant that they will not withdraw from the "Pink Zones", thereby leaving the Serbs to the wrath of the Croats. We have some ideas on how to manage the situation; however, it will require flexibility on both sides and I don't believe that word even exists in Serbo-Croatian.

While all the above is going on up front in Croatia, we at the HQ find ourselves mired in the problems of Bosnia-Herzegovina (BiH). For political reasons, we were directed to locate our headquarters in Sarajevo, the capital of BiH. It was a smart political decision but, as we warned them in New York, very unwise from a military point of view. The airport is one of the most unreliable in Europe due to weather patterns and we are some six hours away from our forward troops by road—when the roads are not blocked. Having our own aircraft resources will help; however, they are at least a month away. We have promises of helicopter casualty evacuation from both sides, which eases my concerns a bit.

Bosnia-Herzegovina has slid into anarchy, with the Serbs abandoning the Presidency and setting up a parallel organization in the hills. When they left the Ministry of the Interior, they took the guns (and most of the armoured cars) with them, leaving the city open to thugs and looters. Each side is now flexing its muscles as the European Community tries to work out a "cantonization" plan, which would see ethnic groups concentrated in specific areas of the republic. It will not work; however, the diplomats are still trying. In the meantime, the three sides and the JNA are destroying the republic and its capital. Everything from 152-millimetre artillery, 120-millimetre mortars, anti-tank weapons and heavy machine guns are methodically destroying most of old Sarajevo and a large number of towns and villages throughout the country. MIG-29s are acting as peacekeepers as they do low passes over the troubled areas in an attempt to intimidate everyone.

The capital is quiet during the visits of the Vances and Carringtons of the world. Everyone gets a good night's sleep and starts afresh on the VIP's departure.

Tragically, there is no solution that I can postulate. Hatred is deep, and everyone has a gun and calls himself a sniper. Hundreds of years of ethnic violence and intolerance are dredged up at each meeting; everyone thinks that theirs is the just cause. From my impartial point of view, there is more than enough blame to go around for all sides, with some left over. We will continue to try and operate from Sarajevo; however, nothing is functioning (including the post, so I will have this mailed from Belgrade or Zagreb) and food and fuel are running short. As a result, numerous humanitarian convoys are regularly hijacked. Naturally, everyone wants us to provide escorts and all we have are staff officers with pistols! In fact, I lie, as we have an outstanding platoon of Swedish military guards who give increased meaning to the term "professionalism". I feel very safe as they escort us in the execution of our duties in some very sensitive parts of town.

As a final point, the work here is by far the most challenging of my career. We have now worked fifty-two days straight and it was all good operational stuff. I am blessed with an outstanding commander, Lieutenant-General Nambiar from India, who is ideally suited to the job. I like to think we make a good team. I have an outstanding personal staff led by a Canadian major, Steve Gagnon, and in spite of the situation, we are enjoying practising our profession. Hopefully, we are doing some good, but only time and CNN will tell.

Warmest personal regards,
Lew

Philippe's French cook outdid himself that day and prepared a magnificent four-course lunch. For a few hours, our Delegates' Club became an oasis of sanity in the midst of chaos. The lunch was a welcome break, made all the more enjoyable by an apparently inexhaustible supply of the local wine from Mostar.

Later in the day, I threw together a few notes for a presentation I had promised to deliver at the NATO Defence College in Rome on July 10. Subject: peacekeeping in Central America! I decided to talk about Sarajevo instead.

16

Damned If We Do...

APRIL 20–21   The actions of the Bosnian Territorial Defence Forces (TDF) throughout the new nation were beginning to have serious repercussions in Sarajevo. On or about April 12, they had been ordered to blockade the JNA's barracks, occupy its weapons depots and communications centres, and attack JNA soldiers and their families with the objective of driving them from Bosnia. The JNA was retaliating by shelling Sarajevo. And, under cover of the conflict, the Croatian Army was invading Bosnian territory in the north and the southwest. All of the ethnic mistrust and suspicion, all of the disinformation and propaganda, were coming together in Sarajevo, and all hell was breaking loose—and we still didn't have a mandate to get involved.

Cedric Thornberry reported from Sector East in Croatia, where he was visiting, that we were about to be hammered by the international media. The Serbs within the UNPA in that area were intimidating the non-Serbs, ordering them to leave their homes and get out of the UNPA. Buses were being provided every morning to deport people; if the non-Serbs didn't leave voluntarily, the next night their houses were fired at by the Serbs. If that didn't convince the occupants to leave, there was a good chance that grenades would be thrown into the houses on the third night.

The previous day, over a hundred non-Serbs had opted for the "free" bus ride out of the UNPA, gathering at the UNPA boundary where there was a minefield to negotiate. The UN observer at the crossing point asked what was going on; the occupants of the buses indicated that they wanted to leave. The observer tried to talk them into returning to their homes but, knowing the danger that would await them, they refused and insisted on proceeding out of the area. The observer, with no other choice, guided the buses through the minefield and out of the UNPA. The event was captured on film, and the headlines in Croatia screamed, "UN Troops assist Serbs with ethnic cleansing!"

Cedric was livid. He had ordered the next convoy of would-be evacuees detained, so we were now caught in the bizarre situation of holding people against their will until we could mobilize Amnesty International, the International Red Cross and the Croatian authorities to verify that the people actually wanted to leave. There was no way that our modest force in the UNPA could guarantee the security of all the non-Serbs. Nevertheless, Cedric was convinced that much more active and ambitious patrolling by the Russian and Belgian battalions would reduce this "ethnic cleansing". I prepared a message for General Nambiar ordering just that. We were learning the hard way that nothing was simple in the Balkans.

Closer to home in Sarajevo, we had a call from the Presidency pleading with us to pick up some serious casualties near one of the battle areas, and to deliver them to the Kosovo hospital in downtown Sarajevo. This was a standard request in many other UN peacekeeping missions and, naively, we complied. Once again, we discovered that the mistrust and hate were so deeply embedded in Bosnia that such humanitarian acts only elicited condemnation from the other side for being biased. It didn't matter that a few hours earlier we might have helped the side doing the condemning. As far as each side in the conflict was concerned, you were there to help them and only them. There were to be times when we would be ordered at gunpoint to unload the dead and wounded of one side in the conflict and leave them unattended beside the road, while we loaded and transported the dead and wounded of the other side. Both the Bosnian Muslims and Bosnian Serbs were guilty of this despicable interference with our humanitarian mission.

It was also getting more and more difficult to make it from the PTT building to the Delegates' Club without incurring the wrath of snipers along the way. Each trip was like a surrealistic scene from a bad movie about the French resistance. All sides had a habit of shifting their roadblocks around; you were never quite sure where you would encounter a new collection of concrete blocks, jagged steel girders welded together to stand upright, or the all-time favourite—abandoned buses or trucks parked at right angles to the traffic with their tires shot out. This last tactic was much preferred by all sides, since it gave the barrier guards a place to smoke and drink during their long and boring sentry duty. If nothing else, it provided me with some entertainment: I kept the accelerator of my large Mercedes pegged to the floor during our slalom runs through the debris of downtown. Steve was very tolerant as he held on for dear life in the passenger seat.

Starting at 1800 hours on April 21, the area across the street from our club was rocked by heavy artillery fire. Over the next six hours, at least a hundred rounds fell in the area of the Old City. Our windows shook, and we gave some consideration to occupying the large walk-in freezer in the kitchen, which doubled as our bunker, but thought better of it and went back to sleep.

Around midnight, the firing stopped. But as if on cue, it started up again precisely at 0300. We were about ten minutes into this fresh barrage when my phone rang. It was Dora. She explained that my career manager, Admiral Porter, had called her and indicated that the commander of our air force, General Sutherland, was taking an early release and that I would probably be promoted in the near future. Thanking her for the news, I explained that I had to return to my vantage point hunched down beneath one of the windows, to try to capture the unfolding drama on my Sony video camera.

APRIL 22 We spent the working day hunched low over our desks, trying to keep below an imaginary line level with the bottom of our windows. It was some consolation knowing that the windows were impervious to small-arms fire; however, the sight of tanks on the JNA-controlled hill a kilometre south of our headquarters was cause for some concern, particularly since the tanks were firing just over our heads at the TDF positions across the street from us.

At approximately 1500, we heard our first air-raid siren, followed a few minutes later by the appearance of two JNA MIG-25s that proceeded to do low passes over the city. Reports over the local radio indicated they were bombing Sarajevo; however, the rockets on their wings were for air-to-air combat and were not fired. Occasionally the pilots released chaff and flares to decoy any ground-to-air missiles that might be fired at them, but all in all, their presence achieved nothing except to remind the TDF and the population of Sarajevo that the JNA controlled the sky.

Keeping UN New York up-to-date on developments was taking most of our time. Officials there were concerned that we were getting involved in the conflict. Frankly, we had no choice: to sit in our headquarters while the city fell apart all around us would have destroyed what little credibility we had. The people of Sarajevo did not understand that we had no mandate in Bosnia and, quite understandably, expected us to help them with their humanitarian needs. Regrettably, every time we tried, we were accused of collaborating with the side we assisted.

At the last minute that afternoon, we decided not to let our colonels try to reach their accommodation at Stojcevac. They had to travel in a bus, but at least two major battles were in progress between our headquarters and the outskirts of town. We made arrangements for them to spend the night at the Rainbow Hotel.

General John de Chastelain, Canada's Chief of the Defence Staff, called and confirmed what Dora had told me during her early morning wake-up call: I would be promoted later in the year, returning to take command of the Canadian Army in Ontario. General John explained that I might not spend the entire year in Yugoslavia; he was considering bringing me home around Christmas. It seemed terribly fitting when I had to duck beneath my desk during our conversation, and a tank round exploded in the field adjacent to our building. One should always be advised of a promotion while under fire.

I was pleased by the prospect of promotion, but it all seemed a little irrelevant in the middle of the deteriorating situation in Sarajevo. Right now, the trick was for us all to survive.

APRIL 23   Philippe Morillon and I made our way to the airport just before lunch to meet with Lord Carrington. General Nambiar had tried to make it in from Sector North by aircraft, but there was too much fighting next to the runway at Sarajevo airport, so he had to divert to Belgrade.

Lord Carrington was meeting his EC special representative, Colm Doyle, to discuss peacemaking in Sarajevo and the potential for arranging yet another ceasefire. Philippe and I told Carrington we thought the Bosnian Presidency was committed to coercing the international community into intervening militarily, and was therefore in no mood to honour a ceasefire. President Izetbegovic argued that Bosnia was an internationally recognized nation, and the world should rescue it from its Serbian enemies. We recommended that Carrington advise the President that he would not receive military intervention and consequently should negotiate a solution with Dr. Karadzic and the Bosnian Serbs. Carrington left the airport for the

Presidency escorted by our full complement of six French armoured personnel carriers.

Thanks to Lord Carrington's involvement, Colm Doyle was able to broker another ceasefire later in the day, following Carrington's departure. As the time for the ceasefire approached, the fighting and shelling intensified, carrying on through the appointed moment and well into the night.

During the afternoon, the French Minister for Health and Humanitarian Affairs, Bernard Kouchner, had arrived at the airport with a substantial entourage. The UN didn't know about his visit, but Philippe had been advised on the "French net", so we were not surprised.

Minister Kouchner is a bundle of energy, charisma and good intentions, and he gets results. He refuses to acknowledge the presence of obstacles blocking his way and forges ahead at full speed, no matter what the consequences or risks to his personal safety. Minister Kouchner is the founder of Médecins sans Frontières and Médecins du Monde, two highly effective French humanitarian agencies that selflessly dedicate themselves to alleviating physical suffering throughout the world. In my army, we would say, "He doesn't have an ulcer but he's a carrier!" Kouchner pops up all over the world, wherever there is a humanitarian need, and always manages to do something to improve the situation for those suffering deprivation. The more I got to know him, the more I was convinced that he would be President of France some day.

We invited Minister Kouchner and his team to the Delegates' Club for dinner. Philippe's cook and the club staff put on a magnificent meal, a much-appreciated break from our normal routine. The club shook violently a couple of times from nearby artillery blasts, but after copious amounts of wine, no one seemed to care.

APRIL 24   "Should have stayed in bed. Wrote off two cars," begins my diary entry for this date.

Philippe had just taken delivery of a brand-new staff car, a Toyota Crown similar to the model assigned to me in Central America. I had assumed sole possession of the black Mercedes. We proceeded to the PTT building at maximum speed in convoy, with me in the lead. It was raining lightly, and as we approached our usual turn to the PTT from the main road, Steve said, "General, you're a great driver, but your eyesight is going—we normally turn here!"

I had been thinking of something else. The accelerator was on the floor, even though we were only fifty metres from the corner. I glanced in the rearview mirrow and thought I saw Philippe's driver signalling for the right-hand turn. I locked up all four wheels on the Mercedes and, when the coefficient of friction of the tires could handle the corner at our reduced speed, I turned right at the last moment. In fact, however, Philippe's driver had *not* indicated or started his turn; through no fault of his own, he slammed into our right front fender at well over 100 kilometres per hour as I cut across his path.

The Mercedes was written off, and the Toyota was never the same. Both vehicles sat in the middle of the junction for some three hours within view of our headquarters, a silent testament to my eroding driving skills. Mind you, I've never had to deal with snipers at any of the racetracks in Canada.

Late in the afternoon, we were advised that 150 Muslim and Croatian women and children wished to leave Hrasnica, a Serb-controlled village southwest of the city, about a kilometre from Stojecvac. After much confusion on the part of the Presidency, Svend Harders departed for the area with three buses provided by the Bosnian government. After six-and-a-half hours of negotiations, which included being held hostage himself and visiting various locations at the insistence of the Bosnian Serbs to confirm there were no Serbs who wanted to leave, he managed to deliver all 150 to safety at a facility downtown. It was a masterful bit of work on Svend's part.

APRIL 25   Two delegations visited me back-to-back, at cross-purposes. First, the International Red Cross representative in Sarajevo explained that it was inappropriate for UNPROFOR to escort ambulances displaying their symbol, since this had a negative impact on the perception of Red Cross neutrality. It disturbed me, but didn't completely surprise me, that we weren't considered as neutral as the Red Cross. She was followed ten minutes later by a doctor from the Bosnian Emergency Medical Centre, who pleaded with me to provide escorts for their ambulances. This was a dilemma with no easy solution. I indicated that we would judge each request on its merits (a response I had picked up from listening to diplomats).

APRIL 26 · 27 · 28   President Izetbegovic called with an urgent request for an UNPROFOR escort to the airport. He was to fly to

Lisbon for negotiations with the European Community, but then his trip was delayed until the 28th.

The next day, a delegation of French ministers visited. After working late at the office, Steve and I were shot at all the way home. My new Toyota was not as fast as the old Mercedes, but at least it presented a smaller target.

President Izetbegovic got away safely to Lisbon on the 28th. Meanwhile, Philippe, who had been visiting Sector East for a couple of days, flew back to Sarajevo. Sergeant-Major Mihilov had been in his party and had driven back, along with a small detachment of French soldiers. When they became a good ten hours overdue, we grew greatly concerned. Fortunately, Mihilov called us around midnight to tell us they were held up for the night in a Bosnian Serb area, but not to worry, as they were being treated very well.

APRIL 29–30   The Bosnian Government formalized its earlier request that the JNA leave Bosnia, by issuing an official directive ordering them to depart. The idea that the JNA would convert and become the Bosnian Army had obviously flopped, so according to President Izetbegovic it was time for them to go—without their weapons and equipment, which they should leave behind for the "Bosnian taxpayers who helped pay for them".

We all knew this was not going to go over well and braced ourselves for a wild night.

April 29 is Camorone Day in the French Foreign Legion. The battle of Camorone was the French equivalent of America's Battle of the Alamo and is celebrated around the world by all Legionnaires, past and present, on the 29th. Both Philippe and Sergeant-Major Mihilov were former Legionnaires, and we had been joined at the club by Philippe's *chef de cabinet*, Colonel Christian Xuereb, who had also served with the Legion.

By coincidence, my birthday is on April 30, so we decided to celebrate the two anniversaries by overlapping at midnight. It was a night of which any French Foreign Legionnaire would have been proud. We sang Legionnaire songs for hours, frequently having to scream our lungs out to be heard above the din of the incessant artillery shelling and the rattling windows. At midnight, Philippe presented me with a beautiful French cravat, so I could be properly dressed at dinner in future.

I was now fifty-two. At 0200 hours, my mother-in-law called

at the height of the artillery barrage. It was nice of Sarah to think of me, I thought.

Later in the day, General Nambiar and I couldn't fly to Belgrade, since Sarajevo airport had been damaged by the worst fighting yet.

MAY 1–2   On the 1st, we were advised that Marrick Goulding, the UN's Undersecretary for Special Political Affairs, with whom we'd met in New York, would be visiting next week. We worked on the program for his visit.

The 2nd was a relatively quiet day; only a couple of hundred rounds of heavy machine-gun fire in and out of the Old City. But the firing continued all night, so I wasn't able to get to a colleague's flat to watch the Spanish Formula 1 Grand Prix. It was just as well—the flat was partially destroyed by artillery fire during the afternoon.

17

The Convoy Incident

MAY 3   "Definitely the worst day of my life," begins my diary
for this date.

Around mid-morning, Bosnian Vice-President Ejup Ganic
came to my office and met with me and Colm Doyle of the EC.
Ganic explained that President Izetbegovic, on his return from
Lisbon, had been kidnapped at the Sarajevo airport; he was being
detained by the JNA at their Lukavica camp, just east of the runway.
Ganic said he was not a strong leader, and needed his President back
in order to control the radical officers within the Bosnian TDF, who
were rapidly getting out of control. TDF forces had General
Kukanjac's headquarters under siege in the eastern part of the city;
Ganic feared that if they attacked the General's barracks, the JNA
would retaliate by levelling Sarajevo.

Our conversation was interrupted by one of our officers, who
reported that the JNA Officers' Club in downtown Sarajevo had just
been attacked, and three JNA officers had been killed. The JNA was
now retaliating with tank fire against the Presidency building and
the Mayor's office. A good deal of downtown Sarajevo was on fire.
Thomas Jarnahed's vehicle had been attacked with an anti-tank
grenade, which had just missed it by a foot.

Ganic was extremely shaken by this news; he almost lost control.
Colm and I decided to go to the JNA camp at Lukavica to find out
what was happening.

Steve Gagnon and I had worn our summer short-sleeved tan
uniforms in celebration of Sunday. We jumped into our 4x4 and
proceeded to Lukavica, followed by the French VBL (armoured car)
and Colm's armoured Mercedes. As we approached the JNA camp

where President Izetbegovic was being held, we could see a crowd of well over a hundred demonstrators in front of the locked front gate. They refused to let us through, and so I got out and worked my way to the front. I assumed they were Muslims protesting the presence of the JNA. I wanted to speak to them but needed an interpreter, and I yelled out, "Can anyone speak English?"

From the back of the crowd, a scruffy individual sporting a Toronto Blue Jays baseball cap shouted, "I'm from London, Ontario. Will I do?"

Over the next ten minutes, in front of a BBC camera that provided footage seen around the world a few hours later, I harangued the crowd, telling them, "We are here to get your sons back. We are here to help you. You must let us in or your wounded will die!"

After ten minutes, it seemed to work. The crowd parted, and we drove into the camp. Steve turned to me and said, "You thought they were Muslims, didn't you, sir?"

"Of course," I replied.

"Nice work, sir—very persuasive. They were Serbs. I think they know Izetbegovic is in here and they want his hide."

Whoops. I was used to serving in areas where you could tell the warring factions apart by their physical features. Well, at least we were inside.

Colm and I were paraded in front of the camp commander, then forced to cool our heels for over two hours. After numerous frustrating attempts to determine if Izetbegovic was in the camp, we threatened to leave. The mood immediately changed, and we were taken across the hall to a room where we found the President, his daughter, Sabina, and his bodyguard. The President was on the phone talking to General Kukanjac and seemed to be in pretty good spirits. As soon as he hung up, he said, "General MacKenzie, General Kukanjac agrees that the two of us should be exchanged. Will you organize it for us?"

Colm and I glanced at each other and nodded. After all, Sarajevo was being destroyed, and this might cool things down. "Just you, your daughter and your bodyguard for General Kukanjac?" I confirmed.

"Yes," replied the President.

I figured that shouldn't present too much of a problem; it could be handled by a couple of vehicles. But I was wrong.

The phone rang; it was General Kukanjac again. He and the

President talked for five minutes. The President was obviously agitated. He took the phone away from his ear and explained, "General Kukanjac now insists that he be permitted to remove his entire staff of 400 along with himself in exchange for my release."

"No way!" I exclaimed, "I can't accept responsibility for those kinds of numbers. I'll have enough trouble just keeping the four of you alive."

Izetbegovic was in a box, and Kukanjac was holding the key. The President looked at me and said very carefully, "General MacKenzie, don't worry. I will accept responsibility for the safety of the JNA personnel."

I was surprised; this was quite a commitment. "You guarantee it?" I asked.

"Yes," he said.

I paused, and Colm and I exchanged glances again. "Okay," I said. "We'll give it a try."

Over the next hour, it was decided that Colm and the President's bodyguard would stay at Lukavica as "collateral". I would take President Izetbegovic, Sabina, Steve, the Swedish guards, the French drivers and twenty-plus empty JNA trucks to General Kukanjac's headquarters in the heart of Sarajevo, where we would load up Kukanjac and his JNA personnel. On our way back out of town, one armoured personnel carrier would break off and deliver Izetbegovic and his daughter to the Presidency, while the rest of us returned to Lukavica.

I called for two French VABs (armoured personnel carriers), which appeared in short order; then we all stood around for over an hour as the JNA organized their truck convoy. After a frustrating wait, we left for Sarajevo with our convoy of vehicles. Once we reached the top of the hill looking down into Sarajevo from the south, we could see the city was well and truly the scene of heavy fighting. The sun was blocked out by the smoke, and the streets were littered with debris, burned-out cars and sparking power lines. As we got closer to the centre of town, we came across numerous destroyed tanks and armoured personnel carriers. One tank engine had been blown a good twenty metres from its chassis, leaving the street still ablaze with burning fuel and oil.

We also started to see bodies, and body parts. Some of the dead were laid out beside the road with their hands folded across their stomachs, as if sunning themselves; others were frozen in contorted postures where they had fallen. A few were still smoldering, having burned to death. I had never witnessed such a graphic condemnation of the stupidity of war.

We arrived at General Kukanjac's headquarters. I rushed to his office, leaving Izetbegovic in one of the armoured personnel carriers. As I entered his office, I was shocked to see Kukanjac having coffee with the commander of Izetbegovic's TDF forces. They explained that the commander was there to accompany Izetbegovic back to the Presidency. I felt pretty good about this: his presence would certainly enhance our security, since it was his soldiers who were blockading Kukanjac's barracks a scant twenty metres away.

I told Kukanjac, "Sir, we leave in an hour. Your soldiers had better get busy loading their stuff."

Kukanjac raised his hand and motioned to me to sit down. "General MacKenzie, we need three hours at least."

"Look, General," I replied, "this could be the first time a one-star gives a three-star an ultimatum: but we've already wasted a minute, and in fifty-nine minutes from now, I'm leaving with or without you and your troops!"

Kukanjac didn't look pleased. He asked me to have Izetbegovic come up for coffee.

While I was out in front of the building, radioing for Izetbegovic and Sabina to be brought in, I also called Thomas Jarnahed on the radio and asked if he could break away from whatever he was doing and join us. He replied that he would arrive in about ten minutes. That was a relief; it would give me a few more sets of eyes to witness whatever was going to happen.

At the appointed time, we left Kukanjac's office and walked towards the convoy, which was forming up, to use the term in its broadest sense, just outside the front gate. Halfway there, I received a call from my headquarters: the deal was off, according to Dr. Ganic.

"What the hell are you talking about?" I thundered. "I've got the President of Bosnia here and his commander of all the TDF forces in the area, and they've guaranteed the safe passage of the convoy—I can't do much better than that. Let me speak to them again."

I ran over to the President and explained the situation. "Who do I listen to, you or Ganic, Mr. President?"

"No problem, General MacKenzie. You have my word and that of our commander," he replied.

I got on the radio and told our headquarters, "We're moving. Tell Ganic."

I moved my VBL to the front of the convoy and placed Steve's Finnish APC (called a SUSI), carrying the President, Sabina, the TDF commander and Kukanjac, directly behind me. We would keep the two key players in the same vehicle, until we got to the point close to the Presidency where Izetbegovic and his daughter would transfer to another APC and drive 300 metres to safety. Thomas's group of Swedish guards, and a couple of Dutch soldiers who had just been rescued from a firefight downtown, took up position so they could join the tail of the convoy when it started to move.

I started off very slowly. The streets were not much wider than the widest vehicle. It would probably be at least fifteen minutes before the last vehicle would start to move.

As we proceeded at a snail's pace along the reverse of our route into town, I could see a number of TDF soldiers down the sidestreets and in the windows of the buildings that overlooked our convoy. Steve and I were standing with our upper bodies outside the top hatches of our vehicles, exchanging hand signals as required.

We had gone about a kilometre when I thought I heard a shot. I turned around and looked at Steve. His SUSI was a lot taller than my VBL and he could see back down along the column of trucks. I knew from the look on his face that something was seriously wrong.

I jumped out of the VBL and started to run back towards the sound of the shooting, which no longer consisted of single shots but sustained bursts of machine-gun fire. I hadn't asked Steve to come, but within seconds he was beside me.

The heaviest shooting was about fifty metres away. I could see TDF soldiers sticking their rifles through the windows of civilian cars that were part of the convoy and shooting the occupants. As Steve and I ran by, we saw blood splattered over the windscreens of some of the cars.

When we reached a crowd of some twenty TDF soldiers, we realized they had driven a car across the road to split the convoy in half. The JNA soldiers were sitting helplessly in the back of their trucks; the TDF were demanding that they throw out their weapons and military equipment. To make the point, one of the TDF soldiers, who had two grenades hanging from his teeth, was threatening to throw a third into the back of the truck full of JNA soldiers if they didn't hurry up and surrender their weapons. Weapons and kit were flying out the back of the truck and landing all around the TDF soldiers. I had visions of a shark-feeding frenzy from the movie *Blue Water, White Death*.

I approached the soldier with the grenades in his teeth and put my hand on his shoulder. When he spun around, I could see he was drunk or high on adrenalin. His pupils were dilated, and he looked wild enough to make me think carefully about what I should do next. A hand grabbed my shoulder; one of the TDF leaders said, "I wouldn't do that if I was you. I certainly wouldn't, and he works for me. All we want are the weapons, no one will be hurt!"

"Somebody has already been hurt—probably killed," I replied. "And your President guaranteed the security of this convoy."

"We gave no guarantee of security. The President is dead or kidnapped," was his response.

"Get your officers and come with me. I've got something to show you," I said as forcefully as possible.

At that moment, we heard the klaxon horn of an approaching emergency vehicle. It was a JNA ambulance driving straight towards us, half on the sidewalk and half on the street. The driver was frantically sawing on the steering wheel, trying to avoid hitting anyone. His task was made all the more difficult by the JNA colonel collapsed on his right shoulder and missing half his face. The Colonel was obviously dead or about to die; every time the driver pushed him away, he immediately snapped upright, then collapsed onto the driver's shoulder again. It was as if the two were attached by a strong rubber band. Everyone stopped and stared for a moment, and then the TDF carried on with their intimidation.

By this time, Thomas had appeared. He was bandaging a TDF soldier who, in his excitement, had shot himself in the thigh. I yelled at Thomas to keep an eye on the immediate area while we went back to Steve's APC with the TDF leaders. It seemed that wherever we were, the killing stopped. The stealing of equipment was still going on, but at least people weren't being executed.

Thomas yelled back that he had just been told on his radio that the TDF had fired through the gun ports of a JNA armoured personnel carrier at the tail of the convoy, and everyone inside had been killed. The Swedish guards at that location were being threatened and shots were being fired all around them, so I told Thomas to have them break off and go back to the PTT. There was no sense having our people killed; they were outnumbered a hundred to one.

Steve and I walked quickly back to his SUSI with four or five of the TDF leaders. I explained that their President was inside. Thinking I was joking, they became even more agitated. I stuck my head through the vehicle's back door and told President Izetbegovic that his people had broken his promise and were ambushing the JNA convoy. General Kukanjac looked shocked and desolate. Izetbegovic retained his composure, however; I told him to open the top hatch of the SUSI and stand up. He opened the commander's hatch and turned to face his TDF officers.

The TDF leaders were dumbfounded. Unable to believe their eyes, they stood silent for a few seconds before clambering onto the SUSI to touch Izetbegovic, wanting to be sure he was really alive. They all immediately broke into animated conversation. Izetbegovic explained to them that he had promised security to the JNA convoy, and that they should immediately stop the ambush and let the convoy past. I couldn't help thinking how surprised the TDF officers would be if they knew General Kukanjac was only fifty centimetres below them as they knelt on top of the SUSI.

After five minutes of conversation with their President, the TDF leaders returned to their troops along the convoy; however, by now the damage had been done. Some 200 JNA soldiers had disappeared. At first I assumed they had bolted for the Serb-controlled area just south of the ambush site; later I discovered they had been taken prisoner. All of the JNA weapons and military equipment of any value had been confiscated by the TDF, and six to seven JNA officers had been killed in cold blood during the incident. Our modest UN presence of ten people had prevented a massive bloodbath; but this was small consolation as we mounted up and started to move again.

A kilometre further on, we came to the bridge where Izetbegovic and Sabina were cross-loaded into another armoured personnel carrier and departed for the Presidency.

At this point, General Kukanjac started pacing back and forth across the street, shouting that he was missing at least 200 soldiers and he had to go back for them. This was the first time he had been able to look outside the bowels of Steve's SUSI since we had started the convoy, and he was devastated. I explained that his soldiers had probably bolted to the Serb area; but he, quite rightly, as it turned out, refused to accept my explanation and insisted on returning to the scene of the ambush. I told him that if he did so, he would be killed for sure, and that I would go back myself to see if anyone had been abandoned. I ordered him back into Steve's vehicle; reluctantly, he obeyed, his face expressing the agony of someone who cared for his soldiers.

I remembered that expression months later, when I saw a story in a Belgrade newspaper that General Kukanjac had abandoned his soldiers and fled the scene in a UN vehicle. That was certainly not the case. Kukanjac had had no control over what happened. He certainly didn't flee, since he was under my direction at all times.

I turned our VBL around and proceeded to drive back towards the scene of the ambush. At the first TDF checkpoint, I stopped to bum a light from a sentry, who insisted I keep his lighter. He spoke English, so I asked him what had happened. He explained that the TDF soldiers had received an order from someone in the Presidency to attack the convoy. We never found out for sure who gave the order, but my suspicion was that Vice-President Ganic was a lot tougher than he wanted to admit, and had given the green light to carry out the attack. On the other hand, it could have been the result of some local commander's initiative. The TDF was very undisciplined at that early stage of its development, and many things didn't go the way they were planned. This might have been one of those times. I suppose we will never know.

I could see back down the road as far as the ambush site; there was no evidence of JNA soldiers or any life whatsoever. The road was littered with clothing, files, bits of uniform and personal belongings. A few trucks were burning, rammed up against buildings, and the scene was one of stark desolation.

I returned to what was left of the convoy, transferred General Kukanjac to my vehicle, and carried on without incident through the ruins of southern Sarajevo to Lukavica.

Needless to say, we were not well received at the JNA camp. Word had been passed that the UN had guaranteed the safety of the convoy, but that we had failed to keep our promise. This was not the time, however, to point out that we were merely accompanying the convoy as impartial witnesses and go-betweens, and that it was the President of Bosnia and his TDF commander who had guaranteed the convoy's security.

I feared for the lives of our personnel; it was obvious that some JNA officers wanted to take revenge on the spot. By now, darkness had fallen, and although we rarely travelled at night, I requested an escort for our UN party to the border of the Serb-controlled area. A JNA captain, who understood we had not been responsible for the convoy's security, volunteered to guide us.

We left Lukavica and turned left. Approximately a kilometre down the narrow track, we came up against a major roadblock constructed from a wrecked truck and oil drums filled with dirt. Our JNA guide went forward in the dark and spent ten minutes conversing with the sentry. When he returned to our vehicle, he explained that we couldn't pass through the checkpoint; the guards had heard we were responsible for the deaths of JNA officers.

Our guide suggested we could try the main route back to the PTT building. There was a minefield on the way, and the safe lane through the minefield was closed at night, but we could give it a try. When we arrived at the minefield ten minutes later, I could tell from the body language of our guide and the minefield sentry that we were not going to get through there either.

Our guide explained we would return to Lukavica and perhaps try again in the morning. So we started towards the JNA camp but, inexplicably, went right past the camp entrance and, a kilometre later, drove smack up against the checkpoint we had encountered on our first attempt.

Once again, our guide went forward to talk with the sentry. A matter of seconds later, in the dark all around us there was the characteristic sound of numerous AK-47 assault rifles being cocked. When I saw our guide being handcuffed and dragged off in the direction of a small schoolhouse doubling as the sentries' accommodation, I knew we were in trouble. "Well, Steve, I guess the day's not over yet," I muttered.

Steve and I were still, of course, in our summer short-sleeved tans—our "Sunday best"—and we were freezing. It was around midnight and as cold as northern Ontario in early spring.

We were surrounded by a number of Bosnian Serb irregulars, who ordered us to move our vehicles into the schoolyard. Once we got there, they ordered us out of our vehicles and stripped us of our weapons, flak jackets and personal equipment. I asked to see the officer in charge; he was introduced to me as "Brigadier". I explained that we wished to proceed to the PTT and wanted our weapons and equipment back. He responded in no uncertain terms: "You, General MacKenzie, are responsible for the deaths of Serb officers. Your people will be held here until you go back to Sarajevo and return with the 200 JNA soldiers who were captured today. You go now!"

If this man considered himself a "brigadier", I thought the best tactic was to appeal to his sense of professionalism. "You realize, of course, as a fellow brigadier, that I cannot leave my people here. I am responsible for them; either I stay, or they come with me." Unfortunately, my high-school psychology didn't work. A number of the "Brigadier's" irregulars pushed me with their rifles into the back of Colm Doyle's armoured Mercedes 4x4.

I turned to Steve and said, "Look after them, you're in charge now."

We drove the kilometre back to the JNA camp at Lukavica. I immediately found General Kukanjac. He was still furious with me, but cooled down enough to listen to my demands. I told him that if my people were harmed, his face would be all over CNN and BBC the next day as the JNA general who had condoned the killing of UN soldiers. If he wanted the true story of the convoy incident to get out, he had better get my people back to me, and the sooner, the better.

While Kukanjac thought this over, I was taken into the conference room, where some of his officers were drinking and eating. Except for a few, their attitudes to the UN seemed to have softened somewhat, and I accepted a drink.

Forty minutes later, Steve walked in with our Swedish guards and our two VBL drivers. I didn't want to show it in front of the JNA officers, but this was, up until that time, the happiest moment of my life. They were all freezing and huddled together in a group. A magnificent tray of steaming cubed beef was brought in for us, along with some fresh bread.

Steve asked, "Have you seen the President's bodyguard?" I looked at Colm Doyle, who shrugged his shoulders. I meant to whisper to Steve, but it came out with sufficient volume that two of the Swedes heard me say it: "We're probably eating him right now." I was just kidding (I think), but only Steve and I ate any of the cubed beef; yet I know that everyone else was starving.

It was still vital to try and get back to the PTT. I didn't want to spend the night at Lukavica; we would only get accused by the Presidency of collaborating with the enemy. Not only that, I didn't trust some of the more agitated JNA soldiers, who might have tried to even the score for the convoy incident.

After a lot of asking, I found someone in civvies who would take us to the minefield and arrange for us to get through. I drove with him in his exhaustless YUGO car with a two-way radio on his lap. The car wouldn't run below 3,000 rpm, and we sounded like a tank as we approached the minefield with our gaggle of white UN vehicles behind us.

Sure enough, after a lot of conversation on the two-way radio, some figures emerged from the bushes and removed the mines on the road. I thanked our guide and joined Steve in our 4x4. We had placed the soldiers in our armoured vehicles. I told Steve that I would drive the 4x4. It didn't surprise me that he insisted he ride with me, rather than jumping into one of the armoured cars or the VAB, which would have been much safer. Steve had done a magnificent job all day, particularly in the way he'd looked after our soldiers and kept their morale up while they were detained. Later I wrote him up for a well-deserved bravery award, and he received a Mentioned-in-Despatches decoration. He deserved more.

On the way to the PTT, we were shot at a couple of times. But it was only a rifle grenade that missed us by twenty metres that got our full attention.

As we turned into the PTT parking area, I said to Steve, "You know, I never thought I'd say this—but I'm really happy to see this building!" We stretched out on our cots on the floor of our offices and slept the sleep of the dead.

MAY 4   The next day, the Bosnian government was obviously feeling guilty about its soldiers' actions in the ambush. I received an early-morning call from the Presidency to say that they were interested in negotiating a prisoner-of-war exchange.

Within a few minutes, I departed for the Presidency with the senior European Community military monitor in Sarajevo, Mr. Santos. On arrival, we met with Bosnian Minister of Defence Jerko Doko, who wanted to do a large POW exchange with the JNA. "And who do you intend to exchange?" I asked.

"Why, the JNA soldiers we captured yesterday," he replied.

"No deal," I said. "You captured those soldiers by breaking a promise of safe passage, promised in front of witnesses by the President himself and the commander of your TDF. You have put the UN and myself in a very difficult position. I want those prisoners back without any matching concessions from the JNA."

After some fifteen minutes of debate, it was decided that all the prisoners who wished to return to the JNA would be released to the UN. In exchange, I would arrange for the return of President Izetbegovic's bodyguard from Lukavica.

Minister Doko and I proceeded to the jail across the street, where we were shown approximately 180 JNA prisoners. They had been split into three groups: those who wanted to go "home"; those who wanted to join the TDF; and those who wanted to return to the

ON DUTY *as a twenty-three-year-old sports officer with Canadian peacekeepers serving the* UN *in Gaza, 1963.*

Above: CYPRUS, **1965**. *The reconnaissance platoon commander and his* NCOS: *(l. to r.) Unidentified; Sergeant Don Ethell (now retired as Colonel); Sergeant Len Quinlan; Sergeant Fred Mueller (retired); Sergeant Ken Snowden (retired); Lieutenant Lewis MacKenzie (retired as Major-General).*
Left: THE CANADIAN PEACEKEEPERS' *encampment at Shams racetrack, Cairo, in 1973. Soldiers' accommodations and office tents in foreground, officers' quarters at upper left.*

Top: LUNCH ON THE *El Salvador-Guatemala border, 1991, while
serving with the UN in Central America. The author, foreground, eats in El
Salvador; his interpreter eats in Guatemala.*
Above: MRS. DORA MACKENZIE, *daughter Kimm and the author
being serenaded on their departure from Central America:
Tegucigalpa, Honduras, 1991.*
Top, right: UNPROFOR'S SENIOR COMMAND *arrives in Belgrade to
take up duties in the former Yugoslavia, March 1992: (l. to r.) deputy
commander Major-General Philippe Morillon of France;
the author; political advisor Cedric Thornberry; commander
Lieutenant-General Satish Nambiar of India.*
Far right: UN SPECIAL REPRESENTATIVE *for Yugoslavia Cyrus Vance
visits Sarajevo for a briefing, April 16, 1992: (l. to r.) Colonel Branko Cadjo
of the Yugoslavian National Army; the author, shaking hands with Mr.
Vance; Cedric Thornberry; Philippe Morillon.*

Top: THE PRIME STRATEGIC OBJECTIVE *during
the civil war in Sarajevo: the airport, seen here in better days
shortly after its opening in 1968.*
Above: SARAJEVO, MAY 14, 1992: *the "Rainbow Hotel" under attack;
(top, right) the effects of the attack on the author's automobile,
the second he'd written off that week.*
Right: THE PTT BUILDING, UNPROFOR's *Sarajevo headquarters, after
the mortar attack of May 15, 1992: the author looks out his
office window to survey the damage.*

Top, left: THE AUTHOR GIVES an early-morning
briefing to French marine commandos serving in Sarajevo, June 1992.
Right: BOSNIAN-SERB TANKS leaving Sarajevo airport
in UN hands, June 29, 1992.
Left: PART OF THE CONVOY of battered and decrepit media
vehicles in downtown Sarajevo, June 1992. Behind the relatively unscathed
TV van is BBC correspondent Martin Bell's car, with the
Union Jack on the smashed-in front door.

Above: FRENCH PRESIDENT *François Mitterand drops in
for a visit during the Bosnian civil war, June 28, 1992: (l. to r.) the author on
the telephone, making arrangements for President Mitterand to
meet Bosnian President Alija Izetbegovic; the author's executive assistant, Major
Steve Gagnon; President Mitterand; French cabinet minister Bernard Kouchner.*

Above: DURING A VISIT *to Sarajevo, July 12, 1992, Canada's
Chief of the Defence Staff, General John de Chastelain (in* UN *helmet), chats
with the BBC's Martin Bell. The author stands in the middle,
while Lieutenant-Colonel Michel Jones looks on.*
Top, right: THE AUTHOR, *left, listens as Yugoslavian Prime Minister
Milan Panic, far right, tries to persuade him to accept a* JNA *tank as a
symbolic peace offering, July 19, 1992.*
Lower, right: TWO OF THE OUTSTANDING *international team serving
with* UNPROFOR *in 1992: British Major Vanessa Lloyd-Davies and Belgian
Commandant Hauben share a toast at Sarajevo airport.*

Above: "I'VE NEVER FELT SAFER." *The author with his French marine infantry bodyguards, Sarajevo, July 1992.*
Right: DURING AN ILL-FATED *attempt to get an aid convoy through to the besieged Muslim community of Gorazde, a* UN *armoured personnel carrier hit an anti-tank mine. This was the incident of July 23, 1992, recounted by Vanessa Lloyd-Davies.*

Top: COLONEL CADJO *of the Yugoslavian National Army (JNA) and author confer outside the Sarajevo military hospital during the evacuation of JNA patients, May 10, 1992*
Lower: A REUNION OF THE GANG *from the Sarajevo Delegates' Club on the author's last night in the former Yugoslavia, August 2, 1992, just before departure from Zagreb: (l. to r.) Major-General Philippe Morillon; Colonel Christian Xuereb; Major Steve Gagnon; Adjutant-Chef Mihilov; the author; Captain José Fernandez.*

Lukavica barracks in buses to be provided by the JNA. The large number in the "I-want-to-go-home" category was rapidly diminishing as word passed that there would be no guarantee of security and no transport provided. Since these JNA soldiers were Serbs in the middle of Muslim-controlled downtown Sarajevo, the prospect of walking out the door on the way "home," which in some cases was hundreds of kilometres away, was not very attractive. About twelve of them were prepared to join the TDF; however, the vast majority wanted to go back to their camp at Lukavica.

We had secretly brought JNA General Milan Aksentijevic with us in our armoured car. I was concerned that the JNA prisoners might refuse to go anywhere with me after their experience the previous day. I discussed the exchange with General Aksentijevic: "It's time to send your buses from Lukavica. But please make sure they bring Izetbegovic's bodyguard with them. I'll meet them at the main road junction just east of the PTT."

I turned to Steve and, for the second time in twelve hours, said, "Steve, you're in charge. You've got a real potential mess here—180 POWs, the Bosnian security forces all armed to the teeth, the Bosnian Minister of National Defence, General Aksentijevic, a couple of Swedish guards and yourself—any problem?" Steve started to open his mouth to reply as I bolted out the door, yelling over my shoulder, "Just try to keep them from killing each other!"

Ten minutes later, my driver and I reached the PTT road junction: no JNA buses were in sight. It was a good twenty minutes before they arrived. I had made a poor choice of a meeting spot, since it was in front of several Muslim-controlled apartment buildings in the old Olympic complex. Sniper fire rained down on the buses as I ran from bus to bus looking for the bodyguard. My heart sank and my stomach turned as I realized he was not there.

I signalled the convoy to follow me on a back route to the jail where the JNA prisoners were. All the way there, my mind raced through the possibilities for getting us out of this mess. I knew that when the Bosnian chief of security saw me arrive without the President's bodyguard, the POW release would be cancelled. We would then be stuck in a large room with a lot of unhappy people, most of whom hated each other, and of whom almost fifty per cent were armed.

When I walked into the jail, I was accosted by the security chief: "Where is the President's bodyguard?"

I had to play my trump card: "Steve, bring General Aksentijevic here." Of all the people in the room, Aksentijevic had by far the most credibility. He was one of the few JNA officers still respected by the Presidency.

I turned to the security chief and said, "For some reason, the bodyguard wasn't on the bus. General Aksentijevic will now promise you to do everything he can to arrange for the bodyguard to be released into my care the moment we get these prisoners back to Lukavica. He will shake your hand while he is making the promise, and Major Gagnon will film the event on my video camera for evidence. It's the best chance you have to get your colleague back. Do we have a deal?"

Within seconds, the security chief nodded agreement. I turned to Steve and didn't like the strained look on his face. We stepped to one side, and Steve whispered, "Sir, the battery is dead! Your camera has stopped filming."

"Fake it, Steve." It was the best idea I could think of in the circumstances.

And so, the deal was consummated, with Aksentijevic pledging that he would have the bodyguard released into my custody. Steve had moved us into better light and was working all the buttons on the dead camera as we "filmed" the event for the record.

All but thirteen of the 180-plus soldiers returned with us to Lukavica. There was a bit of firing at the convoy along the way, but nothing serious; no one was hurt.

On arrival at Lukavica, Aksentijevic and I rushed to see General Kukanjac to discuss the bodyguard. Aksentijevic always spoke in a calm, collected and persuasive manner. This exchange was no exception, except that he was obviously not liking what he was hearing from Kukanjac.

It was time for some crude diplomacy: "General Aksentijevic, please tell the General that it's almost dark and I'm not going to put my soldiers through last night's experience again. I'll be leaving this camp in ten minutes. I want to take the bodyguard with me. If he isn't handed over, I'm going to turn over the tape of your promise and handshake to the international media." By this time, I figured the bodyguard had probably been killed in revenge for the convoy incident.

Steve and I went outside and leaned against the VBL. Aksentijevic joined us, looking disheartened. He apologized, which persuaded me once and for all that the guard was dead. At the ten-minute mark, I opened the door of the VBL and started to climb in. There was a commotion about twenty metres behind our vehicle. Steve yelled, "Here he comes!"

I knew the President's bodyguard from previous encounters. He was about thirty years of age, with thinning blond hair, and looked more Swedish than Bosnian. He was a likeable individual but unfortunately spoke no English. I opened the back door to the VBL and slapped him on the back as he scrambled in, almost breaking my hand: he was wearing a flak jacket with ballistic plates under his suit, and I discovered the hard way that he was not as stocky as I had thought.

By the time we got to the PTT, it was dark again. I called the Presidency's security chief and told him he could pick up his package early the next morning. We shared some French field rations cooked over a heat tablet on my desk. We found a cot for the bodyguard and all settled in for another night on the floor.

Before dozing off, I said, "Steve, you're doing great work. I obviously picked the right guy when I read your file in Ottawa."

There was a long pause before Steve replied, "Sir, you didn't pick my file. You picked Major Gendron, but he had a serious domestic problem and I was sent in his place."

Gendron—Gagnon—I had just assumed I'd recorded the name incorrectly as I skimmed through the files back in Ottawa, seeking an executive assistant. All this time I'd thought it was Steve's file I had picked.

I was briefly upset because my first choice had been changed without my knowledge, yet delighted with Steve's performance. I decided that once again, Lady Luck had smiled on me: "Tough luck, Steve—you stay."

18

Quicksand, Balkan-Style

MAY 5 Marrick Goulding, UN Undersecretary for Special Political Affairs, arrived by JNA helicopter in Pale, headquarters of the Bosnian Serbs. Our effort to meet him there and escort him to Sarajevo almost ended in disaster.

After our initial escort party was held up by heavy fighting in the east of Sarajevo, General Nambiar insisted that he lead the next attempt. Svend and Eric volunteered to go with him, and so I made up one of our documents indicating that we had freedom of movement thoughout Bosnia. Unfortunately, I also signed it. Svend advised me later that the Serbian guards at one of the checkpoints had become highly agitated when they saw my signature on the document. Obviously my credibility with the Serbs was at an all-time low. Fortunately, the entire party, including Mr. Goulding and his assistant, Shashi Tharoor, made it safely to our headquarters by 1830 hours. Following a meeting at the Presidency, we all had dinner at the Delegates' Club.

A ceasefire organized by the European Community for 1930 hours turned out to be a non-event; there was no change whatsoever in the tempo of the fighting. The EC had refused to include the Bosnian Serbs in their ceasefire negotiations, which might have made diplomatic sense to them; but to a soldier it seemed silly not to include one of the major parties to the conflict, particularly one that was initiating a good deal of the fighting.

MAY 6 I spent the full day with Mr. Goulding, briefing him all morning.

In the afternoon, we went on a tour of the city with President

Izetbegovic and came under modest fire in the middle of the Muslim
Old City. There were very strong indications that it was an
orchestrated show for the accompanying media, intended to put the
Serbs in a bad light.

Goulding held a press conference at the end of the day's
activities. We felt it was important that he condemn the TDF attack
on the JNA convoy, and so he made the following statement:

> I also went at my request to see the scene of a particularly
> horrible incident on Sunday evening, where, as I think a
> number of you know, some soldiers of the Yugoslav People's
> Army were killed in cold blood when commanders of the
> Bosnian Territorial Defence had failed to honour a promise of
> safe conduct which they had given our people who were
> evacuating the HQ of the Yugoslavian Army in Sarajevo.

Months later, when I had left Sarajevo for good, I was surprised
to discover just how little media coverage Goulding's strong
statement had received around the world. I couldn't help thinking
that if the JNA had ambushed the TDF, instead of the other way
around, it would have been front-page news. When we returned to
the Delegates' Club, we found some new bullet holes in our
building.

MAY 7 The time had come to make plans to move UNPROFOR
headquarters from Sarajevo. Based on our briefings, Goulding and
I agreed that we would not be able to look after our 14,000 soldiers
in the UNPAs from Sarajevo under the conditions prevailing at that
time. I swore Svend to secrecy and he started working on some
options. Ultimately it was decided that UNPROFOR would relocate to
Belgrade ten days hence.

Later in the afternoon, Steve and I took up an earlier invitation
from Martin Bell of the BBC and dropped by his room at the Hotel
Bosnia, which doubled as an office, production studio and storage
facility. Martin's reports from the war zone had quickly become the
standard against which everyone else in the media judged their
work. He told us this was his ninth war and by far the worst, since
it was so unpredictable. His hotel was now on the line of
confrontation between the Muslims and the Serbs, so he was
frequently able to shoot footage and tape his reports from his own
balcony, with more than enough action in the immediate background

for local colour. We had a nice dinner with pleasant conversation in the hotel restaurant, which, much to my surprise, was still operating.

On the way back to the Delegates' Club, we stopped at a Bosnian Serb checkpoint where my French driver opened the door and mentioned my name. The sentry cocked his weapon, whereupon I told the driver to close the door and get out of there, "Now!" We never opened the door at that checkpoint again.

I was starting to get a little paranoid about the Serbs' attitude towards me. I wondered if I would become totally ineffective as an impartial negotiator. I might have been upset with the TDF for their assault against the defenceless JNA convoy, but I didn't hold the attack against the Presidency because I honestly believed, and still do, that President Izetbegovic and his TDF commander had not ordered or condoned the action. I was prepared to be impartial: the question was, would both sides in the conflict be willing to work with me in the future?

M A Y 8   I had a bad night; infantry attacks reached the grounds of the club, with a few rounds landing in the garden.

In anticipation of the move of our headquarters out of Sarajevo, I asked Colonel Michel Jones of the Van Doos in Daruvar, Croatia, to send a couple of trucks and a handful of soldiers to help us move our Canadian equipment, particularly our satellite telephone system, which was our only guaranteed link with Canada. They would drive from Daruvar the next day.

M A Y 9   Michel Jones knew what he was doing. Anytime a commanding officer is asked by his general to send him some help, it's in his best interests to send the very best. That's exactly what I got—from Captain Guy Belisle, the officer in charge, to Corporal Morin, the gentle giant and junior member of the group. In addition, the Canadian public-affairs officer, Captain Doug Martin, had accompanied the group, along with his cameraman and photographer, Sergeant Christian Coulombe, and an assistant.

On their arrival (four hours late, which had us worried for a while), they backed up their trucks to the club to start loading. We decided to have a beer to celebrate their safe arrival, and were in the midst of bringing each other up-to-date when a dozen explosive rounds detonated in the trees in front of the club and a mortar round landed in the area of the front gate. Our Canadian guests did exactly the right thing, immediately falling flat on the ground and hugging terra firma as only a soldier can. Steve and I looked at each other like a couple of idiots. We were still standing—which told us that perhaps we had been in Sarajevo too long and were no longer capable of taking the goings-on seriously. Someone later reflecting on the day called it bravery—actually it was stupidity, or we were both brain-dead.

MAY 10   I was beginning to dread Sundays. They always started slowly, and then . . . .

I chaired a meeting at 1000 hours, attended by Mr. Abdic, a Croat, representing the Presidency, and General Aksentijevic from the JNA. We discussed the evacuation of the JNA military hospital in Sarajevo. It was under fire by the TDF, and armed JNA soldiers were inside the hospital defending it. Captain Nilsson of the Swedish guard platoon was selected to command the UNPROFOR participants in the evacuation; however, after Mr. Abdic explained that he couldn't guarantee the security of the operation, I advised both representatives that I would run the show.

The JNA were very upset because we had requested the previous day that all their weapons in the hospital be placed in boxes, so that we could put them in the holds of the buses to be used for the evacuation; however, during the night, the TDF had entered the hospital and confiscated the "patients' " weapons, claiming that the JNA generals had agreed to this. Angry over the deception, General Aksentijevic said the JNA would no longer negotiate with Mr. Abdic once this particular operation was completed.

We sent two of our VABs to the JNA camp at Lukavica, where they met up with three JNA buses and accompanied them to the hospital. The operation should have taken thirty minutes maximum; but as usual, the process was interrupted numerous times as the rules were adjusted on the spot. Ultimately we got everyone from the hospital loaded onto the buses, at which time the TDF advised us that there was heavy shelling on the route back to Lukavica, and we would have to cancel the evacuation.

I called our people at headquarters, who could observe part of our route, and they advised me that the shelling was very modest and intermittent. I advised the TDF that we were going ahead as planned. I wasn't particularly comfortable, but with three buses crammed to the gunwales with JNA soldiers, women and children sitting in the open beneath high-rise buildings renowned for their snipers, getting out of there seemed the only thing to do.

We departed for Lukavica and arrived without incident.

MAY 11 The European community had been conducting marathon peace talks over the previous few days. The EC continued to exclude the Bosnian Serbs from the deliberations, and as a result, was becoming less and less popular with them. Meanwhile, the Bosnian Serbs under Dr. Radovan Karadzic were becoming more and more independent of the JNA. There were even reports of Bosnian Serbs attacking any JNA unit that tried to turn its weapons, ammunition and military equipment over to the TDF in exchange for safe passage out of Bosnia.

In mid-afternoon, we were visited by the EC's Colm Doyle, accompanied by Mr. Santos. Colm advised us that his colleagues' lives were being threatened by the Bosnian Serbs, and the negotiations were going nowhere. Accordingly, EC headquarters in Zagreb had directed them to pull out of Sarajevo at 0600 hours the following morning. We agreed that we would try to move their more bulky equipment, such as radios, to Belgrade for them as soon as we had space on one of our trucks. One German monitor who had been the target of death threats had been spirited out on Mr. Goulding's helicopter a few days earlier. The remainder of the EC contingent would try to drive to Zagreb by way of Split as soon as the sun came up.

Like it or not, it seemed inevitable that we would now be getting involved in the peacemaking activities that had been the EC's responsibility until their decision to leave. We realized they had no other choice. Their position with the Bosnian Serbs was untenable, and the fact that their headquarters was located in Zagreb, Croatia, did nothing to temper the Serbs' perception that the EC was biased towards everyone but themselves. It was an unfair and unjustified suspicion; however, perception is often more persuasive than reality.

Later in the day, we moved with some regret from the Delegates' Club to the Rainbow Hotel, for security reasons. One hour later, the TDF moved into the club. There was shelling and tank fire around the Rainbow most of the night. So much for security.

MAY 12 After a restless night in new surroundings, I sat down with General Nambiar, Philippe Morillon and Cedric Thornberry to discuss our expanding peacekeeping role in Bosnia. We still didn't have a mandate from the UN for Bosnia, but with the departure of the European Community, we were the only game in town and, slowly but surely, had already been getting involved. We agreed that we had to involve the Bosnian Serbs in any ceasefire negotiations chaired by UNPROFOR.

Cedric had been advised that a Mrs. Beliana Plavsic, who had been an official in the Bosnian Presidency before the Serbs had walked out, was one of Dr. Karadzic's most trusted deputies and still lived in Sarajevo. Over the next hour, Cedric made contact with Mrs. Plavsic, who agreed to attend a multilateral meeting at our headquarters later in the day. Since she lived in a Serbian neighbourhood and had to drive through a TDF-controlled area to reach us, we arranged for one of our patrols to pick her up.

I started off the meeting by advising Mr. Abdic from the Presidency, Colonel Branko Cadjo from the JNA, and Mrs. Plavsic that UNPROFOR would chair negotiations only if all three parties—the Presidency, the JNA and the Bosnian Serbs—were represented. Mr. Abdic was livid; nevertheless, I insisted, for we were convinced this was the only way we could make a modest contribution to help all sides stop the fighting—provided they really wanted to.

Following the meeting, Mrs. Plavsic took me aside and explained that she lived on the thirteenth floor of a high-rise apartment building with her ninety-two-year-old mother, who was blind. The building's elevator was not working, so she spent a lot of time in transit to and from meetings. As a result, she would be able to spend only an hour at any of our subsequent meetings.

I was disappointed. I had yet to attend a negotiating session in Bosnia where we even scraped the surface of the key issues in the first hour. I could see our meetings going on for ten to fifteen hours as a matter of routine. I asked her, "Is there nothing we can do so you can stay longer?" Mrs. Plavsic suggested that her brother could move into her apartment and look after their mother. He lived close to the Kosovo hospital, in an area firmly controlled by the TDF, so we would have to pick him up and deliver him to his sister's apartment.

We had now been in Sarajevo for two months. We had reaped the condemnation of all sides in the conflict on numerous occasions when we had done anything to assist the "enemy", even if it was in the interests of the peace process. I knew Mrs. Plavsic's request would be no exception and explained to her that it just wasn't possible to do as she asked; something would probably go wrong, and we were permitted to carry non-UN personnel only if they were absolutely essential to our negotiations, or for humanitarian purposes. She agreed to try to find another solution.

I didn't consider our conversation of particular importance at the time; however, a distortion of the facts a month later was used to discredit me and the UN, and continues to the time of writing.

General Nambiar was, quite rightly, becoming concerned about the amount of time I was spending away from my chief of staff job. As a result of my involvement in the convoy incident, the release of POWs and the hospital evacuation, both sides were beginning to treat me as their interlocutor. In the meantime, my primary UNPROFOR responsibilities were frequently being neglected. We agreed that the upcoming negotiations regarding the evacuation of the JNA from Marshall Tito Barracks, located just down the road from the Holiday Inn, should be carried out by our Finnish colleague, Colonel Kerri Hogland. Kerri was our chief liaison officer and ideally suited to the job. He was tolerant, reserved and slow to anger. He would need all three characteristics over the next few weeks.

MAY 13   We began detailed planning of UNPROFOR's temporary relocation to Belgrade. Meanwhile, our convoys were being held up by all sides, as it became increasingly difficult to get around Bosnia.

I was interviewed by CNN about our move to Belgrade, then spent the rest of the day sorting out a civilian staff problem. We had about a dozen very highly qualified young women from Sarajevo working for us as local UN employees (they called themselves "the Sarajevo Girls", so I will also from now on). They were employed as secretaries, interpreters, translators and clerks. Most had university degrees, some had two. They came from all three ethnic communities and were a model of the way Sarajevo society used to function before the outbreak of the Bosnian civil war on April 6.

The Sarajevo Girls had been told earlier in the day that if they wanted to move to Belgrade with us, they could do so. If any were single parents, they could take their children. Most had decided to go.

That evening in the Rainbow Hotel, Fred Eckhardt, General Nambiar's press and information officer, advised me that the order regarding the Sarajevo Girls' move to Belgrade had been rescinded and they would have to stay behind. I was flabbergasted. The girls must have been devastated, I thought, since I knew the majority of them had visited their parents earlier in the day, at considerable risk, to say goodbye.

"Fred, I've got some wine; would you mind rounding up the girls and bringing them here for a chat, please?"

Most of them had gone to bed early after enduring such an emotional roller coaster. I explained, "Girls, I don't have any authority over UN civilian staff. But let me guarantee you that if you want to move with us, you can do so and bring your children. I'll sort out the details with the civilian personnel staff. Now who wants to go?"

They all glanced at each other. I noticed that Alexandria, who had two impressive degrees in mathematics and computer science, was starting to tear up. She quickly regained her composure and said, "General MacKenzie, we don't have any choice. We have to go even if we don't want to."

"Why?" I asked.

Her answer chilled me to the bone: "Because, if we go, you will have to hire some more people from Sarajevo to replace us. And when the next UN evacuation takes place, you will move them out of Sarajevo also. So by leaving now, we will probably save a few more lives in the future." The logic of someone choosing between life and death is powerful stuff.

We were taking only 200 of our UN personnel to Belgrade. One hundred would stay behind in Sarajevo under Colonel John Wilson, with Colonel Kerri Hogland as his deputy. They would conduct any ceasefire negotiations and humanitarian activities as necessary, while the rest of us got on with looking after our soldiers in the UNPAs from a temporary headquarters in Belgrade. John would have to hire some local staff, so Alexandria was absolutely right in her analysis.

Over the next few hours, Fred and I enjoyed being out-numbered by the opposite sex as we eliminated my wine stock. Everyone staggered off to sleep around midnight.

MAY 14   The TDF launched a major assault at exactly 0500 hours into the area just west of the Rainbow Hotel. The preparatory fire for the attack started around 0300. Gradually, the intensity of the shelling and tank fire increased until it was impossible to sleep. The entire hotel was vibrating as two tanks took turns firing from positions under our windows on the east side of the building.

I got dressed and went to the roof with Steve. We sprinted across the gravel roof to the Swedish lookout post and watched the mortars and artillery falling within fifty metres of our location. The volume of small-arms fire suggested there were major infantry attacks being launched in the areas of Ilidza and Stup, just west of our position. Looking towards Stojcevac, I speculated that General Nambiar and our colonels would be stuck there for awhile. The heaviest fighting was taking place between them and us.

I told Steve we'd try to get to the PTT building in the VBL. We ran downstairs to the parking lot and drove at high speed through the smoke and confusion to our headquarters. The night-duty staff of the PTT were all right, but told us that mortar rounds had landed close to the building in the parking lot, and a few of our trucks had been damaged. I tried to call Stojcevac, but no one answered there or at General Nambiar's residence.

I went upstairs to my office on the third floor and prepared an update to New York in longhand. All the power was out, so we would send it as soon as we got the emergency generator working.

Steve had gone to the next floor up for a better view. He yelled down the stairway, "Sir, I think the Rainbow's been hit!" I rushed to the landing just above our floor, where there was a magnificent view to the west. The Rainbow Hotel was enveloped in black smoke that seemed to be originating in the parking lot.

"Steve, you see the base of that pillar of smoke? I think that's where I parked my new Toyota!"

Steve shook his head. "No, sir, I think it's well to the left of that. It should be okay."

I went back to the office and called the Rainbow's front desk—no answer. I raised Thomas Jarnahed on my walkie-talkie and was rewarded with a short, decisive report: "We've been hit. We're moving to the bunker."

An hour earlier, everyone at the Rainbow had been told that breakfast would be served as usual, in spite of the proximity of the fighting. The dining room had been packed when the first artillery round had struck the building. Sergeant Coulombe had his television camera with him and turned it on. The pictures he took over the next ten minutes were seen around the world within twenty-four hours.

His footage shows everyone in the dining room standing up, hunched over, and walking slowly in the direction of the front entrance. As two more rounds strike the building, the pace of the crowd quickens. A few of the children of our civilian single parents start to cry. The camera follows the evacuation to the stairs leading to the bunker. Then a large-calibre round slams into the courtyard beside the reception desk; all the windows are blown inward, and thousands of pieces of glass slice through the air. The camera shows everyone's clothing blown tightly against their bodies by the concussion of the blast. The camera doesn't show any panic, and the camera doesn't lie. Everyone makes it to the relative safety of the bunker.

Steve and I decided to make a run back to the Rainbow to see if everyone was all right. As we approached the building, I said to Steve, "For an old guy whose eyesight is going, I did a pretty good job of spotting where that artillery landed in the parking lot." My second car in three weeks was a write-off. The interior was gutted, the windows blown out, and there were a couple of hundred shrapnel holes in its charred body. I had a flashback to the Toyota television commercials we have in North America. In my case, the salesman could stay on the ground while the car jumped in the air—as it probably did when the artillery shell landed beside it.

We went to the Rainbow's bunker and found everyone in good spirits. They just needed some fuel, since their emergency generator was running low. Steve and I headed back to the PTT.

We'd been back in my office for about ten minutes, discussing the situation with one of our political officers, Adnan Abdelrazek, when a mortar round slammed into our building, impacting about twenty feet from one of my windows. As described in Chapter 1, Steve and Adnan were both knocked down by the blast. Once I'd recovered my cigarettes, we rushed to the bunker.

After hours of trying, we got through to General Nambiar. . Fighting was raging all around his residence; he and Major Philip Campose, his aide-de-camp, were stuck in the basement but fine otherwise. I was also able to speak to Jamie Arbuckle, who set my mind at ease by telling me that the colonels at Stojcevac were all right, but were freezing cold in the mountain bunker adjacent to their motel. He figured their desire for food and heat would soon overcome all other concerns, and they would venture back to the motel. He was right.

Steve and I cooked another meal by heat tablets and, sometime after midnight, dragged out our cots again.

There had been a security scare earlier, when it had been rumoured that looters had entered the Rainbow Hotel just after everyone had gone to the bunker. Captain Guy Belisle organized a house-clearing detail to check every room. A lot of the doors were locked; however, Guy told me afterwards that Corporal Morin had probably established a new standard for *The Guinness Book of World Records* for the number of doors successfully kicked in on the first attempt—somewhere around 150. Morin was still smiling when I saw him the next morning.

M A Y   1 5   By mid-morning, General Nambiar had had enough of sitting in his residence and watching the fighting swirling around his property. He and his aide jumped into their car and, with their Swedish guards, drove straight to the PTT building without stopping. When anyone tried to stop them, they merely waved and bluffed their way through. Fortunately, no one interrupted their brazenness with anything stronger than insults.

The colonels were not so lucky. Led by Svend Harders and Jamie Arbuckle, they had made arrangements to hand over their quarters at Stojcevac to the Bosnian Serbs, who were controlling the area. It was agreed that the handover would occur at precisely 1000 hours. Earlier, the Serbs had swept the complex for weapons and booby traps and left saying they would be back at 1000.

At the appointed time, Svend and a convoy consisting of one bus and numerous UN trucks, loaded down with approximately sixty senior officers and their kit, departed Stojcevac for the PTT. They only got as far as the area around the Hotel Bosnia, when they were stopped and taken hostage by a group of very irate Bosnian Serbs. Some were forced to dismount and were spreadeagled on the ground, while others were held at gunpoint in the backs of their vehicles.

During the remainder of the day, intense negotiations took place to obtain the colonels' release. It gradually became clear that the Serbs had not returned to Stojcevac at the agreed hour of 1000, and as soon as our personnel had departed, the Muslims had smartly moved in and taken over the complex. The Serbs blamed us for their own inefficiency and accused us of having plotted the entire deal with the Muslims. During radio conversations with Svend, he mentioned that my name had been used in vain a number of times by the Serbs, and that it would not be a good idea for me to get involved with the negotiations to obtain the colonels' release.

I had just started to chair my final meeting with representatives from the Presidency, the JNA and the Bosnian Serbs when we received word of the hostage-taking. I vented some of my frustration and indicated that from now on, Colonel Hogland would chair the meetings, since I would be moving to Belgrade; further-more, today's conference would be adjourned, due to the crisis we now had with our people being held hostage. I asked Mrs. Plavsic to see me in my office.

Philippe Morillon joined us. I briefed the two of them on what Svend was telling me on the radio. The situation was extremely tense, and the potential for loss of life was high. The Serbs were convinced we were in cahoots with the Muslims. I also pointed out that it would probably be counter-productive if I showed up to negotiate.

Philippe immediately volunteered to visit the scene of the crisis, and Mrs. Plavsic agreed to go with him. By the time the two of them arrived, the situation had deteriorated even more. One of our Russian colonels had picked up the bodies of some Muslim casualties and, a few minutes later on his way to the hospital, had been forced at gunpoint to unload them so that he could transport Serbian dead and wounded. His actions had been interpreted by the Serbs as further evidence that we were biased in favour of the Muslims.

Over the next six hours, Morillon and Plavsic cajoled, threatened, pleaded and argued, demanding the release of our people. The Serbs were tired, frustrated and irrational. They even threatened Mrs. Plavsic a number of times, which was surprising, given her prominence in the fledgling Bosnian-Serb leadership.

But by 1830 hours, all our officers arrived safe and sound at the PTT building—apart from the two VBL drivers and Captain Belisle, who were searching for dead and wounded as part of the negotiated agreement to release our people. Philippe and Mrs. Plavsic had defused a potentially monumental disaster. We all breathed a final sigh of relief when Captain Belisle arrived back with the two VBLS an hour later.

MAY 16   The first half of the 200 people we were moving to Belgrade departed Sarajevo at 0900. Six hours later, they had gone a mere sixty kilometres because of roadblocks and fighting north of the city. There was no way they were going to make Belgrade before dark.

At midday, I had an interesting call from General de Chastelain. He said, "Lew, be aware that you are rapidly becoming a media star back here. Everything you say is being covered. I just want you to know that. So far, it's all playing pretty well."

Meanwhile, we had no electricity or running water at UNPROFOR headquarters.

19

Back to Belgrade

—

MAY 17 Now it was the turn of the rest of us who were relocating from Sarajevo to Belgrade. We got up at 0500 hours, loaded our equipment and departed at 0900. Our convoy comprised over fifty vehicles, including several large ten-ton trucks that had not been designed to cope with the narrow back roads of Bosnia. Our progress was agonizingly slow, particularly after we were forced to turn the entire mob around when we ran up against a minefield on our primary route.

Around noon, we exited a small village and after a kilometre encountered a massive roadblock created by some ingenious individuals who had blown half a large hill onto the road. This was our last possible route to Belgrade. We surveyed the scene for a couple of minutes, and I asked Captain Belisle, "Guy, what do you think? Can we build a road around the crater and the debris?"

Soldiers never pass up a challenge. Over the next two hours, our Canadian, French and Swedish soldiers, along with our officers and Fred Eckhardt, chopped, dug, piled rocks, moved soil and successfully constructed a good imitation of a road around the obstacle. We placed armed sentries in the surrounding woods in case anyone tried to interfere with our engineering feat, but the only people who showed up were curiosity-seekers from the nearby village, who seemed impressed with our initiative. The event was duly recorded by our accompanying media corps and was beamed to the world that evening. Corporal Morin was the star of the piece as he rolled a 300-pound boulder out of the way.

We arrived in Belgrade at 2000 hours. When we reached the main four-lane highway connecting Belgrade and Zagreb, General

Nambiar and I broke off from the convoy and followed our police escort at over 160 kilometres per hour to the Hotel Yugoslavia. On arrival, we treated ourselves to a bath and a sumptuous dinner in the hotel dining room. I went to bed at midnight but couldn't resist watching television for a few hours. I felt terribly guilty thinking of John Wilson, Kerri Hogland and their hundred people back in Sarajevo, who were probably experiencing the nightly shelling.

I would spend the next twenty-three days in Belgrade. We had moved there so we could turn our full attention to looking after our growing force of UN troops in the UNPAs, but it didn't work out that way. Every day continued to be dominated by events in Sarajevo. John Wilson and his contingent were constantly in danger as the fighting between the Bosnian Serbs and the TDF became more intense. The JNA troops were blockaded by the TDF in Marshall Tito barracks, their release conditional on turning over all their weapons and equipment, which they refused to do. The majority of the JNA troops who had been born in Bosnia left the JNA and became members of the new Bosnian Serb army, under the command of an ex-JNA general, Ratko Mladic. It was becoming more and more difficult to keep track of the players in the conflict without a program.

Looking back over my diary entries for this twenty-three-day period, I find it interesting that they became longer and more comprehensive than the Sarajevo entries. As I grew more bored, with more time on my hands, I wrote more in the diary. In spite of the fact that we were in Belgrade, responsible for 14,000 UN soldiers in Croatia, most of the entries still dealt with Sarajevo. Like it or not, Sarajevo continued to be our focus.

The Belgrade diary entries are fulsome enough over the next two-and-a-half weeks that they speak for themselves:

MAY 18
- No artillery wake-up call.
- First haircut in two months.
- Settled into new office.

MAY 19
- Still spending most of our time on Sarajevo.
- Withdrawal plan to get JNA out of Marshall Tito barracks collapsed.
- Busload of kids being held hostage just down the street from the PTT. I watched the incident live on TV.

- Serbs are expelling non-Serbs from Sector East.
- Croats are expelling non-Croats from Sector West.
- What a sick world.

MAY 20
- Situation bad in Sarajevo. Some of our vehicles mortared. No one hurt. Just a lot of flat tires—miracle!
- Still no deal on evacuating Tito barracks.
- Kids still hostages. They have been stuck in the bus for over twenty-four hours.
- The UN asked us to approach Izetbegovic to see if he would accept a helicopter ride to Belgrade for talks! We don't have to wait for his answer. He would have to be crazy to accept.

MAY 21
- Decided to take a day off. Slept until 0730.
- Svend called at 0800. Seems UN Secretary-General wants us to move our headquarters to Zagreb ASAP. I don't believe it!
- Fifty-two JNA soldiers ambushed today in Tuzla as they were leaving Bosnia. Serbs will probably retaliate in Sarajevo. JNA has stopped withdrawing from Sector East.

MAY 22
- Met with new JNA commander, Admiral Simik, the Yugoslavian Minister of Defence and the Vice-President of the "Serbian Republic of Krejina". I got the definite impression that the Serbs in the Krejina, centred on Sector South, are going to be a force to be reckoned with.
- Svend departed for a few weeks at home in Denmark. He has to turn over the command of his brigade while he is there.

MAY 23
- Tried to organize a half-day in office—left at 1700.
- JNA was ambushed in Sarajevo. This will elicit more retaliation and will probably delay their withdrawal from Bosnia.

- Watching the TV news (BBC and CNN), one gets the impression Serbs are 100 per cent to blame. Some of the reports are unbalanced, based on what we know. Serbs bear majority of responsibility, but Izetbegovic has done an excellent job of mobilizing world opinion on his side, which covers up his hidden agenda. I'm convinced he wants massive international military intervention.
- Dinner with Philippe, José, Steve and Mihilov in floating restaurant on Danube.

MAY 24

- Last three Sundays were disaster: convoy incident, hospital evacuation, and roadblock on move to Belgrade. Today no exception. I was expecting to see Indy 500 on TV and it wasn't covered! That's four Sundays in a row.
- Dora called and gave me the good news that Scott Goodyear came second at Indy by a couple of feet. Made my day!
- Canada recalling its ambassador from Belgrade.

MAY 25

- Met with EC military monitor regarding co-operation in the Pink Zones.
- Attended reception at U.S. Embassy. Met Congresswoman Bentley from U.S.A. She wants to take diplomatic group to Sector East.
- Days are quite boring. I wish I was back in Sarajevo.

MAY 26

- Nambiar off to visit Sector East. Rumours of continuing population intimidation by Serbs.
- Russian Foreign Minister visiting Sarajevo. JNA are talking about opening the Sarajevo airport.
- JNA not withdrawing on schedule from Sector East. They claim it's a misunderstanding. We will see.

MAY 27

- Disaster in Sarajevo. People lined up for bread were attacked, and at least seventeen killed. Presidency

claims it was a Serb mortar attack, Serbs claim it was a
set-up using explosives. Our people tell us there were
a number of things that didn't fit. The street had been
blocked off just before the incident. Once the crowd
was let in and had lined up, the media appeared but
kept their distance. The attack took place, and the
media were immediately on the scene. The majority of
people killed are alleged to be "tame Serbs". Who
knows? The only thing for sure is that innocent people
were killed.
- Evacuation of JNA barracks in Sarajevo a disaster. Five
hours late starting. Convoy got lost in the dark and was
ambushed. One killed and thirty missing.
- Bad road accident involving our Argentine battalion in
Sector West. Two soldiers killed and seven injured.
- Not a good day.

MAY 28
- Keith Walton has been replaced. Needless to say, he is
bitter and didn't accept our invitation to dinner. I
sympathize with him. The UN didn't give him the staff
to do the job and then relieved him when the
administration was screwed up. Jim Baldie will take
over.
- John needed Mrs. Plavsic at Kerri's meetings. They
tried to pick up her brother in the area of the Kosovo
hospital to move him to his mother's apartment, as she
requested me to do weeks earlier. The local Muslims
in the area took exception to this activity and indicated
their intention to lynch the brother and Mrs. Plavsic.
A nasty scene ensued, and only the bravery of the UN
personnel on the scene prevented a cold act of murder.
The mission was abandoned.

[This aborted attempt took on greater significance a few weeks later,
when I was back in Sarajevo. In spite of the fact that I had denied
a similar request from Mrs. Plavsic on May 12, the word was spread
around Sarajevo that I had authorized this latest attempt to move
her brother in one of our vehicles. This was the genesis of the
derogatory term "Chetnik Taxi Service", which the Muslims used
in June to describe UNPROFOR, implying that we constantly did
favours for the Serbs.]

- Heavy shelling in Sarajevo. John and his command are in their bunker. They were shot at twice today in Serbian areas of the city.

MAY 29

- Things heating up. Very heavy fighting in Sarajevo. The talks chaired by Kerri Hogland have broken down. No one can get to the PTT.
- We received a draft of the Secretary-General's report to be released tomorrow. The only thing new is an indication that the UN would like to see a security zone around Sarajevo airport to facilitate the delivery of humanitarian aid. Good luck!
- Sarajevo airport is becoming a popular topic. Cutileiro called New York from the Lisbon talks and said he'd been approached by Karadzic, who suggested the airport be placed under "UN command and control". The Secretary-General thinks the European Community should continue to take the lead in any subsequent airport negotiations. I doubt if that will be possible. They are even more unpopular in Sarajevo than we are.
- We have been advised that Iranian Muslim fundamentalists are infiltrating Bosnia and will attack the UN peacekeepers. I'm not sure why, unless they could make it look like someone else did it.

MAY 30

- All hell has broken loose in Sarajevo. Heaviest shelling yet. Reports are that General Mladic is not responding to Bosnian Serb leadership and is attempting to flatten Sarajevo. Philippe and I went to see President Milosevic and Dr. Karadzic, who is here for talks, and called for an immediate halt to the shelling. They both indicated displeasure with Mladic, but it could have been an act. We worked on a possible ceasefire for 0600 on June 1 if heavy shelling stops now.
- UN imposed sanctions on Serbia today. It's unfortunate the UN document referred to a lack of co-operation between the JNA and ourselves in the UNPAs. In fact, things have been going quite well so far, but that might

change once the JNA reads the Security Council's document.
- Actually saw the qualifying session for the Monaco Grand Prix on TV.

MAY 31
- It's Sunday again and another problem. Nambiar's helicopter back to Belgrade from Sector East has been cancelled for no good reason—retaliation for sanctions, or questionable weather? He is driving.
- Secretary-General has decided to elevate our "good offices" to a mediation role in Sarajevo. It's the first hint of our having a mandate in Bosnia. We will start by trying to obtain an agreement to open the Sarajevo airport. Perhaps I should go back to give it a try.
- Rumours that Karadzic won't last the week.
- President Izetbegovic says he won't deal with Karadzic, only General Mladic, on Sarajevo airport.
- France wants to get involved in airport operation. Would provide 1,000 troops—here we go!
- I saw Monaco Grand Prix—great blocking by Senna during last two laps.

JUNE 1
- Meetings all day on the Pink Zone problems in the Krejina. The Serbs from the Krejina want us to protect their population in the zones. It's not covered in the Vance Plan and will therefore be difficult in the extreme to sell it to the Croatians. I'm not optimistic.
- Someone has to go to Sarajevo to talk to both sides about the possibility of opening the airport. I volunteered to go but Nambiar is sending Cedric. Regrettably, a good choice.

JUNE 2
- Ceasefire scheduled for 1800 yesterday was a flop.
- Met with Nikola Koljevic, another of Karadzic's deputies: a Shakespeare scholar who has taught in U.S. and Canada. I can do business with him. He seems reasonable.
- Cedric flew by JNA helicopter to Sarajevo. Thirty

minutes after he arrived, he was detained at a roadblock close to the PTT. One of our attempts to get some food into Dobrinja adjacent to the airport was fired on by the Bosnian Serbs. The driver was killed and one of our APCs was sprayed with machine-gun fire.

– Svend arrived back from Denmark.

JUNE 3

– Drove to Daruvar at 0730. Went through Vukuvar. Looks like Stalingrad circa World War Two. Stopped and talked to a few of our Canadian combat engineers who were working in the area.

– Visited Michel Jones and saw a lot of his personnel and his battalion area. Visited both of his rifle companies, "N" from the Royal Canadian Regiment and "A" from the Van Doos.

– Had dinner with the officers and NCOs. Guy Belisle presented me with a Van Doos t-shirt. I responded with a few coherent words and asked everyone to forget that I was the guy who said, "Everyone likes you," just before the artillery fire fell on their positions on April 13.

JUNE 4

– Met with the sector commander, Carlos Zabala, at his headquarters in Daruvar. Here it is three months after our arrival, and his people still haven't received the money they are entitled to from the UN. It's his biggest morale problem, and understandably he is both mad and discouraged. I promised to speak to the new chief administrative officer, Jim Baldie, about it. Perhaps he will have more luck than his predecessor had. The Canadians are lucky to have Carlos as their sector commander.

– Got back to Belgrade at 1900.

– Cedric and John are still working on an airport agreement in Sarajevo.

20

Talking my Way into Command

JUNE 5   Cedric Thornberry returned to Belgrade from Sarajevo, bringing with him a trilateral agreement in principle for the opening of Sarajevo airport. After three days of intensive negotiations, Cedric and John Wilson appeared to have pulled off a coup: they had talked the Bosnian Presidency and the Bosnian Serb army into signing an agreement that would see the airport demilitarized and placed under UN supervision for the delivery of humanitarian aid.

Negotiations hadn't gone particularly well until early morning; then the speed with which a final agreement was reached took them all by surprise. Cedric had returned to Belgrade in order to report through General Nambiar to the Security Council over the weekend. He'd explained to Dr. Karadzic that this was an interim agreement and did not mean the Bosnian Serbs were abandoning territory or showing any sign of weakness; on the contrary, it would demonstrate to the world that they were committed to alleviating the suffering of the non-combatants in Sarajevo. Karadzic had presumably seen the tremendous potential for positive press, and his attitude had softened.

By midnight, we had received signed copies of the airport agreement from both the Presidency and the Bosnian Serbs. The text ran as follows:

AGREEMENT ON THE RE-OPENING OF SARAJEVO
AIRPORT FOR HUMANITARIAN PURPOSES

As a first step towards the implementation of Security Council resolution 757 (1992), paragraph 17:

The undersigned have agreed that:

1) The ceasefire declared for 1800 hours on 1 June 1992 in and around Sarajevo is reaffirmed. The ceasefire will be monitored by UNPROFOR, and the parties will provide liaison officers and escorts to assist in its verification.

2) To provide physical guarantees that fire will not be brought to bear against the airport, flying aircraft, or aircraft on the ground they agree that:

A) All anti-aircraft weapon systems will be withdrawn from positions from which they can engage the airport and its air approaches and be placed under UNPROFOR supervision.

B) All artillery, mortar, ground-to-ground missile systems, and tanks within range of the airport will be concentrated in areas agreed by UNPROFOR and subject to UNPROFOR observation at the firing line.

These measures will be established prior to the opening of the airport.

3) The parties undertake not to attempt to interfere in any way with the free movement of UNPROFOR-supervised air traffic into and out of Sarajevo Airport. Such traffic will consist of:

A) Humanitarian and resupply missions.

B) UN and EC or related missions.

C) Official missions.

4) UNPROFOR will establish a special regime for the airport, and will supervise and control its implementation and functioning. This regime will be established at the earliest possible date after the approval of all concerned, with preparatory work beginning immediately after signature. All parties undertake to facilitate these processes, together with the handover of the airport to UNPROFOR.

5) Facilities, organization and security inside the airport, including perimeter security, will be supervised and controlled by UNPROFOR with its civil, military, and police personnel.

6) UNPROFOR will control all incoming personnel, aid, cargo, and other items to ensure that no warlike materials are imported, and that the airport's opening is not otherwise abused in any way. The parties' humanitarian organizations will each establish an office at the airport to facilitate UNPROFOR's related tasks.

7) All local civilian personnel required for the operation of the airport will be employed on a basis of non-discrimination,

and will be supervised and controlled by UNPROFOR. To the extent possible, such personnel will comprise the current employees of the airport.

8) Humanitarian aid will be delivered to Sarajevo and beyond, under the supervision of the UN, in a non-discriminatory manner and on a sole basis of need. The parties undertake to facilitate such deliveries, to place no obstacle in their way, and to ensure the security of those engaged in this humanitarian work.

9) To ensure the safe movement of humanitarian aid and related personnel, security corridors between the airport and the city will be established and will function under the control of UNPROFOR.

10) This agreement shall be without prejudice to the settlement of constitutional questions now under negotiation; and to the safety and security of all inhabitants of Sarajevo and its surrounding area.

JOHN WILSON PULLED OFF yet another coup with the relatively incident-free evacuation of the JNA personnel from Marshall Tito barracks in downtown Sarajevo. The barracks had been crammed with teenage officer cadets, JNA families who had been pushed out of Slovenia and Croatia a year earlier, and a modest number of regular JNA soldiers. They had been blockaded by the Bosnian TDF for months; every time the TDF had killed someone in the barracks with sniper fire, the Serbs had reacted by firing artillery from their Lukavica base into the city.

That vicious circle of retaliation was one of the major problems with this particular war: the TDF would initiate a minor encounter, and the Bosnian Serbs would overreact with their heavy weapons, including artillery and rocket launchers. The Serbs were outnumbered by a less well-trained TDF infantry force; however, they were fixated on their fear of being "overrun" by the Muslim "Green Berets", and chose to fight them from a distance. An old Yugoslavian Army doctrine preached, "Never send a soldier where an artillery round can go first." As a result, the civilian population of Sarajevo was a prime target of Serbian shelling and suffered terrible consequences. The vicious circle was getting worse every day as the TDF became stronger and the Bosnian Serbs became more paranoid.

In order to obtain the safe passage of the JNA occupants out of Marshall Tito barracks, it had been agreed that they would leave behind all their heavy weapons, including artillery, mortars, armoured fighting vehicles and ammunition, for the TDF. It didn't take a genius to predict that as soon their barracks was evacuated, the Serbs would destroy it with artillery and rockets in order to deprive the TDF of the equipment. Since that was the last location where the Serbs had troops in Sarajevo, they would no longer fear retaliation by the TDF and could therefore fire at will. Sure enough, heavy shelling followed the evacuation. Marshall Tito barracks was hit by rocket-launcher attacks and was on fire all night.

Meanwhile, CNN announced a deal had been signed for the opening of Sarajevo airport. I was impressed; their intelligence gathering was a lot better than the UN's.

JUNE 6 The UNPROFOR command cell had an early breakfast meeting in General Nambiar's office. Whenever we had a major problem, Nambiar, Philippe Morillon, Cedric Thornberry and I would get together.

Everyone congratulated Cedric on his achievement and his survival during a particularly violent period in Sarajevo. Implementation of the airport agreement would be difficult, but we all agreed that the longer we waited, the more difficult it would become.

My opportunity had arrived. I had lain awake a good two hours the previous night, putting together my mental script for this exact moment. "General Nambiar," I began, "the plan calls for a thousand-man battalion to take on the security of the airport. You are no longer a stranger to the UN's inability to move troops in a timely manner. Here it is June, some three months after our arrival, and we still don't have all of our forces on the ground. My experience tells me that it will be well over a month before a country could be found to volunteer a battalion and before the UN could move it to Sarajevo. By that time, the window of opportunity could be slammed shut on Cedric's knuckles and all his good work would be history."

I had hit my stride and continued: "The battalion that goes to Sarajevo will have to have presence—by that, I mean lots of armoured vehicles with mounted weapons and highly disciplined and well-led troops. You have two battalions in your command right now that qualify: the French and the Canadians. They both cheated and brought a lot more APCs then the fifteen the UN directed. The French brought eighty and the Canadians managed eighty-three.

"The French are tied up in Sector South, trying to cope with the Serbian Republic of the Krejina. The Canadians are sitting in Sector West along with three other battalions. Carlos wouldn't like it, but Sector West is pretty quiet, and he could do his job with his battalions from Argentina, Jordan and Nepal. You could send the Canadians to Sarajevo until the UN finds another country to replace them at the airport."

No one said anything for ten seconds. Fortunately, Cedric nodded and smiled. Philippe obviously wanted the French to take on the job, but he knew they were critical to keeping the volatile situation in the Krejina in check. Nambiar knew we had to be in Sarajevo with strength very soon, or we'd have to start all over again. "Very well," he said finally, "let's give it a try. Lew, prepare a message to New York asking their approval."

The time had arrived for the next phase of my pitch. "General, there are two parts to my proposal." I paused and caught my breath. "No nation I know would allow one of their units to go to Sarajevo unless one of their officers was in charge of the operation. I doubt if Canada would be an exception. You will need to establish a new sector headquarters in Sarajevo to run the show, and you should send me to command it."

Nambiar smiled. "Absolutely not. Lew, you are the chief of staff, and I need you here to look after the situation in the UNPAS. We can find someone else to look after Sarajevo."

"If that's the case, General Nambiar, you won't get the authority to use the Canadian battalion, I'm sure of it." I didn't want to beg, so I figured threatening the success of the operation would be the most convincing argument.

Nambiar was more than a little shocked. "I don't believe you," he said.

"I'll confirm it for you," I replied. "I'll phone Canada and speak to the Chief of the Defence Staff, General de Chastelain." With that, I took a few quick steps to the door and left Nambiar's office before he had a chance to comment.

I was pretty sure I was right. Like most nations, Canada is sensitive about placing its troops under someone else's command when bullets are flying. This would potentially be our most dangerous operation since Korea, and rightly or wrongly, I felt that the decision to approve Canada's involvement would be a lot easier for the government if the Chief of the Defence Staff could point out that a Canadian general would command the operation. I had persuaded myself. I put my feet up on the desk and lit a cigarette. I didn't call anyone.

Five minutes later, I went back into Nambiar's office and said, "Sorry, sir, I was right. The CDS said that there is very little chance that the government will authorize the involvement of the Canadian battalion in Sarajevo unless I'm placed in charge." (Lest the reader think that I erred, you will be relieved to know, as I was some three hours later following a telephone conversation with General de Chastelain, that he fully endorsed my opinion.)

Nambiar looked me straight in the eye. "Okay, Lew. We discussed it while you were out of the office and agreed that you should go—but I want you back here as quickly as possible!"

Needless to say, I was delighted. I would be able to leave my office and get back to commanding soldiers again. There was an added advantage: Denmark was prepared to promote Svend Harders to brigadier-general, a rank that didn't exist in the Danish Army but that their colonels could receive on UN duty, if the job demanded it. Svend would be the obvious choice for my job as chief of staff, and so his promotion would probably be approved. I told him later the only reason I went back to Sarajevo was to make him a general!

I cranked off two quick messages to New York and my own National Defence headquarters in Ottawa with our proposal. Then I sent a warning order to Michel Jones of the Van Doos to report to our headquarters the following day with his reconnaissance group, ready to proceed directly to Sarajevo on short notice. The main body of the battalion would follow only after the Security Council was satisfied that the operation was viable.

JUNE 7 Michel's reconnaissance team spent all day knitting together a plan to defend Sarajevo airport and secure corridors to the downtown area. I fleshed out my overall requirements and sent them to New York.

If we were to maintain twenty-four-hour observation of the heavy weapons of both sides within range of the airport, we would need at least sixty additional officer observers. It would take too long for them to be mobilized from scratch by the UN, so we asked the UN to lend us officers from other peacekeeping missions around the world.

We received a message from New York indicating that France was prepared to send us a technical team to conduct a thorough evaluation of Sarajevo airport's capacity to handle humanitarian flights. I sent a message saying we would gladly take advantage of their kind offer, and would they please get to Belgrade as quickly as possible.

I needed a modest staff for the new headquarters in Sarajevo, so Svend and I went through our list of officers and selected a few from each branch who could be spared for at least a month. In addition, we sent out the word that all who wanted to volunteer should see their boss, and if the boss agreed to let them go, they should see me.

I was pleased with the result. An overwhelming response came from the Argentine officers led by Lieutenant-Colonel de la Reta, who volunteered en masse for the assignment. I signed up all six of them, plus ten others, including Lieutenant-Colonel Anda from Norway, who would run movement control at the airport, and Lieutenant-Colonel Simon Mbogo from Kenya, who would be the senior operations officer. John Wilson would stay in Sarajevo for a while as my deputy to provide continuity; I would take along Steve Gagnon, Sergeant Traclet and Corporal Leroux to hold everything, including me, together.

I asked Police Commissioner Kjeli Johannsen from Norway to give some thought to how many of his civilian police officers he might be able to lend me for the operation. The airport building itself would have to be policed; there could be a refugee problem if local citizens stormed the airport looking for food or a way out of Sarajevo in the departing empty aircraft; and we would probably have to inspect the incoming aid when it was off-loaded, to confirm that it did not include weapons and ammunition. Our civilian police would be the obvious choice for all these tasks.

Reports from John Wilson in Sarajevo told us that the fighting was intensifying as rumours of the UN takeover of the airport circulated. Regrettably, this is a characteristic of peacekeeping assignments throughout the world: anytime there is a chance that UN action will freeze the status quo on the ground, the parties to the conflict go on a last-minute offensive to make as many territorial gains as possible before the appointed time for the ceasefire arrives. The airport agreement called for a reaffirmation of the June 1 ceasefire, and both sides were trying to improve their positions. I anticipated that both would want control of the airport so they could be the ones to hand it over to the UN. The TDF would have to conduct a large-scale infantry attack at night in order to defeat the Serbian tanks, but I doubted if they had the stomach for such an operation at that stage of their development.

JUNE 8 I knew the UN would try to restrict our force in Sarajevo to the absolute minimum for budgetary reasons. I also knew that we would be in no position to intimidate any potential opponent. After all, if the situation turned nasty and we had to make a break for the Adriatic coast, we would be some 300 kilometres from the nearest border to the west. It would be helpful, however, to be able to hold off the tanks in the area of the airport if they took to disliking us; and so I asked Canada, through the back door, to send us our Tube-Launched, Optically Controlled, Wire-Guided (TOW) anti-tank missile system, which is mounted on an armoured vehicle. It could take out any tank in Sarajevo and would provide a good boost for our soldiers' morale as they watched the Bosnian Serbs' tanks from a distance. The missiles would be able to engage the tanks long before the tanks could fire at us. I hoped the missile system wouldn't be necessary, but there was no sense taking chances.

We had had many problems getting adequate medical support for our initial deployment in March; hence I asked Canada to provide me with a complete surgical team.

The UN never did authorize us to bring the missiles for the TOW. We were authorized to bring the vehicle, as I had stressed that its night- and thermal-vision enhancement systems would be a great help in detecting any developing threats around the airport. In the end, we cheated and brought the missiles anyway. Can you imagine telling soldiers to bring the weapon but not the ammunition? We were also told we could bring mortars, but not high-explosive ammunition—only illuminating rounds to help us see at night. We ignored that order also.

We never did get our surgical team. The UN figured we could get by with a few doctors. If we sustained any serious injuries or mass casualties among our people, we would have to send them to the Bosnian hospital in Sarajevo. Obviously, people in New York were still thinking that this was conventional peacekeeping, and money shouldn't be wasted on luxuries like a full surgical team. What would happen if we became unpopular with the Bosnians? We were to find out.

JUNE 9 I handed over my Chief-of-Staff responsibilities to Svend. The cabinet was still meeting in Ottawa, expressing concerns regarding our operation. They wanted us to have more firepower; they didn't understand that too much force dooms you to confrontation and failure in a peacekeeping operation. We would have just enough if they approved what I'd requested; risk is unfortunately part of the game. I just hoped they'd approve our unit's participation soon, or we would look bad.

I did CNN and Yugoslavian TV interviews late in the afternoon. While cabinet debated, we were off to Sarajevo the next day. Everyone was generous with their best wishes.

21

The Road to Sarajevo

JUNE 10   Our advance force drove to the JNA airfield at Belgrade, but we were told that no flights were possible because of the weather. Once we'd accepted that we couldn't fly to Sarajevo, we headed off by convoy.

We made good progress until we reached an area just outside Pale, the home of Dr. Karadzic's Bosnian-Serb government. The closer we got to Pale, the more belligerent the sentries at the roadblocks became. In one case, the sentry kept muttering, "Mac-Kenzie die." This was not particularly encouraging, so I stayed in my vehicle, unidentified. Obviously there were still a few folks who hadn't heard the true story of the convoy incident.

Our passage around Pale was slow, because we had to be guided along a circuitous route that took us over the top of a mountain to the east of Sarajevo. At the very top of the mountain, we had a magnificent view of Sarajevo airport, which looked immaculate from a distance of six kilometres. So did Sarajevo itself. I decided that we would ask the Bosnian Serbs to put a radio relay antenna at that very location to support our walkie-talkie communications in Sarajevo.

On our way down the mountain into the area of southern Sarajevo and the airport, it turned dark. Just before the bottom of the last foothill, the column stopped; we could hear firing quite close to our front. There was a flurry of activity as a number of Bosnian-Serb ambulances went past us in the opposite direction. Serbian soldiers started to mill around the convoy, and one of them struck up a conversation with the driver of my vehicle. He said in perfect English to my driver, who was French, "MacKenzie won't take the airport from us. We will kill you all if you try."

My common sense was overtaken by my desire to clarify the situation. I blurted out, "Look, I'm MacKenzie, and I'm not going to take anything away from anybody. Why don't you get some of your buddies and we'll discuss it."

Within minutes, we had about twenty Bosnian-Serb soldiers around us, and I had the chance to test my theory that if you can convince a few soldiers of the facts, the word will soon get around. I explained that we were coming to Sarajevo to implement a deal signed by Dr. Karadzic and their commander, General Mladic. But if the soldiers didn't want to hand the airport over to us, it wouldn't happen; our UN force certainly wasn't strong enough to take it from them.

This attempt at logic seemed to satisfy them, but I was disturbed by some insulting references they made to Karadzic and Mladic. Their anger seemed more directed at them than me. They explained that a lot of their colleagues had been killed securing the airport, and so they shouldn't have to give it up.

The convoy started to move again. We inched forward to a large parking lot in a tiny village a few miles east of Lukavica. We had over fifty vehicles filled with supplies for John Wilson's boys, as well as our own kit, and we parked them nose to tail. Sounds of machine-gun fire were joined by the characteristic thump of 82-millimetre mortars exploding; we could see the flashes a short distance away. The TDF was shelling the surrounding area, and we were sitting in the middle.

Over the next hour, we negotiated with a couple of Mladic's officers and decided that we should proceed to their camp at Lukavica. We kept our lights off and crawled along the narrow road to the camp, where we parked our vehicles along the main street facing the front gate. If anything, the shelling was getting heavier; rounds were actually landing inside the camp.

It was impossible to get across the airport to the PTT building. The sky was alive with tracer-fire. Mortars were still landing around the camp as we bedded down for the night in one of the old JNA buildings.

As I settled into my cot and recalled the day's dangers, I realized that for the first time since I'd arrived in Yugoslavia back in March, I was really scared. That was worrisome: what we had just experienced was pretty tame, compared to the convoy incident a month earlier and the subsequent crisis at the roadblock. I wondered if I was losing my nerve. I went to sleep as the building shook every few minutes with concussions from the mortar rounds.

JUNE 11 Because of continued heavy fighting in the mornings, we were not able to move along the normal route to the PTT across the airport. A major battle was in progress in and around Dobrinja, and the Bosnian Serbs at the airport were involved.

During the delay, I had a chance to speak with Mrs. Plavsic, who drove in from Pale. She expressed optimism that the airport agreement was implementable. I suggested that she and the other Bosnian-Serb leaders had better explain that to their soldiers, since I had talked to some of them who had a distinctly different idea.

After hours of negotiations, John Wilson managed to arrange with both sides that we could enter the city from the south, crossing the Miljacka River across from the old Marshall Tito barracks. I led the convoy. Realizing too late that the roadblocks had changed during the last three weeks, I led the first ten trucks down a street that was blocked at the far end. I'd made that mistake once as a young second lieutenant, but it was embarrassing to make it as a general—particularly since somebody was entertaining himself by shooting at us while we turned around.

We finally reached the PTT around 1300 hours; for the second time in my life, I was glad to see the place. Over the past hour or so, I'd felt much more relaxed and back to my old self. I realized that moving into a dangerous situation is a little like jumping into a cold lake: it takes a while for your body to adjust to the temperature. I hadn't experienced fear in my first stay in Sarajevo because the fighting and related danger had started slowly. Last night had been different; we had been away for three weeks and then had jumped right back in. I was relieved, and enjoyed greeting all of John's team, who had endured the previous three weeks on their own. Their morale was great thanks to John's solid leadership.

At 1800 hours, John, Steve and I jumped into the VBL and went to the Presidency. During the drive downtown, I saw that about 20 per cent more of the buildings on the main route had been seriously damaged during my three-week absence. The area around the Presidency was a mess; trees and parts of buildings had been blown into the street. Across from the Holiday Inn, the Congress had been destroyed. The roof of the arena where Katarina Witt had won her gold medal for figure skating in 1984 had completely collapsed.

I met with Vice-President Ganic, who explained that he was the Presidency's representative for the implementation of the airport agreement. He immediately insisted that all Serbian artillery had to be withdrawn out of range of the city, and that Sarajevo had to be demilitarized as a matter of priority. He also stressed that I should not visit Lukavica, since the people of Sarajevo would interpret it as UN collaboration with the aggressor.

I explained to Dr. Ganic that my actions in Sarajevo would be strictly in accordance with the measures detailed in the airport agreement, which his government had signed. Anti-aircraft weapons would be moved out of range of the airport, but all other artillery, mortars, ground-to-ground missile systems and tanks within range of the airport, not the city, would be concentrated under our constant observation. Nothing in the agreement gave me the authority to order the Bosnian Serbs to move their guns out of range of the city, desirable as that might be. I stressed that if that had been the Presidency's desire, they should have included it in the agreement; however, we both agreed that the deal would never have been reached with such a prerequisite.

I pointed out to Dr. Ganic that the measures contained in the airport agreement had to be completed in sequence. The first thing we needed was a genuine ceasefire, as called for in the first paragraph of the agreement. Until we had a ceasefire, it would be impossible for me to proceed with other aspects of the plan. I also stressed that I did not like spending long periods in Lukavica, but as long as the TDF was shelling the area around the camp while I was there, it had been somewhat difficult to get about. Perhaps the next time, he would order his troops to let us into the city. Since the nearest headquarters for the Bosnian-Serb army was in Lukavica, he had to understand and accept that I would be going there on a regular basis for meetings; otherwise the airport would never reopen.

Dr. Ganic indicated that his side would fully co-operate with the UN and that he was available to me twenty-four hours a day.

At approximately 2000, after I'd returned to the PTT, the phone rang in my office-cum-bedroom. The voice at the other end had a very strong accent, which made him very hard to understand; however, I could hear him being coached in the background by a female speaking perfect English.

"General MacKenzie, I command 2,000 soldiers in Ilidza. Many of my people have died capturing the airport. If you go near the airport, we will kill you. No one will take the airport from us. We will kill all your people."

This was not exactly the "welcome wagon", but I decided I might as well talk to him: "I'm not here to take the airport away from you. Your leaders, Dr. Karadzic and General Mladic, have signed a contract with the UN to hand over the airport to us so we can bring in humanitarian aid. This is not my idea, it's yours," I said. I could hear the female translating my remarks.

"Karadzic and Mladic are fools," the voice responded. "I command the airport area and you must stay away."

Obviously I wasn't getting anywhere, so I changed my tack: "Look, why don't we get together and talk about this face-to-face? I'm prepared to come and see you, or you can be brought to the PTT."

"No, no meeting, and you stay away from the airport or you die." And with that, he hung up.

Welcome to Sarajevo, I thought. I went to bed in the "room" that Warrant Officer Traclet and Corporal Leroux had constructed with blankets suspended from wires strung between the walls adjacent to my desk.

JUNE 12 I was deluged with excited media people, who expected the airport to open tomorrow. I explained that the two sides first owed us a ceasefire, in accordance with their promises.

Later, I tried unsuccessfully to get to Lukavica to see General Mladic. Our convoy drew fire at the crossing point between the TDF and the Bosnian Serbs.

I learned Dr. Karadzic had proposed to New York that the Serbs open the airport, and that the UN take over the whole city, with a "Green Line" running down the middle of the river. Another change!

Dr. Karadzic must have visited Cyprus at some time, because he always brought up the subject of a UN Green Line. In Cyprus, the Green Line separated the Greek and Turkish Cypriots and was manned by UN peacekeepers. Karadzic saw a similar solution for Sarajevo, with his Serbs south of the Miljacka, which bisects the city from east to west, and the Muslim and Croat citizens to the north. The idea had absolutely nothing to do with the airport agreement, so I filed it away as yet another proposal that merely clouded the issue at hand.

The suggestion that the Serbs run the airport worried me a lot more. If Karadzic was serious, his army would probably try to expand their influence on the ground around the airport, which would mean more heavy fighting. The TDF controlled two villages very close to the airport, Dobrinja on the north and Butmir on the south, and would not be pushed out of them without a major and prolonged fight. I hoped I would be able to talk Karadzic into following through with the contract he had signed with Cedric.

The day ended with the much-anticipated arrival by road of the French technical team. Led by Colonels Claverie and Forestier, the technicians were well and truly augmented by over thirty excellent French marine commandos. Quite frankly, I was delighted to add the commandos to the modest French Army platoon that was providing our security. The six or so French officers of the technical team, combined with my own air-force and movement-control personnel, would give us all the technical expertise required to evaluate the airport's infrastructure. What we really needed now was more soldiers in case things turned nasty, and by the looks of them, the French commandos were ready for a scrap.

JUNE 13 I met with Dr. Karadzic and General Mladic at Lukavica. The meeting went well. In fact, later in the day, I sent a message to General Nambiar in Belgrade indicating that I thought it had gone too well.

Both Karadzic and Mladic apologized for the difficulties during our arrival in Sarajevo a few days earlier. They explained that their people were feeling very isolated and betrayed by the international community, as a result of the perceived partiality of the EC, the biased reporting of the media, and the sanctions imposed on Serbia by the UN. It was their contention that all foreigners were now mistrusted by the Bosnian Serbs, but they personally would explain our mission to their people and tell them to support us. I silently hoped they would reach my night caller from Ilidza and his "2,000 soldiers".

General Mladic agreed to accept two of my personnel who would stay at Lukavica as liaison officers between his people and mine. I explained that I would also have two liaison officers at the Presidency. He agreed to start working on a plan to concentrate his artillery and move his anti-aircraft weapons out of range of the airport, as per clause two of the airport agreement.

After stressing my concern with the scale of the continuing fighting, I was pleasantly surprised when Dr. Karadzic informed me he was declaring a unilateral ceasefire to be effective at 0600 on Monday, June 15. I indicated that we should inform the other side to give the ceasefire a chance of success, and we agreed to meet at my headquarters at 1400 the following day to discuss the details with the Presidency.

During the day, Lieutenant-Colonel Richard Gray, Michel Jones and the senior members of the French technical team met with officials of the Presidency. Gray, a New Zealander, was John Wilson's senior military observer; we had put him in charge of organizing the centralization of heavy weapons on both sides of the conflict, in accordance with the airport agreement. Colonel Siber, who was deputy commander of the TDF, produced a map showing concentric circles representing where the Presidency wanted the Bosnian-Serb artillery located. Unfortunately, they continued to demand that all artillery, missiles and mortars be moved at least twenty kilometres from the airport. It was pointed out to them, as I had explained the evening before to Vice-President Ganic, that the agreement included no such requirement. Colonel Siber was not happy.

Michel explained to the Presidency officials his plans for securing the airport and delivering aid to the downtown area. The French technical team met with some of the managers who had previously been involved in operating the airport; however, the managers hadn't been there for over three weeks, so their input was considered to be of limited value.

Shortly after returning from Lukavica, I ventured back to the Presidency with John Wilson. Vice-President Ganic expressed satisfaction regarding the level of co-operation evident throughout the meeting earlier in the day between Colonel Siber and our people, but then launched into another demand that all artillery be moved outside range of the city. I congratulated him on his persistence and spent an hour explaining that it was too late to change the agreement that he had signed along with his President.

I brought up Karadzic's intention to declare a unilateral ceasefire and asked Ganic to come to a meeting at the PTT the following day at 1400. Ganic refused to meet with Karadzic, on the grounds that the Bosnian government refused to recognize the "Serbian Republic". The Presidency would send a representative to meet with me, but not with the Bosnian Serbs.

JUNE 14 After hours of separate and seemingly fruitless bilateral discussions with the Presidency and Bosnian-Serb delegations, it was finally agreed that they would sign a ceasefire with me, but not with each other. It would go into effect at 0600 on the following day.

The Bosnian Serbs escorted our thirty-man reconnaissance party to inspect the condition of the airport at 1000. Everyone on the ground was co-operative, and our people were delighted with what they found. Contrary to previous reports, the runway, taxiways and parking aprons were damage-free. The tower equipment looked to be in pretty good shape, but it wasn't possible to check it out, since there was no electricity. The buildings were in reasonable condition, all things considered. A lot of the windows were missing and the place was a mess, but we could clean it up.

On the downside, the fire truck was unserviceable, and most of the heavy equipment required to service aircraft was damaged. There were no fuel trucks around; the condition of the underground fuel tanks was unknown. However, Michel Jones received good co-operation from the Bosnian-Serb military commanders and was promised detailed plans of the minefields and demolitions.

As a confidence-building measure, I had asked our recce team to broach the idea of moving fifty of our people to the airport on June 17. I thought that if UN personnel lived there, they would help satisfy the mounting pressure that we be seen to be moving quickly to open the airport. In addition, they would become familiar with the airport layout in detail. This would turn out to be a dumb idea, but I didn't know it at the time; unfortunately, the Bosnian Serbs agreed to go along with it.

JUNE 15 The firing died down around 0400 hours, and all went quiet at the time arranged for the ceasefire—0600. As the morning progressed, people came out of the cellars and onto the streets. The ceasefire seemed to be effective. Even the firing from the surrounding hills had stopped, and I began to think we might actually have achieved a break in the cycle of madness. But as a realist, I wasn't celebrating yet.

President Izetbegovic said he was concerned about Serbian death threats against me. He felt they were serious.

Late in the day, I had another frustrating meeting with Vice-President Ganic at the Presidency. He continued his attempts to solve all the problems of Bosnia on the back of the airport agreement. Again he wanted to demilitarize Sarajevo and move all artillery completely away from the city.

I tried once more to reason with him: "Dr. Ganic, you've got a war going on here. I know your people are suffering, and I'd love to be able to stop the fighting. But that has to be attempted one step at a time. Right now, my mandate is to try and open the airport and bring in some food and medicine to alleviate the suffering. All you could work out with Karadzic was the airport agreement. Now you won't even talk to him. Quite frankly, I don't know how you are going to resolve this war without talking to the other side. In the meantime, I'm going to try and implement the agreement that you signed. Can we please restrict our deliberations to just that?"

I didn't persuade him. I was beginning to wish that Ganic's education had been in philosophy, like mine, rather than engineering, for which he had a formidable international reputation.

When I returned to the PTT, I noticed that the international media pool surrounding us was growing exponentially every day. There were at least forty journalists patrolling the halls of our building. I recognized Martin Bell of the BBC and Christiane Amanpour of CNN, and realized that the airport story was building momentum in the outside world.

JUNE 16   We arranged to drive to Lukavica at 0900 for a meeting with Dr. Karadzic's close advisor, Professor Koljevic. The Presidency had promised an escort to the line of confrontation with the Bosnian Serbs, just 400 metres northwest of the airport terminal. The escort was two hours late, and when it arrived, its commander decided that the task was too dangerous and refused to budge. I decided that we would go anyway, so Steve and I took the lead in the VBL, dropping off the airport reconnaissance party as we passed along the runway in the direction of Lukavica.

Koljevic and I had a marathon meeting regarding the concentration of heavy weapons and our plans to move a small contingent of our personnel to the airport the following day. Koljevic indicated that he, Karadzic and Mladic were personally visiting the artillery positions to brief their personnel on the details of the airport agreement.

On the way back to the PTT, we picked up the reconnaissance party at the airport. They were pleased with the continuing level of co-operation to date and were starting to get excited about moving to the airport the following day.

Later in the day, I made a trip to the Presidency and had another unproductive session with Vice-President Ganic. He insisted that the UN had condemned the Serbs in the Security Council's most recent resolution, and therefore so should I. I countered with the fact that the UN had condemned Serbia, whereas I was dealing with the Bosnian Serbs—and had to, if the airport agreement was ever to be implemented.

Once again, I took him through the role of a peacekeeping force, which is to be objective and impartial. I explained my assessment that the Presidency was not contributing to a ceasefire by its recent actions. The Bosnian Serbs, supported by the JNA, had started the fighting around Sarajevo, but what we had to focus on now was stopping the carnage; and quite frankly, his TDF forces presented as big an obstacle as the Serbs to achieving that goal.

Ganic revisited his demand that all the artillery be moved at least twenty kilometres from Sarajevo. I listened in silence, convinced that he regretted ever having signed the airport agreement.

22

End of a Ceasefire

JUNE 17 Our magnificent forty-hour ceasefire disintegrated at 0500 hours. The PTT building shook, and the sky was illuminated by fires and explosions. Most of our people just rolled over in their cots, since they had become conditioned to the morning sounds of Sarajevo, but I decided to visit our observers on the roof.

John Wilson's observers maintained a twenty-four-hour presence on the roof of our building. From their vantage point, you could pretty well see the entire city. Their job was to determine who was doing the firing and at what targets. It wasn't an easy task; the favourite weapon on both sides was the mortar, which makes a very modest noise when it's fired. Needless to say, it was easy enough to determine what the targets were; however, that information didn't necessarily help when we were lodging protests. Both sides rarely admitted that their troops had conducted any firing, and on the rare occasions when they did, they would claim that they had been provoked.

The Old City and the airport were both giving off a strong glow, which suggested that the shelling had started some major fires. I could hear shell detonations on both sides about every ten seconds, so there was no doubt that it was an all-out exchange. I rushed back downstairs and told Steve to get the two liaison officers out of bed.

We had persuaded the Presidency and the Bosnian Serbs each to send us a liaison officer from their headquarters. We dealt with the two officers on routine matters such as POW exchanges, reconnecting and repairing the city's infrastructure, and generally any matter requiring co-ordination between the two sides. Captain Indic Milenko, an ex-JNA officer, represented the Bosnian Serbs, and Mohammed Susic represented the Presidency. The two of them got along quite well and probably achieved more between them than all other peacemaking efforts conducted in Sarajevo, including, frequently, our own. Their contributions reinforced my desire to get the sides talking to each other at the highest level. I was convinced that it was the only way to bring the conflict under a modicum of control.

The liaison officers arrived together, wiping the sleep from their eyes. I began, "I don't know what the hell is going on, but the airport agreement is about to go up in smoke—literally! Lukavica, the airport and the Old City are the prime targets, so it doesn't take a genius to see both sides are involved. Our observers on the roof tell me the firing started everywhere at about the same time—0500—so let's not waste time arguing about who started it. I want it stopped. Get on to your people and tell them I want all firing to cease at 0830."

It would take at least two hours to get the word out, provided they could persuade their leaders to agree to stop shooting. They left without saying a word.

The sixty additional observers we had requested from the UN had been borrowed from two other UN missions in Kuwait and Jerusalem. They had been gathering in Belgrade over the last few days; at mid-morning, we were told that they had departed for Sarajevo at first light. They were going to arrive in the midst of a firestorm if we didn't get the fighting stopped.

We tried all day to get to Lukavica but were unsuccessful. Although the shelling died down a bit around 0830, it was certainly not a ceasefire, even by Sarajevo standards. I spoke with President Izetbegovic and Professor Koljevic, and they both stressed that the other side had started it, and they were just defending themselves. I delayed the move of our people to live at the airport.

Just before 1800, our convoy of sixty UN observers, led by a Canadian friend and regimental colleague, Major Ray Honig, arrived on the outskirts of the city, having made the trip from Belgrade in relatively good time. They got as far as Lukavica but, as was becoming the norm, could go no further due to the intense fighting around Dobrinja and the airport. They were in civilian-type vehicles, so I told them to park at the Lukavica camp and be prepared to spend the night there if necessary.

At 2000, I received a call from General de Chastelain to say that I had been promoted to major-general effective five days earlier. He had kindly authorized the promotion six months ahead of the previously announced date, to give me some extra weight when dealing with the local military commanders. I thanked him for his confidence and joined a group of Canadian soldiers and NCOs for a drink to celebrate. Steve Gagnon presented me with a single major-general's rank badge for my flak jacket. Obviously we didn't have any official badges in Sarajevo, so Steve had cut a maple leaf from one of my brigadier's badges and sewn it onto another epaulette to create my new "two-star" rank badge. I still count it among my most prized possessions collected during thirty-three years of serving Her Majesty in the profession of arms.

Halfway through a short presentation to the corporals and privates, in which I thanked them and all their colleagues who had worked for me over the years, Steve reappeared and advised me that Mr. Doko, the Presidency's Minister of Defence, was on the phone.

I picked up the phone in the operations room: "General MacKenzie, this is Doko. You have another group of your people collaborating with the aggressor in Lukavica. If they do not leave immediately, we will shell the camp and destroy their vehicles!"

Great, I thought: my first problem as a major-general, and I don't feel any smarter or more powerful than I had before. "Mr. Doko," I replied, "that convoy is carrying the observers I need to implement the airport agreement. They have come from around the world to help you and your people. They are unarmed and driving soft-skinned vehicles. They can't get beyond Lukavica because of the fighting between you and the Serbs around the airport. I'm not prepared to have them risk their lives driving through a battle at night.

"I'm going to tell them to go into the basements of the buildings in Lukavica right now [a duty officer was speaking to our liaison officer at Lukavica on another line, keeping him up-to-date on what I was saying]. If you want to start shelling, be my guest. But rest assured that every TV station in the world will carry the story tomorrow and you will be condemned for attacking the UN. It's up to you."

During the night, Lukavica camp was indeed shelled; however, it was nothing out of the ordinary, and only a few of our vehicles were hit by shrapnel. Ray Honig and his observers had a noisy night in the basement, but no one was injured.

JUNE 18   During the morning, the shelling died down to its normal dull roar and Ray arrived with his observers at the PTT building at 1000. He had a tremendous cross-section of talent with him. There were officers from sixteen different countries, giving us an excellent reservoir of talent from which to create the team necessary to monitor the concentration of heavy weapons. John Wilson and Richard Gray kept them busy with briefings for the rest of the day. The sporadic shelling in the area of the PTT made them a restless but attentive audience.

Considering the previous evening's threat from Minister of Defence Doko, I asked for a meeting with President Izetbegovic. I made it to the Presidency at 1030 and was surprised by the news that Vice-President Ganic had been taken to the hospital with appendicitis. Ganic is a tall, dark, good-looking individual who would fit right in at any Ivy League university. He had been looking a bit under the weather the last few days; however, I thought it was probably my effect on him. I passed on my best wishes for an early recovery.

I protested the totally unacceptable threat made by the President's minister the previous night. Izetbegovic immediately apologized and explained that it had resulted from an overreaction by some soldiers on the ground. He assured me that he had total faith in our objectivity and, as a gesture of goodwill, would remove their demand that all artillery be moved twenty kilometres away from Sarajevo. I subtly reminded the President that the twenty-kilometre condition had never been a part of the airport agreement, and therefore I couldn't treat its removal as a concession; I thanked him nevertheless.

I went on to object to an official press release from the Presidency the previous day, which had accused UNPROFOR of being biased in favour of the Bosnian Serbs. I stressed the point that this type of unfair allegation would make it even harder for us to open the airport. We had already noticed that a number of the local citizens were giving us "the finger" as we drove through town. Izetbegovic promised to make a statement on Bosnian television that evening stressing his confidence in our impartiality. Later, I wished I'd asked him to make his statement on the radio; not many people had television sets operating at that point in Sarajevo.

We went on to discuss the UN personnel moving to the airport later in the day. We agreed that the move could face problems, particularly with the increased fighting around Dobrinja, but that the advantages would hopefully outweigh the disadvantages. I asked the President to ensure that all his personnel knew that we would have eighty of our people living at the airport starting tonight.

Our "sleepover" group moved to the airport at 1530. Lieutenant-Colonel Anda headed up the team that would actually operate the airport. Michel Jones took his reconnaissance party with him, and Colonels Claverie and Forestier moved in with their French soldiers, providing some security for the group. Needless to say, I was concerned about the team's safety, for they were moving into the eye of the storm. Dobrinja, the scene of heavy fighting on a regular basis, was only a hundred metres across the road from the airport.

J U N E 1 9   We received our all-too-routine wake-up call at 0500. A number of mortar rounds landed directly behind our building in the parking lot, damaging some of our vehicles. Our personnel at the airport were safe, but reported that the battle was raging around Dobrinja, and the Bosnian Serbs at the airport were firing their tanks in response to sniper fire.

Later in the day, we heard the local radio stations accuse us of shielding the Serbs as they fired at Dobrinja from the airport. Doko called again and said he had photographs of our vehicles protecting the Serb tanks as they fired. I said I would send an officer down right away to pick up copies of the photos, and if they actually showed that, I would go on local television that evening and apologize to the citizens of Dobrinja.

Doko explained that he hadn't actually seen the photos but would call me when he did. He never did see the photos, because they didn't exist; however, I was getting concerned that our presence at the airport was turning out to be counterproductive. It certainly wasn't endearing us to the Presidency's people, in spite of the fact that all our actions were designed to get the airport open so we could bring in humanitarian aid.

I spoke to our folks at the airport; they were in good spirits, and I decided to leave them there for one more night and see if things settled down.

J U N E 2 0   The usual early morning shelling was joined by tank fire. The PTT building was hit with shrapnel yet again; our windows were taking a beating.

During the day, the situation around the airport deteriorated seriously. Our people tried to raise a UN flag over the terminal building at 0928 and were fired at by snipers from across the road in Dobrinja. The Bosnian-Serb tanks at the airport started to engage Butmir to the south and Dobrinja to the north. Over fifty rounds were fired, while mortars joined in from both sides. I was fed up and proceeded to make one of the dumbest decisions of my career.

I sent a letter to President Izetbegovic and Dr. Karadzic advising them both as follows: "I intend to withdraw my personnel from the airport as soon as possible. I am terminating all preparation and efforts to open the Sarajevo airport for the delivery of humanitarian aid until there is at least forty-eight hours of continuous ceasefire. Every time there is a breach of the ceasefire, the forty-eight-hour clock will be reset to zero. I cannot impose the ceasefire. That is your responsibility. I suggest you both stop fighting now. When you do, I will start the forty-eight-hour clock."

A press conference was called where I advised the media of my ultimatum to the two leaders.

Following the press conference, I drove to the airport to congratulate our people and thank them for tolerating such an awkward situation. Leading the convoy in a VBL back towards the PTT and past the Rainbow Hotel, I heard the impact of a number of mortar rounds about a hundred metres to our rear. The visibility of the VBL to the rear is very limited, but from what I could see, everyone looked okay. I did, however, notice a jeep pull off to the side just as we turned the corner leading to the PTT.

Five minutes later, I received a report that Major Peter Devlin's jeep had been hit by shrapnel. Major Devlin commanded "N" Company of the Royal Canadian Regiment, which was one of the two large rifle companies in the Van Doos battle group. His driver, Corporal Gordon, had been seriously injured in his left knee but had managed to drive their jeep out of the impact area, in spite of the fact that all their tires, including the rear mounted spare, had been cut to shreds by the flying metal. Major Devlin and the third passenger in the vehicle, Lieutenant Dray, had also been hit, but fortunately their wounds were superficial. We didn't realize how lucky they had been until we saw their jeep. Corporal Gordon was evacuated to our Canadian base in Lahr, Germany, the next day.

Just after lunch, we received word that the American photo-journalist, Jana Schneider, and her colleague, a well-known Sloven-ian reporter, Ivo Standeker, had been engaged by machine-gun fire from a tank as they moved in the open just north of Dobinja. I had met Jana the previous day and was impressed by her dedication and "balls", bordering on foolhardiness. She was a survivor of many conflicts, including the war in Afghanistan, and her photos have appeared on the covers of *Newsweek* and other leading magazines. I remember telling her as she left my office, "Jana, you'll be dead or famous. Be careful."

It was not twenty-four hours later, and Jana was now in my medical centre with half her foot blown off; her colleague, Ivo, was dead. We transferred her to the Kosovo hospital, but when we checked a few hours later, their staff had still not given her the antibiotics we had sent along, so we brought her back to our facility. We weren't supposed to hold non-UN personnel, but some of the rules didn't seem terribly important by now.

Jana was distraught at the idea that we might evacuate her without the body of Ivo, so I promised her I would do what I could. I called Colonel Cadjo at Lukavica and asked him to arrange to move Ivo's body to Pale for the helicopter flight out of the war zone the next day.

The shelling finally died down around 2200, coinciding with a call from Barbara McDougall, Canada's Secretary of State for External Affairs. Mrs. McDougall was on her car phone between Toronto and Ottawa and wanted to wish us all well as we sought to open the airport. I thanked her for the call, making a mental note that she was the first Canadian politician to have made such an effort. It was the first time I'd realized that we hadn't heard from the Minister of National Defence, Marcel Masse.

JUNE 21 I sat up in my cot around midnight and realized that everything was completely quiet. For a few seconds, I thought it might just be a good dream, but I started my forty-eight-hour countdown anyway and went back to sleep.

We had arranged for a JNA helicopter to fly to Pale to evacuate our more serious casualties and Lieutenant-Colonel Anda. I was sending Anda back to Norway on leave. Based on his holiday arrangements made before we'd returned to Sarajevo, he had rented a cottage for a few weeks on the Norwegian coast, and his family was already there. None of us is ever indispensable, so I insisted he take his leave as previously planned. His deputy, Commandant Hauben from Belgium, would take his place in the interim. In fact, a disappointed Colonel Anda was never able to get back to Sarajevo, and consequently Commandant Hauben ran the show at the airport. I don't know if Anda ever forgave me.

I was also sending Thomas Jarnahed to Belgrade for some well-deserved rest. As ever, Thomas had been our eyes and ears around Sarajevo and as a result had been putting himself in considerable danger. I needed his expertise and advice, but to have that, I needed him in one piece, so I decided to give him a break.

Jana Schneider, Corporal Gordon, Colonel Anda, Thomas and a young Serbian boy made their way to Pale under difficult circumstances. Jana was delirious, and her escort was afraid her heart might stop a second time, as it had the previous evening in the PTT medical facility. But they all made it okay; and thanks to Colonel Cadjo, Ivo's body was already waiting on the helicopter.

JUNE 22   An UNPROFOR delegation was scheduled to meet with President Izetbegovic at 1100. We were two minutes late and arrived to witness a scene of carnage that will always be with me.

At 1101, mortars landed directly in front of the Presidency's main entrance, where we normally dismounted from our vehicles. Fourteen people were killed, including elderly citizens and children. Some were still alive as we arrived. One man was trying to drive away in his old Mercedes; his right leg was missing, and his stomach was terribly mutilated. The blood was literally pouring out of the open door of his car as he tried to get the vehicle to move. Mercifully, he died a few seconds later. His car was still there when we left the building after our meeting; the wide path of dried blood from the car to the sidewalk was a graphic reminder of the horror and senselessness of the civil war.

Ambulances were at the scene just after we arrived, so we went straight to the President's office. There was no evidence to suggest that the tragedy was anything but a Bosnian-Serb attack, and I therefore expressed my condolences to President Izetbegovic on yet more loss of life among his people.

I opened the meeting by objecting to a particularly damning article in *The New York Times*, based on statements made by Defence Minister Doko. It contained a number of outright fabrications that placed UNPROFOR in a bad light.

A few days earlier, I had told the President that a convoy of thirty-eight trucks belonging to the UN High Commissioner for Refugees (UNHCR) had gone missing somewhere in eastern Bosnia. The afternoon of that same day, the convoy had shown up at the PTT. According to Minister Doko, the trucks had not been missing, but had been given to the Bosnian Serbs in Lukavica and used to transport Serbian soldiers to Butmir. Doko had alleged that the trucks' white-and-black UN markings had given the Serbs freedom of movement.

I explained as carefully as I could to a shocked Izetbegovic, "Here is a perfect example of disinformation, Mr. President. The convoy in question arrived at the PTT two days ago, off-loaded its food and left the same day. The vehicles were not white, they were a cross-section of colours, and the only markings on them were blue UNHCR decals in the windows. Now, as a result of Mr. Doko's accusations, your people think we are providing logistics support to the Bosnian Serbs!"

Izetbegovic looked at Doko, and Doko looked at the TDF deputy commander, Colonel Siber. Siber didn't have anyone to look at so he stared at the table.

Doko explained that he had received bad information from his military and apologized for the misunderstanding. I found myself feeling a bit sorry for them. After all, they hadn't started the fighting in and around Sarajevo; at this point they were just trying to survive. If survival meant manipulating the media and world opinion to obtain help, I could accept that. What I couldn't understand was their obvious desire to vilify UNPROFOR. It just didn't make sense.

I continued: "Look, gentlemen, for some reason that only you understand, you are convinced that I and my troops are pro-Serb. I can tell you that is not the case, but you won't believe me. We are not here to pass judgment on what is going on. We send objective reports to the UN every day. It's the UN's job to identify the culprits. Our job is to open the airport and ensure the delivery of food and medicine. To do that, we have to negotiate with you and the Bosnian Serbs. If you can't live with that, then my role as a negotiator is impossible.

"I need your co-operation, such as we are getting in our discussions concerning the concentration of heavy weapons. I also need you to tone down the anti-UNPROFOR rhetoric in the media. My command is committed to doing everything within our capability and our mandate to assist the people of Sarajevo, but we can't succeed without your co-operation."

Every time I made a pitch like this one, I had the distinct feeling that President Izetbegovic believed me and accepted that I was impartial. On the other hand, I never had the same impression regarding Vice-President Ganic or Minister Doko. Izetbegovic promised to keep working on improving our image.

THE PREVIOUS DAY, I had decided to send Michel Jones and his reconnaissance team, less a liaison detachment that would remain at our headquarters, back to his unit in Croatia. Michel had completed all preparations for the security of the airport and the delivery of aid, and it made sense to give him some time with his battalion to fine-tune their preparations for coming to Sarajevo. In addition, I felt good about the idea of his personally leading the battalion on the road from Croatia to Sarajevo—if the move was ever approved by Ottawa.

It was also my intention to send the French technical team to Belgrade for reorganization. Colonels Claverie and Forestier had done a great job of evaluating the airport infrastructure and technical requirements; however, they were organized more to duplicate Michel's security task than to take on the technical running of the airport. I was delighted to have their marine commandos for security, but unfortunately the PTT was bursting at the seams.

The building was designed to look after a work force of around 200, whereas we had over 300 living there, twenty-four hours a day. There was only a toilet or two on each floor, and frequently they were out of order, or the water was cut off. We had had a couple of simple showers installed; however, it had meant sacrificing an equal number of toilets, since we'd converted the stalls and plumbing. We tried to avoid using the upper floors of the building because of sniper fire and shelling, and preferred to work and sleep in the offices on the north side, in order to stay away from the main road and potential car bombs. Hence we were crowded, to say the least. Most of the soldiers from the French technical team, the French headquarters company and the Canadian reconnaissance party slept underground in the basement or parking lot. The rest of us slept on the floors of our offices.

With so few showers, they were in use all day. I found the best routine was to get up around 0530 and slip across the hall; most other people preferred to shower before they went to bed, in order to gain a few extra minutes of sleep in the morning. Normally I too love to sleep, and can spend all morning in bed quite happily, but for the first time in my life, I found that four or five hours' sleep was more than adequate; I never seemed to get tired. What made this discovery even more surprising was the combination of lack of sleep with a pack of cigarettes a day and irregular meals. I should have been tired and irritable, but I'd never felt better in my life. It must have been the constant trickle of adrenalin through my system. There was always some emergency: firing at or around you, meetings with the leadership of the combatants, driving through insecure areas, the responsibility for soldiers' lives, or something as relatively straightforward as a press conference. They all produced their own adrenalin kick and, thank God, I always felt alert.

DURING THE AFTERNOON, I met with Dr. Karadzic and Professor Koljevic at the airport. I pointed out in no uncertain terms that the Bosnian Serbs were guilty of an unreasonable and unwarranted scale of retaliation. I acknowledged that the TDF was initiating some exchanges of fire, but blowing a house or an apartment building to pieces with tank fire in response to sniper fire was not the way to sell their case to the world. If they kept up these actions, I would be forced to go public with my condemnation; in the meantime, I would report my observations to General Nambiar, with copies to UN New York.

Professor Koljevic promised to take up the matter with their military leadership.

Finally, I asked for Dr. Karadzic's assistance to evacuate a television journalist, Faridoun Hermani. Arrangements were made, and Faridoun left with our convoy to Belgrade on June 24.

Steve and I returned to the PTT and prepared a message to New York, an excerpt from which follows:

To: NAMBIAR
From: MACKENZIE
Date: 22 JUNE 1992
Subject: FAULT FINDING

1) Until now UNPROFOR in Sarajevo has gone to great pains to give the impression of impartiality. The situation in Sarajevo is so confusing that it is actually easy to say that we do not know who fired at us or who started a particular altercation.

2) We, like most, are under the impression that the President wants massive military intervention to give him back his country and his capital (and unfortunately, comments in the media attributed to Mr. Bush give him cause for optimism in the realization of his dream) whereas Dr. Karadzic wants territory with the UN manning a Green Line through Sarajevo and Bosnia-Herzegovina.

3) It appears that Dr. Karadzic is making more progress in the pursuit of his aim than the President is. The Serbs have the means and, based on their tactical theory of "Never send a man

where a tank or artillery round can go first", they have made significant territorial gains in the municipality of Dobrinja just across the road from the airport. At that location, they have used their tanks against individual houses and apartment buildings. (FACT). As they secure buildings they are *allegedly* herding the population off to detainment centres. Certainly the TDF has initiated some skirmishes and have fired some mortars and perhaps (inherited) artillery into the main Serb army base southeast of the airport. Retaliation, however, has been well out of proportion, with the Serbs shelling non-military targets in the city, including the Presidency.

4) As long as just one side does not see the strategic benefit of a ceasefire, the fighting will continue and we will watch the conflict from the PTT, making occasional forays to the two sides to keep up to date. In the meantime, it appears that the Presidency has condoned an information campaign to discredit UNPROFOR. (As a result [?] the Muslim death threats to yours truly now outnumber the Serb death threats 3 to 2!)

Heavy shelling continued throughout the night. The nightmare I had started with my forty-eight-hour ceasefire ultimatum continued to haunt all of us. Every time an artillery round landed or a machine-gun fired, our phones would ring off the hook with calls from the international media both in Bosnia and abroad. (Don't ask me how the reporters outside Sarajevo discovered so quickly that a few rounds had been fired.) The question was always the same: "What time is it on General MacKenzie's forty-eight-hour clock?"

We decided the best response was, "That's between him and the Security Council." Fortunately, it worked, and the calls dried up within twenty-four hours. I was relieved that I wouldn't be reminded every few minutes of what had turned out to be a lousy idea.

JUNE 23   We made our first trip to the Bosnian-Serb headquarters at Pale, to see Professor Koljevic. Pale is a picturesque Austrian-style village about seventeen kilometres over a major mountain range from Sarajevo. It should have been a thirty-minute drive from the PTT by armoured personnel carrier, but took between three and four hours over a makeshift new road. The main route was too close to the line of confrontation to be passable.

I had a short meeting with Koljevic and Mrs. Plavsic, advising them that they might be winning the war but were losing the media battle. If they didn't stop the shelling and tank fire, they had better be prepared for a major confrontation with the international community. This wasn't a threat; it was merely my personal opinion. As far as I was concerned, we should start with the airport and get it opened as quickly as possible.

Fabrizio Hochschild, the new chief of the UN High Commissioner for Refugees in Sarajevo, had accompanied our delegation and wound up the meeting by discussing procedures for delivery of food once it arrived at the airport. UNHCR would control the scheduling of aircraft into the airport from their office in Geneva. UNPROFOR would operate and secure the airport and land corridors, and UNHCR would look after all the technical aspects related to the actual distribution of the aid. Fabrizio was a young, likeable and highly competent UN officer. We established a good working relationship right off the bat, and I would like to believe the people who said the co-operation between our two organizations was the best the UN had ever experienced in any of its previous peacekeeping missions over the past forty years.

On the way back to Sarajevo, there was a light rain, and our progress was even slower than during our trip out. As we approached one of the Bosnian-Serb checkpoints, I tried to peer between the legs of the French commander of the armoured personnel carrier. We were travelling in the APC rather than the armoured car, because of the size of our group. I was at the very front of the passenger compartment, which was up against a crawlway leading to the crew commander's seat beside the driver. The only way you could see forward out of the vehicle, from my location, was by glancing around or between the driver's legs when he stood on his seat in order to look out his hatch.

I could see movement in the trees. Someone was moving towards the checkpoint with a tubular object resting on his shoulder and pointed in our direction. I immediately thought it might be an anti-tank weapon, so I turned to everyone in the vehicle. I hesitated—what do you tell people in the back of an APC that is about to be fired at? They can't "get down" or leave, so I just stared at them with a hollow feeling in the pit of my stomach.

What followed was horrifying. There was a loud noise and the APC shook; everyone was knocked to the front of the vehicle, and I was thrown along the crawlway up against the crew commander's legs. I kept looking for the flash and explosion from the missile inside the vehicle. There was none; an eerie silence had followed the bang.

One of our French soldiers crawled back to the rear door and lifted the metal shield over its bullet-proof window. He couldn't see outside because the following APC had smashed into us when its brakes had failed and was now fused to our posterior. My anti-tank missile attack had been a standard run-of-the-mill vehicle accident.

I glanced out the driver's window and saw my would-be attacker carrying a small log on his shoulder . . . .

MUCH TO MY SURPRISE, when I met with President Izetbegovic later in the day following our five-hour journey from Pale, only he and his daughter, Sabina, were present. The usual entourage was noticeably absent; I never did discover why.

I told the President that I would like to try to get some food into Dobrinja. The last attempt had resulted in the death of a volunteer Bosnian driver; now, a few weeks had passed, and although a few residents made daring attempts under cover of darkness to sneak out of the area in order to obtain food, it was a very dangerous undertaking. Since most of the residents were in no position to even try to get food, we should send some in. After a lengthy discussion, the President agreed that we should start making arrangements for a relief convoy to Dobrinja.

I broached the subject of yet another ceasefire. Undiplomatically, I pointed out that there were two agendas at work in Bosnia, and unfortunately, they would never coincide. The Bosnian Serbs wanted their own state with a Green Line, manned by the UN, separating them from the rest of the Bosnians; whereas there were strong indicators that he, the President, wanted international military intervention.

At this point, Sabina hid her face in her hands while her father looked shocked. After a few minutes of talking around the subject, the President admitted that he wanted military intervention but did not expect to get it. We agreed that he had a better chance of discovering oil in downtown Sarajevo.

It was a pathetic joke, but we all laughed and felt a little better, knowing that the tragedy had not entirely robbed us of our ability to smile once in a while.

23

From Peacekeeper to
War Criminal

━━━━━

JUNE 24 Our weekly convoy from Belgrade had been stopped
the previous afternoon and had been forced to spend the night
beside the road in Bosnian-Serb-controlled territory. The convoy
personnel were in good shape nevertheless, and I was delighted to
receive a medical advisor, Major Vanessa Lloyd-Davies from the
U.K. My request for a surgical team had been turned down by the
UN, which both surprised and disappointed me. I hoped that if a
second request came from a highly qualified medical officer like
Vanessa, the UN authorities would change their minds. The potential
for mass casualties remained high, so a surgical team could be
invaluable.

As the convoy prepared to return to Belgrade, I said farewell to
John Wilson. He had been a marvellous deputy and a pillar of
strength. John was a natural leader, and everyone had a tremendous
amount of respect for him. He was returning to our headquarters
in Belgrade, where he would once again command all the officer
observers in UNPROFOR.

John was replaced by Colonel Vitali Petrounev from Russia,
UNPROFOR's senior liaison officer in Belgrade. Most of our dealings
with the JNA and the Serbian authorities in Belgrade went through
him; he was to be attached to my headquarters for at least a couple
of months. Vitali was a tough, experienced infantry officer who had
served in Afghanistan. His English was perfect and, not only that,
he had served with the UN Truce Supervisory Organization a few
years earlier in the Middle East. At that stage, I did not know Vitali
very well; however, our short but exciting time together would
make us close friends for life.

Michel Jones and his reconnaissance team departed to marry up with their battalion of Van Doos in Croatia. The unit's morale had been lagging due to the delays in their deployment to Sarajevo. Their commanding officer's return would be a boost to their spirits, and Michel would be able to use his experience in Sarajevo, particularly at the airport, to get them well and truly ready for their mission.

I also said goodbye to Colonel Claverie and Colonel Forestier, who headed up the French technical team. They had done a fine job working with Michel on the security plans for the airport and would now join some new French technical personnel who had arrived in Belgrade. They would return to Sarajevo just as soon as it appeared likely we would take over the airport—if that ever happened.

Around noon, I received an urgent call from Professor Koljevic, who wanted to meet with me at the Sarajevo airport. I disliked announcing the timing of my movements over the telephone, which we knew was monitored. Since Koljevic was a Shakespearean scholar, I decided to try a very low-level code. "Professor Koljevic," I said, "Shakespeare wrote a well-known play for a day of the year which occurred only three days ago. Write the title on a piece of paper."

There was a pause, followed by "Okay—I've written it."

"Professor, I'll give you some letters in the title. Just count the letters starting with the first one as zero, and I'll pass on the time we can meet. For example, in your name, K would be zero, O would be one, L would be two, do you understand?"

"I've got it," he replied.

For the next ten minutes, we tried to make the system work, but to no avail. Frustrated, I asked, "How many words does your title have?"

"Two," he answered.

"That's impossible, Professor. This play was written for the evening of the twenty-first of June, the longest day of the year—does that help?"

"Afraid not," he said.

Obviously my attempt to set a meeting time by using *A Midsummer Night's Dream* as code wasn't going to work. "I'll see you at the airport at 1600," I blurted out.

The Professor was quite excited when we met. He informed me that the Bosnian Serbs were unilaterally declaring that their artillery would no longer shell downtown Sarajevo, and that henceforth they would target only those military forces threatening their positions.

Koljevic assured me that Dr. Karadzic was personally visiting their gun positions as we spoke, passing the orders on to their artillery commanders.

As we appeared to be on a roll, I asked Colonel Tolimir, a very professional ex-JNA officer, if he would consider moving all their artillery at least fifteen kilometres away from Sarajevo. Artillery is just as effective at maximum range as sitting on a hill overlooking a city; therefore such a move would not degrade their operational ability, but would have a tremendously positive effect on public morale in Sarajevo, and might even result in a breakthrough in my attempts to arrange a dialogue between the Presidency and the Bosnian Serbs. Tolimir didn't take the bait, offering instead a number of technical objections. We did agree, however, to accelerate the concentration of heavy weapons, which was already proceeding quite well under Richard Gray's guidance.

Following the main meeting, Pofessor Koljevic asked to see me in private. He indicated that they were having a hard time persuading their military to go along with unilateral gestures in support of the airport agreement. He requested that I give maximum publicity to this new declaration regarding the shelling of Sarajevo. I agreed to do so, pointing out that he had better ensure that the shelling did stop; otherwise, both of us would look very foolish indeed.

I immediately rushed to President Izetbegovic's office. I advised him of the Bosnian Serbs' declaration and my intention to hold a press conference the following day, to put pressure on them to live up to their promises. Izetbegovic was skeptical, as unfortunately was I, but he strongly supported the idea of a press conference to be conducted as soon as possible.

"I will arrange it for tomorrow morning, Mr. President," I said. "In fact, it would have even more impact if I had a similar agreement from your side to engage only military targets."

In peacekeeping, you always try to get matching concessions without the belligerents' knowing it. Frequently, this tactic lets one side to a conflict step back from a confrontation without losing face, provided it appears to be a UN initiative they are accepting, and not a demand from the other side. I hadn't played this card particularly well, however, since I had told the President that the Bosnian Serbs had initiated the gesture. After a few seconds of thought, he would commit himself only to speaking to his military leadership later that evening. I was disappointed that I hadn't handled the opportunity better.

Just before I left his office, President Izetbegovic brought up the subject of the Bosnian Olympic team and its safe passage out of Bosnia en route to the 1992 Olympic Games in Barcelona. This query had been with my staff for weeks. We had told the President's office that Dr. Karadzic insisted on receiving a letter from the Presidency requesting free and safe passage through Serbian lines; if such a letter were received, co-operation would be given. The President steadfastly refused to send any such letter to Dr. Karadzic, since this would be tantamount to recognizing the "Bosnian Serb Democratic Republic".

I explained to President Izetbegovic that the UN had no mandate to get involved in such matters, apart from arranging agreements between the two sides. It was his decision. If he did not intend to send a letter requesting safe passage, there was nothing else I could do, apart from suggesting he contact the International Olympic Committee.

As usual, on a day when we had a new batch of folks in the PTT from the weekly Belgrade convoy, we went to sleep rocked by the sound of heavy shelling.

JUNE 25 At 1000 hours, we told the world that the Bosnian Serbs had agreed to stop shelling civilian targets in and around Sarajevo. It was also announced that the Serbs would have all their heavy weapons concentrated by 1400 on June 29. I was still skeptical that the Serbs would keep either promise, but at least the glare of international publicity would put pressure on them to try.

On our way to Pale for another meeting with the Bosnian-Serb leadership, we were accompanied by a three-man team from Médecins sans Frontières (MSF), the French humanitarian organization founded by French cabinet minister Bernard Kouchner. They were extremely nervous, and rightly so, as the airport was a dangerous area, and we had to drive along the runway to get to Lukavica en route to Pale. In a moment of weakness, three of us lent their party our flak jackets. I told the team leader that I couldn't escort his party officially, but he should stay close to our armoured personnel carrier, since it would provide them some protection. The Canadian Broadcasting Corporation's television reporter, Anna-Maria Tremonti, asked if she could accompany us to Pale and I agreed, telling her to stay glued to the back of our small convoy.

At the eastern end of the airport runway, we were fired on by a TDF machine-gun position in Butmir. A few rounds bounced off our VBL, and our Bosnian-Serb escort fired back. I checked in the rearview mirror; everyone was still with us, so we kept moving until we reached Lukavica about five minutes later.

On arrival, the MSF team was in rough shape and qualified in my book for the Sarajevo "Luckiest People of the Month" award. Their civilian-type 4×4 had been hit by machine-gun fire from the side; the windows were shattered, and bullets were imbedded in the dashboard and door. But apart from some minor glass cuts, everyone was okay. The team decided to wait in Lukavica until things cooled down a bit, since we were told that the next leg of our trip to Pale might be subjected to fire also. We recovered our flak jackets from three very appreciative individuals. I must admit I was developing a healthy respect for the MSF organization.

At Pale, we met with Professor Koljevic and Mrs. Plavsic. I told them it was a good thing my press conference had been held that same morning, rather than the previous night, since the Bosnian Serbs had hammered Dobrinja all night, and what little credibility they had left would have disappeared. I stressed that they had better live up to their promises and stop shelling civilian targets in Dobrinja immediately.

Professor Koljevic responded by saying that they intended to secure Dobrinja in order to facilitate the opening of the airport. I was shocked, to say the least. "Professor, if your side kills people in order to help the UN secure the airport, there is no way we would associate ourselves with such an operation. You have pledged yourselves to a ceasefire. The best way to help the UN is by enforcing the ceasefire on your side. Let *us* worry about Dobrinja. Hopefully, we can work out a deal to demilitarize the entire area. If we don't, I doubt if many pilots will fly into that mess in the first place."

I broached the question of the Bosnian Olympic team's passage out of Bosnia. Koljevic replied that, given the UN sports embargo on Serbia and Montenegro as part of UN sanctions, it would be difficult to convince their people that the Bosnian team should be allowed to participate in Barcelona. If, however, he was to receive a formal request from the Bosnian government, he might be able to react positively. This continuing debate over a letter was becoming tedious; but, considering that the former Yugoslavia was one of the best athletic nations in the world for their size, I realized just how important sports were to the national psyche. The economic sanctions on Serbia seemed to have had far less impact than banning their soccer team from defending its title at the European Cup championships in Denmark.

Within hours, we arrived at the Presidency. I immediately launched into a discussion of the situation in Dobrinja and was disappointed to hear President Izetbegovic say, "We want to control all of Dobrinja!" Great, I thought: both sides had declared on the same day that they wanted to control the same area of town, which currently housed some 27,000 people located across the road from the airport. This had the potential to be a show-stopper.

The President indicated that he would consider a demilitarization plan for Dobrinja, whereby it would be placed under un control. I responded that in due course this might be considered, but it would take at least a month to bring in the necessary additional un troops, and therefore we should get on with implementing the ceasefire that he and Karadzic had signed as part of the airport agreement.

I advised the President that his forces were still firing on our vehicles from the area of Butmir. They had struck the MSF vehicle earlier in the day; our Bosnian-Serb escort had fired back, as had we. I explained that we could not let the perception develop that the UN was being protected by the Bosnian Serbs as we drove through their area. I had therefore decided to cancel any future UN trips to Pale, and from now on, we would meet with the Bosnian-Serb leadership in Lukavica and would drive there without escort. "If we are to have any chance whatsoever of improving the situation in Sarajevo, we have to talk to both sides. You have to get a firm grip on your people and convince them to stop shooting at us," I demanded.

I gave the President the less than encouraging news about his Olympic team's passage out of Bosnia and departed, convinced we were moving backwards in our attempts to open the airport. When I returned to my office, Steve and I prepared a message to Nambiar and Goulding, which included the following comments:

> I fear we have a major crisis on our hands with Dobrinja. Both sides admit they want it. Perhaps we should fold our hands and wait for one of them to call us when it has been decided who won. I advised both sides that they pledged a ceasefire, and therefore fighting over Dobrinja while we struggled with the airport agreement was a major breach of faith. I would appreciate advice on my point that if the Serbs continue to hammer Dobrinja and secure the municipality killing a large number of people in the process, thereby controlling the entire area around the airport, the UN would not probably want to be

associated with any subsequent opening of the airport under such conditions.

Likewise, the President said that his side wanted Dobrinja under their control unless it could be demilitarized and manned by "blue helmets". I am very concerned that both sides intend to fight for Dobrinja and will not be satisfied until the battle is over one way or the other. No matter what the outcome, the un will not be pleased and will be put in a very awkward position.

Perhaps the next step will be to terminate the preparations for the airport opening (we are getting nowhere—in fact, our initiatives have increased the fighting around the airport, particularly in Dobrinja) and to insist that no additional efforts will be undertaken until the two main political sides sit down at the same table.

JUNE 26 This was another day, as I noted in my diary, competing for the honour of being the worst in my life.

Intensive shelling started early in the morning around 0200. All areas of the city were targeted, particularly Dobrinja. At 0700, I received a fax from "Citizens of Dobrinja", who wished me to be tried as a war criminal. I read it twice, wondering how they could so misunderstand our actions and our mandate, which were designed to help all citizens of Sarajevo but seemed to be having the opposite effect:

> General MacKenzie,
>
> We want you to know that we, citizens of Dobrinja, residential area of Sarajevo, will start collecting signatures of our fellow citizens on a document which will bring you to the court.
>
> We all were spending last night and are spending this morning in the basements, because Dobrinja is being constantly shelled and bombed by the Serbian heavy artillery and tanks (located at the Sarajevo airport), in spite of Serbian self-announced unilateral ceasefire which you (again!) declared yesterday, pointing out so proudly that they will stop shelling and destroying Presidential areas. However, knowing you very well now, we're inclined to believe that you will now make a statement in which you will say that "both sides are responsible". . . .
>
> We don't have the proofs that you have been bribed by the Serbian terrorists (which is what they do with everyone

they need on their side), but we don't see any other reason for your disgusting behaviour.

Nevertheless, you, General MacKenzie, are responsible for dozens of civilians killed in the area of Dobrinja only, and we hope that you will be prosecuted accordingly.

That signed document will be sent to all international institutions and bodies which will have to question you for the murder. All the major news agencies will have a copy as well. Thousands of signatures on that document, including our Serbian neighbours, will confirm that this is not an "ethnic war," as you're trying to put it all the time, giving the Serbian side more room to continue killing civilians and destroying their homes.

We also have eye-witnesses who will sign a document which proves that your UN cars and soldiers were collecting dead bodies of Serbian terrorists in our area, while the bodies of civilians and defenders were left behind.

We are very much disappointed that a person like you ever came to our city of Sarajevo.

Citizens of Dobrinja (Sarajevo)

I made a quick trip to the Presidency and advised Izetbegovic that I was on my way to the airport to meet with the Bosnian Serbs to protest the shelling.

At the airport, Koljevic was distraught. Clearly, in my view, they had painted themselves into a corner and didn't know how to get out. He claimed they were being provoked by the TDF and were retaliating. I protested that even if that were true, the Bosnian Serbs were retaliating on a scale out of all responsible proportion to the provocation. Moreover, they were completely ignoring their promise not to shell civilian targets, and I would so advise New York. Koljevic agreed that they would stop shelling Dobrinja. I responded that I was certainly not going to pass that statement on to the international media.

We made our way back to the Presidency, where I briefed Izetbegovic on our protest to the Bosnian Serbs. Both of us were having a bad day, so our meeting was mercifully short.

I vented my frustration by sending a strongly worded message to Nambiar and Goulding:

1) After last night's activities I am convinced that the Serbs

intend to secure all of Dobrinja. They increased their bombardment of the area. Tank, infantry attacks were carried out and heavy artillery was used against the population. The Presidency responded with attacks on Ilidza and Lukavica. The fact remains that the Serbs have the ability to control the situation due to their overwhelming firepower and they are using it. Everything that happened in the Dobrinja area last night and this morning was contrary to their unilateral assurances of 24 June.

2) I would appreciate guidance regarding my assumption that the UN will not associate itself with the airport if the Serbs secure Dobrinja. The desire by the Serbs to control the area around the airport is resulting in some of the bloodiest fighting of the war. We are impotent to stop it. A strong political message is required, and soon, otherwise, Dobrinja will be a bloodbath on the conscience of the world.

3) The Serbs have warned us that the "Green Berets" of the TDF will shell our HQ at 1930 today and will try and make it look like the Serbs did it. We will speak to appropriate Presidency authorities today and will do an emergency "drill" tonight at 1900 hrs.

4) I am even more convinced that a ceasefire is impossible while the fate of Dobrinja is being decided. Somebody has to get through into the mind and conscience of both Mladic and Karadzic—obviously I have not.

Considering what was happening to the city, I took the threat against our headquarters seriously. I always hated it when one side told us that the other side would attack us and would then make it appear that their enemies were responsible. That meant one of two things: either the side that had warned us was, in fact, going to attack us and make it look as if the other side had done it; or the other side *was* going to attack us. The only thing for sure was that the chances of being attacked were fairly good.

I didn't want to upset everyone over what might be a false alarm. So I only advised a few key people and told my operations officer, Simon Mbogo, to organize an "emergency" drill, which would put everyone in our bunker between 1900 and 2000.

Fortunately, we had a quiet hour together that evening, with only a few of us waiting for an attack that never came. I made use of the opportunity to announce Sergeant Traclet's promotion to warrant officer. We had a captive audience.

JUNE 27   The time for the Bosnian Serbs' unilateral restriction of their fire to military targets arrived at 0700, concurrent with a significant reduction of shelling in the city. Throughout the day, we received five reports of the TDF shelling Serbian positions. The Serbs reported that they were taking casualties but were not firing back; this was confirmed by some of our people who were visiting their positions, in preparation for the concentration of heavy weapons. I was upset that the Presidency was not taking advantage of the opportunity to reduce the scale of the fighting and so advised President Izetbegovic and General Nambiar. I also prepared a letter to the President, calling on him to reconsider his refusal to meet with the leadership from the other side:

> President Izetbegovic,
>
> At this stage of the conflict, we appear to have at least a possibility of achieving a ceasefire due to the Serbs restricting the use of their heavy weapons and their commitment to concentrate them by the 29th of June 1992.
>
> What is now required is a dialogue between the Presidency and the Serbs to work out the details. The use of UNPROFOR as a go-between has resulted in painfully slow and relatively superficial negotiations.
>
> In order for UNPROFOR to meaningfully contribute to the peace process in and around Sarajevo, permit me to suggest that the Presidency agree to direct contact with the civilian leadership on the other side regarding the establishment of a proper ceasefire.
>
> As a soldier, I am not involved in the politics of the conflict. I understand that you consider the other side the aggressor; however, it is a war no matter what its categorization, and for a war to stop, there must ultimately be negotiation. This could well be the time or we could slide once again into an all-out confrontation. I solicit your consideration of direct talks and maintain my standing offer of placing UNPROFOR Sarajevo headquarters at your disposal for any and all meetings with the other side.
>
> L.W. MacKenzie
> Major-General
> Sector Commander

At approximately 1900 hours, we FAXed my letter off to President Izetbegovic. I suspected that it would, if anything, be counter-productive, since the President would resent my proposal; however, I felt I had no choice but to confirm my desired option in writing.

UNFORTUNATELY, THE ELECTRICITY was off again. As I walked down the hall to Steve's office, I heard a commotion in the operations room and was nearly bowled over by a French soldier running up the hall in the direction of his colonel's office. As he went, I thought I heard him say, in French, "The President is coming!"

After almost four months in Bosnia, the title of "President" immediately brought to mind President Izetbegovic. For a moment I was dismayed he would try to reach our headquarters so close to darkness, but if that was his intention, at least we would have a chance to debate the current issues on my turf.

Colonel Forestier emerged from the operations centre, his expression a mixture of surprise and concern, but with the makings of a smile beaming through. "*Mon Général,*" he exclaimed, "the President of France will arrive in two hours and twenty minutes!"

"How the hell will he get here? And how do you know?" I asked. They were the only two logical questions that came to mind; however, I had already decided it was going to be another long night.

Colonel Forestier quickly described, with understandable and only slightly masked excitement, that he had just spoken with President Mitterand's aide in the Croatian coastal city of Split. The aide was positioned there awaiting the arrival of the President and his Minister for Health and Humanitarian Affairs, Bernard Kouchner, from the European Community talks in Lisbon. According to the aide, it was the President's intention to fly immediately from Split to Sarajevo in an executive jet and land at the airport. He anticipated they would touch down at approximately 2120 (by this time, only two hours and eighteen minutes hence).

For a few seconds, my thoughts drifted back to my service with the Canadian Armed Forces in Europe. Due to the high level of alert required during the Cold War, we had used a fairly effective system to notify every military member of the command to report to duty immediately. The drill was called "Snowball" and started with a telephone fan-out, whereby one person called two people, and those two called four, etc. The telephone drill was complemented by sound trucks moving throughout the towns and villages where Canadian families were living. The trucks' speakers, operating at full volume in both official languages, and normally around two A.M., would advise everyone (including every German national or anyone else trying to sleep), "Snowball, Snowball, report immediately to your place of duty!"

You might reasonably ask what all this has to do with a visit by the President of France to Sarajevo. Not much, except for the fact that we had a check-back system for the Snowball to verify that it was a legitimate alert exercise. Somehow, in the genetic makeup of soldiers, the sense-of-humour gene has become mutated, and we laugh at things that would drive the average civilian crazy. As an example, if you could initiate an "unofficial" Snowball resulting in a thousand of your fellow soldiers rushing into work at two in the morning, fully equipped and ready to go to war if necessary, only to find the front gate of the barracks and all their unit buildings locked—I mean, what could be funnier than that? Particularly if you didn't get caught?

And so a check-back system was introduced. Everyone had a printout showing who would initiate each and every call. The verification came when you called the individual back immediately after he called you. It was tedious, to be sure, but it thwarted a good number of potential alcohol-induced alert exercises.

I turned to Colonel Forestier and asked "Do you have Mitterand's aide's number in Split?"

"Oui, *mon Général.*"

"Good. Call him back to make sure he is who he says he is. And if you think he's for real, tell him from me that there is major fighting going on right now at the airport involving tanks. There are wrecked cars on the runway, there are holes in the runway, a lot of shrapnel all over the place, both sides of the runway are mined, there is no radar, no landing lights, and it will be dark in less than an hour. Other than that, you can tell him that the airport is in mint condition and we would be honoured to receive the President of France and my good friend, Minister Kouchner. However, I strongly recommend they delay the visit until TOMORROW MORNING."

Forestier disappeared into our operations centre to initiate the contact with the aide in Split. I had my fingers crossed that he would get through, since we could talk to Split only through the civilian telephone system, and damage to the infrastructure caused by the war had reduced the system to a sorry state.

By this time, the word was out. When over 300 soldiers live and work in the same building, it doesn't take long for rumours to make the rounds. Just for fun, we occasionally started some innocent fictitious gossip, such as, "Did you hear that the UN is going to double our allowance from $1.28 a day to $2.56 due to the increase of risk in Sarajevo?" It normally took anywhere from fifteen to twenty minutes for the fabricated rumour to come back to the originator. I swear the word of Mitterand's visit did the loop in under five minutes.

What impressed me more than anything was the excitement it generated. Most of the guard company at our headquarters was French. In addition, we still had a few French technical personnel, logistics and operations staff, and marine commandos. They represented the largest national contingent in my headquarters, and quite frankly, for some of them the prospect of the President of France visiting Sarajevo seemed akin to the Second Coming.

Out of curiosity, I asked some of my "colonial" colleagues how they would feel if, say, the Prime Minister of Australia were to drop in. The anticipated response of "No big deal" was more generous than some of the retorts volunteered by other nationalities who overheard my question. But the French were really excited. I was honestly envious of the unqualified respect they were able to feel for their political leader.

By this time, Colonel Forestier had spoken to his President's aide in Split and to the President's staff in Paris. Slightly bemused at the magnitude of the impending event, he assured me that the President was indeed intent on arriving at the Sarajevo airport that evening.

I had two options: accept the impossibility of the plan and merely await word of the inevitable crash, as the President's aircraft tried to land at night in the middle of a war zone, at an airport controlled by the Serbs, without any landing aids; or try to facilitate his arrival by cleaning up the runway and marking the touch-down area. The thought of having the President of France splattered over a mountainside beside the runway, and having to live with the fact that we had done nothing to reduce the risk, persuaded me to opt for the latter option.

Fortunately, the rumour of Mitterand's arrival had resulted in the migration of virtually every French officer in our headquarters to the operations centre. I turned to Forestier and said, "Get thirty of your soldiers together in the next few minutes. We'll try to get to the airport, stop both sides from fighting, and sweep the runway for debris on foot. If the President's plane touches down and runs over a bit of shrapnel, a tire will blow and he'll skid off the runway into a minefield. Once we clean the runway, we'll position two of our vehicles with their headlights on to mark the touch-down area. We'll also put a couple more at the southeast end of the runway to define the limit of the landing area. In the meantime, our staff will try and get the two sides' liaison officers to stop the fighting around the airport. Even if we succeed, we'll take a lot of sniper fire from both sides. Both will think we're opening the airport for a plane from the other side. Tell your guys to wear all their combat kit."

Once again, I was impressed by the French reaction. Thirty French officers and soldiers treated my directions as a routine order. So what if there was a major battle going on? After all, this was the President of France arriving, and God bless them, the soldiers of France were more than ready to risk their lives to help him.

All of this had taken approximately fifteen minutes. The troops would need another fifteen to sort out their kit and vehicles, and the two liaison officers would need at least forty-five minutes to stop the fighting. We would be able to leave for the airport around 2000. Considering the slow drive in the dark along the three kilometres of road to the airport through three ethnic areas, I figured we would have about an hour to clean up the runway, including removing the wrecked cars, before President Mitterand attempted to land. The French didn't seem to think this was a problem, so why should I?

As I walked across the hall to my office, I was intercepted by Major Jorge de la Reta of the Argentine air force, who was one of my personnel officers. Jorge was a special individual who never failed to amaze me with his compassion for and commitment to the suffering people of the world.

Sarajevo provided Jorge with all too many opportunities to carry out his self-imposed humanitarian mission, and he never hesitated to respond to a challenge. He also did a lot more around the headquarters than his job called for: so when Jorge said, "General, come with me down the hall for a bit, I have something to show you," I was intrigued.

For the past month, we had all been living in our offices and sleeping on cots or air mattresses. Some of us had suspended blankets from the ceiling to define a sleeping area in the office; this technique, while functional, made some of the offices, including my own, resemble a Bedouin encampment.

You can imagine my shock when, led by Jorge, I turned into an office only five doors down from my own and saw a piece of furniture I hadn't seen since my last trip to Belgrade—a bed! A bed with sheets! Jorge and his light-fingered associates had set up a suite for President Mitterand, consisting of an office with a desk, chair and telephone, and an adjacent room complete with bed, chair, bedside table and reading lamp. On the bedside table was a batch of fresh red flowers. I never did find out where the bed came from. Actually, I didn't pursue the issue too vigorously, since I already had thoughts about who could make best use of the two rooms on the departure of President Mitterand. They were both blessed with a thick outer wall, which made them much more sniper- and mortar-"proof" than my own office down the hall. I was also impressed by the fortunate coincidence that placed the "Mitterand Suite" directly across the hall from a toilet and one of the two showers in our part of the building. It would at least help give the President the impression that we knew what we were doing.

By now, about twenty-five minutes had passed since the initial notification of the visit; however, General Nambiar was presumably still unaware of the pending international event and the inevitable media attention. Once I got hold of him via our satellite link, he too was a little reluctant to accept the notification as reliable. I sympathized with his initial skepticism, but thought it might be beneficial for all of us if Philippe Morillon got on the French net to Paris as soon as possible to try to talk the President's staff into delaying the flight until the next morning. Nambiar promised to help.

Over the next half-hour, the usual transportation problems reared their ugly heads. We could only move about Sarajevo after dark in armoured vehicles, and even that was a risky operation; you couldn't see who was shooting at you, and therefore returning fire was virtually impossible.

One of the French VBLs was having an electrical problem, and its radios were acting up. Our departure for the airport was delayed fifteen minutes. Ten minutes after our originally scheduled departure time of 2000, the phone rang in the operations centre. It was the President's aide from Split, advising us that President Mitterand and Minister Kouchner would arrive by plane "early tomorrow morning at the Sarajevo airport". Our collective sigh of relief might not have been heard in Paris, but it certainly was heard at General Nambiar's headquarters in Belgrade.

The thought of unnecessarily risking soldiers' lives to facilitate a political visit was disturbing; however, considering that the visitor was French, and the majority of the soldiers involved in supporting the visit were French, and the fact that they were all psyched up and keen to go, I found it much less of an ethical dilemma. I have often thought of what I would have done if the majority of the soldiers in my headquarters had been Swedish, as they had been a month earlier; in that case, I would probably have refused to deploy a runway cleaning detail to the airport until the next morning.

With the visit delayed, we tried to find out what was going on. Was Mitterand visiting on behalf of the European Community; as President of the nation making the largest contribution of troops to UNPROFOR; at the request of one or both sides in the conflict; as a unilateral personal gesture; or some combination of the above?

Absolutely no one we contacted had any definitive answers. There were some indications that President Mitterand had phoned the UN Secretary-General to advise him of his intentions just before he had left Lisbon for Split. Other EC members attending the Lisbon meeting had apparently expressed shock and disbelief at Mitterand's intentions to fly into Sarajevo. From my vantage point, it appeared we were about to witness the most outstanding act of political one-upmanship by a European statesman since the Second World War. This had the makings of a fun event.

As the excitement died down and the adrenalin flow returned to its normal Sarajevo level, arrangements were put in place to sweep the runway at first light the next morning, provided we could get the two sides to stop fighting for at least an hour. Since I didn't know if the Presidency of Bosnia or the Serbs had been advised of Mitterand's visit, I couldn't tell the liaison officers from either side exactly who would be arriving in the middle of their war the following day. They were both called to my office, and I tap-danced around the identification of our impending guest:

"This is important: tomorrow morning we are expecting a VVIP at the airport. He is coming here to try and help stop the war. If either of your sides do anything to interfere with the visit, it will be seen around the world on CNN and your side will suffer the consequences. I strongly recommend that you get hold of your political and military leaders and tell them to cool it for the next twenty-four hours. There will be a group of UN soldiers on the runway at 0700 hours tomorrow morning to clean up the debris. Don't use them for sniper practice!"

At that point, the telephone in the operations centre went into continuous "send" mode, which lasted for the next nine hours. It seemed everyone and his or her dog wanted to "help" co-ordinate the visit. The President's staff in Paris, his personal staff in Split, the French chargé d'affaires in Belgrade, my own superior headquarters in Belgrade, etc., all had bits of information; unfortunately, few of them matched. I decided to have an early night and get out of the way, confident that the French officers on my staff would sort it all out by morning.

Before bedding down at such an unnaturally early hour, I thought I would try out the new combination surgical-theatre-and-shower-room on the second level of the basement. Our medical advisor, Vanessa Lloyd-Davies, with her characteristic initiative and energy, had discovered a perfectly good laundry room about twenty by thirty feet in diameter. It was fully tiled from top to bottom, with a large drain in the middle of the floor. It hadn't taken long for Vanessa's professional imagination to visualize a mass-casualty operating theatre, and our staff had just put the finishing touches on the layout that afternoon. Elevated stretchers, drip bags, operating tools, and just about everything else needed for emergency surgery, except for the actual surgical team, were all in place. I was proud of Vanessa for having addressed so quickly one of our most serious problems. At the same time, the somewhat surrealistic scene reminded me of the potentially grim consequences of our business.

Three shower stalls were located next to the operating theatre. As I approached them, I could hear water running but no other sounds. I quickly doffed my clothing and, with soap in hand, walked towards the far stall. As I passed the first cubicle, my peripheral vision picked up a sight I had not seen in some four months. The accompanying shriek confirmed that it was a female soldier enjoying the privacy of a quiet shower, while confusion reigned supreme in the operations centre three floors above. I stared straight ahead and muttered a barely audible "Good evening." By this time, I was more than halfway past her cubicle, so, like a good soldier, I carried on to my destination.

For five minutes, she and I showered in silence, separated by three feet and a tile divider. As the general who had been put in charge of developing scientific trials to evaluate the acceptability of women soldiers in Canadian combat units, I began to wonder what all the fuss was about. I let her leave first. After all, chivalry is not entirely dead.

24

President Mitterand
Drops In

JUNE 28 At 0545 hours, after a restless night of worrying about the imminent arrival of my uninvited guest, I unwound myself from my cot and ventured down the hall to the operations centre. Everything was dead calm. The duty officer confirmed that the President of France would be landing at Sarajevo airport in an executive jet at 0830 hours. Just another day.

Following a quick shave and a bite to eat, we had our morning conference. Inevitably, word of President Mitterand's visit had leaked out during the night; the braver and more ambitious members of the international media were already milling about our headquarters, waiting for my vehicle to lead them to the airport.

Steve and I climbed into the VBL and headed up a ragtag convoy that arrived at Sarajevo International around 0800 hours. The French soldiers had done a good job of sweeping the runway, collecting some fifteen steel helmets full of shrapnel—any piece of which could have meant disaster for the President's aircraft.

The appointed time of 0830 came and went, and went, and went. I avoided eye contact with the Bosnian-Serb soldiers occupying the airport. They were not pleased with the idea of turning the facility over to the UN; several of their colleagues had been shot a day earlier while packing their kit in preparation to leave. We had a pretty good professional relationship with the Bosnian-Serb leadership, but at the airport we were most decidedly unpopular with their soldiers.

The relative boredom of hanging about the terminal building was relieved by seven of eight rounds of TDF sniper fire that impacted around us at 0950 hours. Then, at 1000 hours, someone spotted a dark speck just above the horizon to the north. We were surprised at how slowly it was moving, considering that an executive jet, particularly the French Falcon used by the President, has quite a high landing speed. As the speck grew larger, it was joined by another, approximately a kilometre to the rear. Simultaneously, we all experienced a blinding flash of the obvious: the President of France was arriving by helicopter!

While momentarily upset because French soldiers had risked injury sweeping the airport for the arrival of an executive jet, on reflection I much preferred seeing the President approach in a more flexible and controlled manner aboard one of his country's large Super Puma helicopters. As the two helicopters started their final turn towards our location, the media people, who now out-numbered our small military contingent, went into a feeding frenzy. They jostled for position where they thought the President's helicopter would land. Their hunger to be upfront for this top story clashed with their natural fear of exposing themselves to the ever-present threat of sniper fire; professional hunger won out, and as the helicopter began to touch down, they burst onto the parking apron as if starting the Boston Marathon.

Although military protocol dictates that the senior officer present be the first to greet any visiting VIP, I was now separated from the President's descending helicopter by the swarm of journalists. Fortunately, the landing characteristics of the Super Puma solved the dilemma for us. As the pilot changed the pitch of his blades for landing, an enormous wall of air picked up everything in its path, including several journalists and cameramen, and pushed them inexorably backwards until they were once again beside or behind me. Steve, Warrant Officer Traclet and I marched forward unimpeded to the now stationary helicopter, as if we'd planned it that way all along.

I could see the smiling face of Bernard Kouchner in one of the rear windows. I experienced a moment of uncertainty, thinking that the President might be in the second helicopter, which was about to touch down some distance away. Some of the journalists had already made up their minds to that effect and were now sprinting through a moving cloud of dust and debris towards the other helicopter.

Kouchner flung open the door, and with his customary energy sprang from the helicopter, embracing me and planting at least one kiss on my cheek before his feet were firmly on the ground. We gave each other a big hug, and I remember saying something like, "We have to stop meeting like this."

Kouchner then opened the left front door of the helicopter. Up to that point, I had not felt fully persuaded that the President of France would actually visit Sarajevo. I'd become jaded from the lack of precision surrounding arrangements for visiting VIPs; for all I knew, the arrangements for Mitterand's visit to Sarajevo might have been a cover for a clandestine call on Serbian President Milosevic in Belgrade or Croatian President Tudjman in Zagreb.

I was wrong. Kouchner assisted the President of France from the helicopter, all the while maintaining an animated conversation with Mitterand. Once again my comprehension of French failed me when forced to deal with such rapid-fire delivery. I did, however, hear the reassuringly familiar name "MacKenzie" a couple of times in each sentence, so I assumed Kouchner was explaining that I was the guy in charge and that he, Philippe Morillon and I had "dined" together during an artillery bombardment some thirty days earlier.

President Mitterand grasped my hand with both of his. In perfect English, he thanked me for what I had done for Saravejo and for Mr. Kouchner. I was somewhat embarrassed that the President felt it necessary to offer greetings in English, so I responded as best I could in French, saying that I had a wonderful team in Sarajevo doing the real work, and since the majority of my soldiers were from France, my job was easy. Kouchner whispered in my ear that if we were going to get the full benefit of the limited time available, perhaps we should stick to English. I had a momentary thought of my French-immersion teacher, Geneviève, who had been locked in a room with me in Ottawa for three months in 1988 in an attempt to make me fluently bilingual. Although she is a great teacher, I guess I failed the ultimate test. But when the President of France wants you to speak English, you speak English. I figured Geneviève would understand.

My immediate impression of President Mitterand was that he deserved his well-known nickname, "The Sphinx". In spite of the considerable confusion swirling around him, including the inevitable Bosnian VIP welcome consisting of mortar and sniper fire, which had started on schedule from both sides of the runway, you would have thought the President was on a leisurely stroll through the Bois de Boulogne. His face was expressionless, and his eyes always seemed to rest on some point in the distance, immediately in line with the direction in which he was proceeding. He had mastered the technique of maintaining his composure as everyone around him was losing theirs. This trait had a very calming effect, and I instantly liked and admired him.

By this time, we were well and truly engulfed by the media, which slowed our progress towards the waiting column of armoured personnel carriers. It was the first time I'd witnessed a phalanx of cameramen and photographers trying to get pictures at a distance of one metre while their subject moves towards them at a walking pace. It's a dangerous business: those who had muscled their way to the front row of the phalanx shuffled backwards, tripping over the remainder, who were literally draped over them in their attempt to get a closer shot. The resulting chaos, freqently intermixed with verbal abuse in some twenty-plus languages, got expensive as $30,000 cameras and their operators bounced off the tarmac. To my initial surprise, no one stopped to render assistance to a fallen comrade as long as the focal point of the chaos was still within camera range. I was to learn later, however, that when one of theirs was in real danger, media people were as tightly knit and mutually supportive a profession as my own.

As we neared the armoured vehicle designated for the President, a crew member of the second helicopter successfully fought his way through the journalists and advised us that his machine had been struck in the tail by a single round of heavy machine-gun fire on the approach to the airport. The helicopter could not fly until it was repaired. He suggested they ask for the Falcon executive jet to fly from Split to facilitate the President's departure later in the day. Otherwise, some of the French delegation would have to spend the night in Sarajevo. The one good helicopter could get them all to Split, but it would take two trips; and the second trip would have to be delayed until tomorrow due to darkness.

For the first but not last time that day, the President dropped his distant stare, looked me straight in the eyes, and said, "General, what do we do?"

The realization had now sunk in that I was going to be responsible for the President of France until he disappeared over the horizon on his way back to Split. I knew that if Mitterand spent the night with us at our headquarters, we would be subjected to more than the usual shelling; it would be too tempting for one or both sides to try to convince him that the other side was the real culprit in the war. I could do without that.

"Mr. President," I began, "I would appreciate an hour with you before you start your rounds, during which time my staff can make arrangements for any meetings you wish to hold. There will be a lot of 'showtime' today. By that I mean, wherever you go, there will be shelling and fighting. So I doubt you will be finished before 1700 hours.

"I recommend you call for your jet. Your boys cleared the runway this morning—so as long as we don't have any shelling on or near the runway, we should be okay. You should also bring in a repair team as soon as possible, since your second helicopter will be a sitting duck during the night. I'll have a hard time guarding it with our meagre force."

Mitterand, an advisor and his personal bodyguards were loaded into one of the five identical French armoured vehicles. My hope was that anyone trying to ambush the President would have only one chance in five: actually one in six, counting my own armoured car. In fact, I anticipated that most of the locals would assume that the President would ride with me, so Steve and I took off at the head of the column in the direction of the PTT—just a little more uneasily than usual.

Everyone arrived without incident. A high-speed run in the back of a metal box, just after landing by helicopter in a war zone, couldn't have been very comfortable for the President. Yet he appeared quite at home as we walked inside amid the admiring, even worshipful, stares of the French soldiers, who had located themselves in just about every nook and cranny around the entrance to the building.

President Mitterand asked to visit the toilet before we had our chat. I detected an immediate look of concern, bordering on panic, on the faces of my staff. I found out later that the water and electricity had been off for most of the morning while the rest of us had been at the airport, and no one knew what condition the toilet was in. The President disappeared into our crude WC and closed the door as we all took a deep breath. About two minutes later, we exhaled with a collective sigh of relief when we heard the delightful sound of a strong and complete flush. The President emerged, rubbing his damp hands together to dry them. Apparently, our single cold-water tap had also co-operated, for the first time in days. Who says prayer doesn't work on plumbing?

The President, Minister Kouchner, Steve and I entered my office. It was considerably neater than I had left it earlier that morning. I assumed that the French contingent had been embarrassed at the mess on my desk and had seen fit to make it look a little more organized, rearranging the papers and hiding the beer bottles and open French ration packs. (I'd run out of Canadian gum a few weeks earlier and had got into the habit of opening a full ration box every time I needed a few Chiclets. Someone in the French logistics planning staff had determined that every soldier was entitled to only two Chiclets per day, so it took a fair number of ration boxes to keep me supplied.) I also noted that the grey blanket on my cot had been neatly folded; the entire office had a misleading look of austere efficiency.

Kouchner told the President that he should see President Izetbegovic as soon as possible. After all, Izetbegovic was the Bosnian head of state, and protocol dictated that he be visited first.

Mitterand indicated that that one visit would suffice, and therefore they should be able to depart in a few hours. If they could get away early enough, he said, perhaps all of their entourage could make it to Split using the single helicopter before darkness, even if his personal jet was not able to land.

I was shocked. I'd never considered that the President of France would visit Sarajevo and talk with only one side in the conflict. I could just imagine the Bosnian Serbs' reaction; they would take their fury out on the only permanent international mediator present in Sarajevo—me.

It was now or never. "Mr. President, with all due respect, I would appreciate you also seeing the Serbian leader in Bosnia, Dr. Karadzic. It's important for me to be seen as an impartial negotiator by both sides. If you see only President Izetbegovic, it will become virtually impossible for me to deal with the Serbs after you leave. They are about to hand over the airport to us, and I would hate to see anything jeopardize that."

Mitterand turned to Minister Kouchner. There was a disturbingly long visual exchange between the two. Much to my relief, Kouchner came to my rescue: "Absolutely, Mr. President. It would help General MacKenzie if you saw Karadzic. And it would be good to hear what the Serbs have to say."

The President asked me, "Where do you propose we see Karadzic?"

The last thing I wanted was another trip with a VIP to the Bosnian Serbs' camp at Lukavica. I knew the TDF would shoot at us from Butmir, and the Serbian escort would definitely fire back. We'd end up with a major firefight on our hands. Visions of dragging a dead President of France from the back of a burning vehicle played over in my mind.

"Mr. President, the Serbs still control the airport, and they can get there in relative safety from Lukavica. I recommend we tell Dr. Karadzic to meet you there just before you take off for Split."

"*D'accord*," Mitterand replied. "Tell Karadzic that I will see him for only five minutes before I depart. I won't meet with him, I'll just say hello."

Another problem. I was about to push my luck, but I had little choice: "Mr. President, your greetings will turn into a meeting, and the meeting will last at least an hour."

Before I could continue, Mitterand and Kouchner both exclaimed that such an idea was absolutely out of the question. The President had to return to Paris and did not have an hour to spare with Karadzic. It would be five minutes, a quick handshake, and that would be it. In any case, to spend any longer might be misinterpreted by Izetbegovic, who would be upset that Karadzic was getting the last word.

"I'm not suggesting that you *should* spend an hour with Karadzic," I explained. "I'm just saying that you *will* spend an hour with him. Approximately two minutes after you start your five-minute meeting, fighting will break out. There will be a major firefight involving tanks, mortars and machine guns around the airport terminal. We won't be able to move from the building until Karadzic decides your meeting is over."

Minister Kouchner had seen it all before. I knew that he realized I was probably right. The President was not persuaded, however; we agreed that we would play it by ear when the time came.

By now Vitali Petrounev had made arrangements for a meeting between Presidents Mitterand and Izetbegovic. Mitterand was clearly anxious to get on with his visits as quickly as possible; however, I was equally anxious to give him my interpretation of events, and also wanted to solicit his support on a couple of matters with Izetbegovic.

"Mr. President, I realize that you know a lot more about the political situation here than I do. But if you are interested, I could give you a quick synopsis of what I think is happening around town."

All it took was a nod from the French head of state, and I had my opening:

"I won't beat around the bush, Mr. President. I'm not particularly interested in the long and complex history of this region. All that does is complicate the discussions I have with both sides. Our job is to try and achieve some semblance of a ceasefire, so we can deliver food and medicine. That means dealing head-on with the situation in Sarajevo as it stands now.

"In synopsis, the Serbs started the fighting in April, after your country and the rest of the European Community decided to recognize Bosnia-Herzegovina. The Serbs shelled the city, in the hope that the Muslims and Croats would give in to their demands for a state within a state. It didn't work, and both sides have been fighting ever since.

"Izetbegovic is determined that this is a war of outside aggression controlled from Belgrade. Karadzic, on the other hand, insists it is a civil war, and that the Serbs who joined him are Bosnians who have a right to self-determination. Presumably, the Serbs pretty well have what they want by way of territorial gains in Bosnia; they already started with around 60–65 per cent, since many of them are farmers with relatively large tracts of land.

"On the other hand, the Muslims are businessmen and own very little of the countryside. Now that the time has come to measure your success by how much territory you control, the Muslims don't have very much, and have even less every day. In the meantime, the Croatian Army is quietly taking over the area from the Croatian border up through Mostar. They are even bragging about their forward units taking pictures of the Sarajevo airport from Mount Igman, just southwest of the city. It's amazing to me that the international community has been so silent on the Croatian Army operations in Bosnia.

"The Muslims are in a box. Even if they recover the territory they had before the war, they won't have very much. Izetbegovic wants the entire country back. Quite frankly, the only way he can get it is by convincing the international community to intervene with massive military force, ridding him of his Serbian enemies. I have been uniquely unsuccessful in convincing him of the futility of such a strategy. It's in the interests of Izetbegovic to keep the fighting going, in the hope that the world will come to his rescue—provided he can make it look as if the Serbs are solely responsible for perpetrating the chaos. God knows, overall, the majority of the blame does rest with the Serbs; however, whenever we arrange any type of ceasefire, it's usually the Muslims who break it first. In addition, there is strong but circumstantial evidence that some really horrifying acts of cruelty attributed to the Serbs were actually orchestrated by the Muslims against their own people, for the benefit of an international audience.

"There are no good solutions to this mess, Mr. President, only the best of the worst. It's my opinion that face-to-face negotiation is the only way. Karadzic is ready, but Izetbegovic refuses. And while I understand his logic, its implementation will lead to the destruction of himself and his people. I respectfully request that you attempt to convince Izetbegovic that he will not see international military intervention—and having done that, pressure him to sit down in the same room with Karadzic, so we can at least arrange some sort of ceasefire."

Mitterand didn't change his stoical expression during my entire monologue. I thought I detected a glint of understanding in his eyes when I mentioned the very sensitive issue of the Muslims allegedly firing on their own people; however, it was such a tiny and fleeting change to his steady stare that I could have been mistaken.

"*Merci,*" was the full extent of the President's response. I had no idea if he rejected my personal opinion or endorsed it; nor would I ever find out.

I suggested to the President that it would be best if I did not accompany him to see Izetbegovic. Relations between the Muslim leader and me were cordial on the surface, but I thought my presence might inhibit any attempt to convince Izetbegovic to negotiate with Karadzic. Mitterand agreed.

Before departing for the Bosnian Presidency, Mitterand agreed to do a quick walk around our headquarters to meet as many of our people as possible. By now the French officers and soldiers had taken up strategic positions along the route out of the building. They popped out of doorways and corridors as their President approached, and once again I was envious of the respect, bordering on affection, that he elicited from each and every one of them. I was delighted that he also took time to talk with personnel from the other twenty-nine nations represented in our headquarters. He seemed absolutely genuine in his expressions of admiration for the work that this international collection of peacekeepers was doing. It was obvious that, in return, we all admired him for his personal courage and initiative. I hoped he would draw some strength from meeting our merry band, in exchange for the boost his presence gave to our own morale.

As we arrived in the parking lot to the rear of our building, mortars were landing about 300 metres to the north. The President was oblivious to the danger and climbed into the back of his armoured vehicle along with four of our outstanding French commandos, who were specially trained for guarding VIPs. As Marlborough said about his soldiers during the Peninsular campaign, "I don't know if they scare the enemy but they certainly scare me." I felt the same way about our VIP guard team; I made a point of never upsetting them. Little did I know that, within a few weeks, they would be assigned to protect me twenty-four hours a day.

MITTERAND'S CONVOY LEFT FOR the Presidency, surrounded by a motley collection of journalists' vehicles masquerading as cars. Most were missing windows, some had shrapnel and bullet holes for natural ventilation, and a good number had been rammed or rolled over. All four wheels on most of them didn't necessarily face in the direction of travel, and consequently they resembled a row of crabs sidestepping down the street. They did, however, share one characteristic: there were only two known positions for the accelerator—fully off, or flat to the floor with all the strength the driver could muster.

As usual, the more experienced members of the journalistic fraternity anticipated that our VIP was on his way to the Bosnian Presidency; they shot off down sniper alley, in order to set up their cameras in front of the main entrance for his arrival. As we rarely revealed the destination of our guests, some journalists were less confident of Mitterand's destination and so stayed close to the convoy, using the APCs as protection against sniper fire whenever they could. It was a technique that I quietly encouraged, since I was convinced that the media were in more danger than ourselves; driving about Sarajevo in a civilian car without some sort of armoured shield was not beneficial to one's health.

I returned to my office and asked the Bosnian-Serb liaison officer to have Professor Koljevic give me a call. It normally took at least an hour for the loop to be closed; in this case, I received a call back within ten minutes. Presumably, the Bosnian Serbs were anticipating a meeting with our guest.

"As you know, Professor, President Mitterand has arrived and is on a round of meetings in the city. He wishes to meet with Dr. Karadzic, preferably at the airport, on his way out. It will be a short meeting of only a few minutes. The President has to get back to Split well before dark. I suggest you be at the airport manager's old office at 1500. Can you make it?"

"Certainly, General. We will see you there."

Much too easy, I thought. With the Bosnian-Serb army, and their tanks, still at the airport, the potential for a major battle around the President of France and his helicopters remained a disturbing possibility.

I turned on my television set and within a few minutes watched Mitterand arrive at the Bosnian Presidency. The media were out in force. The French President worked the crowd as well as anyone while making his way to the front entrance. Blessedly, no mortars fell in front of the building. It had become almost routine for visiting VIPs to receive a volley of incoming fire; we had begun to refer to them as "calling cards".

The duty officer stuck his head in my doorway and announced that President Mitterand's personal Falcon jet had just landed safely at the airport. At least the shuttle run to Split with the single helicopter would not be necessary. I hoped the Falcon would not be damaged by sniper or mortar fire as it sat out in the open awaiting the President's arrival.

Over the next few hours, Bosnian tv showed Mitterand and Izetbegovic emerge from their meeting and hold a press conference. Izetbegovic did most of the talking. From his body language, I could tell that the Bosnian President was stressing his demands that the Serbs be forced to withdraw, and that the international community intervene on an urgent basis. My Serbo-Croat was pretty limited, but having heard him make the same points with me many times in English, I got the gist of his message. Mitterand remained stoical during the entire performance. Kouchner did not look terribly pleased.

The cameras followed the two Presidents on a drive through downtown Sarajevo. The official car moved at a snail's pace, and the Bosnian security personnel walked alongside, keeping a close eye on the favourite sniper locations. At the shrine to the Bosnian victims of the bread-line massacre, Mitterand placed a flower at the foot of the simple monument, which drew an overwhelming response from the massive crowd following his progress.

I had been advised that the President would visit the Kosovo hospital following his walkabout, so I thought it was about time to go back to the airport. I wanted to be sure that Dr. Karadzic was standing by. After a high-speed run to the airport, Steve and I arrived in the airport manager's office. The Bosnian-Serb soldiers were very agitated and seemed to be running off in all directions. When I looked at Mitterand's Falcon, I was surprised to see a Bosnian-Serb army truck stopped very close—too close—to the port wing.

Professor Koljevic arrived and somewhat sheepishly explained that one of their soldiers had driven into the wing of the aircraft. Tragically, the driver had been critically injured when the wing tip broke through the windshield of the truck and struck him in the head. We walked out to the aircraft and observed a major dent and a twelve-inch hole torn in the leading edge of the wing. Everyone was offering opinions on the Falcon's serviceability.

Occasionally, one's hobby comes to the rescue in one's day job. As a racing-car driver who competes in a fibreglass-bodied Formula Ford, I had done a lot of temporary repairs with "racer's tape" over the past decade. Racer's tape is just an expensive, coloured version of duct tape. We didn't have either back at headquarters, but we did have what the Canadian military affectionately calls "gun tape". If anything, it is even tougher than duct tape. I didn't know if it would stand up to speeds of 400 miles an hour, but if placed on the wing so that the wind pushed the tape onto the damaged surface, it might work. Warrant Officer Traclet jumped into his vehicle and headed back to the PTT building to pick up a roll of gun tape from our private stash of Canadian supplies. We couldn't ask anyone to bring it out for us, since that would mean revealing our hiding place. The UN was incapable of supplying even a modest scale of office supplies, and if a non-Canadian saw Traclet's cache, we would have to put a twenty-four-hour guard on it.

I returned to the airport manager's office. By this time, Dr. Karadzic and General Mladic had arrived. Mladic tried to explain that the accident had been caused by Muslims firing at the truck as it manoeuvred close to Mitterand's aircraft. But I could see that his heart was not really committed to the explanation.

I noticed Colonel Forestier outside the window; he seemed to be subtly trying to get my attention. I strolled over to the window as inconspicuously as possible and leaned on the sill as if to light a cigarette. Forestier spoke in a hushed tone: "The driver of that truck had been drinking. As he was driving past the aircraft, that pretty, dark-haired journalist was walking towards the terminal and he stared at her a little too long. He drove into the wing with the cab of his vehicle. He's hurt pretty bad."

"Well, there's bugger-all we can do about it now, apart from patching up the driver and the wing. I've sent for tape to fix the wing; who's looking after the driver?"

Colonel Forestier explained that Vanessa Lloyd-Davies was tend-
ing to the driver, so there was nothing more we could do. I turned
back to the animated conversation among the three Bosnian-Serb
leaders. This was no time to embarrass them, so I let the matter drop.
I'd never met a soldier who couldn't be distracted by a pretty face.

I took the opportunity to press for their co-operation. "Dr.
Karadzic, with all the activity at the airport today, I'm concerned
you won't be able to pull out your soldiers by nightfall. They have
a lot of personal equipment to remove, let alone all their vehicles—
including those tanks I've been after you to move for the last few
days. If you are not able to turn the airport over to us today, I would
like to move about thirty of my personnel here this afternoon and
they will spend the night. I don't want to lose the momentum started
by the Mitterand visit. We should try to do the handover as early
as possible tomorrow—if not this afternoon, following the
President's departure."

Before Karadzic could respond, the advance guard of the media
convoy screeched to a halt in front of the office. As thunder follows
lightning, Mitterand would not be far behind. I excused myself and
made my way through a maze of Bosnian-Serb soldiers onto the
tarmac.

President Mitterand's convoy of armoured personnel carriers
came to a halt in front of the building. One APC broke from the
convoy and reversed towards the building; this was a regular drill
we used to protect convoy passengers from sniper fire while they
were dismounting.

As the President dismounted, the journalists and cameramen
went into another frenzy. To me, it seemed that we were losing
control of the media mob and the President could well be crushed,
but as usual he appeared oblivious to the chaos, and so he and I
waded into the crowd side by side, going in the direction of the
airport manager's office. After about ten metres at a stumbling pace,
Karadzic, Koljevic and Mladic appeared at the entrance of the
building and moved towards us, approaching the media scrum from
the rear. Obeying some unwritten law of their profession, the media
people parted, allowing Karadzic and his associates to come
face-to-face with the President and create the perfect shot.

I introduced them. Karadzic informed Mitterand that he was
about to hand the airport over to the UN and suggested they go
inside for a short meeting. Mitterand responded that he had to get
on his way to Split and just wanted to say hello.

By now it was two-and-a-half minutes since Mitterand had emerged from his armoured vehicle. As if on cue, machine-gun fire could be heard in the distance, and almost immediately two of the Serbian tanks, no more than fifty metres away from us, fired in the direction of Butmir and Dobrinja. The shock wave from their main guns blasted the crowd around the President and fortunately pushed us all in the direction of the building's entrance. All the Bosnian-Serb weapon systems now opened up. The TDF started to return the fire with vigour. There was no choice: I seized Mitterand by the arm and started to move him, none too gently, towards the door. "Mr. President, I think we should get out of view. Perhaps a short meeting *is* in order."

Once inside the office, Karadzic began a rambling indictment of the "Muslim threat", referring to Izetbegovic's alleged desire to establish a Muslim fundamentalist state on European territory. From there he tried to convince Mitterand that all the "good" Serbs had joined him in his battle against the Muslims, whereas the Serbs who had remained loyal to the Presidency were traitors. All the Serbs desired was the right to establish their own independent territory within Bosnia. As citizens of Bosnia, didn't they have that right?

Mitterand looked Karadzic square in the eye and said, "Perhaps. But you are going about it in the wrong way."

Talk about succinctness. In one sentence, Mitterand had summed up the West's point of view and disarmed Karadzic's arguments.

Karadzic never fully recovered. First he and then General Mladic attempted to make their case. The coherence usually evident in their arguments was missing. If they were looking for some glimmer of understanding or sympathy from Mitterand, they didn't get it. His utterly expressionless response to their pleas for support rattled them. They jumped from subject to subject, searching for that elusive point that would elicit some response from Mitterand.

The President was not prepared to get involved in a debate while a battle was raging, particularly one that could well have been orchestrated by the Serbs themselves. I was disappointed that Professor Koljevic did not intervene, since he was certainly the most articulate of the three. Presumably he was deferring to his leader, but I could tell that he knew a valuable opportunity had been lost.

General Mladic again tried to claim that his soldier who had run into the President's aircraft had done so while under fire from the Muslims and would probably die. He then indicated that three of his soldiers had just been seriously injured "defending the President of France". He wanted us to see them, but his offer was graciously refused. (I discussed the Serb casualties with Vanessa later in the day; she reported that all their wounds had occurred at least three to four hours before the casualties were to be brought before the President, and that one casualty had actually arrived by vehicle. This variation on "showtime" was characteristic of the conflict on all sides, so I was not surprised or shocked.)

Mitterand was now aware that his aircraft had been damaged. He and Minister Kouchner went into a huddle to discuss the possibility of reactivating the plan for a helicopter shuttle to Split. The pilot of the Falcon must have been psychic; he appeared at the door of the office and announced that the aircraft had been repaired and he was ready to fly.

The intensity of the firing had died down a bit, so I suggested to the President that we try to make it to his aircraft. Once outside the office, we were again enveloped by a cocoon of at least forty media people. We hadn't gone more than twenty steps parallel to the building when the tanks opened up and machine-gun fire could be heard less than fifty metres away.

I turned towards the President and encountered a look that got my full attention. Deadly serious, he asked, "Well, General Mac-Kenzie, what do we do now?"

Over the last few years, I've developed the politician's technique of dealing with a question to which the answer is not immediately apparent: you start talking without saying anything of significance, hoping you will think of an adequate response before you bore the person to death. "Well, Mr. President, as I see it we have two choices. We can try to get you and your party back to our headquarters, where we would be honoured if you joined us for the night. The problem is, your presence would tempt both sides to shell the building, in order to persuade you that the other side wants to kill you. Or, we could assume that this fighting is going to get a lot worse, and therefore the best thing is to get to your aircraft so you can fly to Split right now." I had made up my mind. "I recommend you fly."

Mitterand looked at me. He was about to speak when Minister Kouchner once again demonstrated his decisiveness: "General MacKenzie is right. Let's go." The decision had been made.

Mitterand held up his hand just below his chin. There was something he wanted to say before we moved towards the aircraft.

"General," came his voice, almost in a whisper, "what can I do for you?"

I was stunned. We had been visited by quite a few VIPs during my time with UNPROFOR, and I was pretty confident that none of them had asked us if we needed anything.

"Mr. President, thank you for your offer. We will probably take over the airport from the Serbs tomorrow. At that point, all we will have is an expensive piece of real estate. We need a couple of humanitarian aircraft to land here tomorrow to jumpstart the operation. If you were to send in French aircraft with some humanitarian aid on board, no matter how modest, it would embarrass other nations, especially your European allies, and they would rush to be the next in.

"My second request [I was pushing it] is for a company of your outstanding marine commandos. The Security Council will not approve the move of the Canadian battalion from Croatia until we actually take over the airport. That means the earliest they could be here would be around the first of July. In the meantime, I only have a party of thirty to defend the airport. And about all they have for protection is the UN flag."

The President nodded, and we started towards the aircraft. Kouchner grabbed me by the arm and gave me one of his infectious smiles. I had a feeling we might see some French aircraft tomorrow.

As we left the sidewalk and turned to move across the parking apron to the aircraft, the rifle and machine-gun fire intensified around the perimeter of the terminal building. There was little danger to us at that stage, thanks to the media security blanket surrounding us. If any snipers fired at us, they would have to eliminate at least a dozen journalists before they got to the President. While this thought would not have been particularly comforting to the media, it allayed my immediate fears for the President's well-being.

As we passed under the Falcon's wing tip, I glanced up and had a flashback to a motor race through the streets of Halifax, Nova Scotia, in which I'd competed the previous year: I had slammed into one of my competitors when he slowed for a yellow flag indicating an accident, and had spent the entire afternoon taping the mangled fibreglass back into some semblance of its original aerodynamic design. Someone had done the same thing to the Falcon's wing. There, for all the world to see on CNN, was good old Canadian Army gun tape covering the tear in the aluminium. Whoever had made the repair had known what he was doing; the tape had been placed over the leading edge of the wing, with the ends of the tape facing the rear. Tape repair is not nuclear physics, but you'd be surprised how many people apply the tape so that the wind tears it off after only a few seconds.

President Mitterand stopped at the bottom of the steps, grabbed me by both hands, and expressed his appreciation for what we were doing for Sarajevo. I replied that we wouldn't be doing very much if not for his magnificent soldiers and their excellent equipment. I said, "Mr. President, you are a very brave man. Thank you for coming to Sarajevo and thank you for your offer of support."

As the President started up the steps, I realized he would be exposed to sniper fire for a few seconds. I was about to follow him up when Minister Kouchner grabbed me and, in conjunction with a French version of a bear hug, planted a kiss on each cheek. By this time, the President was "safely" inside his aircraft.

Kouchner assured me that I would be seeing him back in Sarajevo in the near future, and I believed him. If it had been anyone else, I would have been skeptical.

Once the presidential party was on board, Steve and I moved back towards the terminal along with the media. The aircraft moved off immediately to the single runway. As it turned northwest, the engines were taken to maximum torque with the brakes fully on. Much like a turbine dragster, at the moment of maximum thrust the pilot released the brake, and the Falcon shot forward and lifted off the tarmac within a few hundred metres. Hot on its tail was the serviceable Super Puma helicopter. The damaged one would stay with us for a few days, along with its crew.

Steve told me that the parts necessary to repair the helicopter should arrive on tomorrow's aircraft. "Tomorrow's aircraft? What aircraft is that?" I asked.

Steve explained, "The French crew told me at least two of their planes are landing here tomorrow."

I never did find out if my request for aircraft had been actioned on the spot by the President, or if it was just coincidence that my request matched his intention to upstage the rest of the European Community two days in row. Quite frankly, I couldn't have cared less. It looked as if we were going to run an airport after all. All we had to do was persuade everyone to stop fighting long enough so the Serbs could hand it over to us.

I went looking for Professor Koljevic—praying along the way that the gun tape would hold until Split.

25

A UN Airport

PROFESSOR KOLJEVIC WAS waiting for me inside one of the terminal buildings. President Mitterand's visit had given the airport takeover a new momentum, so I decided to try and keep it rolling.

"Professor," I began, "the whole world is going to expect the UN to take over the airport, now that the President of France has used it. I'm prepared to put a very modest force here tonight to maintain a UN presence. It's essential that your personnel and equipment leave within twenty-four hours, and that you start packing up right away, so the Presidency's forces can see you are serious. I would like to take over responsibility for running the airport at 1630 tomorrow.

"I can't actually secure the airport until the Canadian battalion gets here. That will probably be around the first of July, in three or four days. Until then, I need a guarantee from you and the Presidency that you will not interfere with the airport's operation or take any tactical advantage of our tiny force."

Koljevic was obviously keen to hand over the airport to the UN, since he realized that the resulting PR for the Serbs would create a small glow in an otherwise dreary international image. "You know, General MacKenzie," he said, "we have only one serious problem with giving up the airport. We are prepared to sacrifice the tactical advantage that it gives us; however, we need to be able to drive our ambulances along the runway when we have serious casualties to evacuate from Ilidza. We have only one field hospital in Lukavica to look after the area. If we can't use the runway, our casualties will have to take a three-to-four-hour journey through the mountains to reach the hospital."

"I understand your dilemma, " I replied. "As you are voluntarily giving up the airport, and a significant advantage on the ground, I will let you transport casualties across the runway—but only after my people have confirmed by inspection that the wounds are life-threatening, and there are no arms or ammunition being carried."

"Agreed," he said. "We will be out of here by 1630 tomorrow."

Steve and I made a quick dash to the Presidency, where we spent the next hour-and-a-half debating the ambulance issue with Izetbegovic. The President was adamant that the Bosnian Serbs should not have the right to transport their casualties across the runway. He repeatedly emphasized that some of his people around the airport had been cut off from proper medical care for months. I sympathized with his argument, but explained that this was a voluntary withdrawal from the airport by the Bosnian Serbs; therefore, in order for the airport agreement to be implemented, I had agreed that critical casualties could use the "shortcut" between Ilidza and Lukavica. If President Izetbegovic wanted me to go back to Koljevic and say there was no deal, and delay the opening of the airport until we worked out another solution, I would be prepared to do so; but I really thought we should take advantage of the window of opportunity presented by President Mitterand's visit.

Izetbegovic was not entirely convinced, but advised me to carry on with our plans to open the airport the following day. Unfortunately, the ambulance issue was to become one of the biggest thorns in my relationship with the Presidency.

We returned to the PTT in time to wish our modest force the best of luck on its way to the airport. Numbering only thirty, the group included several French soldiers to guard Mitterand's helicopter, some of our new UN observers under Ray Honig, a few officers from the French technical team, and the Van Doos who had not returned to Belgrade and Daruvar, plus a small medical team. Commandant Hauben was in charge.

To say I was concerned about their security was an understatement. They would spend the night located with the Bosnian Serbs, who would be packing up and would therefore be a tempting target for the TDF. The citizens of Dobrinja would interpret our presence at the airport as further collaboration with the enemy, which would erode our relationship with the citizens of Sarajevo even more—if that were possible.

Unfortunately, there was no other choice than to have a UN presence at the airport. If we didn't keep our foot in the door kicked open by President Mitterand, it might be slammed shut and locked. I was very proud of Commandant Hauben and his team as they departed. They were all very positive and ready to take the risk.

Later that night, I received a copy of a news release issued the previous day by the UN Secretary-General during his visit to Nigeria. It gave the Serbs some credit and called on the TDF to stop initiating hostilities. This was the first time that the government of Bosnia-Herzegovina had been criticized publicly and I anticipated that they would take it out on us. For the UN, the statement was pretty strong stuff. Here is an excerpt:

STATEMENT BY THE SECRETARY-GENERAL
ISSUED IN ABUJA, NIGERIA

The following statement was issued by the Secretary-General on 27 June 1992 in Abuja, Nigeria:

The Secretary-General has received reports from UN-PROFOR that, following his statement to the Security Council on 26 June, the Serb forces in and around Sarajevo have taken several steps to implement the 5 June agreement. Military attacks have ceased and tanks have been withdrawn from the airport. The Secretary-General welcomes this encouraging development but is greatly concerned to learn that new hostilities have been initiated on Friday and Saturday by the forces of the Government of Bosnia and Herzegovina. While the Serb side, in response to appeals of UNPROFOR, exercised self-restraint in refraining from retaliation, the persistence of military attacks by the Territorial Defence Forces of the Government risks renewed destruction and suffering for the people of Sarajevo.

The Secretary-General appeals to the government of Bosnia and Herzegovina to respect the ceasefire. He calls urgently on all forces in Sarajevo to halt the fighting and urges all concerned to co-operate with UNPROFOR's efforts to reopen the airport. The Secretary-General wishes to recall to all parties that the purpose of the effort underway to reopen Sarajevo airport is strictly humanitarian in nature and hence does not affect the underlying political differences between them.

I flashed a message off to General Nambiar asking that the Security Council authorize the Canadian battalion to start its trek from Croatia to Sarajevo at 2359 the following day. I knew every soldier in Michel's unit would be delighted with the news, having awaited word to move for over two weeks.

JUNE 29   I made my earliest run ever to the Presidency and was waiting for Vice-President Ganic when he arrived at his office. I explained that since we would take over the airport later that afternoon, I needed a signature from the Presidency guaranteeing that their forces would not interfere with its operation as long as the UN flag flew over the complex. I showed Ganic the contract that I had drafted the previous evening:

SARAJEVO AIRPORT RESPONSIBILITIES

At 1800 hours Monday 29 June 1992 UNPROFOR assumed responsibility for the Sarajevo airport from the "Serbian Democratic Republic".

The Presidency of Bosnia-Herzegovina and the "Serbian Democratic Republic" undertake to ensure the security of the airport by guaranteeing that they will not shoot at, shell, attack, or occupy the airport during the presence of UNPROFOR. Any breach whatsoever of this undertaking will be considered a clear indication that the violator does not wish the airport to open and is prepared to accept the international consequences.

Read, understood and agreed:

Dr. Ganic	L.W. MacKenzie	Professor Koljevic
The Presidency	Major-General	"Serbian Democratic
Bosnia-Herzegovina	UNPROFOR	Republic"

Ganic refused to sign any agreement that included the name "Serbian Democratic Republic". I explained that quotation marks around the name indicated an unofficial status. He refused to budge and we debated the point for over an hour. Rather than let the opening of the airport fail because of disagreement over a matter of principle, I told Ganic that I would produce two documents, one signed by himself and me, the other by a representative from Karadzic's side and me. In the document for his signature, I would change "Serbian Democratic Republic" to "General Mladic's Military Forces". Ganic agreed and signed.

We had been asked to drop into the Bosnian Ministry of the

Interior on our way back to the PTT. My suspicions were confirmed a few minutes after Steve and I arrived, when our host played us a tape of an alleged radio conversation between two Serbs plotting my demise. As we listened to the translation of the garbled transcript, I asked myself the inevitable question, "Now, is it the Serbs who want me out of the way, and the Presidency is warning me; or is it the Presidency, and they want to cast the blame for my death on the Serbs?" I took a copy of the tape and the translation for my collection of useless memorabilia, and we departed, driving a little faster than usual, back to the PTT.

The TDF could not resist the targets presented by the Bosnian Serbs as they packed up and prepared to leave the airport. Our personnel on site reported heavy sniper fire coming from the TDF area of Dobrinja; a number of Bosnian-Serb soldiers had been shot during the morning.

Over the next four hours, I held several telephone conversations with Vice-President Ganic, asking him to get a grip on his people in Dobrinja so we could manage the withdrawal of the Bosnian-Serb soldiers and their tanks. As time passed, I became more impatient, and our verbal exchanges became fairly heated. At approximately 1500, the firing virtually stopped, and relative calm settled on the area surrounding the airport. Steve and I immediately drove there for a meeting with Professor Koljevic.

The airport was a scene of frenzied activity. The Serbs had occupied it since April 6, when it had been taken over by the JNA. Any soldier worth his salt can make himself comfortable in some pretty miserable circumstances; the Serbs were no exception and had accumulated a lot of junk designed to assist them in their quest for comfort over the previous eleven weeks. Some of it was being loaded into vehicles, but most of it had been thrown onto the grass surrounding the buildings or left in the hallways, where it augmented the waste left over from the actual running of the airport. There were thousands of files littering the hall floors, which made it almost impossible to walk as they slid around under your feet.

Much to my surprise, the Serbs had lined up their tanks and self-propelled anti-aircraft weapons on the parking apron in front of the terminal. They made a tempting target for the TDF in Butmir and Dobrinja, but I presumed the Serbs were daring the Presidency's forces to engage them and give them an excuse to stay. It was also obvious that they were not going to be organized in time to leave at the appointed time of 1630.

Professor Koljevic and I sat in the airport manager's office and discussed our hopes (soon to be proved hollow) that the withdrawal from the airport would be a start to a meaningful and lasting ceasefire in Sarajevo and perhaps Bosnia. Finally, at 1815 hours, the last of the two armoured convoys departed, accompanied by Richard Gray and a few of our observers. I wanted to wait until all of our airport detachment personnel were gathered before we ran up the UN flag; however, Richard was delayed at Lukavica, so at 1910 we decided to go ahead with the flag-raising ceremony.

The international media were present in large numbers, so I gave some thought to the matter of who should actually raise the flag. Commandant Hauben had spent the previous night at the airport along with his team, and they would be in an even more difficult situation that evening, now that the Bosnian Serbs had departed. If the TDF decided to take advantage of the situation, they could easily occupy the airport, since their front line was only a hundred metres away in Dobrinja; such a move would only cause the Bosnian Serbs to counterattack, and our people would be innocent victims caught in the middle.

Accordingly, I decided that Commandant Hauben would have the honour of raising the flag of the world body. This he did with style. The television cameras caught the rest of us saluting as the blue-and-white flag made its way to the top of the rusty flagpole. I was chewing gum during the event; within a few weeks, I had received dozens of packages of gum from friends and strangers from far and wide, who kindly (and correctly) assumed I might be running short. I was beginning to appreciate the true power of television.

STEVE AND I LEFT THE AIRPORT for the PTT in a euphoric mood, which lasted for about thirty seconds. As we turned onto the road in front of the airport terminal, our VBL was struck by sniper fire. Reality brought us back to earth and we speeded up.

Around 2000 that evening, we had an excited call from our airport personnel advising us that a French Hercules aircraft had arrived unannounced; the crew was already unloading its cargo of humanitarian aid. I gave the order to have the aircraft reloaded, sealed and guarded.

During the past week, we had spent hours negotiating a system whereby humanitarian representatives of the three ethnic communities in Sarajevo would observe our UN civilian police inspecting each aid shipment as it was unloaded. We knew that if such an inspection were not done, we would be accused of smuggling arms and ammunition to one or more sides in the conflict. We had an excellent team of civilian police headed up by Michael O'Riley of the Royal Canadian Mounted Police, and they were on call; but it would be impossible to gather the humanitarian representatives before the following day. If we screwed up this first delivery, we would probably never recover in the eyes of all parties to the conflict. I hated the idea of impounding the French aircraft, given everything that France and President Mitterand were doing to help us in Sarajevo; but unfortunately, there was no choice. I told Commandant Hauben to make the aircraft crew as comfortable as possible. At least he would have five more people to help him "defend" the airport overnight.

After we had resolved the dilemma of the French aircraft, Jorge de la Reta came to my office and asked me to visit our officers' mess. Calling it a mess broadened the definition of the term for the rest of our lives: it was a room with some chairs, a television set, a videocassette recorder and a place to serve coffee. There was a paucity of alcohol, but a few bottles purchased here and there on the black market meant people could have a drink if they seriously wanted one.

As I walked into the mess, I was greeted by a loud round of applause. I was baffled, not knowing for what or whom the applause was intended. Jorge announced, "General MacKenzie, congratulations on opening the Sarajevo airport. We all hope this is the start of a healing process for this city."

It was an interesting observation. I really hadn't considered the impact of running up the UN flag at the terminal. I'd been so immersed in the negotiation process that I'd failed to appreciate that the staff and the observers, who had done most of the work, saw it as a key event .

I mumbled something to the effect of, "Jorge, Vanessa, gentlemen, thank you for everything you have done to make this come to pass—particularly for volunteering to come to Sarajevo in the first place. With your continuing efforts, we will run an airport and keep the heavy weapons under a modest amount of control. Let's all say a personal prayer tonight for our people at the airport."

I checked in with our airport team a few times during the night. They had received a flurry of telephoned death threats, ranging from "We will cut every one of your throats," to "We will burn you alive." They didn't get much sleep, but by sunrise, the airport was still ours, and the shelling had died down to a dull roar.

JUNE 30   Steve and I made an early run to the airport and found everyone in good shape. At 0910, a French C-160 Transall aircraft landed with food and water. By the time it arrived, the previous evening's aircraft had unloaded its food and medicine under observation and departed. At 0923, a French C-130 Hercules landed. It off-loaded some medical supplies and took off with President Mitterand's damaged Puma helicopter safely stowed in the back. Another C-160 touched down at 1155 with five new members for the French technical team and some more humanitarian aid. All in all, 32.6 tonnes of food had arrived during a two-hour period; we were beginning to feel optimistic.

Just after lunch, we visited the Presidency. About five minutes into my discussions with President Izetbegovic, I was called to the phone in his outer office: Commandant Hauben advised me that all hell had broken loose around the airport, and four of our personnel had been injured. A sniper bullet had penetrated the rubber seal between the bullet-proof glass and the armour plate on one of the French armoured personnel carriers. The bullet had exploded when it struck a metal bar inside the vehicle, and four personnel, including Ray Honig, had sustained minor injuries. Commandant Hauben was suspending operations until the fighting died down; he had also restricted vehicle movement in the area of the airport.

I returned to the meeting and told the President in no uncertain terms that the fire had originated from his forces' area in Dobrinja. "If you can't control your snipers, Mr. President, I will," was the way I put it.

The President replied, "Please do, General MacKenzie; those elements are out of control. They do not respond to our direction. If you can stop them from firing by any means, we will be pleased." Great, I thought: now he is authorizing us to kill his own people.

Before I left, Vice-President Ganic asked me to consider the establishment of a security zone around all of Sarajevo, as called for in the UN Security Council resolution containing the airport agreement.

"Dr. Ganic," I replied, "the security zone around Sarajevo is to be considered after the airport agreement is implemented. At this time, we do not have a ceasefire, concentration of heavy weapons, or secure humanitarian corridors—all things promised by you and the Bosnian Serbs when you signed the agreement. The airport is currently open thanks to the personal bravery of the President of France and a handful of UN officers and soldiers. When you live up to the promises you made in writing over three weeks ago, we can discuss the security zone. By the way, I'll be telling the Bosnian Serbs the same thing later today. For now, let's restrict ourselves to trying to make the airport agreement work. It's certainly not getting off to a very good start."

Steve and I decided to take a chance and make for the airport. We arrived without incident and, after checking that everyone was okay, drove to Lukavica. Professor Koljevic was there, along with Colonels Tolimir and Sipcic. The Colonels were obviously depressed; they explained that the TDF was reinforcing its positions in Dobrinja, and the Serbs could do very little about it, since they had turned their defensive positions at the airport over to us. Being outnumbered by the TDF, they would have to use their tanks and artillery if the reinforcing actions around Dobrinja continued. I replied that I would raise the subject with President Izetbegovic later in the day; in the meantime, they should restrain themselves, otherwise the airport would be closed.

Colonel Tolimir brought up the subject of Bosnian-Serb ambulances using the runway on an emergency basis. I explained that the Presidency was against the idea, but, since I had given my word on this matter earlier, I would authorize such traffic. I suggested that they should consider giving freedom of movement to all ambulances from the Presidency in blockaded areas, and left it at that.

I informed the Colonels and Professor Koljevic that we were not happy with the Serbs' concentration of their heavy weapons, as called for in the airport agreement. I was of the opinion that they had actually declared less than 20 per cent of the artillery concerned. The Colonels explained that they had misunderstood which weapons were covered by the agreement, and promised to concentrate the remainder within a few days. I knew they understood the rules that General Mladic had signed, and told them so. We agreed that they should move their offending weapons to concentration areas as quickly as possible, and not later than forty-eight hours hence.

After the meeting, Professor Koljevic mentioned privately that he hoped my remarks would help to bring the Serbs' artillery units under control. He indicated, much to my disappointment, that their artillery units on the east side of the city were not under "proper military control". This was not an encouraging thought; it was those units that were doing most of the damage to the city.

Back at the Presidency, I confronted Vice-President Ganic with the fact that *his* forces were reinforcing Dobrinja. He tap-danced around the issue for a while and finally admitted they were doing so for "various reasons". However, he refused to commit himself to ordering a stop to the activities. So I told him, "Dr. Ganic, if you don't stop, you know the Serbs will use tanks and artillery to even the odds. Perhaps that is what you want, because it will make them look like the villain in this piece. But an awful lot of people will be killed, so please consider very carefully what you are doing."

Ganic concluded the meeting by stating that his forces would fire on any Bosnian-Serb ambulances using the runway, even if they were escorted by the UN. I replied, "That was a big negotiating point that resulted in the Serbs leaving the airport. If you won't agree to it, then presumably we have to let them reoccupy the airport. You know my position: they voluntarily gave up their ability to move critical casualties to their hospital, and therefore it is reasonable to agree to this concession. Without it, the airport closes down again."

Ganic was not pleased, and we agreed to leave the matter for another time. Unfortunately, later that day, he went on Bosnian TV and condemned me personally for permitting such a thing. From that moment, my relations with the Bosnian Presidency and its supporters started down a slippery slope and never recovered.

When we got back to the PTT, I was advised that the first convoy of 274 Canadian soldiers and 100 vehicles, led by Michel Jones, had left the Van Doos' camp at Daruvar for Sarajevo at 0400; the second convoy was scheduled to leave at midnight. Thank God.

26

The Canadians Are Coming

JULY 1 (CANADA DAY!) Our morale was buoyed by a surprise message from New York announcing to all UN personnel around the world that July 1, 1992, had been declared a UN holiday. I told everyone to take a five-minute break sometime during the day to celebrate!

We had very little contact with the Van Doos' convoy en route to Sarajevo. Communication was by ordinary telephone or a series of radio relays, which more often than not didn't reach us. The BBC World Service was reporting that the convoy was held up at a heavily armed Serbian checkpoint a hundred kilometres north of Sarajevo. I called Dr. Karadzic and asked him to intervene. He indicated that he would try, but their communications were as ineffective as ours. Finally, I managed a short radio conversation with Michel Jones; he confirmed that he was having trouble with Serb forces and was going to try another route.

God bless the French! Two aircraft arrived with a 130-man marine commando company led by their unit's operations officer, Lieutenant-Colonel Erik de Stabenrath. His battalion would follow in approximately a month; however, he and his company would give us a hand in the meantime. I was delighted; for the first time, I felt we might be able to hold onto the airport until the Van Doos arrived.

Three more French aircraft, loaded with humanitarian aid, arrived before the end of the day. Off-loading was by hand and painfully slow; however, the arrival of additional French technical personnel gave us a much needed increase to our unloading capacity.

We were still operating without the proper equipment but had hopes that it might be flown in within a few days.

Vice-President Ganic had invited me to walk about Sarajevo with him that afternoon, to try to improve my image with the local population. I wasn't totally convinced that he had my best interests at heart but couldn't very well say no. Steve and I arrived at the Presidency, which was inundated with media people. I jumped out of our VAB, took off my flak jacket and threw it into the vehicle. Even at the time, I knew this was not particularly smart, but Ganic was standing there in his suit, so I decided to match his unprotected appearance.

We strolled along the street surrounded by security police, the media and curious citizens. I shook hands with everyone we passed. Eventually, we reached the site of the bread-line shelling, and I signed the book of remembrance to those who had been killed. Following five minutes at the site, we jumped into my vehicle and drove to the area of the Congress building across from the Holiday Inn. It was a favourite location for snipers; as we started to walk to the building, we came under fire. I grabbed Ganic to pull him out of the way. As my hand fell on his back, I suddenly realized he was wearing a flak jacket under his sports coat! All of a sudden, I felt distinctly unprotected and more than a little foolish.

We proceeded to the Kosovo hospital, where the staff was working under miserable conditions but doing magnificent work. Every inch of space was being used, except those rooms that had windows to the outside and were therefore exposed to sniper fire. The majority of patients were children or the elderly: a graphic statement of the cruel type of war that was being fought.

Our last stop was at a park on the north side of Sarajevo. The park was now a cemetery, and the new, makeshift wooden grave-markers were a clear indication that the graves were fresh. Ganic said, "Our history begins here, General MacKenzie." It was a powerful statement that had a profound impact on all of us.

That evening, I went to the Bosnian television studio, which was only 300 metres down the road from the PTT, and did three interviews back-to-back: with Peter Jennings of ABC, the International Television network, and CNN. I was also interviewed by Andrew Phillips of Canada's *Maclean's* magazine. At one stage, Andrew asked, "Do you think your diary will ever become a book?"

"No way," I replied.

Just before I tucked in for the night, I received word that the Danish Army had promoted Svend Harders to brigadier-general. He had certainly earned it, given that he had taken on my chief of staff position without warning when I'd come back to Sarajevo.

JULY 2   Early in the day, we found out that the second of the Van Doos' convoys had caught up to Michel's lead group. They had bluffed and intimidated their way through a number of problem checkpoints and were making good progress. With any luck, they would arrive in Sarajevo by noon.

The first of two aircraft due during the morning off-loaded its humanitarian aid, plus seventeen journalists, who turned out to have no idea of the situation that existed in Sarajevo. When we explained that we could not give them a lift downtown, they jumped into the back of a UNHCR truck and were promptly arrested at the first Serb checkpoint.

I sat down with our press officer, Fred Eckhard, who had just arrived back from our headquarters in Belgrade. We agreed that any journalists who arrived without a colleague to meet them and get them out of the airport would be sent out on the same plane that had brought them in. This was a bit draconian, but justified; if we didn't take such action, the airport would soon be crawling with non-UN personnel who couldn't get downtown to obtain accreditation. At that stage, just about anyone could pass himself off as a journalist and hitch a ride on a humanitarian flight to Sarajevo, and the situation was quickly becoming a security nightmare for our civilian police.

At 1053, I received word at the PTT that the Canadians had arrived at the airport. Steve and I got there less than ten minutes later, just as Michel was dismounting from his vehicle. I remember saying, "Good trip?" and Michel's replying, "Not bad." Anyone listening in, such as the crowd of media people surrounding us, including our old friend, Martin Bell, would have thought we were discussing a quiet Sunday drive back in Canada.

I bummed a Canadian cigarette off Michel and listened as he told me about his encounter with a drunken Serbian commander the previous day. "He wouldn't let us through," Michel recalled. "So we pulled back about twenty-eight kilometres and waited for the rest of the battalion to catch up to us. This morning I thought we'd give it another try. The same guy was in charge and sober now, but he still wouldn't let us through. He threatened to shoot if we tried to continue. There was the odd bit of sniper fire in the air, so I deployed our TOW system, mortars and our own snipers and told him if we were fired at, we would fire back. He cooled down a bit but started to reinforce his position. I told him, 'If you reinforce with one more person, I'm driving through.' Well, he did, so we drove straight through to Sarajevo. All I can say is, it's a good thing he didn't fire at us, because we had a lot of firepower facing in his direction."

"Well done," I told Michel. "My biggest concern was that no one would take you on face-to-face—they would sit back four or five kilometres and mortar or artillery you."

I went on to explain that we had an unfortunate problem with accommodation. We'd been promised a number of barracks for our troops, plus what was left of the Holiday Inn, but so far we didn't have a firm deal for any of them. "There isn't even anywhere to park your vehicles, so they'll have to stay at the airport tonight. Keep your other 550 people outside of town until tomorrow, otherwise we'll have too much of a 'target-rich environment' here at the airport. The customs buildings have very thick walls, so your people will be well protected there. Just make sure you have lots of sentries. I'll be surprised if you don't get shelled and sniped at overnight."

It was good to see Michel with his battalion around him. Commanding a battalion as a lieutenant-colonel is the best job in any army. It's what anyone who calls himself a combat officer wants to do before he dies; you are really close to the soldiers, and those years in command are usually the best of your military career. To be lucky enough to command in a theatre like Sarajevo made it all the better, and I could easily see that Michel was enjoying the challenge. He was a different person compared to the way he'd been when on reconnaissance with us. Now that he had his boys with him, he knew that anything he ordered would be done and done well.

In addition to his battalion, Michel had a troop of Mike Gauthier's combat engineers. They would be invaluable in helping the unit to dig in and to clear obstacles, including mines and booby traps. They had the best piece of equipment in our army's vehicle inventory—the Badger. It was based on the German Leopard tank chassis, but instead of a main gun, it had an assortment of digging aids; over the following month, these would be in almost constant use. Soldiers should never feel comfortable until they have a place available underground, and with the Badger, digging in didn't take long.

When I got back to the PTT, there was a classified message

waiting for me from a non-UN source, indicating that the Croatian Army's advance was getting dangerously close to Sarajevo. I was aware that a few days earlier, Zagreb TV had shown pictures of the Sarajevo airport allegedly taken from the Croatian front line on Mount Igman. I asked Richard Gray to check with his observers to see if any Serbian artillery was pointing away from the city towards the Croatians. Unfortunately, the reports came back that there was indeed some movement of Bosnian-Serb guns, which could indicate a threat from another direction.

Now we had a new complicating factor. Until that moment, we had been dealing only with the Bosnian-Serb army, consisting largely of ex-JNA officers and soldiers who had been born in Bosnia; and the TDF, made up of Bosnian Muslims, Bosnian Croats and Bosnian Serbs loyal to the Presidency. Enter the Croatian Army, which had been fighting around Mostar, but now appeared to be trying to link up with the TDF at Sarajevo.

I was never persuaded that the Muslim-Croat coalition would hold up under the stress of battle. If the Croatian Army did link up with the TDF, there was a good chance that fighting would break out between them. That would give us a three-way fight to deal with, something I could gladly do without.

J U L Y 3   Now that the Van Doos had arrived, I introduced a daily conference at the airport at 0730 every morning, to keep the various elements in our force co-ordinated. If I wasn't able to make it, Commandant Hauben would carry on without me. Following the airport conference, Steve and I would rush back to the PTT for the regular meeting of our headquarters staff.

We were still having a problem with the Presidency over accommodating the Van Doos at the Holiday Inn. The rooms were supposed to be free of charge except for operating costs, but Presidency officials wanted $38 a night plus meal expenses. When I asked where they would get the food to feed over 300 soldiers, I was told, "We have some reserves as long as you pay for them."

It struck me as bizarre that hundreds of people, including the President of France, had risked their lives to open the airport so that humanitarian aid could fly into a "starving" city, yet here they were, offering to sell us meals at the Holiday Inn. I declined the offer and ordered our people to stop dealing with the hotel staff. Arrangements were ultimately made to move the Van Doos' "N" Company and the unit's administrative company into an old JNA camp renamed "Beaver Camp", located less than a kilometre north of the PTT.

The European Community's representatives, Lord Carrington and Ambassador Cutileiro, arrived for a visit at 1245. After a short stop at our headquarters to discuss the situation in Sarajevo, Lord Carrington proceeded to the Presidency, where the mood was distinctly gloomy. President Izetbegovic insisted on seven full days of ceasefire before he would allow any peace conference in Bosnia. He indicated that Cutileiro's cantonization plan was unacceptable, since his government would only accept a unitary state as a constitutional solution.

Lord Carrington was to meet with Dr. Karadzic and Professor Koljevic at the PTT; however, this was deemed inadvisable when the TDF commander, Colonel Siber, called us and said that Karadzic and Koljevic would be killed if they tried to make it to the PTT—even if they were riding in UN vehicles. We sarcastically thanked the Colonel for his co-operation and decided to take Lord Carrington to Lukavica.

As we crossed the airport towards Lukavica in an armoured personnel carrier, I briefed the Canadian sergeant manning the crew commanders's hatch and its 50-calibre machine gun that we would be fired at from eastern Butmir as we turned south onto the road. "Sergeant," I said, "when we are fired at, you make sure you fire back." What I didn't say, but thought, was: "I'm really sorry you are up there in the hatch with no protection around you, and I'm really sorry your machine gun is mounted in such a way that it can't be fired accurately on the move. When you fire back, I'll be ducking down in the back of this APC, but you are going to have to stay up there to operate the machine gun. I'd like to meet the people in our Department of National Defence who knocked our Multi-Role Combat Vehicle so far down the priority list that it was cancelled three years ago. The only Canadian servicemen getting shot at on a regular basis since the Korean War are in the army, and here we are driving around in APCs designed in the late 1950s. Meanwhile, the navy and air force are taking delivery of state-of-the-art ships and aircraft." By the time I had thought all of that, we had been fired at, the sergeant had fired back from his exposed position, and we had made it to Lukavica.

The meeting was short. Karadzic protested that he couldn't possibly put all his heavy weapons under UN control, since he was outnumbered and had to protect his people.

Before departing, Lord Carrington looked me in the eye and said, "Lew, there is absolutely no consensus here for any type of a dialogue, let alone a settlement. Good luck, your people are doing great work."

A total of nine aircraft made it in with humanitarian aid. That was about the maximum we had thought we could handle in one day, particularly without mechanical off-loading equipment. But Colonel Forestier and Commandant Hauben were keen to try a few more, so the schedule of incoming aircraft was increased for the weekend.

Heavy artillery shelling started all around the city and its outskirts at 2200. Everyone went to their bunkers, wondering if the Croatian Army had arrived on the scene. If they had, there was a pretty good chance that the Serbs would reoccupy the airport. Michel had his own Van Doos company well dug in around the runway. His TOWs and mortars were ready for use, although, according to the UN's directive, they shouldn't have been equipped with missiles or explosive ammunition. Fortunately, of course, we had cheated.

JULY 4   This was the day when I began to lose faith in any realistic hope of a ceasefire. It was also the day when the first Canadian aircraft arrived with aid.

The situation in the city deteriorated following Lord Carrington's visit. Major battles broke out in Dobrinja and Lukavica. Everyone bunkered down at the airport and waited for the sun to arrive, along with the usual reduction in shelling. It did, and twelve aircraft made it in during the day.

During the shelling, our observers were still reporting lots of incoming fire, but neither side was acknowledging that a single gun had been fired from their positions. Both sides were cheating, the Bosnian Serbs being the major culprit because they had the majority of the artillery; but the TDF were guilty of spiriting away some of their recent artillery acquisitions, which they had gained in exchange for the JNA's withdrawal. I met with both President Izetbegovic and Professor Koljevic to protest, but my heart wasn't in it; both sides had lied to me for over a week, saying they had declared all their weapons.

I had requested UN New York to provide us with satellite or reconnaissance-plane imagery, so that I could prove who was cheating and where, but my request had been rejected. I'd even persuaded both sides to ask me to ask the UN for imagery, but that request was rejected also. In the good old days of peacekeeping, it had rightfully been considered bad taste to spy on the people you were trying to help. Bosnia was different, but UN rules hadn't caught up with the new challenges we were facing.

In fact, we had proof that both sides were not living up to the contracts they had signed with the UN. The technical capacity existed to determine more precisely who was cheating and by how much; yet an outdated attitude regarding intelligence kept us from gaining the information we needed. Imagery would also have told us what the Croatian Army was doing in Bosnia. Non-UN sources were trying to help in this regard, but it wasn't easy getting the data to us; and when we did receive it, we weren't allowed to share it with some of the nationalities in our staff.

That evening, I began to receive hints from both UN and non-UN sources that certain nations were standing by with air power to give us a hand, if need be. This was the last thing we needed, unless we were being directly attacked as a matter of policy by one, two or all three sides in the conflict.

I sent a message to General Nambiar stressing that the use of air power on our behalf would clearly associate us with the side *not* being attacked, and thereafter we would very quickly be branded an intervention force, as opposed to an impartial peacekeeping force. If that was to be the case, I wanted delivery of all those weapons and ammunition that the UN had said the Canadian battalion couldn't bring to Sarajevo. I was being sarcastic, but this was a vital issue, much misunderstood by non-military types, and I wanted to make my point before someone came to our "rescue" and got us all killed.

JULY 5   General Nambiar and Cedric Thornberry arrived by UN aircraft early in the morning. We spent the day visiting the Canadian battalion, the French company, the Presidency and the Bosnian Serbs. Nambiar was impressed with Michel's unit and how quickly it had settled in.

Our Canadian units are renowned for their field kitchens, and I was beginning to notice that the PTT staff was a bit thin on the ground around breakfast time, since they were sneaking off to the Van Doos for a great Canadian breakfast. Our mechanics, who had done such a marvellous job getting our vintage APCs to Sarajevo without a major breakdown, were up and running in their new location in Beaver Camp and were the envy of the rest of the force.

Nothing new came up during our talks with Izetbegovic and Karadzic. The same old points were rehashed, although Karadzic placed a new emphasis on the threat posed by the Croatian Army if it were to enter the fray, either on its own or on the side of the Muslims. I stressed to the two leaders that both sides were cheating by not declaring all their heavy weapons to the UN. I don't think Nambiar was terribly appreciative of my frankness of tone, but he was too much of a gentleman to say so.

During the day, a total of seventeen aircraft made it to Sarajevo. We now had a few fork-lift trucks and an adjustable platform with rollers, called a "K" loader. It looked as if we might be able to handle twenty-plus aircraft a day, substantially more than the nine we had anticipated as our maximum. It wasn't just the equipment that made the difference; our French and Norwegian groundhandlers and our UN civilian police were working their butts off and turning the aircraft around in record time. There were more aircraft stacked up in Zagreb waiting to fly in than we could handle, but everyone was voluntarily doing more than I would ever have demanded of them; each day they tried to set a new record. Military folks, no matter what their nationality, are by nature competitive, and I was blessed with some of the most competitive of all.

J U L Y 6 I had reached the point where nothing in Sarajevo surprised me. Just before noon, we received a call from the Presidency informing us that a Serbian member of the Presidency, a "tame" Serb, Mr. Kismanovic, would like to go to Lukavica and meet with the other side. Naturally, I was pleased to assist, since I thought this might be the beginning of a dialogue.

Steve and I took the gentleman across to Lukavica, leaving his bodyguard at the PTT. He met with Professor Koljevic, whom he knew very well, for over an hour. Following their meeting, Koljevic told me, "We want to send Mr. Kismanovic to Belgrade to speak with Mr. Panic, the new American-Serb Prime Minister."

I was a bit suspicious and asked to speak to Mr. Kismanovic, who confirmed that he wanted to go to Belgrade. I said, "Look, your bodyguard is back at the PTT. He is going to be one unhappy camper when I show up empty-handed and tell him you wanted to go to Belgrade. You had better write him a note and include something that convinces him you are telling the truth."

The note seemed to satisfy the bodyguard. In fact, he didn't seem at all surprised, and I had a feeling that he'd expected his boss to stay on the other side all along. The tame Serb never did return to Sarajevo, and his wife became a bit of a pain when she camped at the front entrance of the PTT, lobbying for passage to Belgrade for herself and her children. Once again, we'd been used.

We started firing back at our nemesis, the snipers in Dobrinja. Our Canadian and French marksmen were excellent. Cuban revolutionary leader Che Guevara once said that one of the principles of war is patience, and any good sniper is a living example of that principle.

Except for a few notable and effective exceptions, the snipers on the TDF and Bosnian-Serb sides were not really snipers at all. They would rush about highrise buildings, changing rooms and firing from the windows, rather than camouflaging themselves in the shadows and awaiting their chance. Our snipers would search the building with their powerful scopes and find one of the snipers at work. They would keep watching him or her (the most effective TDF sniper was a female "tame" Serb who had been a competitor in the 1988 Olympics), after deliberately moving into a position where they could easily be seen. When the TDF or Bosnian-Serb sniper spotted them, they would wave, as if to say, "I've got you covered and I found you long before you saw me—so don't do anything stupid." This tactic usually worked, and the sniper disappeared. If it didn't work, and the opposing sniper fired at any member of the UN or at any of our equipment, including the humanitarian aircraft, our man would fire a single, well-aimed shot, which always did the job.

Around midnight, I received a call from General de Chastelain. He was optimistic that he would be able to visit Sarajevo in about five days. I told him it would be great for our soldiers' morale and urged him not to let the UN talk him out of it.

JULY 7　We always started our day with the BBC World Service on shortwave at 0600. Occasionally, it was a surrealistic experience to listen to the BBC's descriptions of events in Sarajevo while watching the events unfold for real outside our windows. Unfortunately, on this day, the BBC was reporting that the TDF intended to launch a major offensive in an attempt to link up with the Croatian forces south of Sarajevo. Since any battle in that quadrant of the city would have a major impact on the airport, I was very concerned. I was also upset that I had to get my intelligence from the BBC. The UN was still following its outdated rules that precluded our even saying the word "intelligence", let alone producing it. Here we were, almost 300 kilometres from the nearest semi-secure border, and we scarcely had the foggiest notion what was going on around us.

Commandant Hauben was returning to Belgrade, having done a marvellous job of setting up and running the airport operation over the past few weeks. As a movement-control specialist, he had expertise that was badly needed back at UNPROFOR headquarters. Colonel Forestier would take over from him. We held a modest ceremony at the airport, and Colonel Forestier paid Hauben the ultimate compliment when he said he would gladly work for him again at any time in the future. A commandant in the Belgian Army is the equivalent of a major, so for a French colonel to say such a thing was clear evidence of the respect that Hauben had earned during his stint as the airport boss.

After the ceremony, I was advised that UNHCR had hired local drivers from all three ethnic communities to drive the aid trucks in and around Sarajevo. This decision sounded okay, but we all knew it had the potential to turn into a disaster, since the drivers would undoubtedly not be able to get along. After all, their communities were killing each other.

On my return to the PTT, there was a message waiting from Nambiar saying that President Izetbegovic would fly to Helsinki the following day for talks with the European Community, and that I should facilitate his movement to and from the airport. The thought of driving from the Presidency to the airport with Izetbegovic in the back of one of our APCs was unnerving, to say the least. He could easily be ambushed and killed, and we would have a catastrophe on our hands.

I told Steve, "Put together three convoys with at least two vehicles each, plus an armoured ambulance. Have two of them drive around the city tomorrow morning making sure they are seen. One of them should pick up Izetbegovic and his party and bring them to our PTT underground parking lot. We will be waiting there with the third convoy. We will transfer the President into one of the vehicles. I don't even want the drivers to know which vehicle is carrying the President. You and I will lead the convoy with him in it." It was all a bit James Bond-ish, but any potential ambush would have only one chance in three to eliminate Izetbegovic.

JULY 8　The BBC reported that fifteen Serbian tanks had been operating in the centre of Sarajevo the previous night. We were all flabbergasted, because it just wasn't possible without our knowledge, not to mention the fact that tanks can't fight in a built-up area without some infantry protection. During the day, we determined that three Canadian APCs had driven past the Holiday Inn, which housed most of the journalists, at approximately 2000 the previous evening. Bosnian radio had reported that Serb tanks were invading the downtown area, and some of the media must have heard our APCs, put two and two together, and got fifteen. In reality, there were no Serb tanks in downtown Sarajevo, but it made a good story just before Izetbegovic's departure. I assumed that the report had been fabricated to elicit some sympathy for the Presidency during the EC talks, which were already underway in Helsinki.

Our deception plan for Izetbegovic's movement worked; he arrived at the airport without incident. I wished him luck and made my standard plea for him to speak, if only unofficially, with the Bosnian-Serb leadership at his meeting in Helsinki.

Later in the morning, Mrs. Ogata, the UN's High Commissioner for Refugees, based in Geneva, arrived for a daylight visit. I was immediately impressed by her toughness and the respect she elicited from her people who were working with us. She and Fabrizio Hochschild spent the day visiting the food-distribution centres in Sarajevo, and she departed at 1600.

That evening, I said goodbye to some members of the French technical team and a squad of the French marine commandos. They sang a marine-commando hymn during our get-together, and we all had tears in our eyes when they finished. No one but a combat soldier can appreciate the affection that can develop among soldiers under the stress of operations. I loved every one of the French contingent because they were true professionals, and I told them I would be honoured to serve with them at any place and time in the future.

There were still a few minutes before nightfall, so I dropped in to our movement-control headquarters, where I had a drink with our hard-working composite unit. It was made up of Norwegian and French personnel, along with a number of Canadians who were not part of the UN, but who had volunteered to stay in Sarajevo after a small task they had been sent to perform was completed a week earlier. They were a great group, and their morale was unmatched. We were now receiving over twenty aircraft a day, and as far as they were concerned, they were ready to handle even more. We had about thirty minutes of "power drinking" before Steve and I returned to the PTT.

As anticipated, the level of fighting escalated dramatically overnight. Izetbegovic was in Helsinki, and therefore it was to his advantage to report that "Sarajevo is burning" to the EC conference. I understood his logic but didn't like our people being in the middle of the firing. The TDF opened up on the Bosnian-Serb positions, and for a while, it looked as if they would undertake a major offensive. Fortunately, as usual, there was much preparation for an attack—preparatory artillery and mortar fire; manoeuvres on the ground; covering fire; etc.—but no final assault materialized. A number of rounds fell on our PTT parking lot, and five of our vehicles were seriously damaged. Everyone spent a few hours in the bunker before turning in for the night.

27

The Hardest Decision
of my Career

JULY 9–10 A year earlier, I had promised to lecture at my alma mater, the NATO Defence College in Rome. I was supposed to speak on my experiences as a UN commander in Central America; however, as Sarajevo was now a hot story, I decided to make a quick trip to Rome to honour my promise with a more current topic.

This was my first trip outside Yugoslavia since we'd arrived on March 8, four months earlier. The visit to Rome went well. I was able to defuse an erroneous story in the Italian press that the Italian Air Force had refused to fly aid into Sarajevo because it was too dangerous. I explained that there were more aircraft stacked up in Zagreb awaiting landing authority in Sarajevo than we could handle; the only reason one of their planes hadn't made the trip a few days earlier was that there was no room in the sky over our airport. To make my point that the Italian Air Force was as brave as any, I cancelled my commercial flight back to Zagreb, and flew there on one of the Italian military relief flights—along with fifteen Italian journalists who got the message.

While in Rome, I stayed with Canadian Colonel Alain Forand and his wife, Axelle, in a blissfully quiet suburb south of the city. After twenty-four hours of peace and quiet, Sarajevo seemed years away. Then a call came through from my headquarters, telling me that Corporal Dennis Reid from "N" Company had landed on a mine when he'd jumped from a fence earlier in the day, and one of his feet had been blown off. I felt guilty hearing about the accident in the safety of Rome and was anxious to get back where my responsibilities lay. I knew that my deputy, Vitali Petrounev, would be keeping a good grip on what was going on; but the sooner I got back, the better I'd feel.

JULY 11 I departed Rome at 0930 on the Italian aircraft, and arrived in Sarajevo at 1230 on a Danish Air Force Hercules from Zagreb. As soon as I arrived, I was called by Vitali, who said there was a delegation from the Bosnian-Muslim political party in our headquarters. They wanted to attend a meeting that "MacKenzie knows all about."

"I haven't any idea what they're talking about. Who are they supposed to meet with?" I asked.

"The Serbs," was Vitali's response.

Great, I thought; perhaps we're getting somewhere. "Call Koljevic and ask him if he knows anything about this meeting."

Five minutes later, Vitali confirmed that the Bosnian Serbs had agreed to meet with the Muslim party at the airport.

We had a dilemma. It was very encouraging that the Muslims and Serbs wanted to meet; however, my interpretation of our mandate gave me the right to mediate only between the two sides in the conflict, i.e. the Bosnian government and the self-styled "Serbian Democratic Republic" based in Pale. Izetbegovic was no longer the head of the Muslim party, having voluntarily given up the position some months earlier to head the Bosnian state. I had to speak to Izetbegovic.

"Mr. President," I told him over the phone, "I'm delighted to hear that your Muslim party will be meeting with the Bosnian Serbs. I think that's a tremendous first step." I was fishing; the resulting pregnant pause at the other end of the line told me the President was probably hearing about this for the first time.

"What meeting?" was his response. I went on to explain, and Izetbegovic said, "I'll call you back."

Thirty minutes later, the President's staff called to explain that the meeting should not take place until the agenda was firmed up. They would call and let me know when they were ready. They never called, and the idea for the meeting died. This was too bad; the Muslim party represented a large segment of the population in Sarajevo, and a dialogue between them and the Bosnian Serbs seemed, at least to an amateur like me, a good idea. Presumably Izetbegovic did not want freelancers undermining his strategy. Once again, I could understand his logic, but I was disappointed.

WHEN I GOT BACK TO THE PTT, I had a chat with Vitali about how things had gone during my absence. What he told me was extremely disturbing. It seemed a number of UN vehicles had been stopped by the TDF and everyone forced to dismount. On each occasion, the TDF soldiers said they were looking for "that f---ing MacKenzie". Vitali had been a passenger in one of the vehicles searched and was genuinely concerned for my safety. "They were really quite irrational when they mentioned your name," he said.

To make matters worse, local newspaper articles had once again started to appear, linking me with the Plavsic incident mentioned earlier, and making fun of our UNPROFOR title by referring to us as "SERBPROFOR" and the "Chetnik taxi service". The accusations were so outrageous and widespread that they had to be part of a deliberate smear campaign.

Later that evening, and without knowing that I had been briefed in confidence by Vitali, Richard Gray told me that one of his UN observers at a TDF gun position had had thirty rounds from an AK-47 fired off beside his ear by an irate member of the TDF screaming, "You work for MacKenzie!"

I was devastated. Ordering people into dangerous situations in war for the overall good of the mission is one thing; but asking them to put their lives at increased risk in a peacekeeping operation because of their association with me was unacceptable. For reasons that only the Presidency understood, they were vilifying me in an attempt to discredit UNPROFOR, and my people were being placed under additional risk as a result. The thought of one of our observers being intentionally shot with my name ringing in his ears before he died was quite honestly horrifying. I decided to sleep on it, if that were possible; if I woke up in the morning convinced that I was an obstacle to UNPROFOR's effectiveness, I would discuss it with General de Chastelain when he visited later in the day.

A few minutes later, my fear for our impartial reputation was reinforced when I was briefed on a heroic act carried out by Michel's boys earlier in the day. Sergeant Forest, supported by Captain Belisle, had risked his life rescuing two Muslim women who had been shot by snipers on the main road through Sarajevo. In spite of this selfless act of bravery, we were condemned for not going back under fire to recover other victims, who had been confirmed dead by Sergeant Forest. All of this happened with the TDF close by; yet the onlookers opted to condemn UNPROFOR officers who had just saved two lives.

I could only assume that the President still wanted massive international military intervention, which I had told him he wouldn't get as long as there was a UN peacekeeping force in his city as potential hostages. Perhaps a campaign to get rid of us had begun, so the door could be opened to intervention.

JULY 12 After our early morning conference at the airport, a Canadian C-130 Hercules landed, carrying humanitarian aid and General de Chastelain's party. The visitors included Lieutenant-General Jim Gervais, Commander of the Canadian Army; Colonel Mike Houghton, Director of Peacekeeping at National Defence headquarters; and Mr. Carroll, our Canadian Forces Chief Warrant Officer. All were good friends of mine, and it was good to see them.

General de Chastelain understood how important it is when senior officers visit that they be seen as much as possible by their soldiers. After a short briefing at Michel's command post, he and his party spent the rest of the day visiting the soldiers of the Van Doos' battle group, accompanying them on a delivery of humanitarian aid to one of the downtown distribution centres. The soldiers were delighted to see their Chief of Defence Staff in their midst, and impressed him in turn with their confidence and initiative.

General de Chastelain's visit was designed to allow him maximum time with the soldiers, so I backed off and let Michel conduct the tour. It was his unit; he didn't need another general to clutter up the itinerary. I went back to the PTT and gave some more thought to my emerging role as an obstacle to meaningful negotiations in Sarajevo.

Michel had told me earlier that one of his APCs had been fired at yesterday with an anti-tank grenade in the TDF-controlled area of the city. The grenade had barely missed the vehicle and had killed three bystanders when it exploded. As we did a great deal of driving in and around Sarajevo, this was a serious development. There was no way we could fire back at hidden assailants in the city without killing innocent people. It never ceased to amaze me that the people you were helping wanted you dead.

It took a while to realize it, but I think to this day that our main problem was our title, UNPROFOR. The term "United Nations Protection Force" was appropriate for the initial deployment of our peacekeepers in Croatia. The 14,000 UN soldiers were sent there to protect the people living in the UNPAs, primarily Serbs, from outside attack. The UN had assumed the responsibility for relieving the JNA of its protection role, thereby permitting it to return to Serbia, and reducing the risk of confrontation between Croatia and Serbia. Things turned out differently, of course; the threat to people living in the UNPAS came from within, particularly from the Serbs, who started to evict non-Serbs from the UNPAS. In addition, many JNA soldiers merely took off their uniforms and stayed put. Nevertheless, the title of UNPROFOR was applicable to the task that the UN had been given in Croatia.

But not in Bosnia. Along came our 1,400-strong force to Sarajevo riding white vehicles and wearing blue helmets and calling ourselves UNPROFOR, because that was the name of the organization we belonged to. The city was frequently the target of heavy shelling, and civilian casualties were high. Most of the damage was done by the Bosnian-Serb guns located in the hills around Sarajevo; but the local citizenry was not aware that the government's TDF forces initiated a good many of the incidents, to which the Serbs usually overreacted with their heavy weapons.

With a name like United Nations Protection Force, it was not unreasonable for the citizens of Sarajevo to expect that our job was to protect *them*. Certainly, the Presidency was perpetuating the idea that we had a responsibility to take their side in the conflict. Their reasoning followed the logical but impractical assumption that as a member of the UN, Bosnians should be able to rely on any UN peacekeeping force to be on their side. As citizens of a new country that started fighting for its existence the day it was born, Bosnians didn't understand, or refused to accept, that an international peacekeeping force had to deal with both sides on a regular basis, and to pass objective judgment on events as they transpired. Any suggestion that anyone but the Serbs or Bosnian Serbs were 100 per cent responsible for each and every incident was unacceptable to the Presidency.

As far as the Presidency was concerned, I represented the impotence of the United Nations. The UN traditionally tries to avoid civil wars like the plague; there is seldom an effective way to bring international pressure to bear on any of the sides in a civil conflict. In the case of Bosnia, the UN was trying to pressure the Bosnian Serbs by imposing economic sanctions on Serbia; however, there was a lack of conclusive evidence that President Milosevic in Belgrade was actually controlling Dr. Karadzic in Pale, or providing him with significant military support. On the other hand, the official government of Bosnia-Herzegovina led by President Izetbegovic, a full-fledged member of the UN, was asking the international body for help, and the best that the UN could offer was to open the Sarajevo airport. Consensus could not be found within the Security Council for a more ambitious intervention. Izetbegovic was understandably disappointed by the lack of military action by the UN, and by the world body's reluctance to lift its embargo on arms shipments to the region. And thanks to efforts by members of his Presidency and the TDF, it appeared that I had become the lightning rod for the dissatisfaction of his people.

Rumours were being circulated that my wife was a Serb, and that she had been introduced to me by the "Serbian terrorist, Mila Mulroney", the wife of Canadian Prime Minister Brian Mulroney. Mrs. Mulroney was indeed born a Serb but left Sarajevo permanently for Canada when she was five years old, and so must have started her "terrorist" career at a very young age. Before I was to leave, various members of the Presidency asked me to pass on their regards to Mila, as they had liked her very much when they had attended university with her in Sarajevo. A terrorist *and* a university student by five years of age—I was impressed.

After some twelve hours of consideration, I kept returning to the same conclusion: UNPROFOR might be unpopular, but it was at least doing some good for the people; I, on the other hand, was an obstacle to the peace process, and the disinformation campaign against me was endangering the lives of everyone who worked with me. Having witnessed the reasonable level of co-operation that had quickly developed between the new UN officers in town, such as Michel Jones, and the Presidency, I reluctantly decided that a new sector commander would probably have a much better chance to advance the peace process than I did. Even more importantly, in my eyes, the hatred being directed towards UN personnel in my name would, I hoped, subside on my departure.

I met with General de Chastelain; he listened to my logic, which culminated in my telling him I intended to ask General Nambiar to replace me. To my pleasant surprise, the CDS said he understood; he'd considered pulling me out earlier. In fact, he thought I should leave as soon as possible.

"Sir, I'd rather not do that," I explained. "I promised myself I wouldn't go until the last soldier from Michel's battalion leaves Sarajevo. That will probably be in early August. There is a definite advantage to waiting until that time: I don't want the Presidency to think they forced me to leave, I don't want to give them that satisfaction. If I leave when the Canadian battalion leaves, we can justify it by saying that the UN has decided the sector should be commanded by a general from one of the countries replacing the Canadians in Sarajevo."

De Chastelain was a four-star general, but he was also an infantryman; he understood what I was asking for. "Okay, Lew, I'll let you stay until the Van Doos leave—but only if you agree to take extraordinary measures for your own security."

"It's a deal," I said. "Thanks."

The CDS and his party got ready to spend the night with Michel and his boys at the airport. I returned to the PTT and sat down to compose the most difficult message I had ever written, and sent it off to General Nambiar:

> To: NAMBIAR BELGRADE
> From: MACKENZIE
> Date: 12 JULY 1992
> Subject: DISTURBING TRENDS
>
> 1) You are aware of the desires of the Presidency to achieve international intervention in order to regain their country and their capital. They are in fact perpetuating the current conflict, while the Serbs are showing considerable restraint (I can only speak for Sarajevo). Obviously, the Presidency does not like to hear me describe the facts as I know them, as this weakens their case with the international media. So far, I have not gone public.
>
> 2) Earlier the Presidency keyed its personal attack on my by using the Plavsic incident. Interestingly, I was in Belgrade at the time of the event; however, everyone in town was made to think that I approved it (reinforced by an erroneous statement in the New York Times). Flyers were produced referring to us as SERBPROFOR, and unwarranted allegations abound suggesting that UNPROFOR is a (Chetnik) taxi service. The people of Dobrinja (some 2,000 of them) have written to 117 newspapers requesting that I be tried as a war criminal for not stopping the shelling of their municipality, and for being "even-handed" with the Serbs. I have received seven death threats and a detailed briefing from the Presidency's Minister of the Interior indicating that the other side intended to do me in, preferably by burning my vehicle. Needless to say, the

thought crossed my mind that the Presidency side was setting me up for an attempt by their people, to be blamed on the Serbs.

When I confronted the President with the growing and unwarranted smear campaign against UNPROFOR, he promised his support and followed through with a short statement to the press.

Unfortunately, the momentum of anti-MacKenzie propaganda has continued to build within the Presidency population in spite of some heroic acts by two Canadians when rescuing two wounded civilian women under fire yesterday.

I can live with all of the above; after all, I'm a soldier; however, over the past few days, some of my personnel have been targeted due to their association with me. My deputy was present in a vehicle when an angry TDF member at a checkpoint insisted in searching a vehicle for "MacKenzie". An UNMO [observer] at one of the Presidency's heavy-weapon positions had a magazine of AK-47 fired next to his head because he "worked for MacKenzie". This I cannot accept nor tolerate, as I am putting my personnel in needless danger.

I will discuss this situation with my Chief of Defence Staff before his departure. I do not wish my country to lose a general officer position in the mission and will suggest Canada replace me with a brigadier-general as sector commander. If this is unacceptable when we do not have a battalion in Sarajevo, then France, Egypt, or Ukraine could be asked to nominate a brigadier-general with a Canadian deputy. Canada could attempt to obtain the Commander Sector West position in February 93.

This has been the most difficult message to write of my career. I have truly enjoyed the challenge of UNPROFOR and it will always stand out as the high point of my life. Regrettably, through no fault of my own, my personnel are being threatened in my name. That I cannot live with.

Regards.

J U L Y I 3   I arrived at the airport at 0630 and joined the CDS and his team for breakfast with Michel. It had been a relatively quiet night, and everyone was in good spirits. The soldiers' morale was definitely boosted by the presence of both Generals de Chastelain and Gervais, and I privately thanked them for finding the time to pay us a visit.

Following the CDS's departure, I made my way to Pale along with Fabrizio Hochschild of the UNHCR, a representative from the International Red Cross, and Martin Bell of the BBC. We had a very nice lunch; nothing of substance was concluded, although the mood was interesting in the sense that the Bosnian Serbs were even more strident than usual in their condemnation of the Presidency for initiating breaches of the "ceasefire". I took General Mladic aside and bent his ear about overreacting with his artillery. He pretty well ignored my comment, reminding me that intervention by the West would be a fatal mistake, and many of our soldiers would return home in body bags. I assumed that something was lost in the translation and didn't rise to the bait; otherwise we would have been there for hours.

At 2003, we were all in the PTT mess enjoying some pasta and the French Army's wine ration. Conversation had been loosened by a good Beaujolais when, all of a sudden, several loud explosions shook the building violently. The noise came from the front of the building; we ran into our large conference room with its solid glass wall, lined up at the window and looked across the street. Cars were burning in the parking lot. There was a lot of debris on the street and black smoke in the air. We could hear screaming, but couldn't see anyone in the area of the shelling. As the screaming continued, I looked straight down the front of the building to the tiny grassy verge two floors below us at street level. What I saw will always be my most lasting and horrible memory of Sarajevo.

Seven teenagers had been accepting chocolate bars through a window on the ground floor from some of our people. One of the mortar bombs had landed in their midst. One youth had lost both his legs, which were now lying on the road and still moving. Another lad had been cut to pieces and would need amputations. A beautiful girl with long, blonde hair was on her back on the grass, staring straight into my eyes. Her hair was fanned out around her head, and I immediately thought of my daughter, Kimm, who is also blonde. The girl was missing half of her head; her brain was exposed. Mercifully, she died minutes later. The entire area was awash with blood. A car drove up, and three of the more slightly injured climbed in and were driven in the direction of the hospital.

Our shock and revulsion lasted only a few seconds. Richard Gray and Vanessa Lloyd-Davies quickly organized a rescue party, who rushed downstairs to the scene and brought the casualties to our medical facility. They were brave to do so, because the favourite trick in this war was to wait until the medical teams arrived and then fire some more munitions to maim the rescuers.

We now had the mass-casualty situation that I had feared. Despite the fact that we had no surgical team, Vanessa and Major Jaegar, from the Van Doos, carried out emergency surgery in our underground operating room. Thanks to Vanessa's foresight, it was all set up and ready to go, and a number of young lives were saved.

An hour later, when our people had done everything they could, a state of shock truly set in around the building. We were all appalled and disgusted to new levels. What made matters worse was that most of the teenagers had come to the PTT in a population exchange organized earlier in the day by Richard Gray. He had delivered some Serbs to Lukavica and, in exchange, had brought back a load of people, including the teenagers, who wished to return to downtown Sarajevo. The Presidency was supposed to send some transportation for them to the PTT, and the teenagers had been milling about our building while waiting to be picked up. Richard was understandably distraught, having risked his own life to lift these kids to "freedom".

The next morning, we conducted a crater analysis of the shell impacts on the street and determined, as usual, that the bombs had been fired from somewhere on the border between the TDF and Bosnian-Serb forces. Either side could have fired them; but the fact remained that, whoever had done it, they had killed some of their own young people.

28

Goodbye to Sarajevo

JULY 14   Early in the day, we were advised that the UN Security Council had approved the despatch of small, 500-man battalions from France, Egypt and the Ukraine to replace the Van Doos. The advance party from Egypt would arrive later in the day, led by the new chief of staff for UNPROFOR headquarters, Colonel Adel Abdelouahab Altahllawi.

General Nambiar had forwarded my request to be relieved to UN New York, and they had agreed that I should depart at a time of our choosing. Colonel d'Avout d'Auerstaedt from France, who had recently arrived in Sarajevo, would take over command from me temporarily until a replacement general arrived.

I was disappointed and angry to receive a blast from the UN through UNPROFOR headquarters about some statements that Michel Jones had made to the media a few days earlier, about opening humanitarian corridors in Sarajevo. It seemed UN New York wanted to make all such announcements. In a foul mood, I drafted a response:

> Corridors are part of the airport agreement as are heavy weapon concentrations. I do not intend to report every new heavy weapon concentration that we observe, nor do I consider it necessary to report every route we open. Jones did exactly what I wanted him to do in order to give some confidence to the population, and was coached by Spokesman.
>
> Considering the media scrutiny that this operation has received—I have been told by those who should know that the airport opening has endured more coverage, and that I have

been interviewed more times, over the previous ten days, than anyone else in the world in the last half of this century—and considering the *positive* image portrayed of the UN, I would appreciate a more supportive attitude by UNNY. If they wish one or both sides of the conflict to make the announcements regarding our operation, with all the potential negative results, and lost opportunities, I request direction to that effect.

In a nutshell, we have handled the media aspect of this operation very well. Fred has helped immensely and has been withdrawn today, leaving me once again without qualified staff. If UNNY thinks they can generate a more positive image of this operation, I would appreciate very much hearing their ideas and benefiting from their expertise. In the meantime, I shall continue to give my subordinates the flexibility to deal with the media, as I see fit. I remind UNNY that the recent coverage of Butmir, Dobrinja, and the rescue of the two wounded female civilians, which received international coverage, were the results of Lt.-Col. Jones' work.

JULY 15 Michel was making good headway with both sides regarding secure land-corridors for the delivery of food, so we decided to up the ante and try for a demobilization of Dobrinja. I visited both sides and ran up against Vice-President Ganic, who wanted any action undertaken in Dobrinja matched by similar activities in Lukavica. As Dobrinja was a municipality and Lukavica was a military camp, I didn't hold out much hope that we could pull it off. Disengagement would probably work only one step at a time; Ganic always wanted to take two.

Later in the evening, I received a cable indicating that a Paris newspaper, *Libération*, had received a leak from a high-level French government source about my departure. Both the UN and Canada were concerned about the lid blowing off the story, so an "appropriate" media response was prepared:

STATEMENT ON CANADIAN CONTINGENT

United Nations Headquarters has confirmed the plan which was announced earlier to have the Canadian battalion in Sarajevo replaced by units from France, Egypt, and the Ukraine at the end of July. At that time, the Canadian battalion will resume its duties around Daruvar in western Slavonia.

Responses to Query

QUESTION: Has MGen MacKenzie resigned as Sector Commander?

ANSWER: No.

QUESTION: Is General MacKenzie being replaced as Commander Sarajevo Sector?

ANSWER: The United Nations will decide when General
MacKenzie is to be replaced in Sarajevo. It would
be expected, given the new configuration of the
forces in Sarajevo Sector, that a new Commander
will be appointed reflecting that new configuration. When that does happen MGen MacKenzie
will return to Canada to take up his duties as
Commander Land Forces Central Area in Toronto.

QUESTION: Does this situation result from threats/accusations
against MacKenzie from parties to the conflict?

ANSWER: In executing his tasks in a professional manner, and
in accordance with the mandate of the Security
Council, MGen MacKenzie (and any UN commander) will inevitably be accused by one side or
the other of being unfair, prejudiced, etc. Such
accusations cannot be allowed to drive UN decisions. In fact, in his report of 10 July the Secretary-General reports "General MacKenzie and the
various elements in Sarajevo under his leadership
are doing a magnificent job under conditions of
great difficulty and danger."

JULY 16   The day was spent explaining to an International Red
Cross delegation the reasons why it would be folly for us to defend
the Kosovo hospital. I said that, in any other peacekeeping mission,
the idea would make sense. But in Sarajevo, as soon as we put our
people around the hospital, the TDF would set their mortars up close
to the facility, fire at the other side, draw retaliatory fire, and then
blame the Serbs for shelling a hospital. If the hospital were on the
Bosnian-Serb side, the Serbs would do the same thing.

The Geneva Convention was being ignored in this war. For
example, ambulances were being used regularly to transfer arms and
ammunition. And even though we were physically checking every
Bosnian-Serb ambulance that used the runways to get to Lukavica

from Ilidza, the TDF was still firing at them and so far had seriously injured a doctor and killed a patient. It seemed that anything we undertook to improve the situation just made matters worse.

The international media called all night about my departure. Each time, I gave our agreed response: "The Canadian battalion is departing, so it is only reasonable that the commander of this sector come from one of the three nations who will provide the replacement units. It's nothing more than that. There is no story here, so I'm going back to sleep."

J U L Y I 7   It was the U.K.'s turn to take over chairmanship of the European Community. Sir Douglas Hurd, the British Foreign Secretary, arrived at 0945 for a day's visit. We spent some time in my office discussing what was happening in Sarajevo, particularly the recent aggressive anti-UNPROFOR attitude within the Bosnian government. I decided my presence would be counter-productive at Sir Douglas's meeting with the Presidency, so he departed with an escort provided by the reconnaissance platoon of Michel's battalion.

On Sir Douglas's arrival, there were ten to fifteen members of the TDF on either side of the building's entrance as a sort of honour guard. Once he had entered the main door, the group of TDF on the right of the entrance joined their colleagues on the left, and the entire group walked around to the west side of the building and took cover. Thirty seconds later, ten mortar rounds landed immediately across the street from the Presidency, and seven innocent citizens were killed or seriously maimed. A pre-positioned pair of ambulances and the local television cameramen on the east side of the building rushed to the scene of the tragedy, collected and filmed the dead and wounded, and moved off in the direction of the Kosovo hospital.

There was only circumstantial evidence, but everyone who witnessed the event had an uneasy feeling that it had been orchestrated by the Presidency to place the Serbs in a bad light in front of Sir Douglas and the international media.

After the meeting, a news conference was held in our large conference room, and Sir Douglas started off with a short statement. When it came time for questions, Martin Bell stepped forward and said, "Sir Douglas, what is your comment regarding the departure of General MacKenzie? His people are doing marvellous work here, and don't you think it's a mistake to replace him? We certainly do."

Sir Douglas turned to me and said, "Perhaps you should answer that, Lew."

All I could think to say was, "It's your conference, sir. Perhaps we should restrict ourselves to issues involving yourself." It was an awkward moment, but the compliment Martin paid to my people and me was worth more than most.

Later in the day, I said goodbye to Vitali Petrounev. He had handed over his deputy's duties to Colonel d'Avout and was on his way back to Belgrade. Vitali and I had become very good friends over the past month, and I hated to see him go. I made a commitment to see him some day in Moscow, which I will honour with pleasure.

During the afternoon, Michel's operations centre at the airport came under fire from a heavy machine-gun. Over thirty rounds penetrated the building and Michel's office. His regimental sergeant-major, Maurice Dessureault, was with Michel; together they rushed down the stairs. As he ran from the office, Dessureault felt a blow to his right hip, but in the confusion thought no more of it until he reached the ground floor. It was a minute or so before he noticed that one of the rounds had struck the handle of the pistol he was wearing, leaving a large indentation in the metal. Even for a regimental sergeant-major, he was more than a little lucky.

JULY 18   Since President Izetbegovic refused to sit down and negotiate with Dr. Karadzic, the arrival on the scene of Milan Panic, the Yugoslavian-born American citizen who had become Prime Minister of Yugoslavia, provided a new opening. Izetbegovic said he would be pleased to talk with Panic; so we made arrangements for Panic to fly from Belgrade to Sarajevo in a UN aircraft the following day.

The European Community was meeting in London on the subject of Bosnia-Herzegovina. Representatives from the country's three ethnic communities were present, and a plan was developed to concentrate all heavy weapons in Bosnia under UN control. Lord Carrington had called the UN Secretary-General and received his approval in principle to proceed, under the assumption that the UN would provide the observers to control the guns.

Considering that the UN had not been able to provide the modest numbers we required to observe the heavy weapons in Sarajevo alone, I was skeptical about the new plan's chances of success. We needed at least ninety observers in Sarajevo, which we didn't have yet; and we estimated the total required for all of Bosnia would be at least 1,600. The idea eventually died a natural death; interestingly, it also caused a confrontation between the Secretary-General and the Security Council, who thought he should have consulted with them before responding to Lord Carrington.

In our continuing attempt to polish our image with the TDF, we had accepted an invitation to play soccer against them in an indoor arena—the only one left standing in Sarajevo. Minister of Defence Doko was in charge of the Bosnian football association and was an avid promoter of the game. Over the years, he had despatched a number of outstanding players to Canada to play with Toronto's Croatia team.

About thirty seconds after the game started, I knew we were in serious trouble. Our side had some good Egyptian and Scandinavian players, but the TDF team was exceptional; they played soccer rather as the Harlem Globetrotters play basketball. When the score reached 15-0, I turned to Doko and said, "Are all your players with the TDF?"

He smiled and replied, "More or less. They're all first-division, and a few of them played on the European Cup championship team last year!"

The final score was 24-5, and would have been worse except that they took pity on us. I told Doko I was going to protest to the UN about too much "shooting" by the TDF. For a few brief hours, relations between us warmed, and we were working together towards a common aim. Sports can do that for people.

Meanwhile, the saga of the Bosnian Olympic team was continuing. I had held a number of meetings with Mr. Kljuic, a Croatian member of the Presidency and also president of the Bosnian Olympic Committee. I had told Kljuic that Dr. Karadzic had agreed to let us fly the team out of Sarajevo on one of our humanitarian flights returning to Zagreb.

The whole matter had fallen into the lap of Mik Magnusson, our new liaison officer for civil affairs. Mik was not particularly diplomatic, but his hard-nosed negotiating style was exactly what we needed in Sarajevo. He had to keep a large and increasing number of demands for evacuation from the city under control; since the UNHCR had yet to issue a policy regarding who could leave and who couldn't, this was no easy task. The Olympic team, however, was another story, and it was driving him mad: it had nothing to do with peacekeeping; the UNHCR, and not ourselves, controlled the loads on the aircraft; and Kljuic was calling him every few hours. Even the Secretary-General had been drawn in. Mik was not amused.

JULY 19 Prime Minister Panic touched down at 1030, along with twenty-six unannounced journalists. It was easy to pick him out from the crowd: Panic is a man in perpetual motion, constantly accompanied by sweeping gestures. He is not a particularly good listener, since he is always preparing what he is going to say next—if he is not already saying it. Yet he has a likeable personality, and I could understand how his business career had benefited from his passion and drive. Unfortunately, the situation in Bosnia was so complex that it didn't lend itself to his quick solutions.

We had brought President Izetbegovic to the PTT for the meeting. Panic strode into the room, walked up to Izetbegovic, who remained sitting, and said, "Mr. President, I am a man of peace. You are fighting my people. We can have peace—if not, I will defeat you!"

Bearing in mind that the Serbs were claiming that Belgrade had nothing to do with the war in Bosnia, I thought that Panic's use of "our people" and "I will defeat you" were revealing. I don't think he appreciated the significance of what he was saying at the time; but perhaps I was beginning to think too much like a diplomat.

We left them alone for about two hours. Frequently, we could hear Panic's voice dominating the conversation, but to the best of our knowledge, no blows were thrown.

When it was all over, Panic stood on the back steps of the PTT with at least forty media representatives pressed in front of him. Unfortunately, he ignored the notes his advisers had prepared for him and introduced a bizarre idea whereby he was going to drive a Serb tank from Lukavica to the PTT and hand it over to me as a gesture of peace. He had tried the same idea on General Nambiar, who had refused the offer, as did I: "Mr. Panic, I wouldn't know where to put the tank. If I park it here, the TDF will shell it and us. If I park it in front of the Presidency, the TDF will use it—I know I would. If you want to make a gesture, get the firing pin from the main gun on one of your tanks and give it to me—better still, take it to London and give it to the EC conference chairman on Bosnia."

As we were discussing the matter in front of the world's media, ten mortar rounds landed to the rear of the PTT and in Camp Beaver. Some of our vehicles were damaged and, in Camp Beaver, a few buildings caught on fire. The attack had a dramatic impact on Panic's news conference, which self-destructed before our eyes.

A few minutes later, President Izetbegovic departed for downtown, while we started back to the airport escorting Panic. After only a few hundred metres, Izetbegovic's French APC was brought under anti-aircraft machine-gun fire, and he was forced to return to the PTT until the firing died down an hour later.

Panic had called General Mladic (about the tank!), and they had agreed not to meet at the airport on his way back to Belgrade. But just as the door of Panic's UN aircraft was closing, Dr. Karadzic and General Mladic showed up on the tarmac, and a short meeting was arranged in my airport office. I decided enough was enough and returned to the PTT, just in time to see Izetbegovic before he left for the second time. "What did you think of the meeting?" I asked.

Izetbegovic stared at me for a few seconds and exclaimed, "A circus!" I made no comment and wished him a safe trip back to his Presidency.

As had become routine after a VIP visit, the city was ablaze with fighting all night. I began to develop the theory that the military on both sides associated such visits with a possible ceasefire or outright end to hostilities. That being the case, they wanted to gain as much territory or carry out as much revenge as possible, before the status quo was locked into place by some agreement. I made a mental note to discourage VIP visits in the future.

J U L Y 2 0   I arrived at the airport at 0715, having driven through the dust of a mortar attack that had preceded my arrival by less than a minute. We started our morning meeting but had to adjourn it when the airport came under mortar fire during major fighting in Dobrinja. Reluctantly, we advised Geneva and Zagreb to hold all humanitarian aid flights until things settled down.

Michel's battalion was scheduled to deliver food and medicine to a Bosnian-Serb area of Sarajevo later that day. The Van Doos despatched a Royal Canadian Regiment reconnaissance party of four APCs and three jeeps in the morning to survey the route. As they approached the Serb area, the RCRs were surrounded by the TDF and ordered to halt. Anti-tank grenades were pointed at them at point-blank range. Our people cocked their weapons and started a pretty good version of a Mexican stand-off.

Major John Collins had been involved in negotiations to obtain his soldiers' release for about an hour when I heard about this incident. I met John at the Presidency; he explained that the TDF were accusing our reconnaissance party of attempting to smuggle Yugoslavian arms and ammunition to the Bosnian Serbs.

I immediately asked to see Minister Doko and was ushered into his office. I explained that this was a very serious situation; I wanted my people released that minute. The Bosnian Serbs had permitted food deliveries to Muslim neighbourhoods over the past few days, and here we were having serious trouble delivering aid to the Serbs.

Doko was defensive, protesting that our vehicles were full of ammunition made in Yugoslavia and destined for the Serbs.

"Balls," I replied. "Our vehicles carry our own ammunition and that's all. This unit has come from Germany and service with NATO, so we have a lot of ammunition on board, but it certainly isn't Yugoslavian. If that's what you think, then let's you and I go there right now and check every vehicle!"

Doko wasn't keen on the idea of an inspection. It was a dangerous situation, and there was a good chance his troops wouldn't respond to his direction. He suggested we wait a while for things to cool down.

"No way," I replied. "Your people are aiming anti-tank weapons at my soldiers as we speak. We can't wait. One idiot will set off a bloodbath." I got up to leave.

Doko said, "Okay, we will send one of my officers if you send Major Collins."

John left, and I sat there for half an hour praying that someone in National Defence headquarters in Ottawa hadn't bought any ammunition from Yugoslavia in the last four years. After what seemed like a lifetime, John and Minister Doko's representative returned. They reported that the vehicles had been checked, and the only non-Canadian weapons were American-made M-72 anti-tank rockets. I stared at Doko; after a few seconds he apologized for the "misunderstanding".

"Mr. Doko," I said, "your media were present during the entire operation. I presume the airwaves will be full of anti-UNPROFOR reports within the hour."

Doko picked up the phone and called the Ministry of Information. After a short chat, he put the phone down and said, "There will be no reports."

"Thank you." I couldn't resist the temptation: "And you've always told me you had freedom of the press."

I thought that was the end of the incident. But that night, the

BBC showed pictures of the hostage-taking on their Sarajevo report. I asked Martin Bell how he had got the pictures, since only the Bosnian media had been present at the event. "You can get anything for a price," was his reply.

When I returned to the PTT, I was delighted to learn that hundreds of French-Canadian Van Doos had volunteered to rescue their anglophone RCR colleagues when they'd heard they were being held hostage. Now that would have been something to watch!

JULY 21   Overnight, a dozen rounds of mortar fire landed in and around the UNHCR hangar at the airport, and seven of their trucks were hit. In addition, the Ukrainian counter-bombardment vehicle's radar was damaged. It was the second of two pieces of such equipment we had requested a month earlier; it had just arrived, and was supposed to be able to tell us who was doing the firing, and from where. Obviously, someone didn't want us to have that capability and had decided to put the vehicle out of action. It would take weeks to get the parts to repair it. Everybody at the airport was a bit shaken, but fortunately there were no casualties.

Early in the afternoon, I drove down to the Bosnian international press centre, located close to the Presidency. I had been invited to meet with the local Bosnian media and had decided to accept, thinking it could do some good for our image.

The place was packed; I noticed some international media people there also. I was flanked by the president of the centre and an interpreter. The questions came hot and heavy for well over an hour, and we strayed into some sensitive areas. For example: "Why did you say both sides are equally to blame, General MacKenzie? We all know who the aggressor is."

"At no time did I say both sides were equally to blame," I responded. "What I did say was that there's plenty of blame to go around. The Serbs started the shelling and therefore have to accept the majority of the responsibility. But the Presidency has to accept a good deal of the responsibility for keeping the fighting going."

As the questions carried on, I noticed tension was developing between our head table and the media. It didn't seem to be directed at me personally; eventually, I realized a number of the journalists were unhappy with the translation of my answers. One Bosnian journalist, with whom I had had a number of interviews, was upset that the interpreter was misrepresenting my words; on at least three occasions, the two of them got into a verbal slugging match.

Near the end of the conference, I was asked, "Why is it so impossible to arrange a real ceasefire in Sarajevo?"

My response was a combination of truth and frustration—something that a soldier/diplomat might think, but should never say: "Because I can't keep the two sides from firing on their own positions for the benefit of CNN. If I could get them to stop, perhaps we could have a real ceasefire." My answer was reported in the print media as: "If I could convince both sides to stop killing their own people to impress CNN, perhaps we could have a ceasefire." I didn't say exactly that, but I certainly thought it.

To my absolute amazement, journalists stopped me on the way out and said they agreed with me, particularly regarding my condemnation of sacrificing lives as part of the disinformation campaign. This made me feel a little better; but it was probably a good thing that I had only a few more days to go in Sarajevo, since I was becoming much too honest in my statements to the press.

Later that day, Mik Magnusson brought me a list of the people whom the Bosnian Olympic team wanted flown to Zagreb. We were shocked; it contained twenty-eight names, of whom only *two* were competitors. I pulled out my dictionary and looked up the definition of "team": "a set of players forming one side in certain games or sports." The definition didn't mention "hostess", "marketing director", "reporter", "cameraman", etc., all of which were listed. "There is no way Geneva will accept this list, Mik. If we cut it down, they just might, so have a try at cutting it down to around fifteen—and leave the two competitors in!"

Mr. Kljuic went ballistic when Mik told him the list was too long. I, in turn, advised UNHCR in Geneva, and was informed that none of the nations providing aircraft for humanitarian flights would agree to fly such a large group containing so few athletes. As far as UNHCR were concerned, even fifteen was too many.

I went to see Kljuic and told him the matter was out of my hands. As far as I was concerned, they'd blown it. Furthermore, I'd wasted a lot of credits with Dr. Karadzic by obtaining his agreement to let the UN fly the Bosnian team out of Sarajevo. "About all I can suggest is that you contact the International Olympic Committee and ask them to send you an aircraft." Kljuic chewed a pretty good hole in his pipe during our short meeting.

Just after dark, Colonel Forestier called from the airport and advised me that two Jordanian officers serving with their battalion in Croatia had shown up on today's last aircraft; they had a letter from King Hussein asking them to find and evacuate a Jordanian student from Sarajevo.

I found this hard to credit. We had strict orders from the UN not to evacuate anyone from Sarajevo: to do so would utterly compromise our neutrality, and the only exceptions made to date had been for life-threatening casualties. But I guess when you get a letter from your King, you try to comply. I told Colonel Forestier to hold the officers there and send them back to Zagreb on the first flight the next day.

JULY 22   The previous afternoon, two soldiers from the Van Doos' "N" Company had noticed the TDF setting up a mortar position fifty metres from the perimeter of Beaver Camp. They notified their commander, and a protest was lodged; however, as the sun went down, the mortars were still in place and manned. Both companies of the battalion were alerted and instructed that if anyone heard the mortars fired, they were to sound the alarm, since retaliatory fire from the Serbs would not be far behind. As mentioned earlier, it was a favourite technique of the TDF to set up their weapons close to our UN positions, in the hope that the opposition would not fire back. If fire was returned, it was still to their advantage, since we would then report that the Serbs were shelling us.

Just after midnight, everyone bolted upright in their cots when the mortars beside their camp were fired. Within a minute, over 300 soldiers were in their bunkers, and not a moment too soon.

The camp was rocked by mortar fire. Rounds exploded in the kitchen, dining area, command post and, unfortunately, the quartermaster's stores. (Every piece of equipment lost by "N" Company over the previous five years was alleged to have been in those stores and destroyed that night—soldiers never change!) A number of rounds landed in the vehicle compound, and 5,000 litres of fuel soaked the ground around the vehicles.

Not one person was injured, thanks to the alertness of the two soldiers who had seen the mortars being set up. It wasn't luck that saved the day, but good training.

The next morning, I had an early appointment with Vice-President Ganic. I got straight to the point: "It is against every rule ever written to set up weapons beside a UN position and use us as a shield. Your people are doing this at Beaver Camp; the mortars are still there. The next time they fire, I will order a patrol of my soldiers to kill every one of your people at the positions. I will not have my people injured as a result of your TDF's actions. I have no more to say."

At least it was a short meeting. The mortars were packed up a few hours later.

JULY 23   At mid-morning, I received a call from General Nambiar, who said that UN New York wanted me to report to Belgrade for consultation. I was pretty sure I knew what was up. I asked, "Should I bring all my kit?"

"I'm afraid so," replied Nambiar. This meant I was being pulled out of Sarajevo for good, and ahead of schedule.

"It sounds like somebody is upset," I continued, trying to keep my voice level and calm.

"Yes, Lew. Your press conference with the Bosnian media has really got New York excited. You might be right, but you can't say those things. In addition, it looks like those exclusive messages you've been sending to New York are not very exclusive—some UN delegations have been getting copies."

"Great," I said. "It would have been nice to know. I'll see you on Saturday."

General Nambiar was a true gentleman and a compassionate commander. He had given me the chance to get back to Sarajevo; now I felt badly that he was getting flak from New York about me. He already had plenty on his plate with the problems in the UNPAs and the Pink Zones, and I was just making his life more difficult. My only consolation was that if I had to do it all over again, I wouldn't have done anything differently. It was a small consolation, but it helped.

There was a terrible accident in the afternoon. A CNN car was hit by sniper fire in the area of the airport. Margaret Moth, a New Zealand cameraperson for CNN, was shot in the face and seriously injured. The CNN producer driving with her in the car was also injured.

I had watched Margaret at work with admiration for over five months. She was a tall, tough lady who always dressed in black, which was appropriate for a citizen of a country renowned for its All-Blacks rugby team. The bullet had torn apart a large segment of Margaret's jaw and neck, and she couldn't speak. She was evacuated along with her producer in short order. (Subsequently, Margaret spent a long period in recovery in the Mayo clinic, but not half as long as most people would have taken, if they had managed to survive such a serious wound. True to form, she went back to work as early as possible, and at the time of writing is serving with Christiane Amanpour in cnn's Paris office.)

After weeks of negotiations, we finally despatched a convoy of relief aid to the besieged city of Gorazde, a Muslim community sixty kilometres south of Sarajevo, where living conditions were desperate because of the three-month siege by the Serbs. Fabrizio Hochschild organized supplies of food and medicine for the city, and members of our French company provided the escort. Vanessa Lloyd-Davies accompanied them to provide medical care if required.

Since I only followed this story from the safe end of a very bad radio connection, I have asked Vanessa to record what happened on the trip to Gorazde. The following is an edited version of her personal account, which does not necessarily express the views of the British government or Ministry of Defence:

"Permission was obtained from the Bosnian-Serb authorities, and we set off at around 0900 hours on July 23 in a convoy consisting of a Serbian police escort in their armoured personnel carrier from Lukavica, two French APCs with French drivers and armed co-drivers, two large trucks filled with food and medical supplies, and one four-wheel-drive "soft-skinned" vehicle with Sir Donald Acheson of the World Health Organization, Fabrizio Hochschild, whose idea the operation was, and Una, a charming diminutive girl in her twenties as the interpreter, whose appearance belied nerves of steel and huge inner resources. The rest of the party was made up of: six Swedish truck drivers, civilians who had been flown into Sarajevo that morning; a photographic team of two French naval personnel to record the event; three un military observers; a British medical assistant, and myself. Altogether our party numbered twenty.

"We set off full of hope and expectation on this particular adventure and very pleased to be going, feeling that perhaps something valuable could be achieved. Although reaching Gorazde with such a small offering would be little in itself, if the route could be established, it could be the start of humanitarian aid convoys going on a regular basis all over eastern Bosnia.

"Our first stop was Pale, the headquarters of the Bosnian Serbs, and in true Bosnian style further negotiations were required. By this time, news of the convoy had filtered through to the media, and several TV people turned up to join the convoy. Finally, at about

1130, we left Pale, and instead of turning southeast, went northeast, as apparently the direct route was mined and the area was being fought over. An hour or so later we reached a town where further negotiations ensued, with another two-hour wait. When we finally left, turning southward, the TV crews were not permitted to accompany us and were turned back for reasons not fully explained.

"It was important that we reach Gorazde in daylight before the night fighting started, so time was of the essence. We passed swiftly along roads over disputed territory without incident and finally back onto Serb-held territory. We then took to tracks, traversing the stunningly beautiful Bosnian countryside, winding our way over mountains and through heavily wooded valleys in glorious sunshine. At about 1730 we were stopped on a track beside a cottage by local Serb forces, who seemed reluctant to let us proceed. The usual negotiations ensued, and some thirty minutes later we set off, moving now very slowly.

"Approximately six kilometres later, we came across a civilian car that had obviously gone over an anti-tank mine; there were three bodies in it. They had been dead for several hours, and it transpired that one of the victims was related to one of the local Serb fighters, who understandably was extremely upset.

"However, we were told it was safe to proceed with caution, which in hindsight may have been foolish, but we were totally in the hands of the local Serbs and had to take their advice on trust. The order of the convoy at this stage was: the Bosnian-Serb police APC, a French APC with myself, two observers and Una, followed by the rest of the vehicles. Una had been transferred from the four-wheel-drive vehicle to the APC on the basis that it would be safer. Some two kilometres further on, disaster struck.

"One moment all was peace and quiet, we were following the Bosnian-Serb police APC, sun shining, birds singing, travelling up a wooded track on the side of a mountain, and the next moment the world exploded. The APC I was in erupted forward with a monumental bang. We were all flung around inside like puppets and landed in a heap on the floor. It happened so quickly that all I can remember is an extraordinary feeling of time becoming elongated and everything being in slow motion. We were certainly all dazed and momentarily deafened. I realized fairly fast that we had been hit by something, but having had no previous experience of anti-tank mines, I was not quite sure what! As the six of us (including the French drivers) regained our senses, we were aware of a great deal of firing going on around us.

"Our first reaction was to see that we were all still alive and that everyone's arms and legs were still attached in the right place. There was a fair amount of chaos; one of the young French soldiers panicked and started to try and hide under a nine-inch-high seat in the body of the APC. There was a lot of blood about, which had come from a minor laceration on Una's head. Water and a field dressing took care of that. Fortunately we were all in one piece.

"The next problem was, what on earth should we do now. When the sound of firing stopped (I have to say it was extremely difficult to tell how much was incoming and how much outgoing), we had no idea what had happened to the rest of our party, and in particular to Sir Donald and Fabrizio in the soft-skinned vehicle behind us. We were desperately worried that the rest of our party were injured or even dead. They, of course, were fairly convinced that we might be.

"Silence reigned for what seemed like hours but was probably only minutes, when finally we heard a shout—but who was shouting? 'Identify yourselves!' we yelled through a surreptitiously opened window. We were extremely relieved to find that it was one of our party. One by one, under covering fire, we ran as fast as possible twenty-five metres back down the track and off into the lower mountainside to join the rest of our party. Being female, I was mildly amused that on this occasion sexual discrimination had no part to play; no one offered to carry my medical bags for me! When my turn came to run, I put thoughts of further anti-tank mines or anti-personnel mines firmly to the back of my mind, grabbed my bags and sprinted off into the bushes!

"We all regrouped safely under the trees and exchanged accounts and theories as to what had happened. We will never truly know. There was the ambush and command-detonated-mine theory, and the 'bad-luck' theory of just happening to encounter forgotten mines. The Bosnian Serbs from Lukavica, interestingly, were extremely worried and seemed very concerned for their and our safety. However, the main point at this stage was that no one had been seriously injured.

"In true British tradition, my medical assistant, Lance-Corporal McHugh, set about making 'a brew' (he had been in the APC at the rear) and generally raising morale. Fabrizio felt very responsible and needed much reassurance that it was not directly his fault. Radio contact with Sarajevo was only possible via Zagreb in Croatia, involving a French/English Chinese-whisper form of communication, which did not make life easy; but we were able to inform Sarajevo of what had happened, and were told to wait for further information.

"It was now beginning to get dark. I redressed Una's wound, which could be sutured in the morning. The local Serbs reappeared, apparently fairly unconcerned, and we tried to move one of the lorries full of relief supplies, which promptly went over another anti-tank mine. At this juncture the mission was abandoned. We decided to spend the night where we were.

"It was a long night. Some spent it outside on guard. I was sent into the Bosnian-Serb APC with the truck drivers and Serbian police. What interested me was how obviously frightened the police were: no smoking, no talking, the fear of further ambush very much in the forefront of their minds. Sleep was impossible; we dozed fitfully and shared a very welcome half-bottle of brandy. During the night we could hear distant sounds of rocket and mortar fire. We were approximately twenty kilometres from Gorazde and estimated that at one stage in the night, a mortar went off every minute, terrifying. I have no doubt I was not the only one contemplating the dreadful conditions endured by the people of Gorazde constantly under such attack.

"At 0445 dawn broke; we had survived the night. Breakfast was taken (at least we were not short of food!) and I put a couple of sutures in Una's head, with her sitting on the bonnet of the four-wheel-drive—real medicine in the field!

"Before leaving, radio contact was established with Sarajevo, again via Zagreb, but unfortunately became somewhat confused due to the language problem. We radioed stating that we were moving on to higher ground. The message that came back was that we should stay where we were and on no account move until ordered to do so. Messages flew back and forth, but in the end we had no choice but to ignore them and proceed. We did not wish to be left on our own. The important issue was that we would need to be rescued at some stage, and it was vital that Sarajevo knew where we were. Crawling at a snail's pace, we finally reached an open area at the top of the mountain: stunning views, with ice-cold, crystal-clear water from a spring which we shared with the cows grazing there, and again, glorious sunshine.

"The local Bosnian-Serb commander appeared at this stage and offered help in the form of an army helicopter to rescue us. This offer, if accepted, would have meant leaving the trucks with all their supplies and the other vehicles with the Serbs. One of the Swedish truck drivers made the unfortunate point within hearing of the Serb commander that, if we were to leave, we must destroy the trucks and their contents so that they did not fall into 'enemy' hands. I do not think the local commander appreciated the reference to him as 'the enemy'. This suggestion had the following effect: the offer of the helicopter was promptly withdrawn; the Bosnian-Serb police from Lukavica, having stated categorically that the return route was unsafe, bade us farewell, jumped into their APC and disappeared at high speed back to Sarajevo; and the Bosnian-Serb commander went off to lunch, leaving us with a few of his soldiers, a pleasant but decidedly tough-looking lot.

"So there we were, stranded! We radioed requesting rescue as soon as possible and could then do nothing but wait. We had a pleasant picnic, but I have to say time dragged somewhat. We were very well looked after by our 'minders', who had a free hand with the slivovitz, and one in particular was most concerned that I should use his coat to sit on the grass. They spoke no English and sported a comprehensive selection of weapons about their persons.

"One of their vehicles I will never forget: it was a white car, a Trabant of some sort, with a piece of plywood placed across the windscreen painted in camouflage colours with Serbian insignia, and two slits cut in it to see through, with a dead eagle proudly mounted on the roof of the car. I thought it marvellous.

"We waited and waited. I have to admit that, for me, coping with the action was fine, but waiting merely ate away at one's resolve and reserves in a slow but inexorable fashion—no fun. Finally at about 1900, the rescue convoy from Sarajevo arrived. Having set out the previous morning with so many high hopes, we were ignominiously rescued. We left the damaged truck with the supplies for the Bosnian Serbs, the French APC was loaded into a large low-bed truck, and we set off bidding farewell to our Serb 'companions'.

"The commander of the rescue operation, a French captain, did not waste any time. Contrary to the usual regulations, we travelled through the night, and later I found out that we had passed through one town at high speed while a battle was being waged! (I was fast asleep at the time.) We stopped for a few hours in the early morning for the drivers to rest, and arrived without further incident at Sarajevo airport at about 1030 on July 25.

"The following day, I went to Lukavica to take the Bosnian-Serb police a bottle of whiskey because, until they had left, they had been very good to us. I asked one of them why they had left so quickly down a route which they had continually stated was unsafe. The policeman, who did speak some English, said that when people had started to talk of blowing up trucks of food, he knew he could no longer guarantee our safety and therefore had to leave.

"I think that going over the anti-tank mine was just bad luck, but I do know that during the day spent on the mountains, we were probably in considerable danger. It would have taken little for the local Serbs to dispose of us and leave with our weapons, food and medical supplies, but that is merely speculation, as we were very well treated. All I do know with any certainty is that we were unable to reach the Muslim people of Gorazde. We all felt a sense of despair and impotence at our inability to provide help. Regrettably, but not surprisingly, yet another relatively straightforward relief operation had turned into a disaster. But we kept trying, and a few weeks later, a humanitarian convoy did manage to reach the besieged city."

JULY 24   Mr. Kljuic was beside himself with happiness. The International Olympic Committee had finally agreed to send a plane for the Bosnian team, and I went to the airport to see them off. Mirsada Buric, their long-distance runner, had become a bit of a celebrity when her picture had appeared in *Newsweek* showing her training in the ruined streets of Sarajevo. She and I had a short chat and I wished her luck.

Kljuic presented me with one of the team's last gold Sarajevo pins, and we all waited anxiously for the IOC aircraft. It was late and could carry only seventeen people. It seemed the IOC had a similar opinion to ours regarding the size and composition of the team. But I was not prepared to see the team humiliated at this late date, after all the excitement surrounding their departure; I authorized the eleven extra "members" of the team to fly to Zagreb on one of our aircraft.

Days later, I was terribly disappointed when I watched the opening ceremonies of the Games on television from Barcelona. I was aware that the majority of the Bosnian team had been training in the relative comfort of Split for the previous month, and that the two athletes we had flown from Sarajevo had been on a proper diet during their training. Imagine my shock when I heard the announcer say, "Now marching into the stadium is the Olympic team from war-torn Bosnia-Herzegovina. We understand they have been living on bread and water for the past month." Who had told them that, I wondered?

We had managed to round up a good deal of alcohol from various sources, and I put on a happy hour at the PTT, compliments of Canada. Among a few members of the staff, there was some suspicion that I was leaving for good; however, the vast majority thought it was just a good party on a Friday night in Sarajevo. It was extremely difficult for me not to be able to say goodbye to people who had been so loyal and supportive over the previous five months. It was unfair, and reflected a lack of understanding of what leadership was all about, for the UN to call me out for "consultation" and not allow me to come back, if only for a few hours. I decided I would return in any case and live up to my promise to see the last Canadian soldier leave Sarajevo. And to make the point with my staff that I would be returning, I decided not to pack all my kit for my trip to Belgrade the next day.

The party finished late. I went back to my office to pack a few things. There was a knock on my door, and I opened it to find the "Sarajevo Girls" en masse, with a bottle of good Mostar white wine. For the next two hours, we talked, and I felt terrible. They knew I was leaving officially around the first of August, and they were upset about it; I felt terrible because I couldn't share with them the real reason for my departure.

I wanted to tell them that my effectiveness as a mediator in their city was approaching zero, and that my people were being put at unnecessary risk due to my vilification by the Presidency. I repeated over and over again that I was leaving because the Canadians were leaving, but my heart just wasn't in it. By the end of the two hours, I was desolate, and subsequently spent a restless night in bed.

JULY 25   I figured I might as well get in some parting shots, so I accepted an invitation from the local television station just down the road for a farewell interview. I was pleasantly surprised when the interviewer spoke positively of the recent news conference at the international press centre. His questions were fair and objective, and I had a chance to express the hope that my successor would be successful in enhancing the UN's reputation in Sarajevo. I departed the station slightly bemused, wishing that this sudden change of attitude had happened a few months earlier.

I spent the rest of the morning wandering the halls of the PTT. I wasn't supposed to be saying goodbye, because everyone was anticipating that I would return in a day or two. It was also my intention to return, but I would have to talk the UN into it, and their agreement was far from certain.

Unfortunately, I started hugging people as I left their office or workplace for the next stop on my "walkabout". I couldn't resist the temptation; I knew I would probably not see some of them again, and together we had shared some of the most exciting moments of our lives.

At the airport, the French contingent was out in strength. Since the day General de Chastelain had ordered that measures for my personal security be increased, Colonel d'Avout had assigned four of his French security men, trained as personal protection specialists, to guard me. I had never felt safer in my life; those were some tough professionals, and I was going to miss them. They pinned their unit's badge on my flak jacket, and we had our pictures taken together. Colonel de Stabenrath presented me with a beautiful silver disk displaying his regimental badge. Colonel d'Avout asked my driver, Sergeant de vau Corbeil, to come forward. To my astonishment, the Sergeant presented me with a miniature model of our VBL, painted in UN colours, with a few black spots indicating where we had been hit by sniper fire during the thousands of kilometres we had spent together on the back streets of Sarajevo. Of all the gifts I received in my years of UN service, the VBL from de vau Corbeil stands out as the one I cherish the most.

By that time, I was convinced that everyone thought I was leaving for good. We started unabashedly hugging and promising to get together in the future. In fact, the chances of a reunion were pretty good. Before leaving the PTT, I "ordered" Commandant Eamon "Coke" Colclough, an outstanding Irish Army UN observer, to organize a reunion for our "Sarajevo gang" five years hence. Knowing Coke, I expect it will happen.

I told Michel Jones I would see him in a few days and not to leave Sarajevo until I got back. With that, I walked into the back of the Russian UN cargo plane taking me to Belgrade, sat down and buckled up. There was only one other person in the back of the plane, a Danish civilian police officer returning to his UNPA.

The ramp of the aircraft closed slowly, shutting out the sunlight and the sound of mortar fire in Dobrinja. The last thing I saw were three or four hands waving above the floor of the ramp just before it locked shut with a thud.

The engines roared, and we taxied off towards the runway. Immediately, my body felt completely drained. I was suddenly overwhelmed by emotion and found myself incapable of stopping the flow of tears. I put my head in my hands and cried like a baby. I felt guilty for abandoning my people and Sarajevo. I felt frustrated because we had not been able to live up to the expectations of the citizens. I felt sorry for myself because I was not able to say a proper goodbye. I swore that I would get back to Sarajevo, if only for a few hours.

The trip to Belgrade took about an hour. I spent the entire trip persuading myself that I had done the right thing. I kept coming back to the safety of our people and, blessedly, by the time we touched down, I knew that I'd had no other choice but to give someone else a chance.

JULY 26   I slept in until the ungodly hour of 0630, then met with General Nambiar at 1000. As usual, he was gracious and understanding. He explained in more detail that my remarks at the news conference, while well-founded, had caused much concern in New York. I made the point that if they'd expected diplomacy, they should have sent a diplomat. The UN had backed into the Sarajevo operation as a result of putting UNPROFOR headquarters there to run the Croatian operation. We had told them back in March, during our few days at UN New York, that it was the wrong place for our headquarters; however, I admitted that at this point I didn't get much satisfaction from saying, "We told you so."

"I described what we all saw in Sarajevo, General Nambiar," I said. "I'm absolutely shocked that the coded messages I sent to you and New York were allegedly read by the parties to the conflict. That's a terrible condemnation of security at the UN, and blatantly unfair to a commander in the field. At the very least, we should have been warned that was going on, and I could have used it to our advantage."

I went on, "I promised I would shake the hand of the last Canadian soldier as he left Sarajevo. I would still like to do that. If you would be good enough to support my proposal, I suggest we tell New York that I'll spend the next four days visiting our Canadian combat engineers in the UNPAS. They've been doing outstanding work and they've been out of the spotlight, due to the media's presence in Sarajevo. I've been unable to visit them since they arrived. We can tell New York I will return to Sarajevo for less than twenty-four hours on the thirty-first. That will give me a chance to see Michel and the last convoy off as the sun comes up on the first of August."

General Nambiar was a soldier first and a general second; he knew how much it meant to me to live up to a promise made to my soldiers. Without hesitation, he said, "Okay, Lew, you prepare the message to New York."

"With pleasure," I replied. "And thank you for your support."

JULY 27–AUGUST I   Over the next few days, Steve Gagnon and I visited the Canadian combat engineers in Sectors West and North. They were involved in everything from lifting mines and booby traps to opening vehicle routes by removing rubble. Both the Serb and Croatian armies had tremendous respect for their professionalism and, in some instances, would not move into a mined area unless they were accompanied by a Canadian soldier.

I visited one location on the afternoon of July 30 where there was a major minefield operation underway, controlled by our engineers. I crawled into the back of one of our APCs that was being used as the command post for the operation. Sitting in front of a large map was a Canadian master corporal with two radios. I asked him, "Who are you talking to?"

He replied, "Well, sir, I have a Croatian colonel on this side and a Serbian lieutenant-colonel on the other."

"And you are controlling the operation by telling them what to do?"

"Yes, sir.

To me, that said it all about the quality of the soldiers we manage to attract and keep in the Canadian Armed Forces. Here was a young man trained on the first rung of the leadership ladder as a master corporal, and he was totally at ease and confident while controlling two foreign colonels in a complex and dangerous operation. There was certainly nothing wrong with the quality of our soldiers; we just needed more of them.

On the morning of July 31, I thanked Mike Gauthier for the visit to see his boys and congratulated him on commanding such a positive and happy unit. My old friend, Alex Morrison, Executive Director of the Canadian Institute for Strategic Studies, was supposed to fly with Steve and me to Sarajevo. Unfortunately, his plane was late arriving from Canada, and so we had to leave without him.

Steve and I stepped out of the aircraft and onto the runway in Sarajevo, and knew we were "home". Dobrinja was still the scene of sporadic fighting; mortar fire and the sound of exploding artillery rounds could be heard around the city. We were briefed that someone from the Presidency had called to say that they had intercepted a Bosnian-Serb radio message giving orders for "Mac-Kenzie and the PTT to be destroyed tonight." Hmmm, I thought, it's nice to be back.

This time I could say a legitimate goodbye to our folks working and living at the PTT building. They were under a lot of pressure following the deaths of two Ukrainian soldiers just before my arrival. The Ukrainian unit had been manning our one remaining counter-bombardment radar position overlooking Sarajevo from the north, and had come under fire. Two were dead and a number of others seriously injured. There was significant circumstantial evidence that their trench had been grenaded by TDF soldiers who had illegally dug in closer than fifty metres to the UN position, in their continuing quest to shield themselves from Serbian fire. As usual, it was never possible to prove which side had actually carried out the cowardly act.

Just before dark, Steve and I went back to the airport to spend the night with Michel and the last group of his Van Doos. We had a quiet meal in the customs building, after which I spoke to most of the soldiers in "N" Company and the battalion's headquarters personnel. Approximately 300 were present, so I had a good chance to tell them all how proud I was of what they had done, and particularly the spirit they had shown while doing it.

Since a lot of firing was going on in Dobrinja, it was difficult to sleep. This was my first and last night at the airport itself, so I stood back from the window and watched the fireworks for hours, mesmerized by the beauty of it all, yet, at the same time, realizing that every explosion represented more deaths and suffering in a war that should never have started, and probably never would end until there was no one left to care.

Naturally, I had just fallen asleep when it was time to get up at 0330. After a quick breakfast, three cups of coffee and a cigarette, we mounted up in Michel's APC and drove 100 metres to the airport tarmac.

It never failed to impress me as a commanding officer how a

few simple words of direction could result in complex operations being carried out so well. Michel had ordered everyone to be on the airport parking apron at 0400 ready to go. Following his order, years of training, practice, knowledge and regimental spirit had kicked in, and 400-plus soldiers had started working to a common purpose. The chain of command from major to captain to lieutenant to warrant officer to sergeant to master corporal to private all sang the same tune, while the sergeants-major kept an eye on everyone and everything. Vehicles were fuelled and maintained, weapons and ammunition checked, equipment stowed, groups within the convoy arranged with individuals designated in charge, route cards prepared, schedules issued, sleeping arrangements made, and sentries posted. And all without fuss or fanfare.

Just before the sun came up, the first convoy group headed off towards Lukavica en route to the main Belgrade-Zagreb highway some twelve hours away. I said goodbye to Michel and wished him well: "You have every reason to be proud of what your unit has done here, Michel. It rates a chapter in your regimental history. Good luck, I'll see you in Canada."

During the next hour, over 100 vehicles crawled off the runway on their way back to Croatia. A red glow from some burning buildings in Dobrinja, less than 200 metres away, complemented the taillights of the APCs as they disappeared into the darkness, creating an eerie atmosphere around the entire scene.

As the last vehicle, an APC, started to move, I stepped in front of it and shook the hands of each member of the crew and their sergeant. I thanked them all for their good work, stepped back and watched them drive off down the runway.

It was without a doubt the happiest moment of my life. They weren't safely back in Croatia yet, but over 800 Canadian soldiers had spent a month in one of the most dangerous places in the world, and they'd all left alive. Corporal Reid had lost his foot, and eighteen others had sustained injuries from shrapnel and snipers' bullets, and that was bad enough—but they were alive. All things considered, that was a pretty good outcome. I thought a small prayer of thanks—to God and our regimental system that produces such good units and soldiers.

Colonel d'Avout and Lieutenant-Colonel de Stabenrath had kindly organized a farewell breakfast for Steve and me in the terminal building. It was a very classy affair, in stark contrast to our surroundings. The media were allowed in, and d'Avout and I signed a certificate of handover of command. He said some overly nice words, and I responded in my halting French: "*Vous soldats de la France à Sarajevo, écrivez une autre chapitre de l'histoire militaire de la France. La France et la reste du monde sont fiers de vous.*"

We were scheduled to depart on a Canadian Hercules; however, following the dictum of changing your routine at the last minute for security reasons, we climbed on board an American aircraft thirty minutes after our scheduled departure time and flew to Zagreb, which would be the new location of UNPROFOR's headquarters.

As we took off from Sarajevo airport for the last time, I watched French soldiers moving into the dug-in positions left by Michel's battalion. The surrounding area was pockmarked with shell craters; the roads were blocked by burnt-out vehicles. Hardly a building was undamaged, and black smoke was rising from the centre of the city. But as we reached a few thousand feet, the city was transformed into a patchwork of red tile roofs and green parks against a blue sky. Sarajevo was beautiful again: my less than perfect eyesight was unable to see the scars of war as we gained altitude. Wouldn't it be wonderful, I thought, if it could look like that again down at street level. I glanced over at Dobrinja. Even from that distance, I could see buildings burning.

29

The Aftermath

STEVE AND I SPENT THE next two days in Zagreb before flying to New York. Everyone at the new headquarters was very kind and supportive, and General Nambiar presented Steve and me with the first two UNPROFOR medals. I quite liked the colour of the ribbon; but then I'd designed it months before in Sarajevo, when I'd been chief of staff.

Philippe Morillon and our old Delegates' Club gang went out to dinner and had a marvellous time reminiscing. It gradually became clear to me that we were really leaving the former Yugoslavia for good; I became a bit melancholy as the evening drew to a close.

Steve and I arrived at UN headquarters in New York on August 4. I met with Marrick Goulding, then had lunch with senior staff. Everyone was very complimentary about the positive UN image projected by the Sarajevo operation; however, I could tell that some of them were uncomfortable with the way I had used the media. After all, they were diplomats and I was a soldier, so I could understand their frustration.

During my private discussion with Goulding, I expressed surprise that the contents of my classified messages had become so widely known, particularly by people involved in the conflict. I also stressed the need for UN personnel in Sarajevo to be mounted in armoured vehicles when they moved about. I had requested that the three battalions that replaced the Canadian battalion be fully mechanized, but to my shock and disappointment they had arrived with only ten to fifteen APCs each and a lot of useless jeeps and truck transporters. Goulding sympathized and promised to look into both problems.

That evening, I set a personal record for media exposure, appearing in the space of four hours on the *MacNeil/Lehrer News Hour*, *Larry King Live* and ABC's *Nightline*. In between, I gave interviews to *USA Today* and *Time* magazine. The following morning, I was up at 0500 and appeared on the CBS and NBC morning news programmes, followed by interviews with CFRB radio in Toronto, *USA Today*, and *The Washington Post*.

I was beginning to realize just how much media coverage the war in Sarajevo had received. While there, I hadn't particularly noticed, because you never saw the results of your interviews. But it seemed the New York media were aware of many interviews I had given, and for the first time, I wished I'd been a bit more circumspect in some of the sound bites.

I had been advised by Department of National Defence headquarters in Ottawa that I should go to Washington to see U.S. Secretary of Defence Dick Chaney and the Chairman of the Joint Chiefs of Staff, General Colin Powell. I indicated that I didn't think this was a good idea; the perception back in Yugoslavia would be that I was "marking the Serb artillery positions on the maps at the Pentagon". I thought it best that I be seen briefing Canadian officials before I went to Washington. I asked National Defence staff to pass on my concerns to General de Chastelain, and was advised within hours to report to Ottawa before visiting Washington.

Steve and I arrived at Ottawa International at 2110 and were met by our wives, Dora and Lynn. They looked great!

Admiral Anderson also greeted us, along with a large number of well-wishers from the Ottawa area. A giant greeting card with thousands of signatures was presented by an Ottawa radio station, CFRA, and I accepted it on behalf of all the soldiers who had earned it in Sarajevo.

The following morning, I spent three hours with the media at the National Press Theatre. A call came from the Prime Minister's Office that Dora and I were invited to the PM's summer residence at Harrington Lake for lunch with Mr. and Mrs. Mulroney. I called Dora, and she was picked up at home. While she was waiting for me outside the Press Theatre, another call came through that the invitation was for me only. Needless to say, I was upset, and tried to talk Dora into coming along anyway. She would have none of it and went home. Unfortunately, the incident cast a pall over what should have been an enjoyable experience for both of us. To this day, I don't think that the Prime Minister or his wife was aware of the mixup.

Over the next few months, I discussed the Yugoslavian situation before the United States Armed Services Committee, met with American Secretary of Defence Chaney and General Powell, appeared in front of our own Senate and House of Commons Defence Committees, and went to Brussels to meet with the NATO ambassadors and the Supreme Allied Commander Europe. I also visited the United Kingdom and appeared in front of the British Parliament's Defence Committee, and had a most enjoyable audience with Her Majesty, Queen Elizabeth.

The question was always the same: "We have to do something to help in Bosnia—what can we do?" And my answer was always the same: "Stop the war. But you can't do that militarily without killing a lot of people, including your own. If you go in with a big military force (and quite frankly, I don't know how, because there is no country next door to Bosnia comparable to Saudi Arabia in the Gulf War, where you can put a coalition force together to do the job), the whole thing will flare up again when you leave. You have to force the three sides to agree to a constitutional solution that will stand the test of time. All solutions in Bosnia are bad, but a constitutional compromise is the best of the worst."

This was my first peacekeeping tour where the conflict followed me home. Within days of my arrival in Canada, various citizens of Croatian origin started to condemn me in articles and letters in the major newspapers. I put up with it for a week, then contacted the leaders of the Croatian-Canadian community and suggested they might want to meet with me.

The meeting took place in the Delta Chelsea Hotel in Toronto. I responded to all the red herrings: the fabrication that my wife is a Serb (she's of Scottish extraction; her maiden name is MacKinnon, although I call her MacKinnovic now); that she was introduced to me by Mila Mulroney (I met Mrs. Mulroney for the first time in August 1992, and I married Dora in 1967); that Mrs. Plavsic was my girlfriend in Sarajevo and that I delivered food and ammunition to her on a daily basis (I met Mrs. Plavsic eight times at various meetings attended by numerous UN witnesses and was in Belgrade when the infamous Plavsic incident took place in Sarajevo); etc., etc. The meeting seemed to have a positive effect, and the letters to the editor dried up for a while.

In November 1992, the Bosnian-Serb soldier Borislav Herak was arrested by the Presidency's forces in Sarajevo and charged with the murder and rape of Muslim citizens. Allegedly, he said under interrogation that he had worked at the "Sonja" prison camp located north of Sarajevo, and had seen me come by and pick up four Muslim girls, who were taken away and presumably raped and murdered. He indicated that I had arrived in a jeep, and the girls had followed my party when we left in a car. The story made headline news during the Islamic conference in Saudi Arabia, attended by President Izetbegovic. Fortunately, the North American press showed an encouraging degree of good taste and at first declined to carry the story. The story did, however, receive wide coverage in the Islamic press, and in Croatia, Germany and Italy.

Given that I hadn't even known that a place called "Sonja" existed; that I had never ventured north of Sarajevo except on one drive to Belgrade with 200 others on May 17; that I never drove around Sarajevo in anything but the VBL armoured vehicle after my return to the city on June 10; and that I didn't go anywhere without UN colleagues as witnesses, I was more than upset over such disgusting fabrications. My greatest concern was the impact these lies would have on the security of our people on the ground, particularly the Canadians. Anyone with a Canadian flag on his sleeve was immediately associated with my reputation as a "rapist and murderer of Muslims" in Bosnia.

The Canadian government and the United Nations decided that their response to these accusations would be low-key until they became a major story in North America. I endorsed this decision, which over time I grew to regret. My phone rang off the hook for weeks with calls from around the world, asking, "Why doesn't your government deny these allegations? Their lack of comment is condemning you, and the UN certainly isn't doing you any favour by their silence." To be fair to Canada and the UN, they were merely following a policy we all thought best at the time. When reporters called, they were given a denial. We just didn't go proactive in refuting the story, which is what various supporters quite reasonably expected us to do.

In my continuing attempt to figure out why the authorities in Sarajevo would perpetuate such a lie, I have come up with only two theories. The first is that it really wasn't the Bosnian authorities, but Herak himself, knowing he would face the death penalty if found guilty of murdering innocent Muslims, who made up the story to delay his execution. At the same time, obviously the Presidency wanted to use him and his story for propaganda purposes to discredit myself and UNPROFOR.

The second theory makes a bit more sense. The Presidency knew I was against international military intervention in Bosnia. They also knew I was appearing regularly in front of some very influential government committees and leaders in the countries that would actually carry out the intervention, if such a decision were ever made. If they couldn't stop me from recommending against intervention on their side, and against lifting the international arms embargo, they would try to destroy my personal credibility.

This vilification campaign put my family under a tremendous amount of unnecessary and unwarranted stress. Having volunteered to go to the former Yugoslavia in the belief that I could some good, and having watched Canadian soldiers risk their lives to help the population of Sarajevo, I was extremely resentful of the campaign to impugn my character and the role of the UN. Mind you, if I had been the President of Bosnia-Herzegovina, perhaps I might have done exactly the same thing—such is the nature of modern "warfare" when you and your people are trying to survive.

In the Canadian military, there is a highly appropriate restriction precluding members of the armed forces from commenting on matters of government policy. Normally, this policy doesn't cause any heartache, because normally, who wants to know what a general thinks anyway? But in my first four months back in Canada, I made over 200 appearances and presentations, which always included a question period, with the media usually present. I tried to be careful not to stray into policy issues, but on the odd occasion when I did, the phone rang off the hook the next day, and understandably so. "You can't say that, Lew, the Minister is upset, you have to stop getting involved in policy," was the usual comment. As my reputation as an outspoken general became exaggerated, I started to be criticized for things that I hadn't said, but that other people had attributed to me.

Although I was accepting only a small percentage of the requests I received for speaking engagements, they were still beginning to interfere with my new job commanding the 14,000 troops of the Canadian Army in Ontario. In February 1993, I made the difficult decision to retire a year early: it would be a lot easier on my superiors, and a lot easier on me. None of us had intentionally created the awkward situation in which I found myself, and so I left the army with no hard feelings or bitterness. I hope my colleagues feel the same way. I will always be a soldier and an unabashed, outspoken supporter of the profession of arms. Soldiers made me look good for thirty-three years, and I will be forever grateful for their loyalty and support.

30

Whither UN Peacekeeping?

SINCE RETURNING FROM Sarajevo, I have been publicly critical of the UN's ability to command, control and support logistically its burgeoning peacekeeping forces in the field. Numerous UN commanders have expressed similar criticisms in the past; however, due to the extensive media coverage given to my command, my views received a considerable amount of attention and, regrettably, resulted in some hard feelings at the UN.

I say "regrettably" because I am a staunch supporter of the UN. I feel it is the only international organization that has the potential to cope with an increasingly complex and unstable world. Unfortunately, it was not possible to encourage the debate needed to bring about a review of the UN's shortcomings without resorting to the strident sound bites that capture the media's, and the public's, imagination.

The vast majority of the people I worked with in UN New York were hard-working, dedicated individuals. They gave me every bit of support within their capacity to do so. Unfortunately, they were handcuffed by systemic inefficiencies within the overall UN bureaucracy.

"If you are a commander of a UN mission, don't get in trouble after five P.M. or on the weekend. There is no one in the UN to answer the phone!" Yes, I said that. My friends and former bosses in the UN were hurt and replied that, indeed, they had talked to me many times after five P.M. They were absolutely right, but they missed my point: they talked to me from home, a reception or, in some cases, from bed, but that isn't the same as being able to report to a command headquarters on a twenty-four-hour basis.

To give the UN credit, communicating with its commanders in the field during office hours was good enough from the first observer mission in 1947 until 1992. Peacekeeping forces were doing just that, keeping the peace; most of the time, except for some violent exceptions in the Congo and Lebanon, there was ample time to react to a crisis during office hours. A UN commander was given a mandate, resources and a budget, and told to get on with it. He didn't need or desire a lot of contact with UN headquarters in New York. I felt exactly the same way when I commanded the UN mission in Central America in 1991.

All of that changed when the UN decided to place the headquarters of its Croatian UNPROFOR operation in Sarajevo in 1992 and was inexorably drawn into the Bosnian conflict. The numerous crises in that city required urgent input by the UN, but the diplomatic technique of exchanging coded cables was not up to the challenge. Soldiers are used to talking to other soldiers at their headquarters— superiors who speak their military language and, more importantly, who understand what's going on, day to day, in the operational theatre.

Over the past few years, the number of UN peacekeepers deployed around the world has grown from fewer than 5,000 to well over 60,000, and yet, at the time of writing, there is still no military-style command centre in UN New York: no one on duty twenty-four hours a day, seven days a week; no communications room with maps of the various operational areas on the wall, and mission-knowledgeable duty officers manning the radios and keeping a log of all the information and requests coming in from the field. No army in the world would deploy its troops with so little direct control over what they were doing. The UN shouldn't either.

The solution is simple, and various nations are ready to take on responsibility for helping to provide it: a full-time UN peacekeeping operations centre should be established as a matter of priority. It should be manned by experienced officers with previous UN peacekeeping service, and it should have planning capability.

Another problem is that the UN is currently incapable of providing adequate logistics support to its various missions around the world. In theory, national military units are supposed to arrive in the theatre self-contained for a period of sixty to ninety days, after which a system of internationally-let contracts is supposed to kick in and provide the necessary logistics support. But unfortunately, many countries are not capable of or willing to send their units self-contained. Within UNPROFOR, as an example, the battalion from Nepal arrived without vehicles. Germany ultimately gave them what they needed, but the requisite spare parts and personnel to maintain the German fleet were not included.

Within UNPROFOR, there were six different headquarters, comprised of individuals from a cross-section of nations. No concerted, overall plan was drawn up to meet the logistics needs of these groups, and obviously they were incapable of being "self-contained". Months after our arrival, they were still missing the basic items to permit them to carry out their responsibilities.

Recent UN missions have experienced dramatic changes to their mandates and responsibilities on a month-to-month basis. The UN is willing to take on expanded roles for its missions, but cannot generate the expanded logistics support in anything approaching a timely manner. In UNPROFOR, the role of the officer observers grew tremendously in importance; however, the vehicles and radios critical to their effectiveness never did show up in adequate numbers. Lives were put at risk as the observers' vehicles were forced to go on patrol singly, when pairs of vehicles were absolutely necessary for safety.

A solution to the logistics problem is not easy, but has to be addressed. A chain of logistics bases is required around the world to support UN peacekeeping operations. They must have the necessary equipment on hand, or at least the ability and the budget to purchase it. Such bases exist today; they are American military bases.

The U.S. is delinquent in payment of its UN dues for peacekeeping purposes. Since the Americans are the largest contributor to the UN budget, their debt has a tremendously detrimental effect on UN operations in the field. The U.S. is not keeping up with its payments because it knows peacekeeping money is being wasted on overly generous allowances and benefits, and a bloated peacekeeping bureaucracy. If I were in the Americans' position, I wouldn't pay all of my UN bills either. Fortunately, their predicament has the makings of a solution.

Among nations, only the U.S. is capable of providing the badly needed logistics support to UN forces in the field. The U.S. manages large logistics problems, both in planning and execution, better than anyone else. If they were to provide the necessary support, two major goals would be achieved: the UN would receive outstanding logistics support; and the U.S. would have an audit trail at the UN, and could be confident that its contributions were being spent in a cost-effective manner.

Even if the U.S. were to assume such a role, the UN would still need a modest peacekeeping logistics staff, including budgeting expertise, at its headquarters. At present, the UN personnel employed in support of peacekeeping do not work for the Undersecretary responsible for peacekeeping. This structural flaw creates tremendous operational problems and is replicated in the field, where the chief administrative officer can thwart the mission commander's direction if he so wishes. This situation is clearly unacceptable; it could easily be resolved by putting one official in charge of all aspects of peacekeeping (including budgeting) at the UN, and one person in charge in the field, i.e. the mission commander. The problem with the UN is that the buck never stops anywhere—it just keeps moving.

Once one person is in charge of these two areas, he or she should sort out the overly generous allowances and perks that have crept into UN peacekeeping over the years. People should not be motivated to volunteer for peacekeeping missions by financial reward; but that is certainly the case in a large number of ongoing missions. A thorough review and reform of current practices could result in significant savings within the UN's peacekeeping budget.

For example, UN civilian staff and officer observers receive large per diem payments to absolve the UN of any additional responsibilities for their accommodation; the per diem rates are based on local hotel rates and restaurant prices. Not surprisingly, many UN officials in receipt of these allowances find their own, less expensive accommodation and prepare their own meals, making a significant profit at the expense of the peacekeeping budget. Some officers have been known to save over $50,000 U.S. in one year. And yet, it should be noted, military members of a peacekeeping unit or headquarters such as UNPROFOR receive the princely sum of $1.28 U.S. per day. This differential between them and the civilian UN staff, who frequently although not always serve under less dangerous and arduous conditions, is not exactly good for the soldiers' morale. In fact, it is the number-one grievance in most missions; it should be resolved by a simple decision to eliminate the disparity and pay people only what they really need to get the job done.

In spite of all the above problems, UN soldiers continue to risk their lives every day, in an attempt (unfortunately often futile) to create conditions whereby political discussions can take place, leading to a lasting peace in areas of armed conflict or tension. When peacekeepers do create such conditions, as they have in Cyprus for some twenty-five out of the last twenty-six years, insufficient pressure is brought to bear by the international community to force the political leaders in the conflict to talk. The soldiers, however, do their job without questioning the political process and, on the whole, thoroughly enjoy the experience. All they ask in return are three meals a day, a place to put their heads down, and good leadership.

The international community gets a good deal when it "borrows" a nation's soldiers for peacekeeping duties. Soldiers rarely question what they are ordered to do until the job is finished. Their loyalty deserves to be repaid from the top. The UN's role and responsibilities are expanding at a dramatic rate, and peacekeeping is a growth industry. It wouldn't take a major effort for the world body to improve significantly the command, control and logistical support of the people doing the dirty work on behalf of us all.

UN peacekeepers deserve nothing less.

Index